Vital Records of New Durham and Middleton New Hampshire 1887-1998

Richard P. Roberts

HERITAGE BOOKS
2008

HERITAGE BOOKS
AN IMPRINT OF HERITAGE BOOKS, INC.

Books, CDs, and more—Worldwide

For our listing of thousands of titles see our website at
www.HeritageBooks.com

Published 2008 by
HERITAGE BOOKS, INC.
Publishing Division
100 Railroad Ave. #104
Westminster, Maryland 21157

Copyright © 1999 Richard P. Roberts

All rights reserved. No part of this book may be reproduced or transmitted in any form or by any means, electronic or mechanical, including photocopying, recording or by any information storage and retrieval system without written permission from the author, except for the inclusion of brief quotations in a review.

International Standard Book Numbers
Paperbound: 978-0-7884-1246-2
Clothbound: 978-0-7884-7046-2

TABLE OF CONTENTS

Introduction	1
New Durham Births, 1887-1998	4
New Durham Marriages, 1887-1998	93
New Durham Deaths, 1887-1998	175
Middleton Births, 1887-1998	260
Middleton Marriages, 1887-1998	305
Middleton Deaths, 1887-1998	358

INTRODUCTION

Early vital records of many New Hampshire towns can be located either through the State's Vital Records Department or on microfilms made available through LDS Family History Centers. Some, however, have been lost or are inaccessible for various reasons. Many of the early vital records of New Durham, primarily marriages, were recently reprinted in the New Hampshire Genealogical Record. A valuable, but time-consuming, source of information for events occurring after 1886 is the vital statistics which are provided in a section of the Annual Town Reports of many New Hampshire towns. Many of these town reports have been collected at the New Hampshire State Library in Concord, as well as more local repositories.

The amount of information published in these Annual Town Reports varies tremendously over time. Early records are far more detailed and comprehensive. Recent records are rather cursory, but issues of confidentiality and sensitivity to the privacy of those residents still living offsets the lack of information of genealogical value.

While the information provided is often very helpful, one must remember that it is not fool-proof or universally accurate, nor is it the primary source or the actual vital record itself. The fact that much of the data is self-reported suggests that it is reliable. However, errors in transcription, spelling, and printing often are obvious. Foreign names often have been hopelessly abbreviated or misspelled. In addition, there may be two children listed as the third child of a particular couple, or the mother's maiden name, age or place of birth differs or is inconsistent from one entry to another. It is also important to note that a birth, marriage or death may have been reported in another town although the subject resided in New Durham or Middleton, or the entry may not have been made in the first place.

Despite these shortcomings, the information contained in the Annual Town Reports can be a valuable tool for the genealogist. Marriage and death records from the late 1800's often identify parents who were married nearly a century before. Many immigrants from Canada, or their children, have lived in New Durham or Middleton during the time period covered by these records. Finally, those families that have remained in New Durham and/or Middleton for several generations can be traced and connected to the present.

Births - To the extent the information is available, the entries in the list of births are given as follows: child's name; date of birth; place of birth (New Durham or Middleton, as applicable, unless otherwise indicated); the number of children in the family; father's name, place of birth, age and occupation; and the mother's maiden name, age and place of birth. The residence of the parents is given when it is other than New Durham or Middleton. As noted above, the amount of information in earlier records is substantially greater. The New Durham birth records for 1890 have not been located and are not included. The Middleton annual reports for 1944, 1981, 1982 and 1983 do not list vital statistics and the reports for 1891 and 1920 have not been located.

At times, the given names of many children are missing from the early reports. In this case, the sex of the child is given and they are listed chronologically at the beginning of the surname heading. On occasion, the child's name can be determined from marriage or death records, as well as secondary sources. These names are shown in brackets where available.

Marriages - To the extent the information is available, the entries in the list of marriages follow this format: groom's name; groom's residence; bride's name; brides residence; date of marriage; place of marriage (New Durham or Middleton, as applicable, unless otherwise indicated); H, signifying husband's information, and W, signifying wife's information, each in the following order - age, occupation, number of the marriage (if other than first), father's name, father's place of birth, father's occupation, mother's name, mother's place of birth, and mother's occupation. The name of the official conducting the marriage has been omitted but is generally provided in the original document. The

New Durham marriage records for 1890 have not been located and are not included. The Middleton annual reports for 1944, 1981, 1982 and 1983 do not list vital statistics and the reports for 1891 and 1920 have not been located.

Deaths - To the extent available, the entries in the list of deaths contain the following information: name of decedent; place of death; date of death; age at death; cause of death; marital status; birthplace; father's name; father's place of birth; mother's name; and mother's place of birth. Later entries give the residence of the individual. An entry which reads (BP) means that the individual was buried in New Durham but died elsewhere. The New Durham death records for 1890 have not been located and are not included. The Middleton annual reports for 1944, 1981, 1982 and 1983 do not list vital statistics and the reports for 1891 and 1920 have not been located.

Most of the entries listing a cause of death are self-explanatory. In older entries, the phrase "senectus" is sometimes used and is essentially equivalent to "old age", and "phthisis" is similar to "consumption" and "tuberculosis". As one would expect, the death records often contain somber entries for young mothers and small children, as well as tragic instances of individuals passing before their time due to accidents, fires or suicide.

In addition to the Annual Town Reports, information regarding several deaths are listed which have been obtained from other sources. Those marked with a single asterisk are contained in the Social Security Master Death Index as having a "last residence" of New Durham, as well as those listed in the Middleton Town Reports but for whom no further information was provided. Those marked with a double asterisk are taken from obituaries in area newspapers.

NEW DURHAM BIRTHS

ADAMS,
Alvah Atwood, b. 3/30/1930; second; Edgar N. Adams (laborer, Augusta, ME) and Verna M. Willey (Alton)
Dennis James, b. 12/6/1959 in Rochester; Alvah A. Adams and Julianne T. Chiasson
Joan Priscilla, b. 5/25/1932; third; Edgar N. Adams (laborer, Augusta, ME) and Verna Willey (Alton)
June Phyllis, b. 10/23/1937; fifth; Edgar N. Adams (laborer, Augusta, ME) and Verna Willey (Alton)
Mary Edwina, b. 7/7/1934; fourth; Edgar N. Adams (laborer, Augusta, ME) and Verna A. Willey (Alton)
Pamela Carlene, b. 8/1/1957; Alvah Attwood Adams and Julianne Theresa Chiasson

AHLIN,
Corey James, b. 4/14/1994 in Rochester; James Stephen Ahlin and Kathleen Mary McSharry

AIKEN,
Carole Ann, b. 6/23/1943; third; Carroll W. Aiken (lumberman, Wilcock, VT) and M. P. Truchon (Warren)

AINSWORTH,
Robert B., b. 10/26/1927; fifth; Harry J. Ainsworth (laborer, Montpelier, VT) and Mildred E. Morgan (Brooklyn, NY)

ALBERT,
Stephanie Ann, b. 12/13/1994 in Rochester; Paul Emile Albert and Michele Lee Dube

ALDEN,
Chad Robert, b. 1/24/1983 in Wolfeboro; Franklin A. Alden, Jr. and Lynne A. Berry
Sarah Lynne, b. 5/30/1981 in Wolfeboro; Franklin A. Alden, Jr. and Lynne A. Berry

ALLARD,
son, b. 1/31/1909; third; Ephraim Allard (carpenter, Carleton, PQ) and Mary Choninard (St. Epiphan, PQ)

AMROL-DAVIS,
Phoenix Myles, b. 11/11/1992 in Rochester; Glenn Clyde-True Davis and Sharon Lynn Amrol

AMROSKI,
Anthony James, b. 3/12/1995 in Rochester; Peter C. Amroski and Janet R. Hebert

ANDERSON,
Avery, b. 10/25/1998 in Boston, MA; Dwight Anderson and Tracy Anderson
Ben, b. 10/25/1998 in Boston, MA; Dwight Anderson and Tracy Anderson
Taryn Kate, b. 12/2/1976 in Dover; Dwight P. Anderson and Bonnie J. Emerson

ANDREWS,
daughter, b. 5/1/1894; first; Frank Andrews (fireman, 24, Canada) and Maud K. Snider (23, NS)

ANZALONE,
Jennifer Mary, b. 3/17/1983 in Rochester; John V. Anzalone and Sharon R. Penney

APPLE,
Emily Pauline, b. 7/24/1996 in Manchester; Mark David Apple and Lea Denise Dufour
Jane Elizabeth, b. 10/7/1993 in Manchester; Mark David Apple and Lea Denise Dufour

ARCHUNDIA,
Ethan Nicholas, b. 8/9/1990 in Dover; Jorge F. Archundia and Audra G. Gilson

ARNOLD,
Lorraine Hilda, b. 12/17/1935; second; Ralph Arnold (shoeworker, Braintree, MA) and Mildred Hulse (England)
Pamela Ellen, b. 12/13/1970 in Rochester; Robert C. Arnold and Pamela J. Skillin
Robin Jean, b. 3/19/1968 in Rochester; Robert C. Arnold and Pamela J. Skillin

AVERSA,
Matthew Scott, b. 3/25/1997 in Rochester; Michael Scott Aversa and Charna Lee Smith

AYERS,
son, b. 12/1/1895; first; Joseph T. Ayers (brush maker, 32, Wakefield) and Belle G. Wallace (18, Alton)
daughter, b. 9/24/1898; second; Joseph T. Ayers (brush manfr., 34, Wakefield) and Belle Wallace (21, Alton)
Esther E., b. 6/26/1906; fourth; Harry C. Ayers (last maker, 31, New Durham) and Mary E. Mitchell (30, Annapolis, MD)

BABB,
daughter, b. 6/24/1889; third; Charles H. Babb (farmer, 34, Farmington) and Jennie D. Lougee (25, Farmington)

BABCOCK,
Soren Ambros, b. 5/21/1998 in Laconia; John Francis Babcock and Elizabeth Ruth Babcock

BAKER,
Thomas S., Jr., b. 12/29/1946 in Wolfeboro; first; T. Sterling Baker (grocery store, Manchester) and E. U. Kittredge (Manchester)

BAND,
Patricia Ann, b. 12/13/1960 in Rochester; Sherwood Lester Band and Violet May Jenness

BARBARISI,
Bradley Connor, b. 10/7/1998 in Rochester; Robert Barbarisi and Kelly Barbarisi

BARBER,
Joseph F., b. 8/24/1924; fourth; Morris Barber (farmer, Wheelock, VT) and Ottie Ingalls (Walden, VT)
Maurice Albion, b. 8/31/1921; sixth; Maurice A. Barber (farmer, Wheelock, VT) and Viotte Ingalls (Walden, VT)
Mildred J., b. 2/28/1919; fifth; Maurice A. Barber (farmer, Wheelock, VT) and Viotte M. Ingalls (Walden, VT)

BARNET,
Robin Elida, b. 1/9/1956; John Barnet, Jr. and Dorothy Fessel

BARTLETT,
Brady Scott, b. 10/28/1989 in Dover; Brooks S. Bartlett and Susan Hopkins
Clarence R., b. 7/6/1950 in Rochester; second; Clarence M. Bartlett (electrician, MA) and Jeannette Maxfield (NH)

BARTON,
Everett Woodbury, III, b. 4/26/1968 in Wolfeboro; Everett W. Barton, Jr. and Jacqueline H. Berter

BARTSCH,
Karl Eric, b. 4/7/1963 in Rochester; Albert Irvin Bartsch and Pauline May Weeks

BASS,
Sara Jane, b. 10/2/1982 in Rochester; Kenneth A. Bass and Jane A. Yurkus

BASSETT,
Daniel Treloar, Jr., b. 5/10/1984 in Laconia; Daniel T. Bassett and Andrea E. Dean

BATES,
son, b. 10/29/1888; first; Charles L. Bates (mechanic, 24, Leeds, ME) and Clara A. Bates (24, So. Leeds, ME)

BAXTER,
Eleanor, b. 7/22/1921; first; Hibbert B. Baxter (farmer, Halifax, NS) and Cora L. Walker (New Durham)
Victoria Nicole, b. 10/21/1997 in Rochester; Charles Edwin Baxter, III and Pamela Ann Wentworth

BEAN,
Angela May, b. 8/7/1989 in Wolfeboro; Kenneth E. Bean and Barbara A. York

BEASLEY,
Evan David, b. 12/28/1989 in Wolfeboro; David G. Beasley and Michele A. Piper

BEAUDET,
Oliver Jane, b. 2/25/1998 in Rochester; Daniel Nelson Beaudet and Victoria Jean McLean-Beaudet

BELLEMORE,
Olivia Kay, b. 9/1/1998 in Rochester; Daniel Marcel Bellemore and Sandra Anne Bellemore

BENNER,
Amy Lynn, b. 10/22/1975 in Rochester; Richard E. Benner and Sara A. Downs
Christene Ann, b. 10/23/1971 in Rochester; Richard E. Benner and Sara A. Downs

BENOIT,
Leon Jon, b. 3/29/1982 in Rochester; Leon A. Benoit and Rozalind J. Howard
Lindy Jean, b. 3/14/1981 in Rochester; Leon A. Benoit and Rozalind J. Howard

BERNARD,
Andrew Christopher, b. 7/18/1986 in Dover; Steven Alan Bernard and Lauryl Anne Eastman
Nicholas Alan, b. 3/27/1989 in Dover; Steven A. Bernard and Lauryl A. Eastman

BERNIER,
Bradley Thomas, b. 4/17/1991 in Wolfeboro; Paul Wilfred Bernier and Tina Michelle Wilcox
Christopher Matthew, b. 11/8/1994 in Rochester; Paul Wilfred Bernier and Tina Michelle Wilcox
Gregory Raymond, b. 9/25/1984 in Rochester; Raymond T. Bernier and Cindy-Sue Martel
Nicholas Thomas, b. 6/13/1986 in Rochester; Raymond Thomas Bernier and Cindy-Sue Martel

BERRY,
daughter [May A.], b. 9/30/1891; first; Willis E. Berry (farmer, 33, New Durham) and Watie M. Joy (27, New Durham)
son [Roy W.], b. 7/18/1899; third; Alberton N. Berry (farmer, 33, New Durham) and Mary A. Jenkins (28, New Durham)
son, b. 7/25/1900; first; John L. Berry (shoemaker, 21, New Durham) and Fannie B. Clough (19, Alton)
daughter, b. 6/17/1903; fourth; Alberton N. Berry (farmer, 37, New Durham) and Mary A. Jenkins (32, New Durham)
son, b. 12/2/1906; third; John L. Berry (knife maker, 27, New Durham) and Fannie Clough (24, Alton)
Alberton Herman, b. 6/3/1916; first; Guy Alberton Berry (farmer, 24, Wolfeboro) and Eva Alice Weymouth (25, Quincy, MA)

Alta T., b. 1/10/1904; second; John L. Berry (knife grinder, 23, New Durham) and Fannie B. Clough (22, Alton)

Amy Lynn, b. 12/22/1976 in Rochester; Elmer N. Berry, Jr. and Alice R. Whitehouse

Anita Louise, b. 11/15/1954 in Rochester; Elmer Nelson Berry and Ellen Elizabeth Bowden

Arthur Phillip, b. 10/29/1958 in Rochester; Elmer Nelson Berry and Ellen Elizabeth Bowden

Barbara Marie, b. 6/2/1928; third; Roy W. Berry (farmer, New Durham) and Christina MacKenzie (Cambridge, MA)

Benjamin Marcel, b. 6/1/1988 in Dover; Paul T. Berry and Marcia D. Houde

Beryl Lucy, b. 8/28/1924; sixth; Guy A. Berry (farmer, Wolfeboro) and Eva A. Weymouth (Quincy, MA)

Christine M., b. 9/18/1921; first; Roy W. Berry (farmer, New Durham) and Christina J. McKenzie (Cambridge, MA)

Deborah Ann, b. 2/27/1974 in Rochester; Dennis E. Berry and Renee Sue Held

Dennis E., b. 5/24/1950 in Wolfeboro; fourth; Elmer N. Berry (farmer, VA) and Ellen E. Bowden (ME)

Dorlis A., b. 1/10/1919; third; Guy A. Berry (farmer, Wolfeboro) and Eva A. Weymouth (Quincy, MA)

Elmer Nelson, Jr., b. 10/25/1952 in Rochester; Elmer Nelson Berry and Ellen Elizabeth Bowden

Elmer Nelson, III, b. 5/22/1980 in Rochester; Elmer N. Berry, Jr. and Alice R. Whitehouse

Eunice M., b. 7/7/1917; second; Guy A. Berry (farmer, 25, Wolfeboro) and Eva A. Weymouth (26, Quincy, MA)

Grace Ellen, b. 9/18/1983 in Dover; Paul D. Berry and Robin E. Wyatt Held

Izah P., b. 2/21/1891; first; Zanello D. Berry (farmer, 34, New Durham) and Magean E. Hale (25, Bridgton, ME)

John M., b. 10/9/1917; first; Nelson M. Berry (farmer, 23, Farmington) and Mabel F. Canney (22, MT)

Joseph Neal, b. 10/19/1953 in Rochester; Elmer Nelson Berry and Ellen Elizabeth Bowden

Kenneth Nelson, b. 9/3/1928 in Rochester; third; Nelson M. Berry (farmer, Farmington) and Mabel F. Canney (MT)

Lon Roy, b. 1/6/1956 in Rochester; Elmer Nelson Berry and Ellen Elizabeth Bowden

Lua May, b. 9/1/1902; third; Zanello D. Berry (farmer, 45, New Durham) and May Hale (35, Bridgton, ME)

Lynne Ann, b. 10/1/1953 in Rochester; Robert Wilmer Berry and Janet Shaw Campbell

Marcy Lee, b. 3/14/1972 in Rochester; Dennis E. Berry and Renee S. Held

Mary Anne, b. 11/13/1957; Elmer Nelson Berry and Ellen Elizabeth Bowden

Mary E., b. 2/2/1939 in Wolfeboro; first; Myron E. Berry (laborer, New Durham) and Elizabeth King (Gloucester, MA)

Mildred, b. 3/15/1920; fourth; Guy A. Berry (farmer, New Durham) and Eva A. Weymouth (Quincy, MA)

Myron Earl, b. 4/19/1893; second; Zanello D. Berry (farmer, 35, New Durham) and Magene E. Gale (26, Bridgton, ME)

Paul Douglas, b. 12/7/1951; Elmer Nelson Berry and Ellen Elizabeth Bowden

Robert Wilmer, b. 6/18/1926; second; Roy W. Berry (farmer, New Durham) and Christina MacKenzie (Cambridge, MA)

Rosemary, b. 6/15/1902; Theodore Berry (carpenter, Canada) and Rose Valley (Canada)

Stella, b. 6/22/1922; fifth; Guy A. Berry (farmer, Wolfeboro) and Eva A. Weymouth (Quincy, MA)

William Joseph, b. 10/10/1951 in Rochester; Willis Herman Berry and Gloria Rita Gelinas

BICKFORD,

daughter, b. 10/28/1897; fourth; Charles D. Bickford (farmer, 34, New Durham) and Mary L. Downs (34, Wakefield)

Barbara J., b. 5/15/1950 in Rochester; first; George E. Bickford (dairy farmer, New Durham) and Eloise R. Wyatt (MA)

Charles Martin, b. 11/18/1952 in Rochester; George Everett Bickford and Eloise Ruth Wyatt

David Allan, b. 9/6/1951 in Rochester; George Everett Bickford and
Eloise Ruth Wyatt
Deborah Elain, b. 9/26/1953 in Rochester; Robert Edward Bickford
and Alta Louise Scott
George E., b. 11/3/1922; first; Harry Bickford (laborer, New Durham)
and Helen F. Goodell (Alton)
George Thomas, b. 1/9/1962 in Rochester; George Everett Bickford
and Eloise Ruth Wyatt
Guy Thornton, b. 1/20/1901; third; Albert A. Bickford (laborer, 34,
Newton) and Ella Peabody (26, Lowell, MA)
Richard Warren, b. 5/29/1954 in Rochester; George Everett Bickford
and Eloise Ruth Wyatt
Robert Edward, b. 12/10/1925; second; Harry Bickford (brush maker,
New Durham) and Helen Frances Goodell (Alton)
Robert Edward, Jr., b. 12/24/1958 in Rochester; Robert Edward
Bickford, Sr. and Alta Louise Scott

BILLSON,
son, b. 5/12/1909; first; Bertha Billson (Providence, RI)

BILODEAU,
Joshua Adam, b. 7/29/1989 in Dover; Romeo R. Bilodeau and Kelly
L. St. Clair

BISHOP,
Matthew Ford, b. 5/23/1988 in Dover; Ford A. Bishop and Pamela R.
Constant

BISSION,
Kevin Guy, b. 6/17/1994 in Rochester; Eric Guy Bission and Laurie
Ann Allen

BLACK,
Amanda Mae, b. 12/26/1992 in Lebanon; Michael Kevin Black and
Elizabeth Emily Riesenberg

Katherine Elizabeth, b. 10/8/1989 in Dover; Michael K. Black and
    Elizabeth E. Riesenberg
Megan Patricia, b. 12/26/1992 in Lebanon; Michael Kevin Black and
    Elizabeth Emily Riesenberg

BLACKDEN,
Kathyrn Elaine, b. 2/11/1991 in Dover; Donald Henry Blackden and
    Vicki Lynn Byron
Taylor Elaine, b. 8/1/1994 in Dover; Donald Henry Blackden and
    Vicki Lynn Byron

BLAIR,
Jessica Ann, b. 2/17/1975 in Rochester; Bernard A. Blair and June E.
    Neaves

BLAIS,
Benjamin Andre, b. 1/13/1988 in Dover; Andre R. Blais and Nancy
    Rose
Hunter Fernard, b. 6/30/1985 in Concord; Andre Raymond Blais and
    Nancy Austin Rose
Juliana Catherine Rose, b. 4/15/1994 in Dover; Andre Raymond Blais
    and Nancy Rose

BLAISDELL,
Robert Paul, b. 1/2/1970 in Rochester; Paul A. Blaisdell and Dianne
    A. Lambert

BLAKE,
Kathaleen L., b. 5/5/1929; second; George O. Blake (laborer,
    Dorchester, MA) and Thelma V. Green (Cornville, ME)

BLANCHARD,
George Arthur, b. 3/7/1945 in Rochester; first; Joseph Blanchard
    (physician, Boston, MA) and May L. Peck (St. Johnsbury, VT)
Kerry Peck, b. 8/7/1981 in Dover; Christopher Blanchard and
    Stephanie Dunn

BLANEY,
Alexander John, b. 1/7/1988 in Rochester; Francis J. Blaney and
Elaine C. Tremblay

BOLSTRIDGE,
Amanda Lynn, b. 6/3/1990 in Rochester; Jeffrey A. Bolstridge and
Kristine M. Elliott
James Patrick, b. 12/24/1976 in Rochester; Larry A. Bolstridge and
Carol E. Rioux

BOOTH,
Randall Cullen, b. 4/9/1987 in Rochester; Ronald C. Booth and Betsy
C. Thompson
Robert Colin, b. 12/31/1981 in Rochester; Ronald C. Booth and Betsy
C. Thompson
Sarah Elizabeth, b. 6/29/1996 in Concord; Frederick Harold Booth
and Diane Marie Auclair

BOUCHE,
daughter, b. 9/12/1892; first; Leon J. Bouche (carpenter, 34, Quebec)
and Alvina Lamontagne (37, Halifax, NS)

BOUCHER,
Irene V., b. 12/4/1913; sixth; Ernest Boucher (lumberman, Canada)
and Maggie R. Mixon (Poland)

BOWDEN,
Donald Arthur, b. 1/24/1959 in Rochester; Harold H. Bowden and
Lorraine L. Martin
Karen Gail, b. 11/5/1961 in Rochester; Harold Raymond Bowden and
Lorraine Lucille Martin

BOZINOS,
son, b. 10/28/1967 in Rochester; James Bozinos and Madelene C.
Bergaglio

BRESCIA,
Meegan Ann, b. 10/23/1985 in Dover; Barry Norman Brescia and Sharon Ann Hughes

BREWER,
Bonita Louise, b. 11/27/1952 in Wolfeboro; Marcus Hamlin Brewer and Bertha Louise Geary

BRIGGS,
Chaim Lee, b. 7/6/1970 in Wolfeboro; Gary L. Briggs and Susan L. Frigon

BRITTON,
Todd Alan, b. 8/9/1964 in Wolfeboro; Harry Waldon Britton and Carrie Taylor

BROWN,
son, b. 3/27/1887; first; Horace O. Brown (lumberman, 23, Danvers, MA) and ----- (19, Barrington); residence - Barrington
daughter, b. 2/6/1907; fourth; John A. Brown (farmer, 31, Alton) and Alice M. Tibbetts (22, Berwick, ME)
son, b. 2/2/1916; fifth; William Harriman Brown (teamster, 33, Madison) and Mabel Rose Schultz (36, Boston, MA)
Abigale Chase, b. 7/12/1994 in Laconia; Alden Clifford Brown, Jr. and Kirsten Marie Peterson
Angela Meghan, b. 2/27/1989 in Portsmouth; Robert E. Brown, Jr. and Nancy M.G. Martinez
Gloria May, b. 4/11/1946 in Wolfeboro; third; Clarence R. Brown (farm foreman, Center Sandwich) and Marcia E. Taylor (Center Sandwich)
Megda Alberta, b. 11/14/1905; second; Albert C. Brown (wood turner, 31, Waltham, MA) and Nellie E. Mitchell (34, New Durham)
Nellie M., b. 7/17/1904; first; Albert C. Brown (knifemaker, 29, Waltham, MA) and Nellie M. Brown (33, New Durham)

BRUNELLE,
Sandra Lynn, b. 1/19/1969 in Rochester; Roland A. Brunelle and
  Mary Jo Cotter

BRYANT,
Edna Louise, b. 4/23/1921; second; Ralph A. Bryant (farmer,
  Rochester) and Amelia Marcotte (Fremont)

BURBANK,
Lyndon, b. 9/22/1920; Frank E. Burbank (laborer, Gilmanton) and
  Sadie Gault (Bridgewater)

BURNS,
Reita Alice, b. 12/2/1938 in Dover; second; Raymond J. Burns
  (finisher w.m., Swanton, VT) and Alice B. Howard (Strafford)

BUSS,
son, b. 9/11/1895; third; George E. Buss (teamster, 36, W. Boylston,
  MA) and Hattie M. Tucker (26, Lancaster, MA)

CAMERON,
Alan Burton, b. 6/7/1954 in Rochester; Lawrence Chester Cameron
  and Kathryne Beatrice Richard
Edward Roscoe, b. 3/16/1935; third; Lawrence Cameron (farmer,
  Greenport, LI) and Ada Kelley (Lynn, MA)
Helda Lee, b. 9/25/1961 in Rochester; Edward Roscoe Cameron and
  Carolyn Jessie Hodgdon
John Buddie, b. 12/17/1935; second; Albert Cameron (carpenter,
  Greenport, NY) and Catherine Colbath (Farmington)

CANNEY,
son [Ralph], b. 8/7/1896; first; Henry J. Canney (farmer, 33, New
  Durham) and Mary E. Willson (31, Rochester)
son [Herbert], b. 4/24/1900; second; Isaac A. Canney (farmer, 44,
  Farmington) and Annie M. Colbath (29, Farmington)

Grace A., b. 10/23/1902; third; Isaac A. Canney (lumbering and teaming, 44, Farmington) and Annie M. Colbath (30, Farmington)

CARDER,
Daniel Eliot, b. 7/13/1954 in Rochester; Walter Adams Carder and Marie Elizabeth Titcomb

CARDINAL,
son [Carroll], b. 6/16/1913; sixth; John B. Cardinal (lumberman, Canada) and Rosie Rock (Epping)
Carroll Ann, b. 4/8/1949 in Wolfeboro; second; Leo Cardinal (trucking, Farmington) and Ethel M. Shaw (Farmington)
James David, b. 4/20/1984 in Wolfeboro; David J. Cardinal and Kathy L. Lizotte
Nicole Davis, b. 3/13/1987 in Rochester; David J. Cardinal and Kathy L. Lizotte
Samuel James, b. 5/27/1983 in Dover; Arthur S. Cardinal and Bonny L. Woodside
Sheila Lee, b. 3/15/1948 in Wolfeboro; second; Leo Cardinal (Socony, Farmington) and Ethel M. Shaw (Farmington)

CARPENTER,
Scott Alan, b. 4/8/1972 in Rochester; Horace H. Carpenter and Gloria J. Hayes
Traci Lee, b. 10/14/1974 in Rochester; Horace H. Carpenter, Jr. and Gloria J. Hayes

CASSELL,
Annette Marie, b. 5/12/1995 in Rochester; Michael A. Cassell, Jr. and Samantha A. Merchant
Michael Andrew, III, b. 6/2/1993 in Rochester; Michael Andrew Cassell, Jr. and Samantha Annette Merchant

CASSIDY,
Robert Arthur, b. 11/29/1949 in Rochester; sixth; Francis Cassidy (woodsman, VT) and Ida M. Taylor (RI)

CATHCART,
Charon Madolyn, b. 1/30/1951 in Rochester; Roland H. Cathcart and Pauline May Laney
Hubert Roland, b. 6/5/1938; first; Hubert R. Cathcart (drier l.b. factory, Farmington) and Pauline M. Laney (Alton)
Janis Marie, b. 10/25/1946; third; Roland Cathcart (laborer, Farmington) and Pauline Laney (Alton)

CHABOT,
Michael Andrew, b. 6/9/1974 in Wolfeboro; Jerry L. Chabot and Shirleen A. Goodrow

CHAMBERL[A]IN,
child, b. 7/5/1955 in Rochester; George Daniel Chamberlin and Carolyn Mae Fogg
child, b. 7/5/1955 in Rochester; George Daniel Chamberlin and Carolyn Mae Fogg
child, b. 7/5/1955 in Rochester; George Daniel Chamberlin and Carolyn Mae Fogg
Carlton Eugene, b. 9/13/1932; fifth; John C. Chamberlain (farmer, New Durham) and Edna G. Blackmer (Madbury)
Charles H., b. 9/3/1898; second; Irving S. Chamberlain (farmer, 30, New Durham) and Edith M. Thurrell (26, So. Berwick, ME)
Daniel Keith, b. 8/17/1952 in Rochester; George Daniel Chamberlin and Carolyn Mae Fogg
David John, b. 8/11/1953 in Rochester; George Daniel Chamberlin and Carolyn Mae Fogg
George Daniel, b. 3/19/1931; fourth; John B. Chamberlain (farmer, New Durham) and Edna Blackmar (Madbury)
Jennie M., b. 5/29/1898; first; John B. Chamberlain (farmer, 28, New Durham) and Annie M. Joy (28, New Durham)

Jennifer Elaine, b. 10/23/1990 in Rochester; John E. Chamberlin and Melynda A. Blair

John Burley, b. 1/31/1992 in Rochester; John Eric Chamberlin and Melynda Adrienne Blair

John Eric, b. 2/23/1967 in Rochester; Nelson E. Chamberlin and Freda M. Smith

Louis B., b. 10/7/1919; first; John B. Chamberlin (farmer, New Durham) and Edna G. Blackmer (Madbury)

Nelson Ellsworth, b. 12/14/1925; second; John B. Chamberlain (farmer, New Durham) and Edna G. Blackmer (Madbury)

Roscoe, b. 3/16/1906; third; Irving S. Chamberlin (farmer, 38, New Durham) and Edith Thurell (34, Berwick, ME)

Ruth Adella, b. 11/23/1928 in Rochester; third; John B. Chamberlin (farmer, New Durham) and Edna G. Blackmar (Madbury)

CHANDLER,
Linwood, b. 10/15/1908; first; Edward L. Chandler (mechanic, Lawrence, MA) and Rosa B. Edgerly (New Durham)

CHARLES,
William Arthur, b. 5/31/1912; seventh; F. A. Charles (dentist, Brimfield, MA) and Ida M. Young (Houlton, ME); residence - Andover, MA

CHASE,
daughter, b. 3/16/1907; fourth; F. H. Chase (laborer, 31, NH) and Ella Blanche Davis (24, ME)

son [Melvin N.], b. 9/28/1908; fifth; Fred H. Chase (laborer, Dover) and Ella Dame (Wells, ME)

daughter, b. 3/31/1912; seventh; Fred H. Chase (farmer, Dover) and Ella B. Davis (Wells, ME)

son, b. 3/13/1917; ninth; Fred H. Chase (farmer, 41, Dover) and Ella B. Davis (34, Wells, ME)

stillborn son, b. 6/18/1922; thirteenth; Fred H. Chase (farmer, Dover) and Ella B. Davis (Wells, ME)

Barbara Jean, b. 4/27/1938; fourth; John E. Chase (sawyer, Hill) and
   Ethelbert Colby (Hill)
John Ivory, b. 3/12/1921; twelfth; Fred H. Chase (farmer, Dover) and
   Ella B. Davis (Wells, ME)
Leslie O., b. 8/19/1915; eighth; Fred H. Chase (farmer, 41, Dover)
   and Ella B. Davis (32, Wells, ME)
Noris D., b. 5/21/1910; sixth; Fred H. Chase (teamster, Dover) and
   Ella B. Davis (Wells, ME)
Vera A., b. 1/25/1920; eleventh; Fred H. Chase (farmer, Dover) and
   Ella B. Davis (Wells, ME)
Victor W., b. 11/15/1918; tenth; Fred H. Chase (farmer, Dover) and
   Ella B. Davis (Wells, ME)
Zane, b. 10/16/1939; third; Victor W. Chase (unemployed, New
   Durham) and Ruth Veno (Rochester)

CHASSE,
Austin Thomas George, b. 1/9/1998 in Rochester; George Chasse and
   Celeste Chasse

CHRISTOFORE,
Lesa Beth, b. 1/20/1978 in Wolfeboro; Richard W. Christofore and
   Elizabeth F. Perkins

COBB,
Judy Ann, b. 10/6/1954 in Rochester; Walter Stevens Cobb and
   Adaline Catherine Vanduzen

COBURN,
Bernice M., b. 6/28/1897; third; Alonzo G. Coburn (knife mfr., 39,
   New Durham) and Annie Adams (39, Farmington)
Floyd P., b. 1/8/1894; second; Alonzo G. Coburn (knife mfr., 36, New
   Durham) and Annie Adams (35, Farmington)
Lena I., b. 10/18/1897; second; Dana Coburn (shoemaker, 35, New
   Durham) and Hannah L. Spinney (31, Portsmouth)
Norma L., b. 8/30/1917; first; Floyd P. Coburn (woodturner, 23, New
   Durham) and Ethel E. Hayes (22, New Durham)

COLBATH,
stillborn son, b. 9/18/1887; first; Samuel E. Colbath (box maker, 26, Alton) and ----- (23, New Durham); residence - Alton
Evelyn, b. 3/5/1914; first; Loren Colbath (shoemaker, Farmington) and Grace G. Thurston (No. Berwick, ME); residence - Farmington

COLE,
Charles Wilcek Iarussi, b. 5/8/1982 in Dover; Douglas S. Cole and Jane M. Iarussi

COLEMAN,
Edward Henry, III, b. 12/10/1974 in Dover; Edward H. Coleman, Jr. and Bonnie L. Sullivan

CONSTANT,
daughter, b. 6/28/1906; sixth; Alma Constant (lumber chopper, 31, Canada) and Mary Ann Mattas (28, Canada)

COOK,
daughter, b. 5/16/1905; third; David R. Cook (farmer, 38, Milton) and Rosa M. Cook (32, Holderness)

CORAN,
Wallace Robert, b. 8/18/1979 in Rochester; Wallace J. Coran and Robin B. Mooney

CORSON,
Amanda Emily, b. 12/20/1984 in Rochester; Richard H. Corson and June E. Carleton
Harris Charles, b. 1/6/1930; fourth; Charles H. Corson (millworker, New Durham) and Gladys E. Miller (New Durham)
James Michael, b. 4/21/1959 in Rochester; Harris C. Corson and Norma E. Woodman
Lawrence R., b. 3/5/1933; second; Willis R. Corson (laborer, Wolfeboro) and Etta S. Thurston (No. Berwick, ME)

Marjorie Louise, b. 12/16/1923; second; Charles Corson (lumber maker, New Durham) and Gladys Miller (New Durham)
Mildred Irene, b. 7/14/1922; second; Charles H. Corson (laborer, NH) and Gladys E. Miller (New Durham)
Richard Harris, b. 2/27/1957; Harris Charles Corson and Norma Evelyn Woodman
Willis A., b. 2/17/1920; first; Willis R. Corson (wood turner, Wolfeboro) and Etta S. Thurston (No. Berwick, ME)

COURNOYER,
Claire Marrie, b. 10/16/1938; ninth; D. J. Cournoyer (woodheel nailer, Manchester) and Mary A. Poisson (Derry)

COUTURE,
Lindsey Mary, b. 6/6/1994 in Portsmouth; Kevin Donald Couture and Diane Maria Paradis
Philip, b. 12/31/1892; first; Philip Couture (wood chopper, 22, Canada) and Mary Couture (15, Canada)

CROCKETT,
daughter, b. 6/5/1894; second; C. T. D. Crockett (clergyman, 61, Greenwood, ME) and Hattie Maria Crockett (38, Canton, ME)

CROTEAU,
Leon Ernest, b. 1/5/1948 in Rochester; first; Joseph R.E. Croteau (truck driver, Rochester) and Mary R. Bolduc (Somersworth)

CROTHERS,
Christina Maria, b. 5/21/1987 in Dover; James M. Crothers and Sharon L. Lapinski
William Michael, b. 6/25/1989 in Dover; James M. Crothers and Sharon L. Lapinski

CROWLEY,
Kelsey Christine, b. 4/2/1996 in Rochester; Frank Warren Crowley and Christine Marie Joy

Krystal Marion, b. 9/20/1997 in Rochester; Frank Warren Crowley
and Christine Marie Joy

CULBERT,
Donald Bruce, b. 7/6/1938; third; Walter R. Culbert (farmer, Mechanicsville, NY) and Edna O. Smith (PEI)

CUMMINGS,
Maurice Andrew, b. 6/2/1903; third; Herbert W. Cummings (clergyman, 39, Middlesex, VT) and Lenora Powell (34, Topsfield, MA)

CUNNINGHAM,
William Michael, b. 4/2/1987 in Rochester; Harvey J. Cunningham and Ardell M. Smith

CUTTER,
Carol Jean, b. 12/24/1967 in Rochester; Frank M. Cutter and Jean A. Hoage
Carroll Elwin, Jr., b. 10/8/1985 in Concord; Carroll Elwin Cutter and Carlene Lynn Carlsons
Necia Kathrynne, b. 3/10/1967 in Rochester; Richard W. Cutter and June R. Newton
Richard William, Jr., b. 4/19/1970 in Rochester; Richard W. Cutter and June R. Newton

CUTTING,
Linda Suzanne, b. 9/15/1949 in Wolfeboro; first; William R. Cutting (merchant marine, Roxbury, MA) and Glenna Blakeney (NS)

DADURA,
Laura Ellen, b. 5/20/1967 in Laconia; Robert J. Dadura and Ellen C. Reinholz
Robert Stasik, b. 7/3/1972 in Laconia; Robert J. Dadura and Ellen C. Reinholz

DALPE,
Christopher Laurent, b. 1/20/1990 in Rochester; Wayne L. Dalpe and Linda N. Peloquin
Elizabeth Rose, b. 1/9/1988 in Rochester; Wayne L. Dalpe and Linda N. Peloquin

DAME,
son, b. 5/30/1899; seventh; Alonzo Dame (laborer, 44, Barrington) and Ella E. J. French (45, Farmington)

DARGAN,
Geoffrey Francis, b. 9/21/1989 in Dover; Timothy F. Dargan and Therese A. Thibodeau

DAVENHALL,
Nicholas William, b. 1/6/1981 in Rochester; William H. Davenhall, III and Gail L. Remick

DAVIS,
Arline, b. 4/21/1917; first; Harry Davis (shoemaker, Farmington) and Alice Chamberlin (New Durham)
Linda May, b. 7/8/1952 in Laconia; Lester Charles Davis and Helen May Joy

DAVOL,
Elizabeth Lorraine, b. 1/4/1988 in Rochester; Bruce W. Davol and Carolyn S. Hathaway

DEELY,
David Jason, b. 5/28/1990 in Rochester; Kevin C. Deely and Nancy M. Pelletier
Erica Lindsey, b. 11/24/1989 in Dover; Mark A. Deely and Patricia L. Bennett

DEMAIO,
Kaytie Lynn, b. 11/14/1997 in Rochester; James Michael DeMaio and
  Rebekah May Lidback

DEMELLO,
Allison Cusack, b. 10/22/1994 in Rochester; Paul Anthony Demello
  and Maura Cusack

DESHON,
Linda Marie, b. 7/15/1947 in Rochester; third; Richard A. Deshon
  (laborer, Lynn, MA) and Catherine J. Walch (Lynn, MA)

DESMARAIS,
Jason Gary, b. 8/13/1985 in Rochester; Gary Paul Desmarais and
  Janet Evelyn Bean

DESROSIERS,
Megan Alicia, b. 6/28/1998 in Rochester; Marc Roger Desrosiers and
  Grace Alice Desrosiers

DEVINE,
Devinne Fallon, b. 5/9/1988 in Dover; Stephen E. Devine and Susan
  M. Haig

DIACO,
Laura Ann, b. 3/26/1991 in Dover; Eugene Diaco and Suzanne Kay
  Smith

DIPRIZIO,
Aaron Edward, b. 9/3/1987 in Hanover; Edward C. DiPrizio and Jane
  E. Brooks
Brett Charles, b. 9/3/1987 in Hanover; Edward C. DiPrizio and Jane
  E. Brooks

DODGE,
Gretchen Emma, b. 3/11/1989; David D. Dodge and Bonnie L. Oickle

DOLAN,
Lisa Louise, b. 8/1/1957; Thomas John Dolan and Clara Louise Blalook

DONNELLY,
Morgan Perry, b. 12/31/1983 in Wolfeboro; Gregg N. Donnelly and Jane E. Perry
Shaun Perry, b. 6/21/1982 in Dover; Gregg N. Donnelly and Jane E. Perry

DORE,
Frank, b. 1/17/1940 in Rochester; second; Frank E. Dore (truck driver, Farmington) and Ethel Burres (Gilmanton I.W.)

DOTY,
Maynard D., b. 2/22/1912; first; Frank E. Doty (mechanic, Bristol, VT) and Bessie F. May (Fitchburg, MA)

DOUGLAS,
Gavin Alexander, b. 10/26/1977 in Rochester; Desmond N. Douglas and Arleen A. Duso
Jessie Danielle, b. 8/21/1988 in Dover; Ronald M. Douglas and Darlene A. Richards

DOWNS,
daughter, b. 11/15/1926; fifth; Frank P. Downs (teamster, Milton) and Edna H. Johnson (Rochester)
Tina Marie, b. 8/27/1974 in Rochester; Larry R. Downs and Vicki J. Garland

DRAPEAU,
Brittany Marie, b. 5/16/1994 in Rochester; Jeffery Phillip Drapeau and Jeanette Marie Berry
Travis Austin, b. 9/3/1996 in Wolfeboro; Jeffery Phillip Drapeau and Jeanette Marie Berry

DREW,
Bonnie Lee, b. 7/11/1948 in Dover; first; Wilbur J. Drew (laborer, Sandwich) and C. M. Willard (Alton)
Lizzie A., b. 12/11/1895; fourth; Philip L. Drew (mechanic, 30, Dayton, ME) and Sadie A. Gould (28, Dayton, ME)

DROVIN,
daughter, b. 10/3/1894; Joseph Drovin (laborer, 31, Canada) and Sarah Peasant (32, Canada)

DUARTE,
David Dario, b. 3/22/1974 in Rochester; Felipe Duarte and Marian C. Ortega

DUMAIS,
Eric Daniel, b. 7/27/1990 in Rochester; Daniel R. Dumais and Tracey A. Durant

DUMAS,
son, b. 1/16/1893; fifth; Joseph Dumas (wood chopper, 27, Canada) and Marie Guillmette (32, Canada)

DUMONT,
daughter, b. 9/2/1902; first; Frank Dumont (laborer, 27, St. Audree, PQ) and Mary Fountain (20, Dixfield, PQ)
Michelle Catherine, b. 1/4/1980 in Concord; Paul W. Dumont and Catherine R. Wilson
Noelle Esther, b. 4/6/1983 in Concord; Paul W. Dumont and Catherine R. Wilson
Shawn Paul, b. 1/4/1980 in Concord; Paul W. Dumont and Catherine R. Wilson

DURAND,
Jacob Scott, b. 8/15/1997 in Rochester; James Roland Durand, Jr. and Lisa Dawn Patat

DURGIN,
daughter, b. 7/17/1887; first; Woodbury J. Durgin (farmer, New Durham) and ----- (Belgrade, ME)

DYER,
Jeanne Marie, b. 2/9/1953 in Rochester; Francis Everett Dyer and Barbara Marie Berry
Keith Paul, b. 4/15/1954 in Rochester; Francis Everett Dyer and Barbara Marie Berry

EATON,
Sandra Anne, b. 8/6/1970 in Rochester; James M. Eaton and Shirley A. Bowden
Stacy Jean, b. 12/30/1971 in Rochester; James M. Eaton and Shirley A. Bowden

EDGERLY,
daughter, b. 7/12/1889; second; Charles Edgerly (farmer, 40, Dover) and Minnie Colomy (23, New Durham)
daughter [Florence M.], b. 11/24/1895; fifth; Charles W. Edgerly (farmer, 46, Dover) and Minnie Colomy (26, New Durham)
son [Earl], b. 1/23/1899; first; Walter C. Edgerly (laborer, 25, Northwood) and Ellen Rice (22, Sterling, Scotland)
son, b. 6/19/1903; seventh; Charles W. Edgerly (farmer, New Durham) and Minnie B. Colomy (42, New Durham)
daughter, b. 8/7/1906; ninth; Charles Edgerly (laborer, 57, Dover) and Minnie Colomy (44, New Durham)
Earle, b. 2/23/1908; first; Annie B. Edgerly (New Durham)
Ella Ruth, b. 5/26/1900; seventh; Charles W. Edgerly (laborer, 51, Dover) and Minnie B. Colomy (34, New Durham)
Frank H., b. 2/--/1892; third; Charles W. Edgerly (farmer, 44, Dover) and Minnie B. Colomy (26, New Durham)
Fred E., b. 8/12/1893; fourth; Charles W. Edgerly (farmer, 45, Dover) and Minnie B. Colomy (27, New Durham)
Helen, b. 7/24/1898; sixth; Charles Edgerly (farmer, 50, Dover) and Minnie Colomy (30, New Durham)

Regina Arlene, b. 6/11/1948 in Wolfeboro; third; Chester G. Edgerly (laborer, Craftsbury, VT) and Ethel E. Hale (Stowe, VT)

EDMUNDS,
Jeremy Samuel, b. 1/5/1977 in Rochester; Christopher H. Edmunds and Brenda Simonds
Julia Anna, b. 8/29/1985; Christopher H. Edmunds and Brenda S. Simonds
Keturah Leah, b. 12/8/1987; Christopher H. Edmunds and Brenda Simonds
Lydia Anna, b. 5/29/1982 in Concord; Christopher H. Edmunds and Brenda Simonds
Mara Beth, b. 11/10/1978 in Rochester; Christopher H. Edmunds and Brenda Simonds
Rebecca Ruth, b. 12/11/1990 in Farmington; Christopher Edmunds and Brenda Simonds
Simeon Nathaniel, b. 12/21/1983; Christopher H. Edmunds and Brenda Simonds

ELDRIDGE,
Charmaine Lacrecia, b. 7/19/1993 in North Conway; Philip Clyde Eldridge and Sonya Marie Eldredge
Daniel Anthony, b. 4/25/1997 in Laconia; Anthony Carl Eldridge and Amy Lynn Langis
Nichols James, b. 2/14/1995 in Laconia; Anthony C. Eldridge and Amy Lynn Langis

ELLEA,
Joseph, b. 10/13/1891; first; Nelson Ellea (teamster, 21, Canada) and Amma King (20, Canada)

ELLIOTT,
daughter, b. 9/14/1911; sixth; D. M. Elliott (farmer, Rumney) and Bertha C. Plummer (West Fairlee, VT)

EMERSON,
Helen Alice, b. 10/5/1912; first; Frank A. Emerson (fireman, Chester) and Ruth Shackford (Somerville, MA)

EMERY,
Arthur Thomas, b. 9/28/1927 in Rochester; fourth; George E. Emery (wood chopper, Farmington) and Lillian Hurd (Lowell, MA)

ESTEY,
Eugene Wallace, 4th, b. 11/19/1965 in Rochester; Eugene W. Estey, 3d and Ruth M. Reany

FIEDERER,
Lola Jeanette, b. 9/7/1952 in Rochester; Frank Fiederer, Jr. and Harriett Moulton Varney

FIELD,
Harold George, b. 12/13/1925; first; Harold George Field (shoemaker, Norway, ME) and Freda M. Miller (New Durham)

FLANDERS,
Francis L., b. 11/19/1943 in Wolfeboro; second; Wesley D. Flanders (tractor driver, Belmont) and D. M. Marden (Laconia)

FLINT,
Jasper E., Jr., b. 3/1/1923; second; Jasper Flint (wood turner, Alton) and Marion Parshley (Strafford)
Murray George, b. 3/18/1928 in Rochester; fourth; Jasper E. Flint (shipping clerk, Alton) and Marion M. Parshley (Strafford)
Raymond H., b. 9/8/1924; third; Jasper Flint (laborer, Alton) and Marion Parshley (Strafford)

FOLAN,
Emily Margaret, b. 7/31/1990 in Dover; Michael P. Folan and Margaret H. Hogan

FONTAINE,
Ashley Rose, b. 8/7/1990 in Wolfeboro; Shawn J. Fontaine and Linda
  E. White
Katelyn, b. 5/21/1988 in Dover; Michael N. Fontaine and Brenda L.
  Goodell
Matthew Glenn, b. 8/12/1988 in Wolfeboro; Shawn J. Fontaine and
  Linda E. White
Megan Ashley, b. 12/1/1990 in Dover; Michael N. Fontaine and
  Brenda L. Goodell

FORD,
Linwood, b. 1/27/1953 in Rochester; Herman L. Ford and Etta
  Elizabeth Gilman
Waneta A., b. 9/24/1948 in Rochester; thirteenth; Herman L. Ford
  (woodsman, Barnstead) and Etta E. Gilman (Derry)
Warren Vernon, b. 4/16/1955 in Rochester; Herman L. Ford and Etta
  Elizabeth Gilman
Wendall Russell, b. 4/16/1955 in Rochester; Herman L. Ford and Etta
  Elizabeth Gilman

FOSS,
Helen Frances, b. 1/6/1912; fourth; Frank G. Foss (merchant,
  Strafford) and Bessie G. Hall (Strafford)
Linda Ann, b. 11/5/1954 in Rochester; Albert George Foss and
  Marjorie Louise Foss
Wayne Russell, b. 6/29/1943 in Rochester; first; Albert G. Foss
  (woodsman, Barrington) and M. L. Corson (New Durham)

FOSTER,
Jeni Lyn, b. 12/9/1986 in Rochester; Jeffrey Alban Foster and Mary
  Alice Hanson

FREEBERN,
Shawn Milo, b. 5/31/1977 in Laconia; Michael D. Freebern and Cindy
  A. Carte

FRENCH,
daughter, b. 6/21/1900; second; Alden C. French (teamster, 20, Farmington) and Laurentina E. Runnals (18, New Durham)
Christina Marie, b. 1/27/1990 in Wolfeboro; Michael P. French and Roberta A. Fontaine
Ida Frances, b. 12/14/1912; first; Benjamin French (baker, Tiverton, RI) and Annie M. Colbath (Farmington)
Lawrence L., b. 6/17/1905; third; Leander H. French (farmer, 47, Farmington) and Nettie B. Tufts (34, Alton)

FRITSCHIE,
Elaine Susan, b. 2/19/1988 in Dover; Ralph Fritschie and Barbara K. Smith

FRYE,
Robert W., Jr., b. 11/27/1915; first; Robert Wilfred Frye (machinist, 25, Lynn, MA) and Miriam Estella Drew (23, Dayton, ME)

FUHRMAN,
Faith Joyce, b. 10/15/1926; second; James J. Fuhrman (farmer, Chelsea, MA) and Emma Joy (New Durham)

FULLER,
Brian Neal, b. 8/20/1981 in Wolfeboro; Mark J. Fuller and Paula M. Thumm
David Howard, b. 12/2/1978 in Rochester; Jeffrey A. Fuller and Ann J. Lang
Keith Mark, b. 5/16/1979 in Wolfeboro; Mark J. Fuller and Paula M. Thumm
Leann, b. 6/10/1989 in Wolfeboro; Mark J. Fuller and Paula M. Thumm

GAFFNEY,
Kelly Anne, b. 8/7/1980 in Rochester; Lawrence P. Gaffney and Cynthia A. Corbin

Kevin Lawrence, b. 8/28/1984 in Rochester; Lawrence P. Gaffney and Cynthia A. Corbin

GAGNE,
Eric Norman, b. 1/14/1976 in Rochester; Edward J. Gagne and Nancy D. Garland

GAGNER,
Andrew Donald, b. 3/20/1985 in Wolfeboro; Donald Raymond Gagner and Louise Helena Mega

GAGNON,
Kathryn Edith, b. 8/21/1975 in Rochester; Hilaire V. Gagnon and Elsie D. Lussier
Kristine Elieana, b. 6/22/1966 in Rochester; Hilaire V. Gagnon and Elsie D. Lussier

GALE,
George Theodore, b. 2/19/1958 in Manchester; Richard David Gale, Sr. and Eleanor Frances Baxter
Mary E., b. 9/19/1950 in Rochester; second; Richard D. Gale (teacher, RI) and Eleanor Baxter (NH)
Richard David, Jr., b. 4/16/1952 in Rochester; Richard David Gale and Eleanor Frances Baxter

GANTT,
Gabrielle Nicole, b. 12/26/1996 in Portsmouth; Gary William Gantt and Doreen Mary Hastings

GARLAND,
Nancy Diane, b. 2/27/1955 in Rochester; Victor Irving Garland and Joan Priscilla Adams
Paul Adams, b. 2/27/1957; Victor Irving Garland and Joan Priscilla Adams
Penny Ellen, b. 7/6/1959 in Rochester; Victor I. Garland and Joan P. Adams

Richard Mark, b. 9/25/1961 in Rochester; Victor Irving Garland and Joan Priscilla Adams

Sarah, b. 6/14/1985 in Rochester; Wendall Robert Garland and Karen Michelle Radcliffe

Vicki Joann, b. 5/22/1951 in Rochester; Victor Irving Garland and Joan Priscilla Adams

GAULT,

Beverly Ann, b. 9/28/1944 in Rochester; first; John Q. Gault (truck driver, Meredith) and Mildred I. Corson (New Durham)

Bonnie Phyllis, b. 12/3/1954 in Rochester; John Quincy Gault and Mildred Irene Corson

Brenda Joyce, b. 2/4/1952 in Rochester; John Quincy Gault and Mildred Irene Corson

Glenn Allen, b. 11/29/1956; John Quincy Gault and Mildred Irene Corson

GAVILL,

Bryan Tyler, b. 7/28/1995 in Laconia; Michael A. Gavill and Diana L. Frawley

GEARY,

Brenda Lee, b. 1/21/1962 in Wolfeboro; Philip Edward Geary and Selma Jane Emerson

Edward Phillip, b. 9/29/1937 in Wolfeboro; third; Anthony Geary (Waterboro, ME) and Bessie Eastman (Middleton)

GEHL,

Kirsten Leigh, b. 7/3/1998 in Portsmouth; Ronald Gehl and Paula Gehl

GELINAS,

Carole Marie, b. 5/22/1955 in Rochester; Paul Roger Gelinas and Alice Alma Gauthier

Christin May, b. 10/2/1988 in Rochester; Michael R. Gelinas and Grace M. Held

Diane Barbara, b. 8/15/1960 in Rochester; Paul Roger Gelinas and Alice Alma Gauthier
Joanne Alice, b. 5/20/1951 in Rochester; Paul Roger Gelinas and Alice Alma Gauthier
John Richard, b. 4/3/1958 in Rochester; Paul Roger Gelinas and Alice Alma Gauthier
Paul Roger, Jr., b. 6/2/1952 in Rochester; Paul Roger Gelinas and Alice Alma Gauthier
Paul Roger, III, b. 7/1/1981 in Rochester; Paul R. Gelinas, Jr. and Elizabeth A. Thomas
Richard Ernest, b. 3/24/1979 in Rochester; Michael R. Gelinas and Grace M. Held
Stacy Ann, b. 11/9/1977 in Rochester; Paul R. Gelinas, Jr. and Elizabeth A. Thomas
Tina Marie, b. 1/18/1974 in Rochester; Paul R. Gelinas, Jr. and Elizabeth A. Thomas

GENDRON,
Christopher Winn, b. 6/25/1964 in Wolfeboro; Philip Louis Gendron and Christine Marian Edwards
Lisa Nicole, b. 3/13/1963 in Wolfeboro; Philip Louis Gendron and Christine Marian Edwards

GEORGE,
Ashley Rae, b. 6/30/1983 in Rochester; Paul E. George and Mary A. Arsenault

GERRISH,
Daniel Wayne, b. 8/10/1986 in Dover; Raymon Robert Gerrish and Sylvia Lee Byrge

GILBERT,
Jeremy Greg, b. 9/3/1996 in Rochester; Eric Donald Gilbert and Andrea Lynn Bilodeau

GILMAN,
Matthew Martin, b. 9/11/1975 in Rochester; Michael V. Gilman and Brenda L. Varney

GIVETZ,
Thomas Walter, Jr., b. 8/17/1988 in Rochester; Thomas W. Givetz and Brenda J. Yianakopolos

GLIDDEN,
daughter, b. 1/26/1888; first; John F. Glidden (laborer, 28, Ashland) and Eldora B. Brown (15, Alton)

daughter, b. 1/13/1889; third; George Z. Glidden (farmer, 26, Gilford) and Lulu Ricker (18, Middleton)

son, b. 2/15/1889; second; James O. Glidden (laborer, 31, Gilford) and Ida Berry (31, New Durham)

son, b. 7/28/1889; second; John F. Glidden (farmer, 29, Gilford) and Eldora Brown (17, Alton)

son, b. 1/1/1892; fourth; James O. Glidden (farmer, 34, Lake Village) and Ida L. Berry (34, New Durham)

daughter [Georgie Ellen], b. 5/19/1892; third; George Z. Glidden (laborer, 30, Gilford) and Lulu Ricker (21, Farmington)

son [Charles], b. 10/30/1894; fifth; James O. Glidden (laborer, 37, Laconia) and Ida L. Berry (36, New Durham)

daughter [Alice P.], b. 6/8/1897; first; Harry F. Glidden (brushmaker, 19, New Durham) and Lilla B. Randall (18, New Durham)

daughter [Beatrice I.], b. 10/5/1898; second; Harry F. Glidden (brushmaker, 20, New Durham) and Lilla B. Randall (19, New Durham)

son [Clyde], b. 5/22/1901; third; Harry F. Glidden (laborer, 23, New Durham) and Lilla B. Randall (22, New Durham)

daughter, b. 2/24/1903; fourth; Harry F. Glidden (brushmaker, 24, New Durham) and Lilla Randall (24, New Durham)

son [Lauriston], b. 3/14/1905; fifth; Harry F. Glidden (brush work, 27, New Durham) and Lilla Randall (26, New Durham)

son, b. 8/20/1907; fifth; Harry Glidden (brush maker, 29, New Durham) and Lilla B. Randall (28, New Durham) daughter, b. 9/8/1909; seventh; Harry Glidden (sawyer, New Durham) and Lilla B. Randall (New Durham)

daughter, b. 12/31/1914; first; Hervey Glidden (laborer, New Durham) and Josephine Dame (New Durham)

daughter, b. 5/5/1915; first; Sidney M. Glidden (woodturner, 23, Farmington) and Alice P. Glidden (18, New Durham)

Ann E., b. 1/18/1887; first; James O. Glidden (farmer, 29, Gilford) and Ida ----- (29, New Durham)

Bernard S., b. 2/21/1918; second; Sidney M. Glidden (wood turner, Farmington) and Alice P. Glidden (New Durham)

Laurel Eleanor, b. 7/21/1924; ninth; Harry F. Glidden (woodturner, New Durham) and Lilla B. Randall (New Durham)

Velma, b. 6/24/1920; third; Sidney M. Glidden (wood turner, Farmington) and Alice P. Glidden (New Durham)

Warren M., b. 3/11/1921; eighth; Harry F. Glidden (sawyer, New Durham) and Lilla B. Randall (New Durham)

GODDARD,
Taylor Alexander, b. 3/17/1991 in Rochester; Timothy Allen Goddard and Susan Priscilla Locke

GOLDBERG,
Skylar Phillip, b. 12/16/1996 in Laconia; Michael W. Goldberg and Dana Marie Ouderkirk

GONYO,
daughter, b. 7/17/1894; third; ----- Gonzo (sic) (laborer, 40, Canada) and Sarah King (26, Canada)

Joseph, b. 8/13/1892; second; Andrew Gonyo (laborer, 35, Canada) and Sarah King (26, Canada)

Mary, b. 1/9/1891; second; Allum Gonyo (wood chopper, 34, Canada) and Sarah King (23, Canada)

GOODRICH,
daughter, b. 7/17/1894; first; Grafton N. Goodrich (farmer, 22, Danville) and Mattie E. Goodrich (19, Kingston)

GOODROW,
Lucille May, b. 1/27/1928; second; Andy Goodrow (laborer, Berwick, ME) and Jessie Colbath (Wolfeboro)
William Joseph, b. 8/27/1982 in Wolfeboro; Joseph L. Goodrow and Juanita A. Mandigo

GOODWIN,
Tarsha Jeanette, b. 5/21/1987 in Rochester; Robert B. Goodwin and Carol J. Cutter

GRADY,
John J., b. 12/23/1910; third; Joseph Grady (laborer, Ireland) and Nora Crosby (Ireland)

GRANT,
Janet May, b. 10/31/1934; first; Frank S. Grant (mechanic, East Rochester) and Frances G. Hughes (Barrington)

GRAY,
son, b. 4/21/1887; fifth; William A. Gray (blacksmith, 42, Alexandria) and ----- (37, Grafton)
child, b. 5/14/1959 in Rochester; William A. Gray and Rita J. King
Alan David, b. 4/28/1978 in Rochester; David A. Gray, Sr. and Sheryl M. Parsons
Bonnie Lee, b. 2/1/1966 in Rochester; Stanley F. Gray and Leora R. Gauthier
Brenda Lee, b. 3/17/1967 in Rochester; Stanley F. Gray and Leora R. Gauthier
Brian, b. 10/12/1960 in Rochester; William Albert Gray and Rita Jeannette King
Calvin Clay, b. 1/27/1966 in Rochester; William A. Gray and Rita J. King
David Allen, Jr., b. 8/21/1975 in Rochester; David A. Gray and Sheryl M. Parsons
Douglas Frank, b. 3/23/1972 in Rochester; Stanley F. Gray and Leora R. Gauthier

Glen Alan, b. 12/6/1962 in Rochester; William Albert Gray and Rita Jeannette King

Joann Marie, b. 1/3/1970 in Rochester; Harold L. Gray and Barbara A. York

John Alan, b. 4/21/1960 in Rochester; Wilbur Marshall Gray, Sr. and Gloria Maude King

Joseph Peter, b. 3/8/1953 in Rochester; Arthur Frank Gray and Marcia Agnes Barber

Joyce Ann, b. 8/8/1964 in Rochester; William Albert Gray and Rita Jeannette King

Linda Darlene, b. 6/7/1951 in Rochester; Arthur Frank Gray and Marcia Agnes Barber

Susan May, b. 5/2/1952 in Rochester; Arthur Frank Gray and Marcia Agnes Barber

Wilbur Marshall, Jr., b. 9/12/1958 in Rochester; Wilbur Marshall Gray, Sr. and Gloria Maude King

GRENIER,
son [Raymond J.], b. 6/24/1905; sixth; John Greenier (farmer, 51, Laboise, Canada) and Mary Perry (36, Laboise, Canada)

son, b. 8/29/1907; sixth; John Grenier (laborer, 52, Canada) and Mary Porrier (38, Canada)

Wilfred, Jr., b. 4/19/1929; third; Wilfred Grenier (mechanic, Rochester) and Nettie Chesley (Farmington)

GRIEVE,
Audrey Melissa, b. 10/6/1988 in Rochester; Douglas R. Grieve and Johanna M. Cadorette

GUERTIN,
Leslie Anne, b. 12/27/1986 in Dover; Gerry John Guertin and Janet Anne Rutherford

HALE,
daughter [Crystal V.], b. 7/24/1893; third; Corie E. Hale (shoe maker, 38, Lee, ME) and Ida M. Rines (25, New Durham)

son, b. 2/6/1897; fifth; Corie E. Hale (shoemaker, 41, Lee, ME) and Ida M. Rhines (27, Rochester)

son [Burton], b. 7/19/1900; seventh; Corie E. Hale (shoemaker, 45, Lee, ME) and Ida M. Rines (32, Rochester)

daughter [Doris V.], b. 8/18/1901; eighth; Corie E. Hale (shoemaker, 46, Lee, ME) and Ida M. Rines (33, Rochester)

son [Corie], b. 4/15/1907; ninth; Corie E. Hale (sole leather cutter, 51, Lee, ME) and Ida M. Rhines (39, Rochester)

Edgar Earl, b. 7/17/1891; first; Corie E. Hale (shoemaker, 36, Lee, ME) and Ida M. Rhines (23, Rochester)

Hazel, b. 9/8/1892; second; Corie E. Hale (shoemaker, 37, Lee, ME) and Ida Rines (24, Rochester)

Iona M., b. 9/30/1898; sixth; C. E. Hale (shoemaker, 43, Lee, ME) and Ida M. Rines (30, Rochester)

Queenie G., b. 1/16/1896; fourth; Corie E. Hale (shoemaker, 40, Lee, ME) and Ida M. Rhines (26, Rochester)

HALL,

Roxanne Marie, b. 2/27/1964 in Rochester; Leon Louville Hall and Ethel Louise Merrill

Roy Michael, 2d, b. 3/24/1965 in Rochester; Leon L. Hall and Ethel L. Merrill

HALPIN,

McKenzie Joyce, b. 3/20/1993 in Rochester; James Power Halpin and Kimberly Ann Johnson

HAM,

son, b. 6/13/1907; sixth; Frank Ham (laborer, 46, Farmington) and Gertie Randall (36, Canada)

Kaitlyn Leigh, b. 6/9/1993 in Rochester; Russell Warren Ham and Tracy Lynne Howard

Mabel A., b. 5/26/1906; fifth; Frank Ham (farmer, 44, Farmington) and Gertie F. Randall (34, Stanstead, PQ)

Nathaniel Russell, b. 8/18/1998 in Rochester; Russell Ham and Tracy Ham

HAMILTON,
Ryan Spencer, b. 9/29/1995 in Rochester; Robert E. Hamilton and Michele L. Lacroix

HARDING,
son [Daniel], b. 9/14/1889; first; Joseph D. Harding (farmer, 28, St. Johns, NB) and Ida Pearl (33, Farmington)
son [Joseph], b. 4/8/1892; second; Joseph D. Harding (farmer, 33, St. Johns, NB) and Ida Pearl (37, Farmington)
son [Herbert], b. 6/27/1895; third; Joseph D. Harding (farmer, St. John, NB) and Ida P. Harding (Farmington)
Gladys M., b. 9/8/1910; first; Joseph D. Harding (farmer, NS) and Mary A. Trafton (ME)
Harold V., b. 7/8/1917; third; Joseph H. Harding (woodturner, 25, New Durham) and Merle Bennett (25, Dover)
Olive, b. 10/25/1915; second; Joseph H. Harding (woodworker, 23, New Durham) and Merle H. Bennett (23, Dover)
S[tanley]. H., b. 11/30/1913; first; Joseph Harold Harding (woodworker, New Durham) and Merle H. Bennett (Dover)

HARRELL,
Ralph Andrew, b. 12/3/1992; James Keith Harrell and Madene Arleen Ramsey

HARRIS,
John Andrew, b. 6/2/1995; Paul A. Harris and Heather E. Levere
Katherine Brooks, b. 10/2/1992 in Rochester; Paul Andrew Harris and Heather Elizabeth Levere

HARTING,
Alexandra Katherine, b. 6/12/1990 in Dover; Bruce G. Harting and Lauren J. Brown

HARTLEY,
Kristen Nicole, b. 3/21/1995 in Laconia; David J. Hartley and Susan C. Sharkey

HASKINS,
William Leslie, b. 7/12/1970 in Rochester; William C. Haskins and Nancy R. Emery

HATCH,
Christine Elizabeth, b. 5/30/1980 in Dover; Richard D. Hatch and Katherine P. Koch

HAWKINS,
Heidi Sue, b. 4/24/1973 in Rochester; Howard W. Hawkins and Belinda J. Nesbitt

HAWLEY,
son, b. 9/1/1907; first; Henry A. Hawley (merchant, 22, Jeffersonville, VT) and Gertrude E. Avery (24, Newbury, VT)

HAYES,
son [Colo Erwin], b. 6/27/1892; fourth; Seth W. Hayes (knife maker, 32, Alton) and Abbie E. Swett (26, East Kingston)
daughter [Ethel E.], b. 11/13/1892; first; George L. Hayes (knife manufacturer, 29, Alton) and Clara E. Swett (24, East Kingston)
daughter [Arvena May], b. 4/29/1894; second; George L. Hayes (knife maker, 30, Alton) and Clara E. Swett (26, East Kingston)
daughter [Ethel E.], b. 3/23/1895; fifth; Seth W. Hayes (knife maker, 34, Alton) and Abbie E. Swett (28, East Kingston)
daughter [Mildred], b. 9/29/1895; first; Charles E. Hayes (farmer, 32, New Durham) and Georgia A. Hurd (18, So. Berwick, ME)
son [Everett W.], b. 7/4/1898; sixth; Seth W. Hayes (manufacturer, 38, Alton) and Abbie E. Swett (32, East Kingston)
son [Archie Lester], b. 12/29/1904; eighth; Seth W. Hayes (laborer, 43, Alton) and Abbie Swett (38, East Kingston)
son [Abbott N.], b. 8/30/1907; ninth; Seth W. Hayes (knife maker, 47, Alton) and Abbie E. Swett (41, East Kingston)
son [Ernest W.], b. 3/10/1909; tenth; Seth W. Hayes (knife maker, Alton) and Abbie Swett (East Kingston)

daughter [Margaret E.], b. 9/22/1911; eleventh; Seth W. Hayes (knifemaker, Alton) and Abbie Swett (East Kingston)

stillborn daughter, b. 9/19/1925; fifth; Everett W. Hayes (truckman, New Durham) and Rosaria Grenier (Rochester)

Altie Evelyn, b. 9/18/1901; seventh; Seth W. Hayes (knifemaker, 41, Alton) and Abbie E. Swett (35, Kingston)

Arnold W., b. 11/15/1945 in Rochester; first; W. Arnold Hayes (lumberman, New Durham) and Virginia Wyatt (Farmington)

Ashmun Stanley, b. 1/11/1930; second; Archie L. Hayes (woodturner, New Durham) and Rachel Peterson (New Durham)

Clarence E., b. 7/16/1887; second; Seth W. Hayes (knife maker, 27, Alton) and Abbie Swett (22, East Kingston)

Colo Erwin, Jr., b. 3/7/1924; fourth; Colo E. Hayes (truckman, New Durham) and Bertha McCarlie (Farmington, ME)

Elizabeth Elaine, b. 4/20/1929; sixth; Everett W. Hayes (mail carrier, New Durham) and Rosaria Grenier (New Durham)

Elizabeth G., b. 9/29/1947 in Rochester; first; John W. Hayes (woodsman, New Durham) and Mazie Demerritt (Sanbornville)

Gloria Jean, b. 1/2/1948; second; Warren A. Hayes (lumberman, New Durham) and Virginia Wyatt (Farmington)

John, b. 9/8/1921; third; Everett W. Hayes (farmer, New Durham) and Rosaria Grenier (Rochester)

Leon F., b. 11/8/1919; second; Everett W. Hayes (teamster, New Durham) and Rosaria Grenier (Rochester)

Mildred E.E., b. 2/15/1918; second; Colo E. Hayes (wood turner, New Durham) and Bertha E. MacCarlie (Farmington, ME)

Rachel Ann, b. 5/26/1955 in Rochester; Warren Arthur Hayes and Virginia Lee Wyatt

Robert LeVin, b. 10/15/1931; eighth; Everett W. Hayes (mail carrier, New Durham) and Rosaria Grenier (Rochester)

Roberta T., b. 11/23/1919; third; Colo E. Hayes (brush maker, New Durham) and Bertha MacCarlie (Farmington, ME)

Rosemary E., b. 1/7/1950 in Rochester; third; Warren A. Hayes (lumberman, New Durham) and Virginia L. Wyatt (Farmington)

Sylvia B., b. 4/15/1888; eighth; Augustus W. Hayes (knife manf'r, 33, Alton) and Martha E. Jewett (33)

Warren Arnold, b. 11/22/1922; fourth; Everett W. Hayes (teamster, New Durham) and Rosaria Grenier (Rochester)

HEALD,
Michael Anthony, b. 4/27/1982 in Portsmouth; Gerald M. Heald, Jr. and Luanne Gordon

HEATH,
Mark Winslow, b. 8/20/1960 in Wolfeboro; Gray Paul Heath and Edna Martha Knowles

HELDENS,
Bennett Kyle, b. 12/7/1998 in Portsmouth; Joachim Heldens and Michelle Heldens

HELFER,
Elizabeth Pauline, b. 3/27/1988 in Laconia; Lawrence B. Helfer and Lorraine J. Drake
Rebecca Jeanne, b. 3/27/1988 in Laconia; Lawrence B. Helfer and Lorraine J. Drake

HEMPEL,
Staci Jean, b. 6/17/1997 in Dover; Douglas Walter Hempel and Janice Marie Smeriglio

HENDERSON,
James Edward, b. 5/1/1928 in Rochester; first; Roland Henderson (laborer, NS) and Evelyn Littlefield (Barnstead)

HENSHAW,
Howard Myron, b. 2/15/1928; fourth; George Henshaw and Gertrude Pender (Northwood); residence - Kingston

HIGGINS,
Andrew Edward, b. 9/5/1976 in Quincy, MA; Edward P. Higgins and Jane P. Webb

Joy Kathryn, b. 6/24/1978 in Rochester; Edward P. Higgins and Jane P. Webb

HILL,
Arlene, b. 2/19/1927 in Farmington; second; Earl A. Hill (mill worker, Barnstead) and Effie M. Thurston (Berwick, ME)
Diane Mary, b. 4/26/1976 in Rochester; Wayne E. Hill and Anna M. Blomstrom
Earline, b. 2/19/1927 in Farmington; first; Earl A. Hill (mill worker, Barnstead) and Effie M. Thurston (Berwick, ME)

HILLSGROVE,
Ashley Nicole, b. 9/3/1991 in Wolfeboro; Royal Allen Hillsgrove and Christine Casey
Charles Raymond, b. 9/19/1959 in Rochester; Harry G. Hillsgrove and Theresa R. Plante
Daniel Gordon, b. 5/2/1958 in Rochester; Harry George Hillsgrove, Jr. and Theresa Reta Plante
Deanna Leigh, b. 12/31/1981 in Rochester; Randy M. Hillsgrove and Deanna L. Poole
George Terry, b. 9/18/1955 in Rochester; Harry George Hillsgrove, Jr. and Theresa Reta Plante
Janice Janine, b. 10/28/1956; Harry George Hillsgrove, Jr. and Theresa Reta Plante
Michael Barry, b. 8/18/1969 in Rochester; Harry G. Hillsgrove and Theresa R. Plante
Royal Allen, b. 11/30/1965 in Rochester; Harry G. Hillsgrove, Jr. and Theresa R. Plante
Suzanne Rose, b. 8/29/1953 in Pittsfield; Harry George Hillsgrove and Theresa Rita Plante
Tina Dee, b. 8/30/1967 in Rochester; Harry G. Hillsgrove, Jr. and Theresa R. Plante

HORNE,
daughter [May Eva], b. 11/19/1894; first; Everett E. Horne (farmer, 28, Middleton) and Emma A. Berry (15, Farmington)

son, b. 9/3/1896; second; Everett E. Horne (farmer, 30, Middleton) and Emma A. Berry (17, Farmington)

HOUSEL,
Kelsey Lee, b. 10/17/1993 in Rochester; Joseph Housel, III and Deborah Jean Rollins

HOVLAND,
Jessica Laurel, b. 8/2/1983 in Concord; Bruce A. Hovland and Kathleen E. Harry
Stephanie Meryl, b. 2/15/1985 in Concord; Bruce A. Hovland and Kathleen E. Harry

HOWARD,
Fred W., b. 12/5/1921; fourth; Fred W. Howard (farmer, MA) and Madeline Ames (NH)

HOYT,
Edith Sue, b. 1/31/1963 in Rochester; Edgar Hoyt and Edna Mae Dawson

HUDSON,
daughter, b. 5/18/1980 in Dover; Harmon P. Hudson and Cheryl J. Cumming

HUGHES,
Robert, b. 8/12/1937; tenth; Henry Hughes (farmer, Dover) and Ruby Labby (East Rochester)

HUME,
Hillary Ann, b. 10/29/1979 in Rochester; John A. Hume and LuAnne Fitzpatrick

HUSSEY,
Caitlin Knight, b. 11/25/1991 in Wolfeboro; David Robert Hussey and Nancy Joan Knight

HUSSON,
Sheri Jo, b. 11/20/1967 in Rochester; David K. Husson and Loneeda
F. Coran

INGHAM,
Jason Robert, b. 11/19/1982 in Rochester; Robert S. Ingham and
Carole M. Gelinas
Mathew Charles, b. 6/13/1979 in Rochester; Robert S. Ingham and
Carole M. Gelinas

INGLIS,
Allison Marie, b. 4/9/1994 in Exeter; Peter Gregory Inglis and Susan
Pauline Price

JACKLIN,
Jason Robert, b. 5/13/1976 in Laconia; Bruce A. Jacklin and June E.
Carleton
Lorraine Louise, b. 2/26/1959 in Rochester; Harry L. Jacklin and
Alma M. Kamps

JACKSON,
Leah Noel, b. 12/17/1989; Herbert R. Jackson and Kerry Clifford
Micah Andrew, b. 5/22/1985; Herbert Roy Jackson and Kerry Clifford

JARVIS,
Rebecca Lea, b. 3/18/1980 in Concord; Mark D. Jarvis and Theresa A.
Murray

JENKINS,
Dorothy A., b. 7/22/1910; first; Ralph C. Jenkins (bookkeeper,
Milton) and Bernice M. Hart (Lebanon, ME)

JENNER,
Drew Frederick, b. 7/29/1969 in Laconia; Frederick V. Jenner and
Bonnie L. Drew

JONES,
son [Frank], b. 9/11/1899; second; George H. Jones (lumber merchant, 28, New Durham) and Myra G. Davis (22, New Durham)
Barbara Frances, b. 1/22/1923; first; Frank Jones (New Durham) and Doris V. Clough (Dover)
George H., Jr., b. 5/9/1917; fourth; George H. Jones (lumber dealer, 46, New Durham) and Myra Davis (40, New Durham)
Harry Erskine, b. 4/17/1898; first; George H. Jones (lumber merchant, 27, New Durham) and Myra G. Davis (21, New Durham)
Lydia Frances, b. 3/23/1905; third; George H. Jones (lumber merchant, 34, New Durham) and Myra J. Davis (28, New Durham)

JOY,
son [Samuel], b. 12/19/1897; second; Samuel Orin Joy (farmer, 38, New Durham) and Mary Ellen Berry (33, New Durham)
daughter, b. 6/14/1899; third; Orrin S. Joy (farmer, 39, New Durham) and Mary Ellen Berry (35, New Durham)
son [Arthur A.], b. 8/11/1902; fourth; Orrin S. Joy (farmer, 43, New Durham) and Mary E. Berry (38, New Durham)
Arthur A., Jr., b. 6/27/1932; fourth; Arthur A. Joy (farmer, New Durham) and Elsie Cilley (Nottingham)
Earl Kenneth, b. 9/5/1933; fifth; Arthur A. Joy (laborer, New Durham) and Elsie C. Cilley (Nottingham)
Earl Kenneth, II, b. 1/9/1967; Earl K. Joy and Marjorie E. Little
Jean Margaret, b. 12/27/1957 in Rochester; Samuel Orrin Joy, III and Jean Margaret Norman
Mary Alice, b. 4/10/1931; third; Arthur A. Joy (farmer, New Durham) and Elsie Cilley (Nottingham)
Mary Ellen, b. 12/17/1964 in Rochester; Samuel Orrin Joy and Jean Margaret Norman
Nellie, b. 11/2/1934; sixth; Arthur Joy (farmer, New Durham) and Elsie Cilley (Nottingham)
Robert Allen, b. 10/22/1935 in Wolfeboro; seventh; Arthur A. Joy (laborer, New Durham) and Elsie B. Cilley (Nottingham)

Samuel Orin, 3d, b. 3/28/1930; second; Arthur A. Joy (farmer, New
    Durham) and Elsie Cilley (Nottingham)
Samuel Orrin, V, b. 10/4/1978 in Dover; Samuel O. Joy, IV and Cindy
    L. Noland
Trevor Allen, b. 4/24/1994 in Dover; Robert Alan Joy, Jr. and Sheri
    Ann Brown

KEEFE,
Michale Jae, b. 3/26/1990 in Wolfeboro; Paul A. Keefe, Jr. and Karen
    L. Lagasse

KEENAN,
Justin Mackenzie, b. 2/15/1997 in Portsmouth; John Joseph Keenan,
    III and Heidi Jean Ryder

KELLER,
Justin Allen, b. 12/17/1988 in Rochester; Terry L. Keller and Carol T.
    Allen

KELLEY,
June Lorraine, b. 6/13/1934; first; Charlotte Kelley (Middleton)

KENISTON,
daughter, b. 3/6/1940; sixth; Elmer Kenniston (sic) (laborer,
    Newmarket) and Georgia Hills (Hill)
Fred Thomas, b. 6/1/1942; seventh; Elmer J. Keniston (odd jobs,
    Newmarket) and Georgia E. Hill (Hill)

KIMBALL,
Dennise Carol, b. 2/19/1953 in Wolfeboro; Marshall Melvin Kimball
    and Charlotte Bernice Geary
Mary Adeline, b. 6/5/1963 in Wolfeboro; Marshall Melvin Kimball
    and Charlotte Bernice Geary

KING,
son, b. 11/30/1892; tenth; Peter King (wood chopper, 39, Canada) and Rose Marcou (38, Canada)
son, b. 4/23/1893; first; George King (wood chopper, 25, Canada) and Anna Bissen (20, Canada)
Alice Frances, b. 6/23/1922; fifth; Francis A. King (tinsmith, Boston, MA) and Beatrice Layton (Fitchburg, MA)
Kaleigh Sandra, b. 8/21/1985 in Dover; Stephen Clyde King and Victoria Marjorie McPhee

KLINCH,
Wendy Lee, b. 1/16/1981 in Wolfeboro; Edward A. Klinch and Corrine L. Judkins

KNIBBS,
Scott Andrew, b. 7/4/1990 in Rochester; Douglas W. Knibbs and Cheryl A. Hillsgrove

KNOWLTON,
son, b. 12/19/1895; second; William G. Knowlton (shoe maker, 21, Concord) and Flora B. Towle (20, Northwood)

KOLB,
Aaron Louis, b. 1/25/1990 in Portsmouth; Timothy L. Kolb and Jennifer G. Waite
Adam Michael, b. 6/17/1994 in Rochester; Timothy Louis Kolb and Jennifer Grace Waite

LABELLE,
Molly Elizabeth, b. 4/28/1997 in Dover; Donald Robert Labelle and Marie Elizabeth Arcano

LABRIE,
Lukas Xavier, b. 12/28/1990 in Rochester; Maurice G. Labrie and Barbara A. Provencher

LAFAYETTE,
Marcus Edward, b. 7/19/1926; third; Lindsay L. LaFayette (poultry husbandry, Whitinsville, MA) and Irene O. Longe (New York, NY)

LAMBERTSON,
Elizabeth Louise, b. 12/31/1928 in Rochester; first; George D. Lambertson (laborer, NS) and Ethel F. Curtice (Concord)
George D., Jr., b. 7/29/1931; second; George D. Lambertson (woodturner, NS) and Ethel Curtice (Concord)

LANCE,
Anthony Franklin, b. 7/10/1985 in Rochester; Gary Norman Lance and Sandra Ann Franklin

LANDOLT,
Zachary William, b. 5/21/1987 in Laconia; David P. Landolt and Patricia A. Wike

LANEY,
Dave Allen, b. 12/17/1949 in Rochester; third; George E. Laney (tannery, Alton) and Geraldine Gorton (Hampstead)
Francis Herbert, b. 4/26/1930; seventh; George Laney (laborer, Skowhegan, ME) and Hazel Nutter (Dover)
George Frank, b. 10/27/1947 in Rochester; second; George E. Laney, Jr. (shaver, Alton) and Geraldine Gorton (Hampstead)
Joan Carole, b. 3/26/1942; second; Frank T. Laney (shoeworker, Alton) and Irene E. Brown (Brockton, MA)
Linda M., b. 9/16/1950 in Wolfeboro; third; Cecil N. Laney (tanner, NH) and Virginia A. Shaw (NH)
Mickie Rae, b. 5/4/1957; Cecil Nutter Laney and Virginia Agnes Shaw
Trina Mae, b. 5/31/1941; first; Frank Tracy Laney (ice man, Alton) and Ilene E. Brown (Brockton, MA)

LANGLEY,
Albert Lyle, b. 3/15/1928; second; Nathaniel R. Langley (laborer, Moultonboro) and Bertha E. Small (Strafford)
Albert Lyle, Jr., b. 8/6/1959 in Rochester; Albert L. Langley, Sr. and Madeline E. Spurling
Patricia Jean, b. 6/20/1930; third; Nathaniel Langley (truck driver, Moultonboro) and Bertha Small (Strafford)

LANZETTA,
Alison Kate, b. 11/15/1979 in Concord; Patrick W. Lanzetta, MD and Marion C. D'Andrea
Joshua Patrick, b. 9/26/1978 in Hanover; Patrick W. Lanzetta and Marion C. D'Andrea

LAPAR,
Rachel Elizabeth, b. 8/11/1996 in Exeter; William H. R. Lapar and Sonya Ruth Maddock

LAPOINTE,
Ricky Jon, b. 8/9/1955 in Rochester; Richard Adelard LaPointe and Dorothy Minnie Murdo
Terry Lee, b. 8/11/1954 in Rochester; Richard Adalard LaPointe and Dorothy Minnie Murdo

LARGE,
Scott Curtis, b. 9/24/1982 in Rochester; Kenneth W. Large and Roberta M. Swallow

LAROCHELLE,
Pauline M., b. 5/24/1930; first; Joseph E. Larochelle (farmer, Rochester) and Eva M. Rand (New Durham)

LARY,
Donald Eugene, b. 6/18/1922; third; Frank G. Lary (farmer, Merrimac, MA) and Marcia E. Lowell (Lebanon, ME)

LASORE,
Clo D., b. 10/17/1892; sixth; L. Lasore (laborer, 34, Canada) and Sarvie Dubois (32, Canada)

LAURION,
Jacob Cody, b. 8/8/1998 in Rochester; Hal Burton Laurion and Nathalli Anne Laurion

LAVOE,
daughter, b. 3/26/1895; seventh; Leizoa Lavoe (blacksmith, 36, Canada) and Elabe Dubois (35, Canada)

LEARY,
Kenneth Robert, b. 5/5/1921; second; Frank Leary (farmer, Merrimac, MA) and Marcia E. Lowell (Lebanon, ME)

LEE,
George Michael, b. 11/24/1952 in Rochester; George Houston Lee and Aline P. Dyer

LEGASSIE,
Shayne Aaron, b. 1/17/1975 in Rochester; Dayne A. Legassie and Bonnie L. Boston

LEHNER,
Ari Sarrau, b. 4/24/1993 in Laconia; Scott David Lehner and Danica Lee Charlton

LEMENSE,
Mary F., b. 9/22/1892; fourteenth; Marselle Lemense (wood chopper, 43, Canada) and Emile Thabarge (43, Canada)

LEO,
Joseph Napoleon, b. 12/24/1891; second; Joseph Leo (wood chopper, 30, Canada) and Mary Lacas (25, Canada)

LEVESQUE,
Adam Paul, b. 8/17/1989 in Rochester; Paul D. Levesque and Laurie A. Buote
Nicole Lillian, b. 5/31/1986 in Rochester; Paul Donald Levesque and Laurie Ann Buote

LINDBERG,
Christine Ann, b. 3/9/1966 in Wolfeboro; David T. Lindberg and Rachel A. Caisse
Ingrid Erica, b. 5/30/1974 in Wolfeboro; David T. Lindberg and Rachel A. Caisse

LINGARD,
Clara Dorice, b. 3/26/1938 in Wolfeboro; first; Elmer Lingard (lumberman, Granville, VT) and Doris Bushway (Newburyport, MA)

LINGEMAN,
Samuel Todd, b. 9/2/1977 in Exeter; Steven L. Lingeman and Joyce M. Casey
Sarah Jeannette, b. 12/10/1979 in Dover; Steven L. Lingeman and Joyce M. Casey

LIST,
Benjamin Thomas, b. 3/30/1974 in Wolfeboro; Paul D. List and June A. McCallum

LIVINGSTONE,
daughter, b. 11/14/1911; second; Irving E. Livingstone (handlemaker, Rochester) and Gladys T. Hayes (Jackson)

LOCKE,
Sandra Nicole, b. 2/13/1982 in Concord; David J. Locke and Colette A. Landry

LOCKWOOD,
stillborn son, b. 12/24/1943 in Rochester; first; John J. Lockwood (farm manager, Marengo, IA) and Priscilla Tillson (Harwich, MA)

LORD,
Hailey Marie, b. 8/16/1985 in Dover; Robert Arthur Lord and Georgette Kamel

LOWELL,
son, b. 12/3/1887; second; Stillman R. Lowell (knife maker, 23, South Hiram, ME) and ----- (29, New Durham)
daughter, b. 9/20/1901; seventh; Stillman R. Lowell (shoemaker, 37, Hiram, ME) and Cora E. Willey (34, New Durham)
Donald Leslie, b. 1/14/1931; third; Fred C. Lowell (laborer, Lebanon, ME) and Marjorie Ryan (Kennebunk, ME)
Fred Clifton, b. 11/30/1927 in Rochester; second; Fred C. Lowell (wood turner, Lebanon, ME) and Marjorie Ryan (Kennebunk, ME)
Gordon Carlos, b. 6/14/1925; first; Fred C. Lowell (lathe turner, Lebanon, ME) and Marjorie J. Ryan (Kennebunk, ME)
L. L., b. 8/12/1889; eighth; James A. Lowell (farmer, 47, Hiram, ME) and Joanna Lowell (41, Hiram, ME)
Sherwood A., b. 2/10/1934; fifth; Fred C. Lowell (woodworker, Lebanon, ME) and Marjorie Ryan (Kennebunk, ME)
Shirley Agnes, b. 8/19/1932; fourth; Fred C. Lowell (wood turner, Lebanon, ME) and Marjorie Ryan (Kennebunk, ME)

LUCKERN,
Marie Nicole, b. 12/7/1998 in Manchester; Maurice Luckern and Patricia Luckern

LUSSIER,
Tiara Rae, b. 12/31/1992 in Rochester; Raymond Frederick Lussier and Melissa Marie Henderson

LYNCH,
Ernest Harold, b. 4/24/1962 in Rochester; Richard Lynch and Sonia Irene Scofield

LYTLE,
Bryan Carl, b. 4/25/1998 in Dover; Gary E. Lytle and Regina Lee Lytle

MAGER,
Morgan Douglas, b. 10/9/1981 in Rochester; Michael B. Mager and Marcelle R. Mater

MAGGIORE,
stillborn son, b. 5/16/1913; tenth; Joseph Maggiore (laborer, Italy) and Rosie Maggiore (Italy)
stillborn son, b. 2/2/1915; fifteenth; Joseph Maggiore (enamel worker, 40, Italy) and Rose Spatafore (40, Italy)

MAHONEY,
Marilyn, b. 6/1/1951 in Rochester; William Edward Mahoney and June Elizabeth Lindahl

MANSFIELD,
Keith Choate, b. 9/19/1958 in Rochester; James Boyd Mansfield and Cynthia Anne Choate

MARCH,
Pamela Ann, b. 7/7/1972 in Dover; Frederic W. March and Margaret T. Goupil

MARCOUX,
Jacqueline Lee, b. 3/15/1937 in Rochester; first; Alfred Marcoux (shoe worker, Wakefield) and Mary Mattocks (Boston, MA)

MARSTERS,
Luke David, b. 6/13/1993 in Rochester; David Charles Marsters and
   Doreen Frances Lamper

MASKELL,
Haley Marie, b. 5/13/1996 in Rochester; Robert Alton Maskell and
   Wendy Marie Lovejoy

MASON,
Thomas Clancy, b. 11/23/1997 in Rochester; Thomas James Mason
   and Ellen Odacier Hardy

McALLISTER,
Grace Blanche, b. 1/30/1949 in Wolfeboro; fourth; Norman
   McAllister (bus driver, ME) and Shirley Richardson (W.
   Lebanon, ME)

McCARTHY,
Patricia Jo-An, b. 11/2/1968 in Rochester; Leo E. McCarthy and
   Patricia F. Garland

McKAY,
Bethany Nancy, b. 2/16/1975 in Wolfeboro; Charles E. McKay and
   Nancy A. Goodwin
Charles Edward, Jr., b. 7/20/1965 in Rochester; Charles E. McKay
   and Donna L. Rand
Fallon Patricia, b. 7/10/1990 in Rochester; Charles E. McKay, Jr. and
   Diana E. Pinckard
Sunny Anne, b. 8/29/1973 in Wolfeboro; Charles E. McKay and
   Nancy A. Goodwin
Thomas Dean, b. 5/22/1968 in Rochester; Charles E. McKay and
   Donna L. Rand

McKEAN,
daughter, b. 5/31/1887; second; Evans McKean (farmer, 45, Lovell,
   ME) and ----- (38, Brookfield)

daughter [Doris L.], b. 9/14/1902; first; James M. McKean (lastmaker, 27, New Durham) and Flora M. Towle (25, New Durham)

McKEEN,
stillborn daughter, b. 11/3/1909; second; James M. McKeen (wood worker, New Durham) and Flora M. Towle (New Durham)
son [Donald M.], b. 7/4/1911; third; James M. McKeen (knifemaker, New Durham) and Flora M. Towle (New Durham)
C. L. (daughter), b. 8/20/1939 in Wolfeboro; second; Donald McKeen (salesman, New Durham) and Mary Miller (New Durham)
Joyce Ann, b. 8/15/1937 in Wolfeboro; first; Donald McKeen (truck driver, New Durham) and Mary F. Miller (New Durham)

McKENZIE,
Michael Mathew, b. 10/26/1980 in Rochester; Douglas P. McKenzie and Rita E. Orama

McLAUGHLIN,
Ryan James, b. 10/1/1983 in Rochester; Thomas J. McLaughlin and Jennifer M. Betts

McLELLAN,
Steve Edward, b. 4/26/1975 in Wolfeboro; Ronald A. McLellan and Louise A. Soldano

McMULLEN,
Nicholas Matthew, b. 3/18/1997 in Dover; Stephen P. McMullen and Katherine R. Currier

MEEHAN,
Mark Adam, b. 6/25/1985 in Wolfeboro; Mark L. Meehan and Martha Jean Croteau

MEINELT,
Curtis E., b. 10/5/1923; first; William E. Meinelt (farmer, Lawrence, MA) and Margaret Entwistle (Darwin, England)

MELANSON,
R. (son), b. 4/9/1940; ninth; Omer Melanson (truck driver, Grafton) and Wilma Knox (Seabrook)
Wayne Edward, b. 3/12/1937; eighth; Omer I. Melanson (truck driver, Grafton) and Wilmer Knox (Seabrook)

METAYER,
Jaclynne Rose, b. 4/6/1991 in Dover; Jeffrey Michael Metayer and Nikki Marie Paquette

MEYER,
Jared Michael, b. 4/23/1993 in Dover; Michael John Meyer and Elizabeth Ann Jordon
Jennifer Whitney, b. 1/22/1987 in Rochester; Michael J. Meyer and Elizabeth A. Jordon

MICHALSKI,
Shyar Louise, b. 10/21/1987 in Rochester; Robert A. Michalski and Vicki Ann Silvestri

MICKLON,
Richard Paul, b. 4/29/1943 in Rochester; second; Vernon F. Micklon (Rep. U Aircraft, E. Northwood) and S. Richardson (W. Lebanon); residence - California
William Charles, b. 6/27/1944 in Rochester; third; Vernon F. Micklon (drafting dept., E. Northwood) and S. L. Richardson (W. Lebanon)

MILES,
Jeffery Scott, b. 6/21/1958 in Rochester; Edmund Walter Miles and Dorothy Mae Hersey

Todd Anthony, b. 12/26/1956; Edmund Walter Miles and Dorothy Mae Hersey

MILLER,
son, b. 8/8/1907; first; Richard Miller (farmer, 26, New Durham) and Eda O. Joy (35, New Durham)
daughter [Eda F.], b. 8/10/1912; fourth; Richard Miller (farmer, New Durham) and Eda O. Joy (New Durham)
Bobbi-Jo, b. 4/4/1979 in Rochester; Robert J. Miller, Jr. and Susan K. Irish
Brandi Lyn, b. 12/19/1982 in Rochester; Robert J. Miller, Jr. and Susan K. Irish
Dorothy C., b. 9/14/1917; third; Grover C. Miller (patrolman, 30, New Durham) and Gresenth Waite (30, Stanton, England)
Freda M., b. 11/12/1908; second; Richard Miller (farmer, New Durham) and Eda O. Joy (New Durham)
Gladys E., b. 6/26/1893; fifth; James A. Miller (farmer, 59, Milton) and Ella J. Glidden (37, Alton)
Grover C., b. 7/16/1887; James A. Miller (farmer, 54, Milton) and Ella J. Glidden (32)
Grover Daniel, b. 5/27/1916; second; Grover C. Miller (farmer, 29, New Durham) and Anna M. Grisenthwaite (28, Beneth, England)
James A., b. 3/14/1914; first; Gladys E. Miller (New Durham)
Lester J., b. 12/15/1910; third; Richard Miller (farmer, New Durham) and Edna O. Joy (New Durham)
Mary F., b. 5/21/1914; first; Grover C. Miller (farmer, New Durham) and Annie Grisenthwaite (England)
Richard, b. 3/4/1915; fifth; Richard Miller (farmer, 34, New Durham) and Eda O. Joy (42, New Durham)

MOHOLLAND,
C. (son), b. 8/21/1939 in Rochester; second; Clinton Moholland (wood cutter, Lynn, MA) and Cora Columbus (Lynn, MA)

MOISON,
stillborn son, b. 3/26/1913; first; Fred Moison (woodchopper, Quebec) and Clara Boucher (New Durham)
Mary L., b. 4/27/1915; second; Fred Moison (woodchopper, 32, Canada) and Clarina Bouche (22, New Durham)

MONTGOMERY,
Adrian Lane, b. 7/2/1970 in Rochester; Robert L. Montgomery and Barbara A. Garofalo

MOODY,
Cheryl Ann, b. 6/20/1964 in Rochester; Willie Henry Moody, Jr. and Joan Patricia Charbonneau
Sharon Marie, b. 1/2/1963 in Rochester; Willie Henry Moody and Joan Patricia Charbonneau

MOORE,
Allen Howard, b. 12/17/1971 in Rochester; Gary F. Moore and Gayle E. Reynolds
Ashley Sherwell, b. 6/21/1982 in Dover; George J. Moore and Elizabeth S. Mead
Seth Michael, b. 12/3/1991 in Exeter; Shawn Michael Moore and Susan Beth Davis

MOORES,
Robyn Alison, b. 6/16/1984 in Dover; Bradley A. Moores and Stacy A. Luneau
Shelby Aaron, b. 9/7/1990 in Wolfeboro; Bradley A. Moores and Stacy A. Luneau

MORIN,
Aloha Lee, b. 5/24/1948 in Rochester; second; Henry E. Morin (truck driver, Effingham) and M. B. Willard (Farmington)

MORRIS,
Brianna Leigh, b. 9/23/1989 in Dover; Richard T. Morris and
  Maureen E. Melanson

MOSES,
Nathan Carlisle, b. 8/13/1987 in Dover; James T. Moses and Dianne
  L. Defrain

MOULTON,
Alden Linbergh, b. 3/17/1929; third; Fred A. Moulton (laborer,
  Middleton) and Vivian E. Grace (Tamworth); residence -
  Middleton
K. A., b. 10/3/1914; first; Charles T. Moulton (machinist, Strafford)
  and Fannie E. Cook (Center Harbor)
Robert C., b. 6/13/1918; second; Charles T. Moulton (farmer,
  Strafford) and Fannie Cook (Center Harbor)

MOYNIHAN,
son, b. 9/16/1903; first; Daniel Moynihan (RR fireman, 23) and Sadie
  Foss (19, Rochester); residence - Portland, ME

MUNROE,
Alison Jeanette, b. 5/28/1987 in Rochester; David L. Munroe and
  Christine V. Torrey
Sheree Lynn, b. 1/24/1986 in Rochester; Darrell Everett Munroe and
  Mary Ellen Joy
Susan Elizabeth, b. 4/30/1983 in Rochester; David L. Munroe and
  Christine V. Torrey
Wendy Leigh, b. 8/10/1968 in Dover; David L. Munroe and Patricia
  A. Williams

MURRAY,
Trevor Patrick, b. 8/18/1994 in Dover; Brian Dennis Murray and Lisa
  Faye Ahlberg

NASON,
Shawn Richard, b. 6/8/1998 in Rochester; Noel Robert Nason and Melissa Louise Nason

NEHRING,
Curtis Glavin, b. 12/8/1948 in Rochester; second; William Hans Nehring (landscape nursery, Northampton, MA) and Viva M. Davis (Northampton, MA)

NELSON,
Kathryn Olivia, b. 10/30/1991 in Rochester; David Allen Nelson and Erika Lee Anderson

NICASTRO,
Angela Lea, b. 11/12/1997 in Dover; John James Nicastro, III and Judith Ann Wengrzynek

NICHOLS,
Parker, b. 11/5/1915; fourth; Parker Borden Nichols (mill hand, 54, RI) and Sophia May Brown (32, Temple)

NICHOLSON,
Wesley Paul, b. 2/15/1956; Norman Nicholson and Violet Jane Rumson

NICKERSON,
Darlene D., b. 5/8/1947; fourth; Leroy S. Nickerson (shoecutter, Stockton Springs, ME) and Violet Woodard (Waterbory, VT)
Ellery Leroy, b. 6/8/1949 in Rochester; fifth; Leroy Nickerson (shoe shop, ME) and Violet Woodard (VT)
Irvin Ellery, b. 3/1/1945; third; LeRoy S. Nickerson (navy yard work, Stockton Springs, ME) and Violet Woodard (Waterbury, VT)
L. (son), b. 10/9/1939; second; LeRoy Nickerson (shoeworker, Stockton Springs, ME) and Violet Woodard (Waterbury, VT)

Levi, b. 4/27/1985 in Wolfeboro; Ellery Leroy Nickerson and Terrie Drew

Nancy Anne, b. 9/27/1936; first; LeRoy Nickerson (shoeworker, Stockton Springs, ME) and Violet Woodard (Waterbury, VT)

NORMAND,

Stacy Danae, b. 9/16/1990 in Rochester; James P. Normand and Patricia A. Tibbetts

NOYES,

son, b. 8/11/1906; sixth; Victor N. Noyes (tool maker, 37, Dixfield, ME) and Dora Snowman (31, Weld, ME)

O'CONNELL,

Jason Paul, b. 6/17/1976 in Concord; Paul V. O'Connell and Martha J. Colburn

Shelley Ann, b. 12/18/1973 in Concord; Paul R. O'Connell and Martha J. Colburn

ORLOWICZ,

Elizabeth Claire, b. 3/22/1991 in Dover; Steven Joseph Orlowicz and Catherine Edna Roy

Martin Stephen, b. 6/6/1993 in Dover; Stephen J. Orlowicz and Catherine Edna Roy

OUELLETTE,

Frederick Louis, Jr., b. 5/2/1985 in Rochester; Frederick Louis Ouellette and Dorothy Edna Downs

Kerry Lynn, b. 4/1/1988 in Rochester; Frederick L. Ouellette and Dorothy Downs

PAGE,

Della Julia, b. 2/14/1929; fourth; Elmer W. Page (woodsman, Loudon) and Julie W. Eaton (Epping); residence - Loudon

PAREDES,
Sara Jade, b. 7/23/1982 in Concord; Juan D. Paredes and Eileen M. Shephard

PARSONS,
Frank Waldo, 3d, b. 10/15/1955 in Rochester; Frank Waldo Parsons, Jr. and Priscilla Alice Wells
Kathy Jean, b. 11/7/1961 in Rochester; Frank Waldo Parsons, Jr. and Priscilla Alice Wells
Sheryl May, b. 11/23/1954 in Rochester; Frank Waldo Parsons, Jr. and Priscilla Alice Wells
Susan Anne, b. 5/17/1951 in Rochester; Frank Waldo Parsons and Priscilla Alice Wells
Terri Lynn, b. 5/19/1960 in Rochester; Frank Waldo Parsons, Jr. and Priscilla Alice Wells

PATRIACCA,
Mark Allen, b. 12/11/1962 in Newton, MA; Raymond L. Patriacca and Marion A. Mandile

PELLETIER,
Robert John, b. 4/14/1975 in Rochester; Robert A. Pelletier and Susan L. Barnet

PELOQUIN,
Eric Paul, b. 6/28/1991 in Rochester; Paul Gerard Peloquin and Charlene Marie Belisle

PENN,
Kirsty Sahara, b. 8/25/1991 in Rochester; Craig William Penn and Agnes Marie Goodwin

PERKINS,
son [Herbert], b. 8/20/1896; second; Chang Perkins (laborer, New Durham) and Hattie Kimball (Wolfeboro)

daughter, b. 11/5/1902; second; Harry Perkins (laborer, 26, Dover) and Lena Willey (23, Middleton)
Allison Elizabeth, b. 4/11/1998 in Rochester; Douglas P. Perkins and Kathryn Denise Perkins
Amanda Lynn, b. 1/25/1989 in Wolfeboro; Charles E. Perkins and Jewel L. Wilkins
Cathrin L., b. 11/27/1934; second; Charles L. Perkins (laborer, Meredith) and Mary Austin (Canaan)
Donald Andrew, b. 5/23/1937; fifth; Charles Perkins (laborer, Meredith) and Mary Austin (Canaan)
Ella May, b. 7/17/1942; eighth; Charles E. Perkins (woodchopper, Meredith) and Mary C. Perkins (West Canaan)

PETERSEN,
Evan Thomas, b. 9/9/1991 in Wolfeboro; Mark Thomas Petersen and Patricia Grace Hartman
Mitchel Dayne, b. 3/26/1990 in Wolfeboro; Mark T. Petersen and Patricia G. Hartman

PETERSON,
Rachel, b. 6/15/1912; first; N. Jacob Peterson (wood turner, Sweden) and Elsie K. Peteysen (Denmark)

PHILBROOK,
Joshua Forrest, b. 10/20/1986 in Portsmouth; Thomas Dean Philbrook and Kathi-Jane Brooks
Nicholas Thomas, b. 10/20/1986 in Portsmouth; Thomas Dean Philbrook and Kathi-Jane Brooks

PICOTT,
Michelle Leda, b. 8/18/1975 in Dover; Frederick E. Picott and Patricia L. Poulin

PIGEON,
Donald Wiley, b. 8/5/1944; eighth; Moses B. Pigeon (lumberman, Canada) and Fannie E. Wiley (Warren, ME)

PINKHAM,
daughter, b. 2/7/1887; second; Kingman Pinkham (farmer, 37, Rochester) and ----- (--, Alton)

PITTS,
Andrew Wyatt, b. 6/9/1987 in Portsmouth; Todd F. Pitts and Diane L. Veno

Heather Renee, b. 11/16/1982 in Portsmouth; Hal R. Pitts and Penny Lee Dow

Sarah Elizabeth, b. 1/15/1993 in Dover; Todd Farrar Pitts and Diane Lyn Vend

Travis Michael, b. 8/7/1989 in Portsmouth; Todd F. Pitts and Diane L. Veno

PLACE,
Alicia Jo, b. 9/22/1967 in Rochester; Terry Place and Nancy L. Worster

Tina Marie, b. 8/11/1966 in Rochester; Terry Place and Nancy L. Worster

PLANTE,
Angela Marie, b. 11/21/1972 in Rochester; Philip A. Plante and Elizabeth G. Hayes

Katherine Ann, b. 5/16/1960 in Rochester; Raymond Joseph Plante and Elizabeth Rose Kelley

POLLARD,
Fallon Brooke, b. 11/8/1998 in Dover; Michael Pollard and Andrea Pollard

POLOZZOLO,
Mark Albert, b. 10/7/1976 in Dover; John J. Polozzolo and Jacqueline A. Sparks

PONCHAK,
Amy Marie, b. 11/23/1998 in Rochester; Robert Ponchak and
   Deborah Ponchak

PORTER,
Mackenzie Aja, b. 12/22/1992 in Rochester; Chester Lee Porter, III
   and Nancy Jean Strout

PORTIGUE,
Adam Lee, b. 11/23/1976 in Rochester; Rodney A. Portigue and
   Sheila M. Wilmot
Amy Lou, b. 11/25/1977 in Rochester; Rodney A. Portigue and Sheila
   M. Wilmot

POTTER,
Jeannie Gay, b. 1/8/1953 in Rochester; Lester Frank Potter and
   Alberta Ettola Staples
Theresa Lynn, b. 5/1/1955 in Rochester; Lester Frank Potter and
   Alberta Ettola Staples

POULIN,
Crystal LaShay, b. 8/9/1982 in Rochester; Claude J. Poulin and Kellie
   A. McKuhen
Joseph John, b. 6/4/1989 in Dover; Robert J. Poulin and Laurie K.
   Borggaard

PRIDHAM,
Kenneth Tracy, b. 7/10/1963 in Wolfeboro; Lawrence Melvin Pridham
   and Paula Ann Laney
Scott Noel, b. 4/18/1966 in Rochester; Lawrence M. Pridham and
   Paula A. Laney

PRINCE,
Nichole Nakia, b. 4/7/1984 in Rochester; Luke J. Prince and Waneta J.
   Cutter

PRUITT,
Ashley Marie, b. 5/8/1989 in Rochester; Gary D. Pruitt and Angela M. Silvestri
Gary Dean, Jr., b. 5/17/1985 in Rochester; Gary Dean Pruitt and Angela Marie Silvestri
Tyler James, b. 8/2/1986 in Rochester; Gary Dean Pruitt and Angela Marie Silvestri

PULCIFER,
Andrew Scott, b. 3/23/1974 in Dover; Paul R. Pulcifer and Joan E. Lucas

PURRINGTON,
Granville N., b. 1/14/1888; second; C. W. Purrington (clergyman, 38, Bowdoin, ME) and Hattie M. Newman (27, Weld, ME)

QUIGLEY,
Cameron James, b. 10/22/1990 in Rochester; Kenneth J. Quigley and Sheila G. Scott
Scott Andrew, b. 4/12/1992 in Rochester; Kenneth James Quigley and Sheila Gaye Scott

RAAB,
Bruce Pollard, b. 8/28/1969 in Rochester; Bruce P. Raab and Beatrice M. York

RAND,
son, b. 5/16/1889; fifth; Oscar A. Rand (farmer, 24, New Durham) and Eliza McDonald (25, Portland, ME)
daughter [Eva May], b. 10/18/1911; eighth; Jacob P. Rand (teamster, New Durham) and Mary Pierre (Canada)
Clifton Dona, b. 6/7/1935 in Wolfeboro; first; Joseph D. Rand (mechanic, New Durham) and Dorothy Garland (Sanbornville)
Clyde LeRoy, b. 4/12/1933; fourth; Nathaniel Rand (laborer, New Durham) and Mabel Bean (Ossipee)

RANDALL,
daughter [Mildred], b. 12/25/1897; fifth; Charles A. Randall (farmer, 47, New Durham) and Martha J. Woodman (42, Gilmanton)
son, b. 4/26/1901; fourth; Gertie F. Randall (27, Stanstead, PQ)
Benjamin Martin, b. 8/13/1979 in Rochester; Clayton R. Randall and Susan B. Martin
Charles Herbert, Jr., b. 5/24/1926 in Rochester; first; Charles H. Randall (laborer, New Durham) and Ruth M. Labby (East Rochester)
Cheryl Darlene, b. 5/16/1956; Samuel Erwin Randall and Jane Gale St. Cyr
John Edward, b. 12/7/1943 in Rochester; fifth; Charles H. Randall (shoe worker, New Durham) and Ruth M. Labby (East Rochester)
Joseph Aaron, b. 12/12/1996 in Rochester; Roswell R. Randall and Tammy Marie Coran
Linda M., b. 9/6/1950 in Rochester; fourth; Roger M. Randall (woodchopper, NH) and Beatrice Chaisson (Canada)
Raymond Edward, b. 10/7/1951 in Wolfeboro; Roger Miles Randall and Beatrice Amanda Chaisson
Raymond Thomas, b. 6/28/1928 in Rochester; second; Charles H. Randall (laborer, New Durham) and Ruth M. Labby (East Rochester)
Roger Miles, b. 6/11/1930; third; C. Herbert Randall (handle worker, New Durham) and Ruth M. Labby (East Rochester)
Roger Miles, b. 6/18/1949 in Rochester; third; Roger M. Randall (shoe shop, NH) and Beatrice Chaisson (Canada)
Roswell R., b. 3/3/1946 in Rochester; sixth; Charles H. Randall (shoe shop emp., New Durham) and Ruth M. Labby (East Rochester)
Samuel Erwin, b. 8/29/1935; fourth; Herbert C. Randall (farmer, New Durham) and Ruth Labby (East Rochester)
Samuel Erwin, Jr., b. 5/16/1956; Samuel Erwin Randall and Jane Gale St. Cyr
Shayna Marie, b. 6/4/1987 in Rochester; Aidyl C. Randall and Linda C. Murphy

Sheila May, b. 9/10/1948 in Wolfeboro; first; Charles Randall, Jr. (woodsman, New Durham) and R. S. Thurston (New Durham)

RANSOM,
Brandon Michael, b. 7/11/1993 in Exeter; Donald Raymond Ransom, Sr. and Christine Marie Patrick

REED,
Ryan Tyler, b. 10/12/1990 in Rochester; Bruce R. Reed and Donna M. Vonericken

RHINES [see also Rines],
son [Charles P.], b. 10/31/1905; fifth; Willie E. Rhines (farmer, 35, New Durham) and Gracie Joy (29, New Durham)
son [Everett], b. 8/20/1907; sixth; Willie E. Rhines (teamster, 36, New Durham) and Gracie Joy (30, New Durham)
Evelyn, b. 7/14/1906; first; Hermon A. Rhines (teamster, 27, New Durham) and Lucie B. Dow (23, Dorchester)
Ruth L., b. 8/4/1914; third; Herman A. Rhines (teamster, New Durham) and Lucy B. Dow (Dorchester)

RHOADES,
Casey May, b. 7/1/1998 in Dover; Peter C. Rhoades and Nancy M. Rhoades

RICE,
son, b. 9/1/1898; first; Edward E. Rice (manufacturer, 35, Freedom) and Laura Ayers (39, Barnstead)

RICHARDS,
daughter, b. 9/17/1906; third; James Richards (farmer, 30, England) and ----- (28, England)

RICHARDSON,
Alicia Marie, b. 6/7/1995 in Rochester; Thomas E. Richardson and Denise L. Cobb

RICKER,
daughter [Ruby May], b. 5/11/1889; eighth; Charles H. Ricker (merchant, 39, Barrington) and Emma A. Stevens (39, New Durham)
son [Raymond Winfield], b. 9/21/1895; second; Leslie W. Ricker (station agt, 35, New Durham) and Wendella Tash (27, New Durham)
son [John, Jr.], b. 2/3/1916; second; John H. Ricker (machinist, 37, New Durham) and Florence Dame (30, New Durham)
Etta G., b. 4/11/1906; first; John S. Ricker (farmer, 27, New Durham) and Florence Dame (20, New Durham)
Marion [Leslie], b. 7/3/1893; first; Leslie W. Ricker (station agent, 32, New Durham) and Wendella Tash (25, New Durham)
Ralph, b. 1/17/1900; first; Helen A. Ricker (17, Alton)

RINES [see also Rhines],
son [Albert], b. 10/4/1900; first; Alonzo G. Rines (farmer, 59, New Durham) and Dora M. Berry (18, Freedom)
son, b. 8/22/1909; second; Herman A. Rines (teamster, New Durham) and Lucy B. Dow (Dorchester)
Eric Hartley, b. 5/5/1985 in Rochester; Ricky Carpenter Rines and Diane Barbara Gelinas
Mark Allen, b. 5/15/1998 in Rochester; Mark Rines and Tammy Rines
Shelley Lee, b. 4/22/1988 in Concord; Ricky C. Rines and Diane B. Gelinas

RING,
Gloria June, b. 6/2/1945; first; Ernest F. Ring (shoeworker, Belmont) and Ethel Shaw (Farmington); residence - Farmington

ROBINSON,
son, b. 3/23/1896; second; George H. Robinson (farmer, 48, Kingston) and Minnie C. Nutter (35, Boston, MA)

ROGERS,

Elmer Eugene, b. 6/30/1921; first; Leon E. Rogers (mechanic, Fitchburg, MA) and Evelyn G. Dore (Barrington); residence - Lynn, MA

Robert W., b. 9/17/1950; fourth; Paul C. Rogers (taxi driver, ME) and Elinor M. Hall (NH)

ROHAN,

Edgar A., b. 4/7/1899; third; George F. Rohan (knife maker, 39, Northampton, MA) and Josie Galbreith (PEI)

George F., b. 4/19/1895; third; George F. Rohan (knife maker, 35, Northampton, MA) and Josephine Galbraith (31, PEI)

Leon W., b. 6/21/1892; first; George F. Rohan (machinist, Northampton, MA) and Josephene P. Rohan (PEI)

ROLLINS,

Estelva L., b. 4/17/1917; first; Harold E. Rollins (clerk, 21, New Durham) and Addie M. Morse (24, Alton)

Harold E., b. 10/18/1895; first; Elmer Rollins (laborer, 24, New Durham) and Ella M. Dore (16, New Durham)

K. L. (son), b. 7/15/1939 in Rochester; first; Everett B. Rollins (farmer, Gilmanton) and Effie Fowle (Newburyport, MA)

Marshall Elmer, b. 5/23/1925; second; Cyrus Carl Rollins (clerk, Alton) and Bessie M. Thurston (Milton)

Shirley Phyllis, b. 3/11/1924; first; Cyrus C. Rollins (merchant, New Durham) and Bessie M. Thurston (New Durham)

ROLPH,

Julie Lyn, b. 2/24/1979 in Concord; David F. Rolph and Lynda A. Warren

ROTHERMEL,

Justin Ray, b. 7/10/1987 in Dover; Raymond H. Rothermel and Sherry L. Stillings

Meghan Rae, b. 5/16/1992 in Dover; Raymond Harold Rothermel and Sherry Lee Marie Stillings

ROUILLARD,
Nancy Lee, b. 7/21/1948 in Wolfeboro; second; Ralph E. Rouillard (shoeworker, Farmington) and Doris M. Burres (Gilmanton I.W.)

ROY,
Alison Elizabeth, b. 8/2/1992 in Rochester; Daniel Richard Roy and Nancy Elizabeth Specker

Brandon Allen, b. 8/16/1992 in Rochester; David Allen Roy and Susan Ann Young

ROYAL,
stillborn son, b. 4/26/1925; fourth; Ulmer Royal (manufacturer, Ellsworth, ME) and Bessie L. May (MA)

James, b. 10/23/1921; first; Ulmer L. Royal (machinist, ME) and Besse May (MA)

RUNNALS,
Jillian Marie, b. 12/9/1991 in Rochester; Scott David Runnals and Linda Sue Hogan

RUPPRECHT,
Laura Louise, b. 8/8/1963 in Rochester; Charles Robert Rupprecht and Julia Ann Moon

RUSSELL,
Charlie Edward, b. 3/30/1912; first; Charles R. Russell (steam fitter, Claremont, NH) and Bertha M. Rose (Ipswich, MA); residence - Haverhill, MA

ST. GEORGE,
Michele Lee, b. 3/25/1973 in Rochester; Leo H. St. George and Paula M. Hillsgrove

SALTZMAN,
Sarah Jane, b. 7/4/1993 in Rochester; Danny Myron Saltzman, Sr. and Justine Lynn Roy

SANFORD,
Grant Delmane, b. 9/23/1926; ninth; Edgar W. Sanford (lumberman, NS) and Ellen Moore (NS)

SAWYER,
Marion Frances, b. 11/19/1936 in Sanford, ME; sixth; Sewell Sawyer (shoeworker, Lagrange, ME) and Venus Smith (Springvale, ME)
Ralph Cornelius, b. 10/5/1935 in Sanford, ME; fourth; Sewell B. Sawyer (shoeworker, Lagrange, ME) and Venus Smith (Sanford, ME)

SCOFIELD,
Karen Lee, b. 7/22/1948 in Rochester; first; Irene S. Scofield (Farmington)

SCOTT,
John Leonard, b. 7/20/1923; second; Leonard Scott (carpenter, Worcester, MA) and Hilda Messinger (Beverly, MA)

SCRUTON,
Douglas James, b. 9/25/1947 in Rochester; second; Lloyd H. Scruton (garage, Newburyport, MA) and Norma Coburn (New Durham)
Elaine Sylvia, b. 8/11/1936 in Wolfeboro; second; Everett R. Scruton (minister, Newburyport, MA) and Yola L. Turner (Chicago, IL)
Gilbert Gordon, b. 10/19/1934 in Rochester; first; Everett Scruton (minister, Newburyport, MA) and Yola Turner (Chicago, IL)

SERVETAS,
Cody James, b. 12/11/1989 in Wolfeboro; Charles J. Servetas and Theresa A. Arsenault

SEVIGNY,
Nicole Ruth, b. 9/6/1993 in Rochester; William Eugene Sevigny and Nora Bertha Ouellette
William Mark, b. 7/20/1997 in Rochester; William Eugene Sevigny and Nora Bertha Sevigny

SHAW,
Donald A., b. 10/6/1944; first; Barbara L. Shaw (Farmington)

SHEDD,
Vira M., b. 4/23/1895; first; Albert H. Shedd (farmer, 30, Lowell, MA) and Susan V. Murray (24, Boston, MA)

SHEEHAN,
Henry A., b. 8/31/1917; second; Henry J. Sheehan (farmer, 33, Natick, MA) and Grace E. Pike (28, Farmington)
Margaret Agnes, b. 5/16/1916; first; Henry J. Sheehan (farmer, 31, Natick, MA) and Grace Pike (26, Farmington)

SHERIDEN,
R. (son), b. 3/28/1940; fourth; Edwin Sheriden (civil engineer, Nashua) and Evelyn Drane (Malden, MA)

SILVIA,
Sarah Rose, b. 4/11/1989 in Dover; John J. Silvia, III and Judith M. McGuirk

SIMONDS,
son, b. 9/26/1891; first; Eugene F. Simonds (farmer, 23, Sharon, VT) and Ethel M. Boodey (23, Alton)
Eugenia Irene, b. 10/3/1959 in Wolfeboro; Richard E. Simonds and Olive M. Wells

SMALL,
Reginald H., b. 8/3/1913; sixth; Leslie F. Small (machinist, Brighton, ME) and Lena E. Flint (New Durham)

SMITH,
Alfred James, b. 2/9/1972 in Rochester; Alfred W. Smith and Norma R. Cutter
Alfred William, b. 9/12/1931; third; Alfred Smith (laborer, Roxbury, MA) and Freda Miller (New Durham)

Alfred William, b. 7/10/1994 in Wolfeboro; Alfred James Smith and Rhonda Gaile Henderson

Freda Mary, b. 7/3/1928; second; Alfred Smith (shoemaker, Boston, MA) and Freda M. Miller (New Durham)

James Richard, b. 3/22/1951 in Rochester; Alfred William Smith and Betty Lucille Cardinal

Kenneth Joel, b. 10/22/1934; sixth; Irving E. Smith (laborer, Alton) and Beatrice I. Glidden (New Durham)

Linwood N., b. 11/30/1929; sixth; Irving E. Smith (sta. engineer, Alton) and Beatrice Glidden (New Durham)

Rae-Anne Mai, b. 4/7/1993 in Rochester; Brian Kent Smith and Cynthia Lynn Dingley

Ryan Taylor, b. 12/22/1991 in Wolfeboro; Brian Kent Smith and Cynthia Lynn Dingley

Tabitha Lee, b. 10/31/1978 in Rochester; Steven A. Smith and Deborah L. Bailey

Tammy Jean, b. 10/28/1970 in Rochester; Alfred W. Smith and Norma R. Cutter

SNELL,
Jason Robert, b. 6/5/1983 in Dover; Robert R. Snell and Darlene A. Brown

SNYDER,
Samantha Marie, b. 4/27/1990 in Rochester; Eric J. Snyder and Joanne M. DiPrizio

SPATAFORE,
Kate, b. 8/21/1915; third; Salvatore Spatafore (laborer, 26, Minie, Italy) and Lucy Bellino (26, Minie, Italy)

SPINNEY,
son [Bernard], b. 2/1/1910; third; Clarence A. Spinney (shoemaker, Raymond) and Nellie M. Rand (Alton)

SPONGBERG,
Jane, b. 1/14/1938 in Wolfeboro; first; Ernest Spongberg (dairy farmer, Gotenburg, Sweden) and Eleanor Gridley (Cambridge, MA)
M. (daughter), b. 3/24/1940 in Wolfeboro; second; Ernest Spongberg (carpenter, Sweden) and Eleanor Gridley (Cambridge, MA)

SPRAGUE,
Daniel Bruce, b. 2/24/1987 in Dover; Dale R. Sprague and Kendra J. Bruce
Lindsey Dale, b. 5/25/1983 in Dover; Dale R. Sprague and Kendra J. Bruce

STANLEY,
son, b. 9/28/1906; first; Alderwin R. Stanley (enameler, 19, Bangor, ME) and Myrtie Baker (19, Laconia)

STAPLES,
Charlene Ann, b. 12/13/1960 in Rochester; Charles Frank Staples, Jr. and Evelyn Carol Woods
Marie Elaine, b. 6/3/1959 in Rochester; Frank M. Staples and Thelma M. Beshaw
Roland Ormand, b. 1/16/1951; Roland Ormand Staples and Evelyn Grass

STEVENS,
Joshua John, b. 11/25/1986 in Rochester; Mark Edward Stevens and Margaret Ann Chamberlin
Matthew Mark, b. 5/10/1982 in Rochester; Mark E. Stevens and Margaret A. Chamberlin

STILLINGS,
son, b. 6/18/1888; third; Rufus I. Stillings (37, Wolfeboro) and Jennie N. Stillings (34, West Newfield, ME)

STOCK,
daughter, b. 11/24/1926; fifth; Hubert Stock (caretaker) and Eva Jones (Gilmanton); residence - Gilmanton

STUART,
Donald Jerald, b. 11/1/1988 in Rochester; Donald J. Stuart and Tammy M. Marcinkoski
Forrest Allan, b. 8/4/1993 in Dover; David Forrest Stuart and Robin Lynn Hamel
Judi Merle, b. 5/25/1970 in Rochester; Richard D. Stuart and A. Lorene Currier
Kristopher Robin, b. 7/31/1992 in Dover; David Forest Stuart and Robin Lynn Hamel

SUCCI,
Ryan Neal, b. 5/18/1988 in Dover; David N. Succi and Bonnie J. Potter

SULLIVAN,
Dorothy May, b. 11/29/1948 in Wolfeboro; third; Martin W. Sullivan (hatchery supt., Lowell, MA) and Mary E. Gardener (Boston, MA)
Helen Julia, b. 8/8/1928; ninth; Thomas F. Sullivan (factory worker, Woonsocket, RI) and Mary G. Corbett (Boston, MA)

SWETT,
Alexandria Whitney, b. 4/27/1992 in Rochester; Thomas Earl Swett and Donna Lynn Walker
Barbara E., b. 12/6/1948 in Stoneham, MA; Fred A. Swett, Jr. (mechanic, Boston, MA) and Mildred Roberts (Malden, MA)
Elizabeth Ann, b. 2/8/1982 in Rochester; James E. Swett and Cherine A. Nelson
James Edward, b. 11/15/1954 in Rochester; Fred Atwell Swett and Mildred Elizabeth Roberts
Janet Ellen, b. 12/13/1961 in Rochester; Fred Atwell Swett, Jr. and Mildred Elizabeth Roberts

Jessica Ellen, b. 11/6/1984 in Rochester; James E. Swett and Cherine A. Nelson

John Ernest, b. 12/23/1950 in Rochester; second; Fred A. Swett, Jr. (mechanic, Boston, MA) and Mildred Roberts (Malden, MA)

Katherine Elizabeth, b. 8/18/1993 in Rochester; Thomas Earl Swett and Donna Lynn Walker

Marjorie Ann, b. 1/14/1958 in Rochester; Fred Atwell Swett, Jr. and Mildred Elizabeth Roberts

Michael Alan, b. 1/22/1977 in Rochester; James E. Swett and Claire M. Deane

Peter Aaron, b. 2/25/1975 in Wolfeboro; John E. Swett and Marion A. Bierweiler

Thomas Earl, b. 5/8/1964 in Rochester; Fred Atwell Swett, Jr. and Mildred Elizabeth Roberts

SYLVESTER,

daughter, b. 2/12/1898; third; Charles Sylvester (farmer) and Grace Chesley

Charles Wesley, b. 5/15/1903; Charles B. Sylvester (farmer, 38, Sanford, ME) and Grace F. Chesley (29, New Durham)

SYLVIA,

John Joseph, b. 2/10/1935; first; John Sylvia (shoeworker, CA) and Alice M. Pinkham (Alton); residence - Farmington

TAYLOR,

Diana Marie, b. 11/25/1954 in Wolfeboro; Stanley Maynard Taylor, Jr. and Ruth Lavenia Thurston

Patricia Louise, b. 12/8/1951 in Wolfeboro; Stanley Maynard Taylor, Jr. and Ruth Lavenia Thurston

Stanley Maynard, 3d, b. 7/27/1953 in Wolfeboro; Stanley Maynard Taylor, Jr. and Ruth Lavinia Thurston

TEBBETTS,

son, b. 3/17/1892; sixth; Albinus B. Tebbetts (farmer, 40, New Durham) and Mary F. Tebbetts (36, Milton)

TETREAULT,
Madison Rey, b. 4/6/1998 in Rochester; Ryan Joseph Tetreault and Lori Ann Tetreault

THERRIEN,
Keith Richard, b. 6/11/1991 in Rochester; Keith Edward Therrien and Jamie Lynn Meyer

THIBEAU,
Frances A., b. 12/3/1917; second; Maurice Thibeau (teamster, 50, Canada) and Ada B. Elliott (19, Rumney)

THIBEDEAU,
son, b. 12/27/1914; first; Morris Thibedeau (laborer, Canada) and Addie B. Elliott (West Rumney)

THOMPSON,
daughter, b. 1/25/1898; first; Hervey J. Thompson (farmer, 31, Farmington) and Florence J. Foss (22, Rochester)
daughter, b. 11/18/1899; second; Hervey J. Thompson (farmer, 33, Farmington) and Florence J. Foss (23, Rochester)
son [Stillman], b. 7/17/1901; third; Hervey J. Thompson (farmer, 34, Farmington) and Florence J. Foss (35, Rochester)
son [Elmer], b. 11/29/1904; first; John C. Thompson (carpenter, Concord) and Julia Emerson (20, Farmington)
Berin Alexander, b. 7/17/1991 in Dover; Brian Walton Thompson and Diane Patricia Stemmer
Esther Holbrook, b. 4/7/1965 in Rochester; Charles C. Thompson and Katharine E. Baker
Joseph David, b. 4/16/1976 in Rochester; Peter R. Thompson and Janice J. Hillsgrove

THOROUGHGOOD,
son [Wesley], b. 7/28/1906; fifth; George Thorogood (wood chopper, 35, England) and Maud Perkins (26, Luke City, NE)

THURSTON,
Albert Josiah, b. 8/28/1921; first; Walter S. Thurston (farmer, Wells, ME) and Viola B. Eaton (West Newton, MA)
Calvin W., b. 9/11/1932; fourth; Walter Thurston (laborer, Berwick, ME) and Viola B. Eaton (West Medford, MA)
Charles Henry, b. 11/16/1946; second; Walter S. Thurston (soldier, New Durham) and Virginia Shaw (Farmington)
Danielle Lee, b. 3/24/1984 in Wolfeboro; David K. Thurston and Carolyn C. Cousins
David Allan, b. 1/30/1960 in Rochester; Donald Henry Thurston and Geraldine Theresa Avery
Joseph A., b. 10/11/1944; first; Walter S. Thurston, Jr. (laborer, New Durham) and Virginia A. Shaw (Farmington)
Julie Lynn, b. 11/4/1986 in Wolfeboro; David Karl Thurston and Carolyn Christine Cousins
Ruth Lavenia, b. 8/28/1930; third; Walter S. Thurston (laborer, Berwick, ME) and Viola Eaton (West Newton, MA)
Walter Scott, b. 6/27/1927; second; Walter S. Thurston (farmer, Berwick, ME) and Viola B. Eaton (West Newton, MA)
Wendy Layne, b. 11/11/1958 in Rochester; Donald Herbert Thurston and Geraldine Theresa Avery

TIBBETTS,
child, b. 5/11/1889; fifth; Albinus B. Tibbetts (farmer, 37, New Durham) and Mary F. Tibbetts (33, Milton)
Flossie Pearl, b. 12/20/1894; seventh; Albinus B. Tibbetts (farmer, 43, New Durham) and Mary F. Amazeen (39, Milton)

TOPLIFFE,
Alexander Lee, b. 12/3/1996; Jeffrey Scott Topliffe and Ranee Lee Miliner

TOWLE,
daughter, b. 12/18/1893; first; George L. Towle (shoe maker, 22, New Durham) and Phebe E. Leighton (19, Farmington)

son [Floyd], b. 7/27/1898; first; Charles F. Towle, Jr. (brushmaker, 24, New Durham) and Henrietta Woodman (19, Alton)

Lucine Ruth, b. 11/27/1938; sixth; Warren H. Towle (farmhand, Pittsburg) and Lucille Hutchinson (Vinal Haven, ME)

Stanley L., b. 12/16/1911; second; Charles F. Towle (brushmaker, New Durham) and Henrietta Woodman (Alton)

TRACEY,
Beatrice C., b. 12/25/1923; third; John Tracey (laborer, NS) and Ruby Hutchinson (New York, NY)

TRAFTON,
Frederic O., Jr., b. 8/5/1918; first; Frederic A. Trafton (enameler, So. Berwick, ME) and Bernice M. Coburn (New Durham)

TREMBLAY,
Brandan Michael, b. 6/18/1989 in Rochester; Michael S. Tremblay and Denise T. Charron

Bryant Thomas, b. 12/29/1991 in Dover; Gary Paul Tremblay and Deborah Ann Thibodeau

TROIANO,
Matthew Ernest, Jr., b. 9/26/1987 in Dover; Matthew E. Troiano, Sr. and Sharon E. Bisson

TUCK,
Shawn Allen, b. 10/31/1979 in Dover; Larry J. Tuck and Rose Mary J. Potvin

TUFTS,
Jamey Aaron, b. 7/29/1981 in Dover; Michael A. Tufts and Brenda J. Hayward

TURCOTTE,
daughter, b. 12/2/1937; ninth; Thomas Turcotte (lumberman, Canada) and Leona Marcou (VT)

L. (daughter), b. 1/10/1939 in Rochester; tenth; Omer T. Turcotte (lumberman, Canada) and Leona Marcou (Walden, VT)
Ryan John, b. 10/23/1985 in Dover; Stephen John Turcotte and Paula Ann Fenton

TURNER,
Christelle Marie, b. 7/29/1982 in Wolfeboro; Paul W. Turner and Mary B. Curtis

TUTTLE,
daughter, b. 11/4/1897; sixth; William B. Tuttle (farmer, 54, Middleton) and Mazina M. Colomy (29, New Durham)
son, b. 2/6/1901; seventh; William B. Tuttle (laborer, 55, Middleton) and Mezina Colomy (33, New Durham)
James Alfonzo, b. 4/19/1928; fourth; Clarence Tuttle (laborer, New Durham) and Mary Patch (Alton)
Lilla D., b. 3/29/1887; second; William B. Tuttle (laborer, Middleton) and ----- (New Durham)

TWITCHELL,
Arthur James, b. 3/7/1993 in Rochester; Kenneth Allen Twitchell and Bertha Rose Arsenault
Dale Donna, b. 7/8/1961 in Rochester; Franklin Wesley Twitchell, Sr. and Nellie Joy
Franklin Wesley, Jr., b. 5/12/1959 in Rochester; Franklin W. Twitchell, Sr. and Nellie Joy
Franklin Wesley, IV, b. 9/11/1984 in Rochester; Franklin W. Twitchell, III and Terri L. Parsons
Kenneth Allen, b. 5/30/1960 in Rochester; Franklin Wesley Twitchell, Sr. and Nellie Joy
Timothy Neal, b. 7/3/1964 in Rochester; Franklin Wesley Twitchell and Nellie Joy

UPTON,
daughter, b. 9/7/1898; first; Elmer E. Upton (machinist, 37, New Castle) and Emma F. Towle (32, Alton)

VACHON,
Gregory Ernest, b. 8/20/1981 in Rochester; Ernest R. Vachon and
Patricia F. Foote

VALLEY,
son, b. 3/18/1898; second; Lewis Valley (laborer, 26, Canada) and
Lezil Lumbar (19, Canada)
son, b. 4/5/1899; third; Lewis Vallie (sic) (wood chopper, 29, Canada)
and Lizzie Lambien (23, Canada)
daughter, b. 9/24/1899; thirteenth; Felix Valley (farmer) and Jennie
Champaign
daughter, b. 10/--/1902; fourteenth; Felix Valley (farmer, 52, Canada)
and Jennie Champaign (36, Canada)
Joseph M., b. 3/8/1898; first; John Valley (laborer, 24, Canada) and
Phoebe Goodnow (18, Canada)

VANMALDEN,
Jacob Scott, b. 8/28/1992 in Rochester; William Nicholas VanMalden
and Dolores Grace Mauer

VAN ROSSUM,
Liam Mulkern, b. 10/18/1996 in Dover; Reed B. Van Rossum and
Kathleen Mary Mulkern
Mae Mulkern, b. 10/18/1996 in Dover; Reed B. Van Rossum and
Kathleen Mary Mulkern

VAN VLECK,
son, b. 1/27/1907; third; Gustav B. Van Vleck (RFD mail carrier, 33,
Brooklyn, NY) and Blanche N. Schoch (30, Reading, PA)
daughter, b. 10/13/1908; fourth; Gustav B. Van Vleck (farmer, NY)
and Blanche M. Schoch (Reading, PA)

VARNEY,
stillborn son, b. 2/22/1897; first; Thomas Varney (farmer, 25, Alton)
and Sarah Tenney (22, Boston, MA)

daughter [Eleanor F.], b. 5/6/1898; second; Thomas S. Varney
(farmer, 26, Alton) and Sarah E. Tenney (22, Chelsea, MA)
Benjamin H., b. 8/30/1921; third; Benjamin Varney (farmer,
Farmington) and Esther E. Thompson (New Durham)
Kenneth H., b. 12/12/1917; first; Benjamin E.W. Varney (farmer, 21,
Farmington) and Esther E. Thompson (18, New Durham)
Marc Daniel, b. 12/25/1969 in Rochester; Harold H. Varney, Jr. and
Betty J. Gates
Michael Richard, b. 7/25/1985 in Rochester; Peter Richard Varney
and Elizabeth Marion Camage
Mildred Elaine, b. 9/3/1922; fourth; Benjamin Varney (farmer,
Farmington) and Esther Thompson (New Durham)

VISCARIELLO,
Amanda Lynn, b. 8/22/1997 in Rochester; Michael Ralph Viscariello
and Deanne Marie Viscariello

VOTER,
Laura Anna, b. 6/22/1909; fourth; Louis A. Voter (wood turner, New
Vineyard, ME) and Sadie Billson (Providence, RI)

WALDRON,
son, b. 12/3/1935; first; Robert Waldron (shoeworker, Farmington)
and Evelyn Pinkham (No. Lebanon, ME); residence - Farmington
son, b. 12/3/1935; second; Robert Waldron (shoeworker, Farmington)
and Evelyn Pinkham (No. Lebanon, ME); residence - Farmington
Gardner H., b. 11/13/1950 in Wolfeboro; first; Samuel G. Waldron
(musician, MA) and Shirley E. Smith (MA); residence - Hyde
Park, MA

WALKER,
daughter [Grace N.], b. 5/7/1888; fourth; John N. Walker (farmer, 65,
Farmington) and Emma F. Burnham (35, Charlestown, MA)
daughter, b. 5/8/1891; fifth; John N. Walker (farmer, 68, Farmington)
and Emma F. Burnham (38, Charlestown, MA)

son [Lawrence], b. 8/17/1910; first; Charles E. Walker (carpenter, Farmington) and Ethel M. MacDade (Parrsboro, NS)

WALLACE,
Beverly A., b. 2/19/1938 in Exeter; second; Henry E. Wallace (wool heeler, Raymond) and Emma C. Barnaby (Stratham)

WALLINGFORD,
son, b. 9/22/1902; fifth; Charles Wallenford (sic) (laborer, 35, Alton) and Carrie Randall (28, New Durham)

WARD,
Evelyn M., b. 8/23/1904; third; Alphonso E. Ward (laborer, 27, Harrison, ME) and Mary Knight (22, Naples, ME)

WARREN,
Emily Rose, b. 12/28/1989 in Rochester; Mark A. Warren and Susan L. Tarbox
Sarah Lyn, b. 6/15/1988 in Rochester; Mark A. Warren and Susan L. Tarbox

WATSON,
David Spencer, b. 11/16/1991 in Rochester; Sherwood David Watson and Leeann Brown

WEBSTER,
Chester W., b. 7/6/1912; first; William R. Webster (laborer, Lee) and Effie A. Willey (New Durham)

WEIDMAN,
Shannyn Marie, b. 1/9/1991 in Portsmouth; Edward Allen Weidman and Darlene Anne Vandermolen

WENTWORTH,
son [Lewis A.], b. 2/13/1892; first; Robert W. Wentworth (farmer, 31, Barnstead) and Mabel Marston (36, Nottingham)

daughter, b. 10/16/1914; first; Edwin I. Wentworth (laborer, Ossipee) and Alice Mooring (Laconia)

Bernice Irene, b. 8/26/1916; first; Lewis A. Wentworth (farmer, 24, New Durham) and H. Irene Nutter (16, Farmington)

George Hawley, b. 10/25/1923; sixth; Lewis A. Wentworth (farmer, New Durham) and Irene Nutter (Farmington)

Kelly Ann, b. 1/1/1998 in Wolfeboro; Ernest Lorin Wentworth and Sunny Ann Wentworth

Lewis A., Jr., b. 10/21/1918; third; Lewis A. Wentworth (farmer, New Durham) and H. Irene Nutter (Farmington)

Lurene Iris, b. 7/20/1934 in Rochester; eighth; Lewis Wentworth (farmer, New Durham) and Irene Nutter (Farmington)

Mabel L., b. 9/11/1917; second; Lewis A. Wentworth (farmer, 25, New Durham) and H. Irene Nutter (17, New Durham)

Mark Robert, b. 8/2/1995 in Wolfeboro; Ernest L. Wentworth and Sunny A. McKay

Nelson Edward, b. 1/4/1922; fifth; Lewis A. Wentworth (farmer, New Durham) and Irene Nutter (Farmington)

Ralph Daniel, b. 5/11/1957; Ralph Nutter Wentworth and Dorothye Irene Smith

Ralph Nutter, b. 8/5/1929; seventh; Louis A. Wentworth (farmer, New Durham) and Irene Nutter (Farmington)

Rebecca Lou, b. 4/3/1954 in Rochester; Ralph Nutter Wentworth and Dorothye Irene Smith

Rene Joseph, b. 3/17/1955 in Rochester; Ralph Nutter Wentworth and Dorothye Irene Smith

Reuben Lewis, b. 4/13/1961 in Rochester; Ralph Nutter Wentworth and Dorothye Irene Smith

Robert, b. 1/27/1920; fourth; L. A. Wentworth (farmer, New Durham) and Irene Nutter (Farmington)

WENZLAU,
William Thomas, b. 5/29/1991 in Wolfeboro; Thomas John Wenzlau and Judith Lynn Rapp

WHEELER,
Jarrod Michael, b. 5/18/1988 in Dover; David M. Wheeler and Holly L. Stuart
Kasey Lynn, b. 8/24/1984 in Dover; David M. Wheeler and Holly L. Stuart

WHELDEN,
Roy M., III, b. 9/5/1950 in Laconia; second; Roy M. Whelden, Jr. (geologist, ME) and Evelyn E. Merritt (PA)

WHITE,
Richard Drew, II, b. 8/21/1984 in Rochester; Richard D. White and Tammy E. LeMay
Shelley Lee, b. 1/15/1974 in Rochester; Sidney W. White and Nancy J. LaVallee
Trista Nichole, b. 4/4/1983 in Wolfeboro; Richard D. White and Tammy J. LeMay

WHITEHOUSE,
Judith Darleen, b. 11/27/1965 in Rochester; Bertram O. Whitehouse and Dorothy F. Pierce
Tiffany Ann, b. 7/7/1982 in Rochester; Warren P. Whitehouse and Karen A. Cronier

WHITING,
Savannah Kate, b. 10/1/1990 in Wolfeboro; Jonathan P. Whiting and Susan M. Michaud

WICHMAN,
Elizabeth, b. 8/4/1951 in Rochester; Henry F. Wichman and Marie Reyneke

WILLETT,
Harriet, b. 11/17/1903; first; Joseph Willett (laborer, 40, Canada) and Bessie Ayers (25, New Durham)

Jessie, b. 5/17/1908; third; Joseph Willett (laborer, Canada) and
   Bessie J. Ayers (New Durham)
Lloyd, b. 8/1/1906; second; Joseph Willett (laborer, 45, Canada) and
   Bessie J. Ayers (28, Wakefield)
Neil A., b. 2/7/1913; fourth; Joseph Willett (woodturner, Canada) and
   Bessie J. Ayers (Union)

WILLEY,
stillborn son, b. 12/8/1887; first; Charles F. Willey (shoe
   manufacturer, 30, New Durham) and ----- Willey (29, Natick,
   MA); residence - Joliet, IL
daughter, b. 9/17/1891; second; Edward M. Willey (knifemaker, 29,
   New Durham) and Mary A. Randall (20, New Durham)
daughter [Effie A.], b. 2/4/1893; third; Edwin M. Willey (knife maker,
   New Durham) and Mary A. Randall (New Durham)
son [Leslie L.], b. 4/22/1896; Edward M. Willey (knifemaker, 32,
   New Durham) and Mary Randall (24, New Durham)
George Edward, b. 9/14/1888; first; Edward M. Willey (New Durham,
   25) and Mary A. Randall (17)

WOOD,
Dawn Eleasha, b. 8/10/1993 in Wolfeboro; Kevin S. Wood and
   Charlene L. Pelletier
Mark Olden, b. 6/27/1989 in Wolfeboro; Kevin S. Wood and Charlene
   L. Pelletier

WOODMAN,
son, b. 5/27/1891; first; Will C. Woodman (farmer, 33, Alton) and
   Valeria M. Lowell (16, Hiram, ME)

WOODS,
Carleton Winthrop, Jr., b. 12/20/1967 in Rochester; Carleton W.
   Woods and Patricia M. Adams
Jon Matthew, b. 5/4/1970 in Rochester; Carleton W. Woods, Sr. and
   Patricia M. Adams

Patricia Ann, b. 12/1/1949 in Rochester; first; Bernard C. Woods (shoeworker, ME) and Selma Bridges (NH)

Sara Marie, b. 4/15/1971 in Rochester; Carleton W. Woods and Patricia M. Adams

WORSTER,

Jason Carl, b. 4/13/1973 in Wolfeboro; Carlton R. Worster and Sharon A. Cameron

Jeffrey George, b. 6/6/1975 in Wolfeboro; Carlton R. Worster and Sharon A. Cameron

June Clara, b. 10/16/1944 in Rochester; first; George O. Worster (US Navy, Farmington) and Doris M. Burres (Gilmanton I.W.)

YORK,

Barbara Ann, b. 12/5/1949 in Rochester; second; Clarence R. York (woodsman, NH) and Mary A. Dionne (NH)

Beatrice Marie, b. 3/11/1951 in Rochester; Clarence Ray York and Marie Anna Dionne

Bonnie Lee, b. 3/12/1952 in Rochester; Clarence Ray York and Mary Ann Dionne

George Arthur, b. 11/1/1936 in Rochester; first; George A. York (laborer, Belmont) and Barbara Wyatt (Barrington)

Janet Louise, b. 3/24/1941 in Farmington; third; George Arthur York (truck driver, Belmont) and Barbara T. Wyatt (Barrington)

Richard, b. 7/29/1939 in Rochester; second; George A. York (truck driver, Belmont) and Barbara Wyatt (Barrington)

Shirley May, b. 4/12/1953 in Rochester; Clarence Ray York and Mary Anna Dionne

YOUNG,

Curtis E., b. 3/3/1938 in Wolfeboro; second; Elbridge G. Young (shoecutter, Fremont) and Ruth M. Guyett (Barton, VT)

Fred Sidney, b. 12/8/1936; third; Herman F. Young (farmer, Middleton) and Nellie A. Fogg (Gilmanton)

Herman F., b. 5/11/1934; first; Herman F. Young (laborer, Middleton) and Nellie A. Fogg (Gilmanton)

John Henry, b. 12/17/1938 in Wolfeboro; third; Herman F. Young
(truck driver, Middleton) and Nellie A. Fogg (Gilmanton)
Robert Lewis, b. 11/19/1935; second; Herman F. Young (farmer,
Middleton) and Nellie A. Fogg (Gilmanton)

NEW DURHAM
MARRIAGES

ADAMS,
Alvah A. m. Julianne T. **Badger** 8/15/1953 in Chichester
Alvah A. m. Carol N. **Perry** 8/16/1980
Alvah Atwood m. Sylvia Marie **Morrison** 7/3/1971 in Gilmanton Iron Works
Edgar N. of Farmington m. Verna **Willey** of New Durham 6/30/1923 in Farmington; H - 21, shoemaker, b. Dover, ME, s/o Alvah A. Adams (MN, carpenter) and Emma Forbus (Solon, ME, housewife); W - 18, shoemaker, b. Alton, d/o Edward Willey (New Durham, knifemaker) and Mary Randall (New Durham, housewife)
Freddie m. June C. **Lepene** 4/5/1980 in Farmington
George H. of New Durham m. Almeda **McIntire** of Great Falls 9/1/1891 in Alton; H - 32, mechanic, b. Farmington, s/o Charles Adams (Newport, VT, mechanic) and Betsey E. Farnsworth (Haverhill, housekeeper); W - 35, housekeeper, 2d, b. Great Falls, d/o Joseph L. Page (deceased) and Eliza A. Horne (deceased)

AHLIN,
James Stephen m. Kathleen Mary **McSharry** 9/8/1990 in Alton

ALBERT,
Paul Emile m. Michele Lee **Dube** 5/14/1994 in Alton

ALDEN,
Charles H. m. Kathy A. **Huppe** 5/17/1980 in Alton
Franklin Allen, Jr. m. Lynne Ann **Berry** 7/5/1975
Seldon E. m. Kathy J. **Parsons** 6/14/1980 in Alton

ALLAIRE,
Joseph of New Durham m. Celina **Gagnon** of Canada 10/20/1891; H - 32, teamster, 2d, b. Canada, s/o Marcia Allaire (Canada, wood chopper) and Philaemon Cruches (Canada, housekeeper); W - 19, housekeeper, b. Canada, d/o Peter Gagnon (Canada, wood chopper) and Lucretia Chamgam (Canada, housekeeper)

ANDERSON,
Dwight P. m. Tracy A. **Whitcher** 8/6/1993

ANDREWS,
Jeffrey G. m. Gloria F. **St. Onge** 3/22/1980 in Manchester
John A. of New Durham m. Gladys E. **Miller** of New Durham
 10/9/1916 in Portsmouth; H - 35, farmer, b. Vernon, CT, s/o
 George H. Andrews (So. Windsor, CT, carpenter) and Ella A.
 Ogden (Vernon, CT, housekeeper); W - 23, housework, b. New
 Durham, d/o James A. Miller (Acton, ME, farmer) and Ella J.
 Glidden (Alton, housekeeper)

ARGUIN,
Peter B. m. Brenda L. **Spinney** 11/22/1986 in Hampton

ARSENAULT,
Scott A. m. Deborah J. **Dow** 11/23/1991

AUBERT,
Paul Roland of New Durham m. Joyce Ethelyn **Woodman** of New
 Durham 3/13/1997

AUSTIN,
Dale A. m. Sandra Lee **Parsons** 3/25/1972 in Alton

AVALLONE,
Thomas Paul m. Sandra Clark **Sims** 8/4/1973 in Kingston

AVERSA,
Michael S. m. Charna L. **Smith** 9/14/1985 in Rochester

AYERS,
Charles A. of Barrington m. Lucy **Kendrick** of New Durham
 3/15/1899; H - 45, laborer, 2d, b. Barrington, s/o Richard Ayers
 (deceased) and Susan C. Leighton (deceased); W - 25, housewife,

2d, b. New Orleans, LA, d/o Wesley Sheffield (deceased) and Mary M. Remey (deceased)

Charles H., Jr. m. Karen P. **Fontaine** 4/16/1988

Joseph T. of New Durham m. Belle G. **Wallace** of New Durham 6/24/1893 in Union; H - 29, brush maker, b. New Durham, s/o J. Frank Ayers and Harriett S. Downs; W - 16, seamstress, b. Alton, d/o Russell Wallace and Rilla McKean

BAKER,
James Samuel m. Lorraine Lucille **Perrault** 9/15/1974 in Springfield
Thomas G. m. Anita L. **Berry** 7/1/1972

BANKS,
Howard William m. Martha Melchier **Laney** 9/12/1951 in Hampton Falls

BARNET,
John James m. Diane Marie **Wyman** 4/29/1967 in Concord

BARSANTI,
Stephen William m. Bonnie Jean **Emerson** 8/30/1992 in Gilford

BARTLETT,
Bruce William m. Marilyn **Hills** 10/2/1957 in Farmington
Clarence of New Durham m. Jeanette A. **Bonser** of Rochester 10/2/1949 in Dover; H - 40, electrician, 2d, b. MA, s/o William H. Bartlett (MA) and Fannie LaFarge (MA); W - 22, shoeworker, 2d, b. NH, d/o Henry Maxfield (NH) and Lena Poisson (NH)

BASSETT,
Daniel T., Jr. m. Andrea E. **Dean** 6/2/1984 in Alton

BASTON,
Richard L. m. Lisa J. **Bleau** 11/30/1983

BATES,
Timothy m. Linda Marie **Hanley** 6/3/1989 in Alton Bay

BAXTER,
Oliver C. of New Durham m. Sadie F. **Walker** of New Durham 10/18/1906; H - 30, wood turner, b. Windsor, NS, s/o Daniel Baxter (Scotland, retired) and Margaret Ferguson; W - 22, housework, b. New Durham, d/o John N. Walker (Farmington, farmer) and Emma F. Burnham (Charlestown, MA, housewife)

BEAN,
Kenneth Edward m. Tammy Marie **Coran** 8/26/1978

BEARD,
Russell Paul m. Cathy Rae **Jones** 8/12/1977 in Wolfeboro

BECK,
Charles W. of New Durham m. Mamie **Stetson** of New Durham 4/18/1911; H - 31, engineer, 2d, b. Gilmanton, s/o James H. Beck (Gilmanton, farmer) and Marie Sanderson (Gilmanton, teacher); W - 31, housewife, b. Hartford, CT, d/o August Stetson (Germany, brass finisher) and Mary Connors (England, laundress)

BEDARD,
Raynold of Rochester m. Priscilla R. **Crateau** of New Durham 1/1/1949 in Farmington; H - 25, seaman, b. Sanford, ME, s/o Arthur Bedard (Canada) and Isola M. Dubois (Canada); W - 24, waitress, b. Rochester, d/o Ernest J. Crateau (Gonic) and Killa R. Lefebrve (Rochester)

BELLEMORE,
Daniel M. of New Durham m. Sandra Ann **Eaton** of New Durham 8/3/1996

BENNER,
Patrick E. m. Sandra A. **Morin** 9/27/1986 in Farmington
Robert George m. Evelyn Ann **Blamy** 10/3/1975

BERNARD,
Robert A. m. Gwendolyn M. **Belanger** 9/29/1989 in Las Vegas, NV

BERNIER,
Michael J. m. Sue A. **Bertrand** 5/31/1986 in Ossipee
Shawn Charles m. Anne Kristyn **Rogers** 6/22/1991 in Wolfeboro

BERRY,
Charles M. of New Durham m. Annie V.A. **Coburn** of New Durham 4/26/1908 in Alton; H - 33, brushmaker, 2d, b. Farmington, s/o Stephen W. Berry (Bangor, ME, farmer) and Hannah J. Edgerly (New Durham, housewife); W - 44, housekeeper, 2d, b. New Durham, d/o Charles Adams (painter) and Betsy Farnsworth (housewife)
Charlie M. of New Durham m. Kate W. **Strout** of Yarmouth, ME 1/11/1896; H - 20, brushmaker, b. Farmington, s/o Stephen W. Berry (Bangor, ME, farmer) and Hannah J. Edgerly (Middleton, housekeeper); W - 25, housekeeper, b. Yarmouth, ME, d/o Nathan A. Strout (Raymond, ME, farmer) and Ellen M. Wiggin (deceased)
Elmer N. of New Durham m. Ellen E. **Woods** of Farmington 2/4/1950 in Farmington; H - 23, farmer, b. VA, s/o Joseph N. Berry (New Durham) and M. Satterwhite (Havellette, VA); W - 27, shoeworker, 2d, b. ME, d/o Roscoe Bowden (ME) and C. A. Richardson (VT)
Elmer Nelson, Jr. m. Alice Rose **Whitehouse** 6/30/1973
Izah P. of New Durham m. Edna J. **Peavey** of Farmington 11/12/1914 in Farmington; H - 23, farmer, b. New Durham, s/o Zanello D. Berry (New Durham, insurance agt) and Magene E. Hale (Bridgton, ME, housewife); W - 23, teacher, b. Farmington, d/o Henry K. Peavey (Farmington, foreman) and Josephine Jenkins (New Durham, shoe stitcher)

John L. of New Durham m. Fannie B. **Clough** of New Durham 7/4/1900; H - 21, shoemaker, b. New Durham, s/o John Berry (New Durham, shoemaker) and Carrie Savage (New Durham, housewife); W - 19, housekeeper, b. Alton, d/o Daniel B. Clough (Alton, shoemaker) and Lydia F. Young (Alton, housewife)

John M. of New Durham m. Shirley M. **Otis** of Center Barnstead 6/2/1942; H - 24, farmer, b. New Durham, s/o Nelson M. Berry (Farmington, farmer) and Mabel F. Canney (Helena, MT, housewife); W - 19, at home, b. Center Barnstead, d/o Lewis L. Otis (S. Barnstead, machinist) and Gladys Brady (Lynn, MA, waitress)

Joseph E. of New Durham m. Annie W. **Winn** of Farmington 12/24/1889; H - 21, farmer, b. New Durham, s/o Joseph Y. Berry (New Durham) and Betsey O. Scruton (New Durham); W - 21, maid, b. Lebanon, ME, d/o Caleb W. Winn (Farmington) and Sarah Wentworth (Farmington)

Joseph E. of New Durham m. Gertrude M. **Berry** of Alton 5/30/1934 in Alton; H - 64, farmer, 3d, b. New Durham, s/o Joseph Y. Berry (farmer) and Betsey D. Scruton (Farmington, housewife); W - 51, at home, b. Alton, d/o William H. Berry (Alton, blacksmith) and Martha Garland (Barnstead, housewife)

Lon R. m. Eileen F. **Sullivan** 9/27/1980

Lyman E. of New Durham m. Laura A. **Straw** of Barnstead 9/8/1887 in Gilmanton; H - 24, farmer, b. New Durham, s/o Eben E. Berry (farmer) and Lucy M. Berry; W - 19, school teacher, b. Barnstead, d/o Thomas S. Straw (farmer) and Laura A. Straw

Lyman E. of New Durham m. Ella A. **Ellis** of New Durham 12/28/1895; H - 32, farmer, 2d, b. New Durham, s/o Eben E. Berry (New Durham, farmer) and Lucy M. Chesley (New Durham, housewife); W - 38, housekeeper, 2d, b. Gilmanton, d/o Ruben W. Page (Sandown, farmer) and Abigail T. Sanborn (Gilmanton, housewife)

Myron E. of New Durham m. Elizabeth **King** of Somerville, MA 9/21/1929 in Alton; H - 36, farmer, b. New Durham, s/o Zanello D. Berry (New Durham, ins. agent) and Magene E. Hale (Bridgton, MA, housewife); W - 29, housework, b. Gloucester,

MA, d/o Marshall King (St. Mary's, Azores Islands, fisherman) and Mary Marshall (Ireland, housewife)

Nelson M. of New Durham m. Mabel F. **Canney** of Gonic 1/12/1915 in Farmington; H - 20, teamster, b. Farmington, s/o Irving N. Berry (Farmington, farmer) and Lizzie A. Jones (Farmington, housekeeper); W - 19, school teacher, b. Rochester, d/o George Canney (Rochester, mill hand) and Emma S. Darby (MT, housekeeper)

Paul D. m. Robin E.W. **Held** 9/18/1982

Robert Wilmer m. Janet Shaw **Campbell** 7/5/1952

Theodore of New Durham m. Eliza **Valley** of New Durham 11/21/1899; H - 25, laborer, b. Canada, s/o John Berry (Canada, carpenter) and Mary Champaign (deceased); W - 17, housewife, b. Canada, d/o Felix Valley (Canada, wood chopper) and Jennie Loubert (Canada, housewife)

Willis Herman m. Gloria Rita **Currier** 2/6/1951 in Farmington

BICKERSTAFFE,

R. D., Jr. of New Durham m. Claire M. **Coyne** of Farmington 7/22/1948; H - 21, student, b. Boston, MA, s/o R. D. Bickerstaffe (England, jeweler, optician) and Margaret Berry (Jersey City, NJ, housewife); W - 19, shoe worker, b. Cambridge, MA, d/o William J. Coyne (Cambridge, MA, foreman fac.) and Catherine Hogan (Cambridge, MA, housewife)

BICKFORD,

Charles Martin m. Deborah Jeanne **Jordan** 2/1/1975 in Rochester

George E. of New Durham m. Eloise R. **Wyatt** of New Durham 1/22/1949 in Farmington; H - 26, dairy farmer, b. New Durham, s/o Harry Bickford (New Durham) and Helen F. Goodell (Alton); W - 23, registered nurse, b. MA, d/o William C. Wyatt (PA) and Ruth L. White (Stoughton, MA)

Harry of New Durham m. Helen F. **Goodell** of Alton 1/24/1922 in Alton; H - 31, farmer, b. New Durham, s/o Charles D. Bickford (New Durham, farmer) and Mary L. Downs (Wakefield,

housewife); W - 23, at home, b. Alton, d/o James W. Goodell (Alton, farmer) and Annie T. Grimes (Ireland, housewife)
Robert E. m. Elaine T. **Scott** 5/30/1987
Robert Edward m. Alta Louise **Scott** 12/10/1952 in Farmington
Robert Edward m. Barbara Joyce **Brogan** 8/26/1972 in Farmington
William H.H. of Wolfeboro m. Emma **Rhines** of New Durham 7/10/1919 in Wolfeboro; H - 68, laborer, 2d, b. Fryeburg, ME, s/o James Bickford (Newfield, ME, farmer) and Delnah Cook (Conway, housewife); W - 75, housewife, 2d, b. Haverhill, MA, d/o David I. Giles (Madison, carpenter) and Anna Huckins (Freedom, housewife)

BILODEAU,
Arthur Allen of New Durham m. Janet Collen **Schepp** of New Durham 7/4/1997

BISSON,
Eric Guy m. Laurie Ann **Allen** 8/12/1992 in Wolfeboro

BOBER,
John J. of Rochester m. Jennifer K. **Wade** of New Durham 12/12/1998

BOLSTRIDGE,
Jeffrey Allen m. Kristine Marie **Elliott** 12/1/1989 in Rochester

BONANNO,
Anthony Michael, Jr. of New Durham m. Debra Kay **Descoteaux** of Seabrook 7/12/1997

BOOTH,
Frederick Harold m. Joy Lynne **Perkins** 6/10/1978 in Moultonboro
Frederick Harold m. Diane Marie **Auclair** 6/17/1989

BORNSON,
William Kirk m. Betsy Rupert **Schaper** 10/21/1989 in Durham

BOUCHIE,
Walter Francis m. June Phyllis **Adams** 1/18/1958

BOUDROW,
Robert Leo m. Paula Hayes **Goodwin** 2/16/1963 in Alton

BOURASSA,
Robert Lawrence m. Jennifer **Nola** 7/29/1995

BOWKER,
Rodman Paul m. Donna Lee **Buehler** 11/3/1973 in Laconia

BOWLES,
John Lewis m. Rachel May **Hilton** 5/28/1993

BOYD,
Donald Thomas m. Jeanne Anne **Kowalski** 9/4/1994

BRACEY,
Robert J. of New Durham m. Ruth F. **Dunlap** of Antrim 7/10/1937 in Antrim; H - 24, minister, b. Franklin, ME, s/o Frank E. Bracey, Sr. (Amherst, ME, light keeper) and Idis H. Clark (Franklin, ME, housewife); W - 24, at home, b. Nashua, d/o Fred A. Dunlap (Salisbury, MA, mechanic) and Abbie F. Shaw (Salisbury, MA, housewife)

BRACKETT,
Erwin H. of New Durham m. Blanche M. **Butler** of New Durham 3/6/1930 in Farmington; H - 51, painter, 2d, b. New Durham, s/o Hiram Brackett (Ossipee, farmer) and Augusta French (Farmington, at home); W - 37, housework, b. Port Hood, NS, d/o Peter Butler and Jennie McLean (Port Hood, NS, housewife)

Horatio N. of Lexington, MA m. Blanche C. **Ayers** of New Durham 8/28/1901; H - 22, sailmaker, b. Charlestown, MA, s/o Jeremiah T. Brackett (Milton, farmer) and Emma Southward (Salem,

housewife); W - 20, b. New Durham, d/o Joseph T. Ayers (Kittery, ME, farmer) and Harriet Downs (Rochester, housewife)
William C. of New Durham m. Bertha A. **Hayes** of New Durham 6/25/1889 in Dover; H - 41, brush maker, 2d, b. Westbrook, ME, s/o Thomas Brackett and Emma Cobb; W - 20, housekeeper, b. New Durham, d/o Nehemiah Hayes and Martha Durgin

BREWER,
Marcus Hamlin m. Bertha Louise **Gerry** 12/22/1951 in Derry

BRIDGE,
Raymond E. of Weare m. E. Miriam **Berry** of New Durham 3/16/1935; H - 19, wood worker, b. Deerfield, s/o Austin W. Bridge (Nottingham, farmer) and Mary Simpson (Deerfield, housewife); W - 17, at home, b. New Durham, d/o Guy A. Berry (New Durham, farmer) and Eva A. Weymouth (Quincy, MA, housewife)

BROWN,
Albert C. of New Durham m. Nellie E. **Mitchell** of New Durham 12/31/1901 in Wolfeboro; H - 27, teamster, b. Waltham, MA, s/o James H. Brown (Waltham, MA, carpenter) and Annie E. Ferish (Fitchburg, MA, housewife); W - 30, teacher, b. New Durham, d/o Thomas E. Mitchell (New Durham, farmer) and Lydia Perkins (New Durham, housewife)
Charles R., Sr. m. Veronica A. **Whites** 2/12/1982 in Farmington
David P. m. Dawny J. **Rand** 8/21/1993
Peter m. Madelyn Adelle **Pike** 1/23/1954

BROWNE,
Lansing Gilbert, IV m. San-Dee **Coleman** 10/12/1991 in Newmarket

BRULOTTE,
Michael Roger m. Barbara Joyce **Lamper** 10/27/1973 in Milton

BUCKINGHAM,
David J. of Springfield, MA m. Ann M. **Ashe** of Springfield, MA 7/3/1920; H - 21, reporter, b. So. Windham, VT, s/o C. L. Buckingham (Clinton, CT, clergyman) and Linnie E. Carter (Clinton, CT, housewife); W - 23, stenographer, b. No. Wilbraham, MA, d/o John J. Ashe (Springfield, MA, paper maker) and Mary Leahy (Springfield, MA, housewife)

BURGER,
William Christopher m. Judi Merle **Stuart** 6/27/1992

BURNHAM,
George D. of New Durham m. Carrie A. **White** of New Durham 5/3/1902; H - 27, farmer, b. New Durham, s/o James A. Coburn (New Durham, storekeeper) and Emma F. Burnham (New Durham, housekeeper); W - 33, housework, 3d, b. Keene, d/o Edward S. Griffiths (Swanzey, chairmaker) and Hattie J. Lappan (Boston, MA, housekeeper)

BUTLER,
Alexander Bruce m. Dorothy Cortney **Stewart** 10/11/1957 in Newport

CALDON,
William B. m. Lucy B. **Poulin** 6/26/1982 in Alton

CAMERON,
Lawrence E. of New Durham m. Ada E. **Kelley** of Lebanon, ME 8/22/1929 in Union; H - 20, farmer, b. Greenport, NY, s/o John B. Cameron (London, England, machinist) and Hilda E. Robottom (England, housewife); W - 18, housework, b. Lynn, MA, d/o Chester Kelley (Allenstown, farmer) and Ada Kelley (Lynn, MA, housewife)

CANN,
Arthur E. of New Durham m. Melvenia J. **Krisiak** of New Durham 7/1/1935 in So. Berwick, ME; H - 27, machinist, b. Lynn, MA, s/o Oscar E. Cann (Lynn, MA, machinist) and Nettie M. Little (Portland, ME, housewife); W - 15, at home, b. E. Templeton, MA, d/o John Krisiak (Poland, deceased) and Rosanna Montbriant (Gardner, MA, housewife)

CANNEY,
Alfred B. m. Carmen M. **Gordon** 7/3/1980
Henry J. of Gilmanton m. Helen A. **Nelson** of New Durham 6/21/1904; H - 41, hotel, 2d, b. New Durham, s/o Thomas Canney (farmer) and Belle Dolby; W - 36, housewife, 2d, b. Plymouth, d/o James C. Nelson (clergyman) and Helen Lynch

CAPONE,
Alfred James m. Brenda Joyce **Gault** 1/2/1972 in Alton

CARDINAL,
David J. m. Kathy L. **Lizotte** 7/31/1982 in Rochester
Leo of New Durham m. Ethel M. **Ring** of New Durham 1/22/1949 in Chichester; H - 33, trucking, 2d, b. NH, s/o John Cardinal (NH) and Rosana Rock (Epping); W - 22, housewife, 2d, b. Farmington, d/o William H. Shaw (NH) and Mabel Ricker (Farmington)

CARON,
Roland N. of Rochester m. Kathleen **Campbell** of New Durham 12/30/1950 in Rochester; H - 21, bus driver, b. NH, s/o Ernest Caron (NH) and Alberta Welch (NH); W - 19, shoe factory, b. NB, d/o Basil Campbell (Canada) and Delia Young (NS)

CASSIDY,
Carlton Douglas, Jr. m. Frances Edna **Fox** 5/12/1978 in Portsmouth

CATHCART,
Herbert R. of Farmington m. Pauline **Laney** of New Durham 11/20/1937 in Alton; H - 25, pipe ftr. hlpr, b. Farmington, s/o Fred Cathcart (Farmington) and Bernice Haddock (Farmington, shoe worker); W - 21, shoe stitcher, b. Alton, d/o George Laney (Skowhegan, ME, laborer) and Hazel Nutter (Dover, shoe stitcher)

CHABOT,
Henry Joseph m. Linda Diane **Morgan** 12/28/1970 in Farmington
Jerry Lee m. Shirleen Ann **Goodrow** 10/5/1972 in Center Barnstead

CHAMBERLIN,
Arthur D. of New Durham m. Bertha J. Berry **Roberts** of Rochester --/--/1907 in Rochester; H - 30, farmer, s/o H. E. Chamberlin (New Durham, farmer) and Sadie M. Tucker (Hopkinton, housewife); W - 35, nurse, 2d, d/o Lovell M. Berry (Strafford, farmer) and Melissa Hartford (Somersworth, housewife)

Charles A. of New Durham m. Ellen M. **Gault** of Farmington 9/13/1917 in Deerfield; H - 19, farmer, b. New Durham, s/o Irving Chamberlin (New Durham, farmer) and Edith M. Thurrell (No. Berwick, ME, housewife); W - 23, shoe stitcher, b. Gilmanton, d/o Charles W. Gault (Gilmanton, merchant) and Ida L. Varney (Gonic, housewife)

George Daniel m. Carolyn Mae **Fogg** 1/6/1952 in Manchester

John B. of New Durham m. Annie M. **Joy** of New Durham 6/12/1894; H - 24, farmer, b. New Durham, s/o Jonas Chamberlin (New Durham, farmer) and Mary S. Burley (New Durham, housekeeper); W - 24, teacher, b. New Durham, d/o Joseph F. Joy (New Durham, clergyman) and Addie F. Berry (New Durham, housekeeper)

John Eric m. Melynda Adrienne **Blair** 9/30/1989 in Farmington

Lewis of New Durham m. Irene W. **Duff** of New Durham 11/5/1949; H - 30, farmer, b. NH, s/o J. B. Chamberlin (NH) and E. G. Blackmar (NH); W - 29, at home, b. Canada, d/o Martin Duff (Canada) and B. M. Henderson (Canada)

Nelson of New Durham m. Freda M. **Smith** of New Durham 11/14/1946; H - 20, mechanic, b. New Durham, s/o J. B. Chamberlin (New Durham, retired) and Edna Blackmer (Madbury, housewife); W - 18, clerk, b. New Durham, d/o Alfred Smith (Boston, MA, laborer) and Freda Miller (New Durham, housewife)

CHANDLER,
Edward L. of New Durham m. Rosa E. **Edgerly** of New Durham 1/25/1908; H - 47, millwright, 2d, b. Lawrence, MA, s/o Edward L. Chandler (Warren, millwright) and Elizabeth Margrett (London, England); W - 23, housekeeper, b. New Durham, d/o Charles W. Edgerly (New Durham) and Minnie B. Colomy (New Durham, housekeeper)

CHASE,
Curtis W. of Rumney m. Mildred L. **Smith** of New Durham 12/15/1934 in Plymouth; H - 26, student, b. Wentworth, s/o Walter E. Chase (Wentworth, laborer) and Mary B. Smith (Orford, housekeeper); W - 17, at home, b. Alton, d/o Irving E. Smith (Alton, mill foreman) and Beatrice I. Glidden (New Durham, housewife)

Fred M. of New Durham m. Priscilla L. **Curtis** of Farmington 7/5/1931 in Farmington; H - 25, wood worker, b. Dover, s/o Fred H. Chase (Dover, wood worker) and Ella B. Davis (Wells, ME, housewife); W - 18, shoe worker, b. Farmington, d/o Willie B. Curtis (Farmington, farmer) and Bessie J. Gilman (Hallowell, ME, nurse)

Melvin N. of New Durham m. Albina O. **Parent** of Farmington 10/10/1931 in Farmington; H - 23, plane operator, b. New Durham, s/o Fred H. Chase (Dover, wood worker) and Ella B. Davis (Wells, ME, housewife); W - 19, shoe worker, b. Salmon Falls, d/o Edward Parent (Canada, laborer) and Celina Caron (Canada, housewife)

Richard F. of New Durham m. Irene L. **Sauerbrey** of E. Rockaway, NY 6/13/1944; H - 18, US Navy, b. Rochester, s/o Fred H.

Chase (Dover, manufacturer) and Ella B. Davis (Wells, ME, housewife); W - 21, clerk, b. E. Rockaway, NY, d/o P. J. Sauerbrey (Germany, watchman) and C. R. Reuther (Brooklyn, NY, housewife)

Roger William of New Durham m. Shirley Ann **Wentworth** of New Durham 10/4/1997

CHASSE,

Arthur John, III m. Samantha Kirsten **Ellsworth** 2/17/1991 in Belmont

George Michael of New Durham m. Celeste Marie **Garland** of New Durham 8/24/1996

CHESLEY,

John E. of Cisco, TX m. Fannie E. **Sampson** of New Durham 10/13/1891; H - 40, ranchman, b. New Durham, s/o Moses H. Chesley (New Durham); W - 28, farmer's daughter, b. New Durham, d/o Ivory P. Sampson (New Durham) and Mary Sampson (New Durham)

CHISHOLM,

Richard A. m. Jane M. **Fox** 7/30/1967 in Dover

CLARK,

Kelvin Herbert m. Janice Paulette **Beaulieu** 10/26/1962 in Portsmouth

CLAYTON,

Glen A. m. Denise L. **Brown** 11/24/1984

COBURN,

Charles H. of New Durham m. Etta F. **Allen** of Somerville, MA 3/3/1898 in Farmington; H - 23, knife maker, b. New Durham, s/o Charles H. Coburn (deceased) and Druzilla Corson (deceased); W - 22, housework, b. NS, d/o Hazen Allen (deceased) and Eliza Rayworth (deceased)

Floyd P. of New Durham m. Ethel E. **Hayes** of New Durham

8/--/1913 in Alton; H - 19, woodworker, b. New Durham, s/o Alonzo G. Coburn (New Durham) and Annie V. Adams (Farmington); W - 18, housekeeper, b. New Durham, d/o Seth W. Hayes (Alton) and Abbie Swett (East Kingston)

Franklin W. of New Durham m. Luella **Hayes** of New Durham 1/24/1891 in Revere, MA; H - 56, knife maker, 3d, b. Pelham, MA, s/o Jesse Coburn (deceased) and Abigail Hardy (deceased); W - 31, housekeeper, 2d, b. New Durham, d/o William H. Tash (deceased) and Frances Randall (New Durham, housekeeper)

Franklin W. of New Durham m. Sarah E. **Gould** of Lynn, MA 4/18/1892 in Dover; H - 57, knife maker, 4th, b. Pelham, s/o Jesse Coburn (deceased) and Abigail H. Hardy (deceased); W - 42, housekeeper, 2d, b. Cambridge, MA, d/o Hiram F. Wright (deceased) and Sarah B. Fracy (Wells River, VT, housekeeper)

Oren B. of New Durham m. Ellen S. **Towne** of Groveland, MA 4/30/1887 in Groveland, MA; H - 56, laborer, 2d, b. Pelham, s/o Jesse Coburn (farmer) and Nabbie Coburn; W - 42, housekeeper, 2d, b. Groveland, MA, d/o Manly Hardy (carpenter) and Rebecca Hardy

COLLINS,
Richard Dennis m. Bonnie Phyllis **Gault** 11/22/1974 in Rochester

CONARD,
Ronald Dean m. Nancy Donna **Boyden** 5/7/1960 in Portsmouth

CONNOR,
William Frederick m. Florence Elsie **Eldredge** 7/14/1973 in Farmington

CORAN,
Wallace James m. Nancy Rose **Lacerte** 6/19/1993

CORRIVEAU,
Philip Michael of New Durham m. Denise Dorothy **Tower** of New Durham 3/1/1997

CORSON,
Charles H. of New Durham m. Gladys E. **Miller** of New Durham 6/26/1921 in Dover; H - 42, laborer, b. New Durham, s/o Henry A. Corson (New Durham, shoemaker) and Mary J. Gilbert (Milton, housewife); W - 27, housekeeper, 2d, b. New Durham, d/o James A. Miller (Acton, ME, farmer) and Ella J. Glidden (New Durham, housewife)

Harris Charles m. Norma Evelyn **Woodman** 8/30/1952 in Farmington

Richard H. m. June E. **Jacklin** 6/16/1979

Willis R. of New Durham m. Etta S. **Thurston** of New Durham 4/5/1919 in Farmington; H - 36, wood turner, b. Wolfeboro, s/o George A. Corson (Farmington, shoemaker) and Emma J. Willey (New Durham, housewife); W - 24, housekeeper, b. No. Berwick, ME, d/o Josiah W. Thurston (Effingham, farmer) and Sylvia A. Newhall (Wells, ME, housewife)

COULIMORE,
H. W. of Stacyville, ME m. Bernice **Wentworth** of New Durham 11/30/1943; H - 28, clergyman, b. Clydebrook, Scotland, s/o L. C. Coulimore (England, carpenter) and Janet M. Pearson (Scotland, housewife); W - 27, at home, b. New Durham, d/o L. A. Wentworth (New Durham, laborer) and Hazel I. Nutter (Farmington, housewife)

COUTURE,
Earl David m. Michele Kristen Marie **Ham** 11/10/1990

Philias of New Durham m. Mary **Duprey** of New Durham 1/11/1892 in Rochester; H - 21, wood chopper, b. Canada, s/o Francis Couture (Canada, farmer) and Virginia Lacare (Canada, housekeeper); W - 15, housekeeper, b. Canada, d/o Louis Duprey (deceased) and Agnes Nadeau (deceased)

COVEL,
Gary Earl m. Robin Elida **Barnet** 10/21/1978

CREPEAU,
Gary R. m. Sheila A. **Heath** 6/30/1984 in Alton

CRONIER,
Mark S. m. Marie H. **Stevens** 8/23/1986 in Alton

CROWLEY,
Frank Warren m. Christine Marie **Joy** 7/29/1995 in Concord
Robert James, II m. Stephanie N. **Schmid** 7/30/1994 in Sandwich

CUNNIFF,
John Timothy of New Durham m. Sandra Jean **Wynn** of New Durham 12/12/1997

CURRIER,
David John m. Rebecca Jeanne **Dupuis** 9/14/1991 in Rochester

CUSHMAN,
Gardner S. m. Judith K. **Daly** 10/10/1981

DADURA,
Robert James m. Ellen Carroll **Reinholz** 9/4/1965 in Laconia

DAMON,
Walter Ernest m. Jeanne Alice **Gelinas** 5/23/1970 in Alton

DAVENHALL,
William Henry m. Gail Louise **Remick** 11/25/1977 in Rochester

DAVIS,
Glenn Clyde m. Sharon Lyn **Amrol** 12/24/1989
Harry W. of Farmington m. Alice D. **Chamberlain** of New Durham 4/15/1916; H - 21, shoeworker, b. Farmington, s/o Charles Davis (laborer) and Ella Bunker (Farmington, housewife); W - 20, shoeworker, b. New Durham, d/o Irving Chamberlin (New

Durham, farmer) and Edith Thurell (No. Berwick, ME, housekeeper)

John of New Durham m. Helen **Tucker** of Farmington 3/9/1887 in Farmington; H - 60, farmer, 3d, b. New Durham, s/o John Davis (farmer) and Lydia Davis (housekeeper); W - 29, stitcher, d/o George Tucker (farmer) and Lucinda Tucker (housekeeper)

DENSMORE,
Gary K. m. Lisa E. **Prince** 8/5/1979 in Concord

DESROSIERS,
Marc Roger of New Durham m. Grace Alice **Quinney** of New Durham 6/16/1996

DEVINCENTI,
James Anthony m. Deborah Ann **Harris** 10/15/1994

DILLWORTH,
Robert T., Jr. m. Kristine E. **Gagnon** 5/11/1985 in Alton

DIONNE,
Greg Stephen m. Rachel Kay **Shields** 4/14/1991 in Strafford

DOLLIVER,
Charles H. of New Durham m. Rossanell **Lowe** of New Durham 10/26/1939; H - 70, poultryman, 3d, b. S.W. Harbor, ME, s/o Hiram Dolliver (S.W. Harbor, ME, sea captain) and Fanny Whitmore (S.W. Harbor, ME, housewife); W - 68, at home, 3d, b. Lunenburg, VT, d/o Arthur Wright (Canton, NY, physician) and Ellen Harris (Albany, NY, at home)

DONNELL,
Edward of Sanford, ME m. Ethel **Patch** of New Durham 8/13/1936 in Springvale, ME; H - 23, laborer, b. No. Berwick, ME, s/o Henry Donnell (York, ME, caretaker) and Lydia Hamilton (No.

Berwick, ME, none); W - 19, none, b. Sanbornville, d/o Reed Lang and Eva Landos (West Newfield, ME, housewife)

DONNELLY,
Gregory N. m. Jane E. **Perry** 1/30/1982 in Wolfeboro

DORE,
Frank E. of New Durham m. Ethel L. **Burres** of New Durham 12/28/1939; H - 37, truck driver, b. Farmington, s/o Eugene Dore (Alton, farmer) and Etta Davis (New Durham, housewife); W - 25, housekeeper, b. Gilmanton, d/o Orman Burres (Gilmanton, laborer) and Eva Jones (Gilmanton, housewife)

Ira L. of New Durham m. Alice **McCormick** of Freeport, ME 9/16/1902; H - 44, farmer, 2d, b. Alton, s/o Thomas L. Dore (Alton, farmer) and Nancy Wadleigh (Alton, housewife); W - 19, housekeeper, b. Milan, d/o Samuel McCormick (Scotland, farmer) and Ellen Murphy (MI, housewife)

William H. of Alton m. Grace L. **Rollins** of New Durham 7/28/1894 in Farmington; H - 24, shoemaker, b. Alton, s/o Alvin H. Dorr (Alton, shoemaker) and Flora L. Hill (Canada, housekeeper); W - 20, housekeeper, b. New Durham, d/o Cyrus C. Rollins (New Durham, farmer) and Laura French

DORR,
John F. of New Durham m. Amy J. **White** of New Durham 12/31/1887; H - 60, farmer, 2d, s/o George Dorr and Jane Dorr; W - 25, housekeeper, d/o Alvah P. White (miner) and Catherine White

DOW,
Lewis Raymond, Jr. m. Yvonne Linnes **Shearer** 6/3/1960

DOWNS,
Larry Richard m. Vicki Joann **Garland** 9/20/1969

DRAPEAU,
Jeffrey Phillip m. Jeanette Marie **Berry** 8/7/1993

DRAPO,
Joseph C. of New Durham m. Minnie Larock **West** of New Durham 8/10/1908; H - 41, laborer, 2d, b. Stanfaul, Canada, s/o Charles Drapo (laborer) and Phoebe LeClare (housewife); W - 39, housekeeper, 2d, b. West River, Canada, d/o George Larock (laborer) and Delia Martin (housewife)

DREW,
Wilbur John of New Durham m. Caroline M. **Willard** of New Durham 6/21/1947 in Milton; H - 24, laborer, b. Sandwich, s/o William P. Drew (Dover, laborer) and Lena Tappan (Sandwich, housewife); W - 17, at home, b. Alton, d/o Frank N. Willard (Alton, laborer) and Ettola Bubier (housewife)

DRUGE,
Robert Bruce m. Rose Marguerite **Gregoire** 8/19/1972 in Rochester

DURAND,
James Roland, Jr. m. Lisa Dawn **Patat** 9/5/1995 in Alton

DURGIN,
Chase H. of New Durham m. Frances E. **Tinker** of East Alton 11/9/1898 in Wolfeboro; H - 21, farmer, b. New Durham, s/o Enoch Durgin (deceased) and Ida F. Durgin (Milton, housekeeper); W - 17, housekeeper, b. Wolfeboro, d/o Charles A. Tinker (E. Lamoine, ME, farmer) and Elizabeth A. Tinker (Lawrence, MA, housekeeper)

DYER,
F. Everett, Jr. of New Durham m. Barbara M. **Berry** of New Durham 8/8/1948; H - 22, carpenter, b. Melrose, MA, s/o F. Everett Dyer, Sr. (Avon, MA, store mgr) and Jeanne Perrin (Rouen, France, housewife); W - 20, at home, b. New Durham, d/o Roy W. Berry

(New Durham, farmer) and C. MacKenzie (Cambridge, MA, housewife)

EASTMAN,
Roger Lewis m. Maryalice **Joy** 6/25/1955

EDGERLY,
Charles W. of New Durham m. Minnie B. **Colomy** of New Durham 4/7/1889; H - 40, laborer, 4th, b. Dover, s/o Shadrach Edgerly (New Durham, farmer) and Ann Bunker; W - 23, housekeeper, b. New Durham, d/o Abram Colomy and Sarah Twombly (Jackson)
Shadrach A. of New Durham m. Sarah J. **Jones** of West Medway, MA 1/13/1889; H - 65, farmer, 2d, b. New Durham, s/o John Edgerly and Lettie Nute; W - 52, housekeeper, 2d, b. W. Medway, MA, d/o Jesse New and Martha Ayer
Walter C. of New Durham m. Ellen **Rice** of Farmington 2/23/1897; H - 23, brushmaker, b. Northwood, s/o Charles W. Edgerly (farmer) and Eliza Drew (housekeeper); W - 20, housekeeper, b. Sterling, Scotland, d/o James Rice (deceased, doctor) and Kathleen Rice

EDIN,
Ronald E. m. Patricia M. **Knibbs** 6/28/1974 in Farmington

EDWARDS,
Michael G. m. Donna M. **Barry** 5/27/1991 in Wolfeboro

EGELER,
Corey Jedadiah of New Durham m. Angela Hope **Hilabridle** of New Durham 7/18/1998

EIDSON,
James Lawrence m. Joanne **Taylor** 4/29/1990

ELDRIDGE,
Edward Arnold m. Cheryl Ann **Brochu** 2/23/1973
Stephen Frank m. Carol Jean **Laplante** 6/19/1970 in Manchester

ELLIOTT,
Laurence E. of Alton m. Mabelle L. **Hoyt** of New Durham 3/19/1938 in Farmington; H - 29, laborer, b. Alton, s/o Willie E. Elliott (Rumney, farmer) and Etta L. Plummer (Groton, housewife); W - 35, shoeworker, b. Northwood, d/o Martin E. Hoyt (Northwood, RR engineer) and Alice Dandelin (Chicago, IL, housekeeper)

Roger T. m. Sheila E. **Dalgety** 4/11/1987 in Rochester

EMERSON,
Russell Wallace, Jr. m. Elizabeth Ann **Brewster** 1/22/1960 in Pittsfield

ESTES,
Richard A., Jr. m. Patricia C. **Theberge** 4/9/1988 in Rochester

FANTASIA,
Stephen James of San Antonio, TX m. Lisa Helena **Kaplan** of San Antonio, TX 12/31/1997

FARR,
Dana G., Jr. m. Donna J. **Gogeun** 4/2/1987 in Alton

FAVART,
Philip Paul m. Bonnie Sue **Oelschlager** 10/15/1988

FENDERSON,
Melvin Clarence, Jr. of Limerick, ME m. Wendi J. **Coran** of Limerick, ME 8/1/1998

FERGUSON,
James of Milton, MA m. Ellen B. **Colbath** of New Durham 9/26/1906; H - 25, RR fireman, b. Scotland, s/o John Ferguson and Catherine ----; W - 28, teacher, b. Farmington, d/o Francis Colbath (Farmington, farmer) and Ellen M. Boody (New Durham, housewife)

FERNALD,
Frederick Sutherland m. Helen Elizabeth **Evans** 7/8/1978 in Nottingham

FIELD,
Harold G., Jr. of New Durham m. Dorothy M. **Hunter** of Farmington 8/2/1946 in Milton; H - 20, shoeworker, b. New Durham, s/o Harold G. Field, Sr. (Haverhill, MA, navy yard) and Freda M. Miller (New Durham, housewife); W - 20, shoeworker, b. Somerville, MA, d/o C. O. Hunter, Sr. (Charlestown, MA, bus driver) and Jennie Magee (Arlington, MA, housewife)

FILLMORE,
David Lewellen of New Durham m. Roberta Ann **Dixon** of New Durham 11/2/1996

FLAHERTY,
William T. m. Lynn A. **Wheeler** 8/11/1979 in Alton

FLINT,
Jasper E. of New Durham m. Marion M. **Fowler** of New Durham 8/20/1921 in Alton; H - 34, machinist, 2d, b. Alton, s/o Edwin H. Flint (Danville, PQ, merchant) and Eva M. Dore (Wakefield, housewife); W - 24, housekeeper, 2d, b. Strafford, d/o Charles E. Parshley (Strafford, farmer) and Mary E. Jewell (Strafford, housewife)

FONTAINE,
Shawn J. m. Linda E. **White** 9/24/1983 in Wolfeboro

FORBES,
Douglas L. m. Cindy L. **Young** 7/27/1980 in Farmington

FORD,
Herman L. m. Etta E. **Cournoyer** 1/12/1952 in Stratham

FOREST,
George F. m. Roxanne L. **Burleigh** 10/18/1981 in Farmington

FOSS,
Albert George m. Madeline **Emerson** 4/9/1955 in West Milton

FOSTER,
Charles Alban, Jr. m. Arlene Frances **Hill** 9/2/1959

FOURNIER,
Gideon Felix m. Florence M. **Pinsonneault** 7/14/1955 in Auburn, MA

FOWLER,
William H. of New Durham m. Bertha G. **Shackford** of East Wakefield 1/3/1897 in Barrington; H - 26, lumberman, b. Rockland, ME, s/o Leroy Fowler (Fort Fairfield, ME, farmer) and Ella Whitney (housewife); W - 16, housekeeper, b. Freedom, d/o Stephen F. Shackford (Eaton, farmer) and Ada L. Smith (housewife)

FRENCH,
Alden C. of New Durham m. Laurentina E. **Runnals** of New Durham 9/7/1899; H - 20, teamster, b. Middleton, s/o Leander H. French (Farmington, teamster) and Jennie M. Tufts (Middleton, housewife); W - 17, teacher, b. New Durham, d/o Caleb R. Runnals (New Durham, farmer) and Laurentina Berry (Middleton, housewife)
Andrew J. of New Durham m. Clara A. **Tufts** of Alton 2/5/1895 in Farmington; H - 29, blacksmith, b. New Durham, s/o Levi French and Mary J. Sawyer; W - 21, shoe stitcher, b. Alton, d/o Samuel Tufts and Susan E. Chamberlin (New Durham, housekeeper)
Benjamin of New Durham m. Annie M. **Canney** of New Durham 12/24/1910 in Dover; H - 37, baker, b. Tiverton, RI, s/o Edward French (Braintree, MA, farmer) and Hannah Manchester (Tiverton, RI, housewife); W - 39, teacher, 2d, b. Farmington, d/o

Francis J. Colbath (Farmington, farmer) and Ella A. Boodey (New Durham, housewife)

Leander H. of New Durham m. Nettie B. **Rollins** of New Durham 9/19/1900 in Portsmouth; H - 43, farmer, 2d, b. Farmington, s/o Jeremiah B. French (Farmington, farmer) and Mary J. Hodsdon (Tuftonboro, housewife); W - 30, housekeeper, 2d, b. Alton, d/o Samuel Tufts (Alton, farmer) and Susan Chamberlin (Alton, housewife)

Michael P. m. Roberta A. **Fontaine** 4/26/1986 in Wolfeboro

FRITSCHIE,
Ralph m. Barbara K. **Smith** 7/14/1979

FULLER,
Fred F. of New Durham m. Glenda L. **Getchell** of Dover 9/25/1944 in Dover; H - 26, ship fitter, b. Springfield, OH, s/o A. F. Fuller (Masedon, NY, hardware) and Edna C. Schaefor (Springfield, OH, housewife); W - 25, at home, b. Dover, d/o H. C. Getchell (OR, trucking) and Bertha Raitt (Eliot, ME, housewife)

Mark John m. Paula Marie **Thumm** 3/5/1977

GAFF,
Henry J. of New Durham m. Louise V. **Cotting** of New Durham 2/14/1942 in Salem; H - 40, b. Chelsea, MA; W - 33, 2d, b. Somerville, MA

GAGNE,
Dennis P. m. Kathryn A. **Buckley** 9/24/1988 in Dover

GAGNER,
Donald R. m. Louise H. **Kelley** 8/6/1983 in Wolfeboro

GAGNON,
Kenneth H. m. Bonnie E. **Parker** 9/2/1984

Leon of Sanbornville m. Eda F. **Miller** of New Durham 8/8/1934 in Farmington; H - 29, laborer, b. Sanbornville, s/o Ernest Gagnon

(Canada, laborer) and Georgina LeGeary (Sanbornville, housewife); W - 21, shoe worker, b. New Durham, d/o Richard Miller (New Durham, farmer) and Eda O. Joy (New Durham, housewife)

GALE,
George Theodore m. Carol-Anne **Holyoake** 7/4/1993

GALIBOIS,
Francis L. m. Virginia G. **Glidden** 7/30/1983

GAMBELL,
Jeffrey J. m. Cynthia J. **Clarke** 6/21/1986 in Alton

GANTT,
Gary William m. Doreen Mary **Hastings** 4/8/1995 in Rochester

GARDELLA,
James J. of Haverhill, MA m. Marie **Bourbeau** of Haverhill, MA 9/26/1937; H - 24, salesman, b. Haverhill, MA, s/o James A. Gardella (Genoa, Italy, retired) and Clara Catermania (Genoa, Italy); W - 21, dancing teacher, b. Haverhill, MA, d/o Alfred Bourbeau (Haverhill, MA, clerk) and Bertha Milot (Exeter, heel coverer)

GARLAND,
Victor I. of Farmington m. Joan P. **Adams** of New Durham 8/27/1949 in Farmington; H - 23, shoeworker, b. Malden, MA, s/o R. I. Garland (NH) and Emily M. Alfrey (England); W - 17, at home, b. New Durham, d/o Edgar N. Adams (ME) and Verna M. Willey (NH)
Wayne Douglas m. Sharon Lee **Call** 6/11/1978 in Farmington

GASSETT,
Leon Elwin m. Jennie Alden **Gassett** 5/28/1971 in Gorham

GAULT,
John G. of New Durham m. Mildred I. **Corson** of New Durham 11/22/1941 in Rochester; H - 25, B.S. operator, 2d, b. Meredith, s/o Sidney N. Gault (Holderness, fireman) and Ethel M. Perkins (Meredith, housewife); W - 19, shoe worker, b. New Durham, d/o Charles Corson (New Durham, laborer) and Gladys E. Miller (New Durham, housewife)

GEARY,
Philip Edward m. Selma Jane **Emerson** 5/20/1961
Philip Edward m. Joan Anne **Guay** 5/31/1974 in Laconia

GEHL,
Ronald Werner of New Durham m. Paula Jane **Kneeland** of New Durham 6/28/1997

GEHMAN,
George Field, Jr. of New Durham m. Cheryl Lynn Marie **Hackett** of New Durham 1/11/1997

GELINAS,
Michael Robert m. Grace May **Held** 6/5/1976 in Alton
Paul R. m. Lois A. **Lord** 6/6/1982
Paul Roger, Jr. m. Elizabeth Ann **Thomas** 3/4/1972 in Wolfeboro

GIBBONS,
Robert Anthony of Wolfeboro m. Dorothy Edna **Ouellette** of New Durham 6/21/1997

GILE,
Thomas J. of New Durham m. Mattie M.L. **Babb** of Strafford 3/15/1894; H - 40, lumberman, b. So. Hampton, s/o Thomas J. Gile and Lucinda F. Bachelder (Raymond, housekeeper); W - 18, school teacher, b. Strafford, d/o Joseph D. Babb (Farmington, farmer) and Melvina Ham (Milton, housekeeper)

GILLIS,
David W. m. Jeanne L. **Gillis** 5/23/1988
David Wayne m. Linda Ellen **Tufts** 7/23/1994

GINAIX,
Peter of E. Sherbrooke, PQ m. Victoria **Goinville** of New Durham 6/1/1889; H - 46, laborer, 2d, b. St. Dignore, Canada, s/o A. Ginaix and L. Pichette; W - 38, housekeeper, 2d, b. St. Barthernie, Canada, d/o Oliver Goinville and Magrite Marse

GIVETZ,
Roy Wesley of New Durham m. Stacie Elaine **Carignan** of New Durham 9/4/1998

GLEASON,
Benjamin F. of New Durham m. Nellie M. **Roberts** of Alton 10/14/1924 in Alton; H - 63, farmer, 2d, b. Oakland, ME, s/o Benjamin Gleason (Canaan, ME, farmer) and Caroline McIntyre (Bingham, ME, housewife); W - 58, hairdresser, 2d, b. Corinna, ME, d/o James H. Sawyer (Durham, minister) and Ellen R. Taylor (Hermon Pond, ME, nurse)

GLIDDEN,
Bert of New Durham m. Hattie M. **Ricker** of Dover 3/7/1895 in Alton; H - 24, farmer, 2d, b. Dover, s/o Joseph F. Glidden (Alton, farmer) and Hannah Evans (Alton, housewife); W - 20, housekeeper, 2d, b. Middleton, d/o Jethro Horne (New Durham, farmer) and Laura Horne (Dover, housewife)

George Z. of New Durham m. Mary J. **Brown** of Dover 7/3/1922 in Alton; H - 61, laborer, 2d, b. Gilford, s/o Freeman Glidden (Gilford, laborer) and Hannah Evans (Alton, housewife); W - 76, housekeeper, 3d, b. New Durham, d/o William H. Corson (New Durham, farmer) and Drusella Jones (Middleton, housewife)

Harry F. of New Durham m. Lilla B. **Randall** of New Durham 7/26/1896; H - 18, brushmaker, b. New Durham, s/o Joseph F. Glidden (Alton, farmer) and Hannah H. Evans (Alton, housewife); W - 17, housekeeper, b. New Durham, d/o Charles Randall (farmer) and Martha J. Woodman (housewife)

James O. of New Durham m. Myra E. **Hanscom** of Dover 6/22/1903 in Rochester; H - 45, laborer, 2d, b. Gilford, s/o Joseph F. Glidden (farmer) and Hannah H. Evans (Alton, housewife); W- 40, dressmaker, 2d, b. Kennebunk, ME, d/o Samuel Hanscom (shipbuilder) and Myra Hanscom (Kennebunk, ME, housewife)

John F. of New Durham m. Dora **Tibbetts** of New Durham 10/23/1902; H - 43, brushmaker, 2d, b. Meredith, s/o Joseph F. Glidden (Alton, farmer) and Hannah Evans (Alton, housewife); W - 30, housekeeper, 2d, b. Underhill, VT, d/o Ed Flint and Lucy A. Magoon

Sidney M. of New Durham m. Alice P. **Glidden** of New Durham 2/20/1915 in Farmington; H - 23, wood turner, b. Farmington, s/o Martin V.B. Glidden (Alton, farmer) and Frances A. Tibbetts (Farmington, school teacher); W - 17, housekeeper, b. New Durham, d/o Harry F. Glidden (New Durham, wood turner) and Lilla B. Randall (New Durham, housewife)

GLOVER,

Archie of New Durham m. Hattie **Perkins** of New Durham 11/28/1936; H - 20, wood chopper, b. Vershire, VT, s/o Bert Glover (Bangor, ME, lumberjack) and Gertrude Asbury (Vershire, VT, housewife); W - 33, housekeeper, b. Meredith, d/o George Perkins (Meredith, deceased) and Annie Clark (Meredith, deceased)

GOODWIN,

Robert George m. Patricia Lee **Ghirelli** 9/18/1976

GOULD,

George W. of New Durham m. Maud S. **Coburn** of New Durham 6/24/1897 in Dover; H - 29, brass moulder, b. Dayton, ME, s/o William H. Gould (Dayton, ME, clerk) and Sarah E. Wright (Reading, MA, housewife); W - 20, seamstress, b. New Durham, d/o Franklin W. Coburn (Pelham, knife mf'g) and Mary J. Willey (deceased)

George W. of New Durham m. Elizabeth V. **Shadduck** of Lowell, MA 6/23/1931 in Chichester; H - 62, retired, 2d, b. Dayton, ME, s/o William H. Gould (Dayton, ME, agent) and Sarah E. Coburn (Reading, MA, retired); W - 43, milliner, 2d, b. Lowell, MA, d/o Ed D. Shadduck (Meadville, PA, merchant) and Richie McLaughlin (Old Town, ME, housewife)

Robert H. of Boston, MA m. Florence **Edgerly** of New Durham 3/12/1922 in Alton; H - 27, fireman, b. Henniker, s/o Frederick A. Gould (Henniker, painter) and Mittie F. Clark (Henniker); W - 26, housekeeper, b. New Durham, d/o Charles W. Edgerly (Dover, farmer) and Minnie B. Colomy (Milton, housekeeper)

GRAY,

David Allen m. Sheryl May **Parsons** 12/2/1972

David Allen, Jr. m. Dana Marie **Martin** 11/21/1994 in Alton Bay

Francis E. of New Durham m. Adeliza **Dickie** of Barnstead 11/28/1895; H - 22, mechanic, b. New Durham, s/o Wendell S. Gray (New Durham, farmer) and Hannah E. Foss (Strafford, housewife); W - 18, housekeeper, b. New Brunswick, NS (sic), d/o Adam Dickie (NS, teamster) and Mary Watson (NS, housewife)

Peter H. of New Durham m. Deborah J. **Nash** of Meredith 11/14/1998

Stanley Frank m. Leora Rose **Gauthier** 5/14/1960 in Rochester

Timothy E. m. Linda A. **Michaud** 10/30/1982 in Dover

GREEN,

Dale R. m. Sherri A. **Housel** 8/22/1986 in Rochester

GRENIER,

Raymond G. of New Durham m. Elizabeth **Langley** of New Durham 10/13/1940; H - 35, carpenter, b. New Durham, s/o John Grenier (Canada, deceased) and Mary Perry (Canada, at home); W - 30, shoeworker, b. Moultonboro, d/o Albert Langley (Lakeport, deceased) and Mabel Hoyt (Malden, MA, housewife)

Rene J. of New Durham m. Ethel **Coburn** of New Durham 2/10/1942 in Berwick, ME; H - 38, laborer, b. New Durham, s/o John Grenier (Canada, deceased) and Mary Perry (Canada, at home); W - 46, at home, 2d, b. New Durham, d/o Seth W. Hayes (Alton, deceased) and Abbie Swett (East Kingston, at home)

Wilfrid of New Durham m. Nettie E. **Chesley** of Farmington 12/24/1921 in Farmington; H - 25, laborer, b. Rochester, s/o John Grenier (Canada, laborer) and Mary Parry (Canada, housewife); W - 17, student, b. Farmington, d/o Herbert J. Chesley (shoemaker) and Annie Kimball (Wolfeboro, housewife)

GRIGG,
Peter Carr of New Durham m. Melissa Marion **Erickson** of New Durham 8/3/1996

GUIDO,
Anthony Joseph m. Brenda Jo-Ann **Hayward** 6/3/1993 in Milton

GUISINGER,
Donald Joseph m. Deborah Ann **March** 4/22/1961 in Rochester

HAGERTY,
Kevin Daniel m. Susan Celia **Trafton** 10/29/1978

HAINES,
Willard B. m. Mabel E. **Adjutant** 12/9/1965 in Wolfeboro

HALL,
William J., Jr. m. Janet E. **Swett** 10/9/1982

HALLER,
Robert W. of New Durham m. Glenna V. **Lanoix** of Gonic 7/4/1948 in Gonic; H - 25, student, b. Lawrence, MA, s/o Walter Haller (Lawrence, MA, shoeworker) and Hilda L. Berger (Manchester, housewife); W - 22, office clerk, b. Gonic, d/o Elphage J. Lanoix

(Gonic, mill foreman) and Hilda V. Bowie (W. Baldwin, ME, housewife)

HAM,
Frank of New Durham m. Gertie F. **Willey** of New Durham 11/30/1901; H - 40, laborer, b. Middleton, s/o Moses Ham (Alton, farmer) and Elizabeth Nutter (Barnstead, housewife); W - 28, housekeeper, 2d, b. Canada, d/o Ezekiel T. Randall (New Durham, farmer) and Melissa Towle (New Durham, housewife)

Frank of New Durham m. Frances M. **Carlin** of New Durham 6/23/1920 in Farmington; H - 58, laborer, 2d, b. New Durham, s/o Moses Ham (Alton, farmer) and Elizabeth Nutter (Barnstead, housewife); W - 39, housekeeper, 2d, b. Melrose, MA, d/o Daniel Carlin (Boston, MA, laborer) and ----- Hurd (Newport, housewife)

Harvey Preston m. Barbara Jean **Morgridge** 1/20/1990

HAMER,
Alan Randall m. Dianna Lee **White** 10/27/1991 in Wolfeboro

HAMILTON,
Robert E. m. Doris A. **Nelson** 2/14/1993 in Lakeport

HANCHETT,
George Franklin m. Gloria Mae **Moulton** 8/11/1951 in Farmington

HANCOCK,
Francis L. m. Donna L. **Dubois** 1/20/1984 in Rochester

HARDING,
Joseph D. of New Durham m. Mary E. **Trafton** of New Durham 10/30/1909 in Haverhill; H - 48, farmer, 2d, wid., b. Rexton, NB, s/o Robert Harding (Rexton, NB, farmer) and Rachel Haywood (housework); W - 28, housework, b. Brownfield, ME, d/o Henry W. Trafton (Acton, ME, clergyman) and Mary Jose (Hartford, ME, housewife)

HARMON,
Thomas Dean of New Durham m. Lori Ann **LeClair** of New Durham 7/19/1997

HARRIS,
Paul Andrew m. Heather Elizabeth **Levere** 8/26/1990
Wayne Guy m. Loneeda Fay **Husson** 8/9/1975

HARTFORD,
Robert M., Jr. m. Carolyn A. **Boardman** 3/5/1988

HARVEY,
Edward W. of New Brunswick, NJ m. Mabel V. **Hoitt** of New Brunswick, NJ 8/12/1919; H - 26, agriculturist, b. Parsons, KS, s/o G. F. Harvey (England, physician) and Eleanor Cole (England, housewife); W - 26, stenographer, b. Tilton, d/o Louis A. Hoitt (Northwood, paper mfg) and Angeline Gray (New Durham, retired)

HASKINS,
William Clifton m. Nancy Rae **Emery** 6/27/1970 in Middleton

HAWKINS,
Howard Harold m. Linda Dianne **Rose** 8/6/1976 in Farmington

HAYES,
Abbott N. of New Durham m. Gladys M. **Parsons** of New Durham 12/20/1945; H - 38, laborer, b. New Durham, s/o Seth W. Hayes (Alton, knife manuf) and Abbie E. Swett (East Kingston, retired); W - 33, housekeeper, 2d, b. Gilmanton, d/o Orman Burres (Gilmanton, laborer) and Eva Jones (Gilmanton, housewife)
Archie Lester, Jr. m. Patricia Jean **Langley** 7/3/1954
Augustus W. of New Durham m. Emma **Pinkham** of Farmington 6/20/1891 in Farmington; H - 36, knifemaker, 2d, b. Alton, s/o Samuel Hayes (deceased) and May P. Hayes (Middleton,

housekeeper); W - 41, shoe stitcher, 3d, b. Farmington, d/o Isaac Laurens (deceased) and Mary J. Laurens (deceased)

Charles E. of New Durham m. Georgia A. **Hurd** of Acton, ME 2/20/1895 in Milton; H - 31, farmer, b. New Durham, s/o Elihu Hayes and Sarah E. Colbath; W - 18, teacher, b. So. Berwick, d/o Edwin N. Hurd (Acton, ME, farmer) and Jennie E. Leavitt (Shapleigh, ME, housewife)

Clarence E. of New Durham m. Sadie M. **Knight** of New Durham 8/16/1905; H - 18, brushmaker, b. New Durham, s/o Seth W. Hayes (New Durham, knife mf'g) and Abbie Swett (E. Kingston, housewife); W - 17, housework, b. Naples, ME, d/o George W. Knight (Naples, ME, blacksmith) and Olive M. Bean (Naples, ME)

Colo E. of New Durham m. Bertha E. **MacCarlie** of Berwick, ME 11/18/1912 in Alton; H - 20, wood turner, b. New Durham, s/o Seth W. Hayes (Alton, knifemaker) and Abbie E. Swett (Kingston, housewife); W - 18, sales woman, d/o Robert E. MacCarlie (Dennysville, ME, wool sorter) and Elizabeth E. Banfill (Madison, housewife)

Ernest W. of New Durham m. Edith R. **Langley** of New Durham 10/6/1942 in Lakeport; H - 33, clerk, b. New Durham, s/o Seth W. Hayes (Alton, knife mfg) and Abbie Swett (East Kingston, at home); W - 30, shoeworker, b. Moultonboro, d/o Albert L. Langley (Moultonboro, engineer) and Mabel L. Hoyt (Malden, MA, housewife)

Everett W. of New Durham m. Rosarie **Grenier** of New Durham 1/11/1918 in Alton; H - 19, teamster, b. New Durham, s/o Seth W. Hayes (Alton, knifemaker) and Abbie E. Swett (East Kingston, housewife); W - 18, b. Rochester, d/o John Grenier (Canada, woodchopper) and Mary R. Perry (Canada, housewife)

Frank of New Durham m. Doris B. **Curtis** of Farmington 7/28/1921 in Dover; H - 18, foreman, b. Farmington, s/o Guy G. Hayes (New Durham, shoeworker) and Clara A. Horne (Farmington, housewife); W - 17, student, b. Farmington, d/o William B. Curtis (Farmington, farmer) and Bessie J. Gilman (Hallowell, ME, housewife)

Grover C. of New Durham m. Bessie E. **Gleason** of Alton 6/8/1918 in Alton; H - 33, postmaster, b. New Durham, s/o Seth W. Hayes (Alton, knifemaker) and Abbie E. Swett (East Kingston, housewife); W - 31, stenographer, b. Sidney, ME, d/o Benjamin F. Gleason (Oakland, ME, farmer) and Lena M. Hallett (Sidney, ME, housewife)

John W. of New Durham m. Maizie **Demerritt** of Farmington 5/7/1947; H - 25, sawmill worker, b. New Durham, s/o Everett W. Hayes (New Durham, sawmill worker) and Rosaria Grenier (Rochester, housewife); W - 17, at home, b. Sanbornville, d/o William H. Demerritt (Berwick, ME, shoeworker) and Mary Eva Hatch (Union, housewife)

Leon F. of New Durham m. Mildred F. **Dow** of Alton 11/17/1940; H - 21, truck driver, b. New Durham; W - 22, housework, 2d, b. Lowell, MA

Maurice F. of New Durham m. Annie M. **Caswell** of New Durham 10/25/1908; H - 19, fireman, b. New Durham, s/o Seth W. Hayes (New Durham, knife maker) and Abbie E. Swett (Kingston, housewife); W - 20, waitress, 2d, b. Lee, d/o James A. Sheaton (Lee, herb dealer) and Madora E. Watson (Lee, housewife)

Maurice F. of New Durham m. Bernice C. **Trafton** of New Durham 8/17/1927 in Farmington; H - 38, mill worker, 2d, b. New Durham, s/o Seth W. Hayes (Alton, mail carrier) and Abbie E. Swett (East Kingston, housewife); W - 30, mill worker, 2d, b. New Durham, d/o Alonzo G. Coburn (New Durham, millworker) and Annie V. Adams (Farmington, housewife)

W. Arnold of New Durham m. Virginia L. **Wyatt** of Milton 11/19/1944; H - 21, laborer, b. New Durham, s/o E. W. Hayes (New Durham, laborer) and Rosaria Grenier (Rochester, housewife); W - 19, typist, b. Farmington, d/o Ralph F. Wyatt (Farmington, laborer) and E. E. Thompson (Barrington, housewife)

HAZELTON,
Thomas Baird m. Catherine Jean **Burroughs** 9/13/1988

HEAD,
Calvin of New Durham m. Angie **Shorey** of Rochester 5/29/1916 in Farmington; H - 50, farmer, 2d, b. Madison, s/o Rufus Head (Albany, farmer) and Betsy Fletcher (Albany, housekeeper); W - 50, nurse, 2d, b. Rochester, d/o Dana Perkins (Rochester, farmer) and Alice Shorey (Somersworth, housekeeper)

Calvin H. of Conway m. Fanny M. **Wright** of New Durham 11/25/1898; H - 33, lumberman, 2d, b. Madison, s/o Rufus Head (deceased) and Betsey R. Fletcher (deceased); W - 24, housework, 2d, b. New Durham, d/o Andrew J. Walker (deceased) and Hannah Berry (deceased)

George R. of New Durham m. Sadie **Newbert** of Bath, ME 7/30/1921 in Farmington; H - 44, ship moulder, 2d, b. Conway, s/o Calvin Head (Conway, farmer) and Ida M. Durgin (housewife); W - 55, housework, 2d, b. Berlin Mills, d/o James Watson (Berlin Mills, farmer) and Lucy Mink (Berlin Mills, housewife)

George R. of New Durham m. Eva **Canney** of Rochester 4/25/1925 in Alton; H - 50, farmer, 2d, b. Conway, s/o Calvin Head (Madison, farmer) and Ida M. Durgin (Madison); W - 27, housekeeper, b. Rochester, d/o Benjamin Canney (Michigan, OH, flagman) and Ella Hoyt (Madison, housewife)

HEALD,
Gerald M. m. Luanne **Gordon** 1/1/1982 in Wolfeboro

HEALEY,
Donald Nelson m. Gladys Louise **Hartford** 9/7/1957 in Dover

HEBERT,
Ryan D. m. Rita E. **Bombard** 8/23/1975 in Laconia

HEGER,
Stuart J. m. Joanne V. **Murphy** 6/7/1985

HELDENS,
Joachim of Hamburg, Germany m. Michelle Ann **Chiasson** of New Durham 7/17/1997

HENDERSON,
Roland A. of New Durham m. Evelyn V. **Littlefield** of Barnstead 10/22/1927 in Center Strafford; H - 22, truck driver, b. NS, s/o James Henderson (NS, carpenter) and Gertrude Sangster (NS, housewife); W - 19, housework, b. Barnstead, d/o George Littlefield (Presque Isle, ME, farmer) and Susie Lyons (NS, housewife)

HENDRICKX,
Jeffrey W. m. Sandra J. **Hanks** 1/28/1984

HENRY,
Harold Edward of Providence, RI m. Virginia Anne **Blandford** of Providence, RI 9/27/1997

HIGGINS,
Edward Paul m. Jane Patricia **Webb** 10/17/1975

HILDRETH,
John H. m. Kathy L. **Gray** 9/1/1984 in Union

HILL,
Allen Wayne m. Michelle Dawn **Perreault** 12/31/1995
Earl A. of New Durham m. Effie M. **Drown** 1/1/1927 in Farmington; H - 27, laborer, b. Barnstead, s/o Sylvester J. Hill (New Durham, farmer) and Effie J. Wentworth (Barnstead, housewife); W - 35, housework, 3d, b. Berwick, ME, d/o Josiah W. Thurston (Effingham, sawyer) and Sylvia A. Newhall (Wells, ME, housewife)
Sylvester of New Durham m. Effie J. **Wentworth** of Barnstead 12/24/1891 in North Barnstead; H - 24, farmer, b. New Durham, s/o Joseph Hill (Gloucester, MA, farmer) and Maria Sumner

(New Durham, housewife); W - 26, housekeeper, b. Barnstead, d/o Jackson Wentworth (deceased) and Jane Wentworth (housekeeper)

HILLSGROVE,
George Terry m. Marla May **Estabrook** 11/1/1975
Royal A. m. Christine **Casey** 5/27/1987

HOAGE,
Thomas James m. Gail Louise **Remick** 6/17/1992

HOCKADAY,
Richard m. Andrea Susan **Hammond** 9/4/1988 in Gilmanton

HODGKINS,
Allan F. m. Mary Ann **Burdett** 9/11/1982

HORNE,
David Alan m. Melody Gail **Ingham** 2/14/1978 in Wolfeboro
Harry E. of New Durham m. Gertie E. **Hawkins** of Biddeford, ME 5/19/1897; H - 24, teamster, b. Middleton, s/o Jethro E. Horne (Middleton, farmer) and Laura Horne (New Durham, housekeeper); W - 18, housekeeper, b. Biddeford, ME, d/o Ansel Hamilton (So. Waterboro, ME, butcher) and Jenny S. Kimball (deceased)

HOUSEL,
William J., Jr. m. Christine M. **Huntress** 6/27/1980 in Farmington

HOVLAND,
Luke Arthur Seavers of New Durham m. Janice Gail **Dozois** of New Durham 9/5/1998

HOWARD,
Bruce Edward m. Susan E. **Waskiel** 6/10/1995

HOWE,
Charles McIntosh m. Sarah Adams **Breck** 7/27/1974

HOYT,
Ray Allen m. Evelyn Carol **Woods** 8/16/1958 in Farmington

HUNT,
Charles F. m. Donna M. **Gray** 4/12/1980 in Rochester

HUNTER,
Charles O., Jr. of Milton m. Virginia B. **Staples** of New Durham 9/19/1947; H - 23, mill man, b. Somerville, MA, s/o Charles O. Hunter (Charlestown, MA, retired) and Jennie Magee (Arlington, MA, housewife); W - 18, at home, b. Tuftonboro, d/o Charles F. Staples (Wolfeboro, mill man) and Doris Willard (Alton, housewife)
Rockie J. m. Darlene D. **Allen** 2/16/1985 in Rochester

HUSSEY,
David Robert m. Nancy Joan **Corriveau** 10/1/1988

HUSSON,
David Kenneth m. Loneeda Fay **Coran** 4/22/1967 in Farmington

INGHAM,
Robert Stephen m. Carole Marie **Gelinas** 8/31/1974 in Alton

JACKLIN,
Peter Lawrence m. Susan Mary **Gormley** 10/8/1966 in Alton
Peter Lawrence m. Barbara Louise **Barnes** 4/21/1973 in Farmington

JENKINS,
Ronald E. m. Susan C. **Pillsbury-Flood** 8/23/1986 in Rochester

JINES,
Joseph Stephen m. Janine Joyce **Lemay** 1/18/1976 in Alton

JONES,

Arthur R. of New Durham m. Lucy A. **Worster** of Rochester 9/3/1905 in Farmington; H - 22, clerk, b. New Durham, s/o Howard S. Jones (Boston, MA, farmer) and Ella M. Davis (Alton, housewife); W - 27, clerk, b. Somersworth, d/o George Worster (Somersworth, farmer) and Eliza J. Hartford (Berwick, ME, housewife)

Dana P. of New Durham m. Ella M. **Jones** of New Durham 5/20/1905 in Farmington; H - 52, farmer, 2d, b. New Durham, s/o John Jones (New Durham, farmer) and Ann Berry (Alton, housewife); W - 51, housekeeper, 2d, b. Alton, d/o James Davis (Alton, farmer) and Martha Cloutman (New Durham, housewife)

Donald Kimbell of New Durham m. Jeanne Franciszka **Bronisz** of New Durham 4/12/1997

Frank of New Durham m. Doris V. **Clough** of Dover 11/15/1921 in Plymouth; H - 22, shipping clerk, b. New Durham, s/o George H. Jones (New Durham, lumber dealer) and Myra J. Davis (New Durham, housewife); W - 20, teacher, b. Dover, d/o Warren B. Clough (Dover, bookkeeper) and Emily Varney (Dover, housewife)

George H. of New Durham m. Myra J. **Davis** of New Durham 6/22/1897 in Rochester; H - 26, clerk, b. New Durham, s/o George F. Jones (New Durham, trader) and Jennie E. Savage (New Durham, housewife); W - 20, teacher, b. New Durham, d/o John Davis (New Durham, farmer) and Jane Bailey (deceased)

Harry E. of New Durham m. Blanche M. **Downing** of Alton Bay 5/29/1920 in Alton; H - 22, lumberman, b. New Durham, s/o George H. Jones (New Durham, lumber dealer) and Myra J. Davis (New Durham, housewife); W - 22, asst post office, b. Alton Bay, d/o Fred H. Downing (Alton Bay, postmaster) and Minnie I. Barr (North Weymouth, NS, housewife)

Harry T. of New Durham m. Rossillah **Roberts** of Farmington 8/19/1906 in Farmington; H - 27, clerk, b. New Durham, s/o Howard S. Jones (Boston, MA, farmer) and Ella M. Davis (Alton, housewife); W - 26, clerk, b. Farmington, d/o Winfield S.

Roberts (New Durham, shoemaker) and **Oceanna P. Fall** (Farmington, housewife)

JOY,

Arthur A. of New Durham m. Elsie B. **Cilley** of Rochester 7/28/1928 in Milton Mills; H - 25, truckman, b. New Durham, s/o **Samuel O. Joy** (New Durham, mail carrier) and Mary E. **Berry** (New Durham, housewife); W - 18, at home, b. Nottingham, d/o George J. Cilley (Nottingham, truckman) and Alice **Harvey** (Nottingham, housewife)

Arthur Alberton, Jr. m. Ann Mary **Nihan** 6/27/1955 in Woodsville

Earl Kenneth m. Marjorie E. **Little** 8/3/1965 in Wolfeboro

Robert Allen m. Cathleen Hilda **Gervais** 6/22/1963 in Wolfeboro

Samuel Orrin m. Judy Lee **Thibedeau** 8/22/1992

KAPPES,

Anthony Clare of St. Jacob, Canada m. Sonja Alice Jackson **Arsenault** of New Durham 11/28/1997

KEEFE,

Paul Alfred, Jr. m. Karen Lee **Lagasse-McAlpin** 6/25/1988

KEENE,

Orin M. of New Durham m. Martha E. **Gooch** of Alton 10/5/1904; H - 23, laborer, b. Marlboro, MA, s/o Edward Keene (Smithfield, RI, carpenter) and Carrie Leighton (Farmington); W - 20, at home, b. Alton, d/o Page D. Gooch (Lee, farmer) and Emma J. Pinkham (New Durham)

KEEVAN,

Michael D. m. Suzanne R. **Laurion** 9/16/1989 in Rochester

KEITHLY,

Joseph T. of New Durham m. Mary E. Tufts **Willey** 6/22/1910; H - 51, laborer, 2d, b. Saco, ME, s/o William Keithly (England, laborer) and Catherine Boule (Scotland, housewife); W - 64, housewife, 2d, b. Middleton, d/o Davis Tufts (Middleton, laborer) and Adeline Horne (Middleton, housework)

KELLER,
John M. m. Desiree E. **Knibbs** 6/21/1975
Terry Lee m. Carol T. **Allen** 5/6/1988 in Middleton

KENNY,
Michael J. m. Kathy I. **Robbins** 6/28/1986

KING,
Stephen C. m. Victoria M. **McPhee** 5/30/1987 in West Nottingham

KINSLEY,
Eric George m. Jane Ann **Cameron** 9/1/1990

KLEEB,
Albert Emil of Beverly, MA m. Marion Leslie **Ricker** of New Durham 10/7/1913; H - 27, station agent, b. W. Wareham, MA, s/o Leonard Kleeb (Luzerne, Switzerland, florist) and Albertina Gassman (Baden, Germany, housewife); W - 20, musician, b. New Durham, d/o Leslie W. Ricker (New Durham, station agent) and Wendella Tash (New Durham, housewife)

KNOWLTON,
H. C. of New Durham m. Stella C. **Chamberlain** of New Durham 5/1/1893; H - 20, shoe maker, b. Concord, s/o F. S. Knowlton and A. E. Buzzell; W - 18, teacher, b. New Durham, d/o H. E. Chamberlain and Sarah M. Tucker

KNOX,
Daniel Delbert of New Durham m. Sandra Lee **Philbrick** of New Durham 6/27/1998

KNUTSON,
Earle R. m. Mildred E. **Goller** 7/23/1983

KOLACZ,
Stephen J., Jr. m. Lisa M. **Lambert** 6/5/1982 in Alton

KONDRUP,
David Alfred m. Judy May **Cardinal** 3/7/1969 in Rochester

KOSKO,
James Jay of New Durham m. Susan Ellen **Uttal** of New Durham 7/6/1996

KROEPEL,
Robert Howard of New Durham m. Janice Elizabeth **Draper** of New Durham 7/14/1996

KURKIER,
John S. m. Corrine L. **Klinch** 6/27/1981 in Exeter

LABELLE,
Donald Robert of New Durham m. Marie Elizabeth **Arcard** of New Durham 11/23/1996

LABRECQUE,
Michael Gerard of New Durham m. Jean Alice **Laudenbach** of New Durham 2/14/1997

LACROIX,
Donald Arthur m. Darlene Debra **Nickerson** 3/12/1966

LACY,
Robert Dean m. Diane Rachel **Mountain** 9/2/1972

LAFAYETTE,
Lindsay L. of New Durham m. Laura M. **White** of Cambridge, MA 10/11/1936 in Farmington; H - 48, investigator, 3d, b. Whitinsville, MA, s/o Moses M. LaFayette (Woodstock, VT, crossing tender) and Flora Myott (Swanzey, housewife); W - 41,

at home, 2d, b. Cambridge, MA, d/o Edward White (So. Hero, VT, deceased) and Julia LaRoche (So. Hero, VT, deceased)

LAMBERT,
Oscar E. of New Durham m. Freda A. **Hoyt** of Farmington 8/19/1944 in Farmington; H - 31, lumberman, b. PA, s/o C. M. Lambert (PA, farming) and Margaret Haines (PA, housewife); W - 21, shoeworker, b. Laconia, d/o Marshall J. Hoyt (Gilmanton, wood chopper) and Alice L. Danford (Belmont, housewife)

LAMBERTSON,
George D. of S. Framingham, MA m. Edith A. **Hayes** of New Durham 11/18/1898 in Alton; H - 23, clerk, b. NS, s/o William Lambertson (Barton, NS, officer) and Louisa Verress (Woodstock, NB, seamstress); W - 19, teacher, b. New Durham, d/o Augustus W. Hayes (Alton, knife maker) and Martha Kehoe (deceased)

George D. of New Durham m. Ethel F. **Curtice** of Norwood, MA 11/22/1927 in Rochester; H - 52, wood turner, 2d, b. NS, s/o William Lambertson (Barton, NS, pension officer) and Louisa Veness (Woodstock, NB, seamstress); W - 38, nurse, b. Concord, d/o Amos H. Curtice (Bethlehem) and Elizabeth Rogers (Isle of Wight, England, housework)

LAMERE,
Denis Clifford m. Barbara Jean **Bickford** 9/26/1970 in Alton

LAMOUREUX,
Rheaume Joseph m. Marilyn Lee **Ditzler** 9/17/1988 in Dixville Notch

LAMPER,
George F., Jr. m. Barbara Joyce **Garland** 7/23/1967 in Alton
George F., Jr. m. Mary E. **Harris** 5/26/1979

LANEY,

Cecil N. of New Durham m. Virginia **Thurston** of New Durham 7/10/1948 in Farmington; H - 27, laborer, b. Alton, s/o George E. Laney (Skowhegan, ME, laborer) and Hazel Nutter (Dover, shoe shop worker); W - 20, at home, 2d, b. Farmington, d/o William H. Shaw (Farmington, shoe cobbler) and Mabel Ricker (Farmington, housewife)

Francis Herbert m. Mary Kathleen **Dolliver** 7/4/1954 in Farmington

Frank of New Durham m. Ilene E. **Brown** of Melrose, MA 12/14/1940 in Melrose, MA; H - 26, foreman, b. Alton, s/o George Laney and Hazel Nutter; W - 18, at home, b. Brockton, MA, d/o Herbert Brown and Dora Betts

George E. of New Durham m. Geraldine **Shannon** of Farmington 6/7/1947 in Strafford; H - 23, tanner, b. Alton, s/o George E. Laney (Skowhegan, ME, laborer) and Hazel Nutter (Dover, shoeworker); W - 19, shoeworker, 2d, b. Hampstead, d/o Clifford A. Gorton (Essex, MA, shoe cutter) and Norma Harvey (South Lee, housewife)

LANGLEY,

Albert L. of New Durham m. Madeline **Spurling** of Rowley, MA 2/11/1950 in Farmington; H - 22, shoeworker, b. NH, s/o Nathaniel Langley (NH) and Bertha Small (NH); W - 22, uniwinder, b. ME, d/o Kenneth Spurling (MA) and Etta M. Maker (NH)

Nathaniel R. of New Durham m. Bertha E. **Small** of Rochester 7/16/1927 in Alton; H - 21, enameler, b. Moultonboro, s/o Albert L. Langley (Manchester, engineer) and Mabel L. Hoyt (Malden, MA, housewife); W - 19, waitress, b. Strafford, d/o Frank Small (Barrington) and Nellie F. Howard (Dover, housewife)

LAPAGE,

Edward James m. Dana L. **Popp** 7/6/1991

Kenneth E. m. Debra A. **Jones** 6/4/1988 in Gilmanton Iron Works

LAPANNE,
Norman Everett m. Anna Marie **Jepson** 10/21/1978 in Barrington

LAPIERRE,
Ernest M. m. Brenda L. **Dow** 3/26/1994

LAROCHELLE,
Joseph E. of Rochester m. Eva May **Rand** of New Durham 1/1/1930 in Rochester; H - 29, RR worker, b. Rochester, s/o Adolph Larochelle (Canada, RR worker) and Sara Lessard (Canada, housewife); W - 18, at home, b. New Durham, d/o Jacob P. Rand (New Durham, teamster) and Mary Parre (Canada, housewife)

LAURION,
Hal Burton m. Nathalli Ann **Talbot** 8/26/1995 in Rochester

LEE,
Henry M. of New Durham m. Margaret H. **Stone** of Stratford 9/7/1938 in Weirs; H - 72, gardener, 2d, b. West Milan, s/o Michael H. Lee (England, railroadman) and Jane Cole (Milan, housewife); W - 64, housewife, 2d, b. Yorkshire, England, d/o John W. Hall (England, railroadman) and Charlotte K. Ellis (England, housewife)

Perley I. of New Durham m. Rena E. **Gale** of No. Stratford 9/10/1923 in No. Stratford; H - 28, carpenter, 2d, b. Stark, s/o Henry M. Lee (West Milan, farmer) and Lillian Minor (Stark, housewife); W - 27, at home, b. Lancaster, d/o Eugene C. Gale (Whitefield, contractor) and Lottie L. Lunt (Newport, ME, housewife)

LEHNER,
Scott David m. Danica Lee **Charlton** 8/27/1988 in Wolfeboro

LEMIEUX,
Timothy Joseph m. Susan Grace **Fontaine** 11/17/1991

LEONARD,
Stanley Ralph m. Arlene **Treadwell** 9/12/1958

LEPENE,
Peter Allen m. Janice Jannine **Thompson** 6/10/1978 in Farmington

LEVEILLE,
David J. m. Vickie L. **Desrosiers** 10/6/1982 in Wolfeboro

LEVESQUE,
Michael D. m. Patricia R. **Reno** 6/4/1988

LEVINE,
Daniel Jay m. Jean Pier **Boucher** 10/1/1994

LEWIS,
William S. m. Lorraine L. **Jacklin** 8/23/1980

LIBBY,
Joseph W. m. Denise P. **McNulty** 3/27/1982 in Alton

LILJEGREN,
Karl Raymond m. Patricia Helen **Kelly** 3/11/1961 in Rochester

LINDBERG,
Kevin W. m. Donna R. **Dunbar** 2/14/1982 in Laconia

LORD,
Bert W. of Rochester m. Amelia F. **Lee** of New Durham 7/21/1920 in
  Rochester; H - 20, machinist, b. Union, s/o Hiram Lord (Acton,
  ME, sawyer) and Lilla M. Temple (Shapleigh, ME, housewife);
  W - 19, mill operative, b. Farmington, d/o Edward M. Lee
  (Moultonboro, farmer) and Nellie Berry (Moultonboro,
  housewife)

LORING,
Melvin Linwood, Jr. m. Auralie Maude **Senter** 9/23/1955 in Farmington

LOWE,
Carrol H. of New Durham m. Clara F. **Leining** of Manchester 8/25/1928 in Manchester; H - 34, school teacher, b. Waltham, MA, s/o Frank C. Lowe (Fitchburg, MA, operator) and Rose N. Wright (Lunenburg, VT, housekeeper); W - 26, school teacher, b. Manchester, d/o Frederick Leining (Roxbury, MA, retired) and Susan Magoon (Danville, PQ, housewife)

LOWELL,
Fred Clifton of New Durham m. Marjorie Julia **Ryan** of Canaan 11/15/1924 in Enfield; H - 31, miner, b. Lebanon, ME, s/o Stillman R. Lowell (Hiram, ME, cook) and Cora E. Willey (New Durham, cook); W - 16, at home, b. Kennebunk, ME, d/o Carloo H. Ryan (Richford, VT, laborer) and Fannie M. Pelton (Lyme, housewife)

Philemon S. of New Durham m. Eva S. **Rand** of Alton 5/30/1891 in Alton; H - 21, laborer, b. Hiram, ME, s/o James A. Lowell (Hiram, ME, farmer) and Johanah Parker (Hiram, ME, housewife); W - 16, housekeeper, b. Alton, d/o Charles E. Rand (farmer) and Ida E. Young (housewife)

LUNDY,
Richard J. m. Gail A. **Bourke** 10/19/1984 on Lake Winnipesaukee

LUTZ,
Todd Leroy m. Barbara Frances **Allwood** 3/5/1977 in Wolfeboro

LYTLE,
Gary Edward of New Durham m. Regina Lee **Cough** of New Durham 10/4/1997

MACEK,
Christopher Joseph of Dedham, MA m. Stephanie Shanti **Archer** of Dedham, MA 8/31/1997

MACGOWAN,
Samuel Thomas m. Kemberley Jean **Sheridan** 8/14/1993 in Bristol, ME

MACKAY,
Daniel Ernest m. Mary Ann **Kimball** 10/6/1962 in Alton
John Forsey m. Nancy Eldora **Glidden** 5/21/1960 in Alton
Robert Carl m. Gertrude Ann **Cassola** 6/4/1955
William Robert m. Florence Laraine **Philbrick** 9/22/1962 in Pittsfield

MANGAN,
Michael Robert m. Jennifer Anne **Hoover** 8/5/1989 in Wolfeboro

MANNING,
Fletcher N. m. Nancy M. **Prince** 12/23/1984 in Concord
Ryan P. of New Durham m. Lori **Cohenno** of New Durham 3/14/1998

MANSFIELD,
James Boyd m. Cynthia Anne **Choate** 2/2/1958

MANSUR,
John Percival, Jr. m. Mildred Ethel **McAlister** 1/27/1956

MARCH,
Frederic Walter m. Cynthia Joan **Bulter** 7/16/1966 in Barnstead

MARKS,
Nicholas William of New Durham m. Merrie Kelly **Gimskie** of New Durham 9/5/1998

MARTINEAU,
Daniel Reed m. Terra Marie **Scruton** 8/27/1994 in Rochester

MASON,
Thomas James m. Ellen Odacier **Hardy** 7/15/1989 in Tilton

McALISTER,
Elmer J. of Sanford, ME m. Mildred J. **Berger** of New Durham 9/19/1947; H - 39, floor man, 3d, b. Hanover, s/o Elmer McAlister (Orford, mill worker) and Mary E. McRae (Ontario, housewife); W - 32, at home, 4th, b. Dover, d/o Chester B. Price (Keene, ry mail clerk) and Ethel Peterson (S. Sherburne, MA, housewife)

McALLISTER,
Norman of Exeter m. Shirley L. **Micklon** of New Durham 12/15/1947 in Exeter; H - 34, bus driver, 2d, b. Auburn, ME, s/o L. W. McAllister (Stoneham, ME) and Grace E. Moore (Albany, ME, shoe shop); W - 34, clerk, 2d, b. W. Lebanon, d/o William Richardson (VT, store mgr) and Blanche Daudelin (Chicago, IL, housewife)

McKAY,
Charles Edward m. Donna Lee **Rand** 12/26/1964 in Stratham
Charles Edward, Jr. m. Diana Ellen **Pinckard** 9/17/1988 in Milford
Charles Edward, Jr. m. Bobbie-Jo **Bloomfield** 12/31/1993 in Alton
Michael Thomas m. Donna L. **McKay** 12/21/1974 in Alton

McKEEN,
Donald M. of New Durham m. Mary F. **Miller** of New Durham 5/23/1936 in Chichester; H - 24, truck driver, b. New Durham, s/o James M. McKeen (New Durham, machinist) and Flora M. Towle (New Durham, housewife); W - 21, nurse, b. New Durham, d/o Grover C. Miller (New Durham, patrolman) and Annie Grisenthwaite (England, housewife)

James M. of New Durham m. Flora Maud **Towle** of New Durham 4/19/1902 in Alton; H - 26, lastmaker, b. New Durham, s/o James M. McKeen (farmer) and Mary A. Smith (Gorham, ME, housekeeper); W - 24, housekeeper, b. New Durham, d/o William

A. Towle (Wolfeboro, farmer) and Mary J. King (New Durham, housewife)

McKEON,
Robert James m. Margaret Ruth **Hilton** 7/27/1956 in Farmington

McNEIL,
Ronald Joseph m. Linda Elaine **Cardinal** 9/27/1969 in Rochester

MEATTEY,
Richard R. m. Alice C. **Gansecki** 6/29/1979

MEEHAN,
John E. m. Lynn D. **Webster** 10/14/1983 in Wolfeboro

MEEK,
Curtis R. m. Beverly L. **Perkins** 5/4/1990 in Wolfeboro

MELLER,
Joseph Norman m. Patricia Jean **Benham** 8/21/1968 in Alton

MELOON,
Harold C. m. Sandra A. **Cronier** 7/18/1980

MERKLEY,
Daniel Clifford m. Laurel Ann **Moltedo** 12/31/1994

METAYER,
Jeffrey Michael m. Nikki Marie **Paquette** 9/28/1990 in Rochester

MILES,
Jeffrey S. m. Deborah J. **Mansfield** 12/22/1978 in Rochester

MILLER,
Ernest H., Jr. m. Janna L. **Carroll** 2/16/1974 in North Hampton
Ernest Howard, Jr. m. Carol Lucille **Blackstock** 5/31/1969 in Alton

Grover C. of New Durham m. Bernice M. **Foss** of Middleton 8/12/1911 in Brookfield; H - 24, farmer, b. New Durham, s/o James A. Miller (New Durham, farmer) and Ella J. Glidden (Ashland, housewife); W - 17, at home, b. Barnstead, d/o Haven B. Foss (Rochester, farmer) and Hattie C. Varney (Farmington, housewife)

Grover C. of New Durham m. Annie M. **Grisenthwaite** of Fall River, MA 3/1/1913; H - 25, laborer, 2d, div., b. New Durham, s/o James A. Miller (New Durham) and Ella J. Glidden (Ashland); W - 25, nurse, b. England, d/o Daniel Grisenthwaite (England) and Mary Ann Ridley (England)

Harley W. of New Durham m. Ethel **Joynson** of Fall River, MA 6/18/1917 in Dover; H - 34, farmer, b. New Durham, s/o Russell R. Miller (New Durham, farmer) and Mary E. Brackett (New Durham, housewife); W - 29, nurse, b. England, d/o William Joynson (England, stone mason) and Catherine Cooper (England, housewife)

Henry B. of New Durham m. Angie D. **Lowell** of New Durham 3/19/1887; H - 27, knife maker, b. New Durham, s/o James A. Miller (farmer) and Lydia M. Miller; W - 16, housekeeper, d/o Wesley M. Lowell (farmer) and Hannah Lowell

Richard of New Durham m. Eda O. Joy **Sampson** of New Durham 7/18/1906; H - 25, farmer, b. New Durham, s/o James A. Miller (Milton, farmer) and Ella J. Glidden (Alton, housewife); W - 33, housekeeper, 2d, b. New Durham, d/o Joseph F. Joy (New Durham, clergyman) and Addie F. Berry (New Durham, housewife)

Walter H. of New Durham m. Carrie E. **Morse** of Alton 9/15/1900; H - 26, teacher, b. New Durham, s/o Russel R. Miller (New Durham, farmer) and Mary E. Brackett (New Durham, housewife); W - 28, teacher, b. Alton, d/o John S. Morse (Alton, farmer) and Jane Grant (Gilford, housewife)

MILLS,
Garold m. Lois Elaine **Barnes** 7/17/1964 in Tamworth

MITCHELL,
James Karl m. Gracellen Marie **Lomonte** 8/28/1993 in Rochester
Joseph F. of New Durham m. Etta **Clough** of Kennebunk, ME 6/21/1893 in Alton; H - 50, farmer, b. New Durham, s/o Samuel Mitchell and Sally Drew; W - 38, housekeeper, b. Kennebunk, ME, d/o Nahum Clough and Mary Ann Morrill

MOORE,
Shawn Michael m. Susan Beth **Davis** 7/7/1991 in Salem

MORRILL,
Matthew J. m. Ellen K. **Jensen** 8/8/1987

MOULTON,
William D. of New Durham m. Mabel E. **Nightingale** of Rochester 10/2/1915 in East Rochester; H - 46, shoemaker, 2d, b. Detroit, MI, s/o William Moulton (farmer) and Mary Moulton (housewife); W - 37, housekeeper, 2d, b. Rockport, MA, d/o Stephen Poole and Minnie Carlton (housewife)
William D. of New Durham m. Marilda A. **Crapo** of Brockton, MA 8/18/1917 in Alton; H - 48, shoemaker, 2d, b. Detroit, MI, s/o William D. Moulton (Detroit, MI); W - 52, housewife, 3d, b. Platsmouth, NE, d/o Thomas W. Barnes (Platsmouth, NE, farmer) and Elizabeth Moore (KY, housewife)

MUNROE,
David L. m. Christine V. **Torrey** 7/25/1980

MURPHY,
Daniel John m. Karen Anna **Gustartis** 10/2/1977

MURRAY,
Brett James of New Durham m. Kimberly Susan **Pidro** of New Durham 8/30/1997
Brian Dennis m. Lisa Faye **Champoux** 11/25/1993
John Francis m. Elizabeth **Ewer** 9/16/1961

MYATT,
Thomas Nathan m. Geraldine Wheeler **Murray** 8/9/1975 in Laconia

NASON,
Noel Robert of New Durham m. Melissa Louise **Jenness** of New Durham 7/26/1997

NATALINO,
Frank Anthony m. Laureen Marie **Ballance** 9/10/1994 in Hampton

NEAL,
Horace Upton of New Durham m. Susan M. **Williams** of New Durham 11/4/1916; H - 50, farmer, 2d, b. Hyde Park, MA, s/o Samuel M. Neal (Henniker, contractor) and Abbie H. Storer (Fryeburg, ME, housewife); W - 41, housekeeper, 2d, b. Andover, MA, d/o William A. Meldrum (Aberdeen, Scotland, wool sorter) and Francis Wilson (Aberdeen, Scotland, housewife)

NEHRING,
William Ellsworth m. Penny Lee **Gile** 5/7/1967 in Rochester

NEISTER,
S. Edward m. Elizabeth Mary **Goss** 7/15/1989

NEWCOMBE,
Robert Allen m. Deborah Ellen **Clock** 8/29/1992

NICHOLSON,
Wesley Paul m. Janley Elizabeth **Hall** 8/15/1992 in Concord

NILES,
Marshall J. of New Durham m. Ida M. **Chamberlin** of Hartford, CT 1/30/1912 in Dover; H - 42, wood turner, 2d, b. New Portland, ME, s/o Charles Niles (Embden, ME, farmer) and Mary J. Jordan (housewife); W - 40, demonstrator, 2d, b. Keene, d/o Allen A. Craig (Lea Merchant) and Ruth Marsh (housewife)

NORMAND,
James Paul m. Patricia Ann **Tibbetts** 12/10/1988

NORTON,
Rodney S. of New Durham m. Darby C. **Grigg** of New Durham 10/3/1998

NOYES,
C. Russell, Jr. m. Doreen Lynn **White** 2/14/1976 in Wolfeboro

NUTTER,
Harry W. of New Durham m. Jessie L. **Willett** of New Durham 5/22/1940 in Chichester; H - 29, carpenter, b. Farmington, s/o Charles Watson (shoeworker) and Hazel Nutter (Dover, shoeworker); W - 31, shoeworker, b. New Durham, d/o Joseph Willett (Canada, carpenter) and Bessie Ayers (Wakefield, brush maker)

O'CONNEL,
Paul Vincent m. Martha Jane **Colburn** 11/4/1972 in Weare

OIKLE,
William A. of Alton m. Gladys O. **Smith** of New Durham 7/23/1935 in Rochester; H - 32, electrician, b. Shelburne, NS, s/o Allen Oikle (Shelburne, NS, farmer) and Martha Buchanan (Shelburne, NS, housewife); W - 18, at home, b. Lynn, MA, d/o William Smith (Wilkshire, England, laborer) and Annie Olden (Breabury, England, housewife)

ORLOWICZ,
Stephen J. m. Catherine E. **Roy** 4/22/1989

O'TASH,
James E. m. Joyce M. **Couture** 11/27/1986

OUELLETTE,
Frederick L. m. Dorothy E. **Downs** 10/21/1983 in Rochester
Wilfred J. of Salem, MA m. Laura T. **Voyer** of New Durham
 11/27/1937 in New Durham; H - 45, elec. engineer, b. Salem,
 MA, s/o Oliver Ouellette (Canada, mechanic) and Mary Belanger
 (Canada, housewife); W - 30, clerk, b. Salem, MA, d/o Alfred
 Therriault (Canada, textile wkr) and Mary L. Martin (Canada,
 housewife)

PALMER,
Frank Leroy of New Durham m. Myra Grace **Palmer** of New Durham
 11/28/1900; H - 21, laborer, b. Rochester, s/o Edgar L. Palmer
 (Rochester, shoemaker) and Annabel Rogers (Rochester,
 housewife); W - 21, housekeeper, b. New Durham, d/o James N.
 Palmer (New Durham, farmer) and Joan Smith (Shapleigh, ME,
 housewife)

PARADIS,
Lucien George, Jr. m. Beverly Ann **Gault** 12/29/1962 in Rochester

PARFITT,
James N. of New Durham m. Margaret **Bunker** of Farmington
 7/3/1948 in Farmington; H - 65, antiques dealer, 2d, b. So.
 Hadley, MA, s/o James Parfitt (England, furniture maker) and
 Mary H. Craven (England, housewife); W - 60, gift shop owner,
 2d, b. Lincoln, MA, d/o John R. Hartwell (Lincoln, MA, farmer)
 and Edith H. Allen (Blue Hill, ME, housewife)

PARKER,
Albert Lauren m. Patricia Lucille **Lindsay** 7/28/1973 in Alton
Robert E. of Portsmouth m. Elizabeth **Hayes** of New Durham
 6/25/1948; H - 24, mechanic, b. Portsmouth, s/o Elmer E. Parker
 (Ellsworth, ME, navy yard) and Hazel Belle Ames (Alexandria,
 housewife); W - 19, brushmaker, b. New Durham, d/o Everett W.
 Hayes (New Durham, truck driver) and Rosaria Grenier
 (Rochester, housewife)

Robert Stanley m. Nancy Diane **Gagne** 5/28/1977

PARSONS,
Frank Waldo, III m. Joy Marlene **Temple** 8/6/1994 in Farmington
George Rufus m. Nancy Ruth **Madeya** 12/18/1954 in Farmington

PATRY,
Gilbert G. m. Mary E. **Kennedy** 12/27/1986

PELLETIER,
Robert Archie m. Susan Laurie **Barnet** 8/31/1973 in Wolfeboro

PELLOWE,
Douglas J. m. Karen L. **Chase** 11/5/1982 in Alton

PENN,
Craig William m. Agnes Marie **Godwin** 10/21/1989

PERILLO,
Dwain Thomas m. Wendy Lee **Sabol** 9/23/1995 in Wolfeboro
Randy Thomas m. Vanessa **Smith** 9/1/1990 in Wolfeboro
Todd Thomas m. Sara Louise **Rawn** 2/4/1989 in Wolfeboro

PERKINS,
Douglas Paul m. Kathryn Denis **Hynes** 12/11/1993 in Farmington
Harry O. of New Durham m. Lena G. **Willey** of Middleton
    10/23/1897 in Farmington; H - 21, farmer, b. Dover, s/o Samuel
    Perkins (Middleton, farmer) and Abbie J. Goodwin (Rollinsford,
    housewife); W - 17, seamstress, b. Middleton, d/o Edward
    Labonte (Canada, shoemaker) and Annie A. Willey (Middleton,
    housewife)
Samuel, Jr. of New Durham m. Bridget **McNamara** of Union
    1/8/1895 in Wakefield; H - 25, mill hand, b. Middleton, s/o
    Samuel Perkins (Middleton, farmer) and Abbie J. Goodwin
    (Rollinsford, housewife); W - 20, mill hand, b. Ireland, d/o
    Michael McNamara and Penelope Carey (Ireland, housekeeper)

Warren E. m. Karen J. **Underwood** 11/18/1978

PERRY,
Herbert P. m. Kathryn J. **Bowman** 7/12/1986
Paul Patrick m. Dianna Lynn **Serrano** 3/18/1989 in Rochester
Timothy M. m. Jane M. **Murray** 10/17/1987 in Alton

PIERCE,
Steven J. m. Debra A. **Parker** 9/10/1983 in Rochester

PIKE,
Cecil Maurice of Rochester m. Lua May **Berry** of New Durham 9/26/1926; H - 23, clerk, b. Brookfield, s/o Caleb Hodgdon Pike (Ossipee, farmer) and Lydia E. Clow (Wolfeboro, housewife); W - 23, teacher, b. New Durham, d/o Zanello D. Berry (New Durham, insurance agent) and Magene E. Hale (Bridgton, ME, housewife)

PINKHAM,
Alan W. m. Diane Virginia **Hunter** 4/17/1976

PITRE,
Christopher Gene m. Sunna Lee **Buckley** 9/18/1993 in Rochester

PLANTE,
Philip Alan m. Elizabeth Gail **Hayes** 12/20/1969 in Pittsfield

POLITO,
Carl W. m. Nancy L. **Polito** 8/17/1985

POLLINI,
John E. m. Kelly Eileen **Ramsey** 10/6/1990 in Farmington

PONCHAK,
Robert Joseph m. Deborah Ann **Theberge** 10/21/1995 in Dover

POTTER,
Lester Frank m. Alberta Ettola **Staples** 4/13/1952

POULIN,
Robert John m. Laurie Kay **Borggaard** 7/17/1988

PRATT,
Daniel R. of New Durham m. Michele A. **Robinson** of New Durham 5/1/1998

PRELLI,
Lawrence John m. Terri Sue **Winters** 10/12/1991

PRINCE,
Luke J. m. Waneta J. **Cutter** 5/3/1980 in Farmington

PROVENCAL,
George Alden m. Tina Marie **Gelinas** 8/25/1994 in Alton

PRUITT,
Gary D. m. Angela M. **Silvestri** 8/24/1984 in Alton

PUTNEY,
Dwayne E. m. Holly B. **Lineweber** 2/18/1984 in Rochester

RABB,
Alan Howard m. Nancy Avis **Green** 11/20/1971 in Concord

RALEIGH,
George J. of Chicago, IL m. Janet **Weeks** of Somerville, MA 7/9/1928; H - 28, chemist, b. Clyde, KS, s/o Stephen M. Raleigh (Peoria, IL, farmer) and Mary Sinnott (Randon Lake, WI, housewife); W - 21, at home, b. Somerville, MA, d/o Asa H. Weeks (Wakefield, wholesale produce) and Frances Meldrum (Aberdeen, Scotland, housewife)

RAND,

Dona of New Durham m. F. E. **DesJardin** of New Durham 10/29/1949 in Farmington; H - 42, truck driver, 2d, b. NH, s/o Newell J. Rand (NH) and Mary Grenier (NH); W - 40, at home, 2d, b. ME, d/o Charles H. Allen (ME) and Alice L. Earle (ME)

Jacob P. of New Durham m. Mary **Lessard** of Canada 12/31/1895; H - 20, farmer, b. New Durham, s/o Ira Rand (Alton, farmer) and Abigail C. Ham (New Durham, housewife); W - 20, housekeeper, b. Canada, d/o Peter Lessard (Canada, chopper) and Julie Lessard

Joseph D. of New Durham m. Dorothy M. **Garland** of Sanbornville 2/15/1935 in Sanbornville; H - 27, mechanic, b. New Durham, s/o Jacob P.N. Rand (New Durham, farmer) and Mary Perry (Canada, housewife); W - 19, housework, b. Sanbornville, d/o Fred Garland (Brookfield, laborer) and Hattie M. West (Brookfield, housework)

Natt H. of New Durham m. Rose **Camiry** of Lewiston, ME 11/19/1901; H - 22, laborer, b. New Durham, s/o Ira Rand (Alton, laborer) and Clarissa A. Ham (New Durham, housewife); W - 20, housekeeper, b. Lewiston, ME, d/o John Camiry (Sherbrook, PQ, chopper) and Selena Gilbert (Lewiston, ME, housewife)

RANDALL,

Charles H. of New Durham m. Ruth **Labby** of East Rochester 10/17/1925 in Farmington; H - 44, laborer, 2d, b. New Durham, s/o Charles Randall (New Durham, farmer) and Martha J. Woodman (Gilmanton, housewife); W - 20, shoemaker, b. East Rochester, d/o Thomas Labby (Canada, woolen mills) and Edna Chisholm (East Rochester, housewife)

Charles Herbert of New Durham m. Hazel Vivian **Lowell** of New Durham 6/20/1915 in East Rochester; H - 34, farmer, b. New Durham, s/o Charles A. Randall (New Durham, farmer) and Martha Woodman (Gilmanton, housewife); W - 18, housekeeper, b. Lebanon, ME, d/o Stillman R. Lowell (So. Hiram, ME, farmer) and Cora Willey (New Durham, housewife)

Ira of Gonic m. Annah S. **Durgin** of New Durham 1/29/1919 in Gonic; H - 75, retired, 2d, b. Alton, s/o Burnham Rand (Alton, farmer) and Sally Rand (Canada, housewife); W - 62, housework, 2d, b. New Durham, d/o Isaac Willey (New Durham, farmer) and Lovisa Bickford (Dearborn, ME, housewife)

John E. m. Phyllis J. **Clifford** 10/20/1984

John F. of New Durham m. Ina M. **Glidden** of New Durham 11/17/1914 in Rochester; H - 32, brushmaker, b. New Durham, s/o Charles A. Randall (New Durham, laborer) and Martha Woodman (Gilmanton, housekeeper); W - 30, housekeeper, b. Farmington, d/o Martin Glidden (Alton, farmer) and Frances Tebbetts (Farmington, school teacher)

Raymond Thomas m. Carrie Elizabeth **Woodard** 10/17/1958 in West Milton

Roger M. of New Durham m. Beatrice **Chaisson** of Farmington 5/14/1949; H - 19, shoeworker, b. New Durham, s/o Charles H. Randall (NH) and Ruth M. Labby (NH); W - 26, housewife, 2d, b. Canada, d/o Simon Chaisson (Canada) and Matilda Roche (Canada)

Roswell R. m. Tammy M. **Coran** 4/23/1992

Samuel Erwin m. Jane Gayle **St. Cyr** 9/23/1955 in East Rochester

REED,
John Bruce m. Tammera Ann **Thurman** 9/12/1992 in Center Ossipee
Wayne Austin m. Donna Jean **Durkee** 7/17/1966 in Brookfield
William E. m. Julie R. **Cox** 12/28/1982

REILLY,
Mark Thomas m. Maureen Patricia **Fuller** 6/6/1992 in Portsmouth

REINHAGEN,
Robert C., Sr. m. Marjorie M. **Vieira** 7/27/1979 in Farmington

RHINES [see also Rines],
Lafayette of New Durham m. Fannie B. **Brock** of Rochester 10/8/1887 in Milton; H - 25, shoemaker, b. New Durham, s/o

Charles H. Rhines (farmer) and Sarah L. Rhines; W - 16, d/o James N. Brock (shoemaker) and Julia A. Brock

RHOADES,
Peter Charles m. Nancy May **Robinson** 12/26/1994

RICE,
Kenneth W., Jr. of CA m. Christina M. **Berry** of New Durham 3/9/1946; H - 28, metalsmith, b. CA, s/o Kenneth W. Rice (CA, printer) and Delia Sutherland (CA, housewife); W - 24, at home, b. New Durham, d/o Roy W. Berry (New Durham, farmer) and C. MacKenzie (Cambridge, MA, housewife)

RICHARDSON,
Thomas Edward m. Denise Lynn **Cobb** 1/15/1994

RICHEY,
William Sheldon, Jr. m. Judith Lee **Bryan** 6/11/1975 in Concord

RICKER,
John H. of New Durham m. Florence **Dame** of New Durham 12/17/1905; H - 26, laborer, b. New Durham, s/o Charles Ricker (New Durham) and Clara Young (Farmington, shoe shop); W - 19, housework, b. New Durham, d/o Alonzo Dame (Farmington, laborer) and Etta French (Farmington, housewife)

Leslie W. of New Durham m. Wendella **Tash** of New Durham 12/7/1889 in Alton; H - 29, station agent, b. New Durham, s/o Ira S. Ricker (Dover) and Mary E. Hall (Barrington); W - 21, shoe stitcher, b. New Durham, d/o John F. Tash and Almira B. Ham (Alton)

RINES [see also Rhines],
Alonzo G. of New Durham m. Dora M. **Berry** of Freedom 6/19/1899; H - 58, farmer, 2d, b. New Durham, s/o Henry Rines (deceased) and Mary H. Babb (deceased); W - 17, housewife, b. Freedom,

d/o Ai Berry (deceased) and Emma Giles (Lowell, MA, housewife)

Herman A. of New Durham m. Lucie B. **Dow** of New Durham 8/24/1904; H - 25, laborer, b. New Durham, s/o Alvah C. Rines (farmer) and Lydia French (New Durham); W - 21, housework, b. Rumney, d/o John K. Dow and Ella F. Morrill

Mark Allen m. Tammy Jean **Smith** 5/28/1994 in Farmington

Ricky C. m. Diane B. **Gelinas** 6/21/1980

Willie E. of New Durham m. Gracie **Joy** of New Durham 7/3/1895 in Milton; H - 24, shoemaker, b. New Durham, s/o Alvah C. Rines (Alton, farmer) and Lydia French (New Durham, housewife); W - 18, artist, b. New Durham, d/o Joseph Joy (New Durham, minister) and Addie Berry (New Durham, housewife)

RING,

Ernest F. of Belmont m. Ethel May **Shaw** 8/8/1944; H - 21, shoeworker, b. Belmont, s/o Charles E. Ring (Loudon, shoemaker) and Martha A. Haines (Loudon, housewife); W - 18, shoeworker, b. Farmington, d/o William H. Shaw (Farmington, shoemaker) and Mabel Ricker (Farmington, housewife)

ROARK,

John J. of New Durham m. Hattie **Geiger** of New Durham 10/16/1922 in Farmington; H - 44, fireman, 2d, b. Albany, NY, s/o John Roark (Ireland, mason) and Margaret Deavaney (Ireland, housewife); W - 42, housework, 2d, b. New Durham, d/o Charles W. Edgerly (Dover, laborer) and Annie E. Drew (Gilmanton, housewife)

ROBBINS,

William Leroy, Jr. of Topsham, ME m. Cynthia Ann **McCarthy** of New Durham 11/1/1997

ROBERTS,

Charles Edson m. Earline **Palmer** 12/2/1962

ROGERS,
Bruce Tryon m. Patricia Jeanne **Taylor** 6/13/1964 in Naugatuck, CT
Kenneth Gordon m. Joanne Carol **Bean** 12/7/1968 in Rochester
Kenneth Gordon m. Paula Irene **Muder** 11/24/1991 in Auburn

ROLLINS,
Cyrus Carl of New Durham m. Bessie M. **Thurston** of New Durham 10/16/1922 in Milton Mills; H - 18, clerk, b. Alton, s/o Elmer Rollins (New Durham, teamster) and Ella M. Dore (Alton, housewife); W - 18, housework, b. Milton, d/o Josiah W. Thurston (Effingham, farmer) and Sylvia A. Newhall (Wells, ME, housewife)

Elmer of New Durham m. Ella M. **Dore** of New Durham 4/3/1895; H - 23, laborer, b. New Durham, s/o Cyrus C. Rollins (farmer) and Laura J. French; W - 16, housekeeper, b. Alton, d/o Eugene Dore (teamster) and Etta Davis (housekeeper)

Eri of New Durham m. Fannie L. **Dore** of Wolfeboro 5/4/1889; H - 25, shoemaker, b. New Durham, s/o Elisha Rollins (Alton, farmer) and Mary Corson; W - 16, housekeeper, b. Wolfeboro, d/o Jonas E. Dore (Ossipee, farmer) and Sarah A. Yeaton (Alfred, ME)

Harold E. of New Durham m. Addie F. **Morse** of Alton 3/11/1916; H - 20, clerk, b. New Durham, s/o Elmer Rollins (New Durham, teamster) and Ella M. Dore (New Durham, housewife); W - 22, housekeeper, b. Alton, d/o Frank D. Morse (Alton, clerk) and Dora B. Lamper (Alton, housewife)

Harold E. of New Durham m. Doris L. **McKeen** of New Durham 3/26/1921 in Milton; H - 25, grocer, 2d, b. New Durham, s/o Elmer Rollins (New Durham, teamster) and Ella M. Dore (New Durham, housewife); W - 19, housekeeper, b. New Durham, d/o James M. McKeen (New Durham, machinist) and Flora M. Towle (New Durham, housewife)

John L. of Alton m. Eva M. **Berry** of New Durham 6/11/1894; H - 24, shoemaker, b. Middleton, s/o Solomon Rollins (Alton, shoemaker) and Lucinda Tufts; W - 17, housekeeper, b.

Farmington, d/o Stephen W. Berry (Bangor, ME, farmer) and Hannah J. Edgerly (Middleton, housekeeper)

Samuel of New Durham m. Joan L. **Lowell** of New Durham 6/23/1898; H - 50, laborer, 2d, b. Somersworth, s/o John P. Rollins (farmer) and Martha C. Rollins (deceased); W - 19, housekeeper, b. New Durham, d/o Alonzo Lowell (Augusta, ME, farmer) and Joan L. Lowell (Augusta, ME, housekeeper)

Winslow C. of Farmington m. Beatrice **Coffin** of New Durham 8/31/1929 in Farmington; H - 48, laborer, 2d, b. Caratunk, ME, s/o Dudley C. Rollins (Pleasant Ridge, ME) and Elizabeth R. Doile (Carryang, ME); W - 22, domestic, b. Berwick, ME, d/o Charles H. Coffin (Berwick, ME, milkman) and Cora E. **Remick** (Somersworth, housewife)

ROLPH,
David Fuller m. Lynda Ann **Warren** 9/9/1978 in Meredith

ROTE,
John R. of Concord m. Valerie J. **Poole** of Meredith 10/3/1998

ROTHWELL,
Peter George m. Sandra Gail **Hunter** 1/23/1971 in Alton

ROUCKEY,
George A. of New Durham m. Gertrude E. **Ricker** of New Durham 6/28/1924 in Farmington; H - 20, laborer, b. Lebanon, ME, s/o George Rouckey (Guinea, ME, laborer) and Mary E. Blaisdell (Lebanon, ME, housewife); W - 18, housewife, b. New Durham, d/o John H. Ricker (New Durham, mechanic) and Florence Dame (New Durham, housewife)

ROUSSEAU,
Leon John m. Cheryl Ann **Toof** 8/6/1988

ROWELL,
Wayne L. m. Theresa A. **McDermott** 8/22/1987 in Alton

ROY,
Arsene of Farmington m. Vinnie **Goodrow** of New Durham 4/6/1929 in Farmington; H - 35, laborer, b. Canada, s/o Leon Roy (Canada, farmer) and Mary Caureau (Canada, housewife); W - 44, housework, 2d, b. Berwick, ME, d/o Joseph Nalar (Canada, laborer) and Nellie Mayo (Canada, housewife)
Daniel Richard m. Nancy Elizabeth **Specker** 9/1/1990 in Amherst
Jon D. m. Cynthia A. **Blaisdell** 2/18/1984 in Rochester
Thomas J. m. Catherine M. **Rupprecht** 4/3/1982 in Alton

ROYAL,
Ulmer L. of New Durham m. Bessie M. **Doty** of New Durham 4/19/1918 in Alton; H - 30, wood turner, b. Ellsworth, ME, s/o Clifford G. Royal (Ellsworth, ME, teamster) and Louise Bartlett (Ellsworth, ME, clerk); W - 30, housekeeper, 2d, b. Fitchburg, MA, d/o Charles H. May (Fitchburg, MA, wood turner) and Isabel A. Neff (Randolph, VT, housekeeper)

RUSSELL,
Ralph E. of Farmington m. Mary E. **Adams** of New Durham 7/8/1950 in Farmington; H - 22, shoeworker, b. MA, s/o L. Richard Russell (MA) and Etta Wentworth (MA); W - 15, at home, b. NH, d/o Edgar N. Adams (ME) and Verna M. Willey (NH)

RYAN,
Walter Ambrose m. Shirley Leora **Waterman** 10/22/1960 in Alton

SALIS,
George L. m. Rebecca Jean **Belanger** 11/28/1992

SAMOISETTE,
Richard A. m. Shirley **Phillips** 8/11/1992 in Alton

SAMPSON,
Frank M. of Alton m. Eda O. **Joy** of New Durham 6/6/1896; H - 21, farmer, b. New Durham, s/o Nehemiah J. Sampson (New Durham, farmer) and Clara A. Corson (Milton, housewife); W - 23, teacher, b. New Durham, d/o Joseph F. Joy (New Durham, clergyman) and Addie F. Berry (New Durham, housewife)

SAUCIER,
Lucas Jacques m. Ann-Marie **Bourgault** 10/1/1993 in Alton

SCRUTON,
Everett Ray of New Durham m. Yola Littlefield **Turner** of Pocasset, MA 6/8/1932 in Dover; H - 22, minister, b. Newburyport, MA, s/o Chester C. Scruton (Rochester, farmer) and Lena May Howard (Strafford, housewife); W - 21, b. Chicago, IL, d/o Edward B. Turner (Wolfsboro, NC, minister) and L. Maude Littlefield (Berwick, ME, housewife)
Lloyd H. of Strafford m. Norma L. **Coburn** of New Durham 1/29/1937; H - 22, cloth finisher, b. Newburyport, MA, s/o Chester Scruton (Rochester, poultryman) and Lena Howard (Strafford, housewife); W - 19, shoe worker, b. New Durham, d/o Floyd P. Coburn (New Durham, machinist) and Ethel E. Hayes (New Durham, housewife)
Lloyd Howard m. Irene Beth **Merrill** 9/9/1951 in Hampton Falls

SHANNON,
Edward A. of New Durham m. Lovisa Durgin **Hart** of New Durham 1/17/1910 in Alton; H - 29, laborer, b. Alton, s/o Stephen Shannon (Alton, laborer) and Nellie Rollins (Alton, housewife); W - 22, housewife, 2d, b. New Durham, d/o James W. Durgin (New Durham, laborer) and Anna S. Willey (New Durham, housewife)

SHAW,
Robert M. of New Durham m. Sylvia B. **Hayes** of New Durham 4/19/1908 in Alton; H - 18, laborer, b. Haverhill, MA, s/o

Jeremiah F. Shaw (Ireland, stone mason) and Agatha F. Sheridan (Ireland, housewife); W - 19, b. New Durham, d/o Augustus W. Hayes (Alton, knife maker) and Martha E. Kelm (Portland, ME, housewife).

SHEING,
Chris A. m. Deanna L. **Portigue** 9/28/1985

SHOREY,
Samuel A. of New Durham m. Florence M. **Eaton** of New Durham 8/10/1910 in Farmington; H - 29, woodman, 2d, b. Enfield, ME, s/o Benjamin Shorey (Lowell, ME, mason) and Emily Daunn (Enfield, ME, housewife); W - 21, housework, b. Auburndale, MA, d/o Albert R. Eaton (NS, farmer) and Mary Woodward (England, housewife).

SILVA,
Manuel F. m. Patricia A. **Ardizzoni** 8/8/1981

SIMONDS,
Eugene F. of New Durham m. Cynthia J. **Varney** of Alton 3/13/1906 in Farmington; H - 38, merchant, 2d, b. VT, s/o William A. Simonds (VT, farmer) and Mary E. Smith (VT, housewife); W - 25, housekeeper, 2d, b. Alton, d/o Oscar E. Davis (Alton, carpenter) and Elizabeth ----- (Alton, housewife)

SLATTERY,
James Paul m. Joyce Ann **McKeen** 6/23/1973 in Chichester

SMALL,
Albert W. m. Shirleen A. **Chabot** 2/12/1982 in Middleton

SMESTAD,
James Edward m. Diana Lynn **Klardie** 7/31/1976

SMITH,
Alfred Wallace m. Norma Ruth **Knox** 4/23/1960 in West Milton
Brian Kent m. Cynthia Lynn **Dingley** 6/15/1991
David S. m. Maureen E. **Black** 8/17/1969 in Laconia
Edward W. of New Durham m. Altie E. **Hayes** of New Durham
    6/28/1922 in Alton; H - 19, laborer, b. Alton, s/o Edward P.
    Smith (No. Berwick, ME, manufacturer) and Mabel L. Gerrish
    (Milton, housewife); W - 20, clerk, b. New Durham, d/o Seth W.
    Hayes (Alton, knifemaker) and Abbie E. Swett (East Kingston,
    housewife)
Harold E. m. Melinda Ann **Joy** 1/16/1971 in Pittsfield
James Richard m. Denise Josephine **Lafontaine** 9/15/1972 in
    Rochester
Loran Edward m. Nancy Jane **Pearson** 8/6/1960 in North Barnstead
Martin B. of New Durham m. Mary Francis **Gleason** of New Durham
    1/22/1901; H - 52, carpenter, 2d, b. Wallace, NS, s/o Benjamin
    Smith and Mary E. Smith; W - 42, dressmaker, 2d, b. Newport,
    d/o Hial Hurd (Newport, butcher) and Beulah Sargent (Orange,
    housekeeper)
Steven Allen m. Deborah Lee **Bailey** 9/11/1976
Walter H.H. of New Durham m. Hannah F. **Thurston** of New Durham
    5/22/1915 in Farmington; H - 19, mill man, b. New Sharon, ME,
    s/o George S. Smith (W. Farmington, ME, chef) and Mildred E.
    Kelgor (Chesterville, ME, cook); W - 16, housekeeper, b. Wells,
    ME, d/o Josiah W. Thurston (Effingham, millwright) and Sylvia
    A. Newhall (Wells, ME, housewife)

SNELL,
Robert R. m. Darlene A. **Brown** 11/28/1982 in Alton

SNOW,
Francis L. of New Durham m. Ethel L. **Hargreaves** of Newmarket
    8/31/1940 in Berwick, ME; H - 21, shoeworker, b. Northwood,
    s/o Donald Snow (Northwood, shoeworker) and Florence
    Daudelin (Chicago, IL, shoeworker); W - 19, at home, b. New

Bedford, MA, d/o James Hargreaves (Haverhill, MA, millworker) and Maude Morrison (Taftville, CT, housewife)
William E. m. Donna E. **Chagnon** 6/23/1979

SPERANZA,
James S., Jr. m. Rachel T. **Tourigny** 10/22/1988

STALK,
Darren Johnson m. Linda Kay **Walker** 5/22/1993

STANFORD,
John Wayne m. Mary Dianne **Johnson** 4/29/1961

STANLEY,
James C. m. Cornelia **Warchk** 7/24/1982

STERLING,
Arnold A. of Newton, MA m. Daisy B. **Sanderson** of Newton, MA 7/29/1938; H - 32, farmer, b. Sackville, NB, s/o Arnold Sterling (Sackville, NB, farmer) and Lucy Corson (Sackville, NB, housekeeper); W - 23, laundress, b. Newton, MA, d/o Guy B. Sanderson (W. Bedford, MA, gardener) and Della Gannon (Dublin, Ireland, housewife)

STEVENS,
Mark E. m. Margaret A. **Chamberlin** 9/21/1979

STIMPSON,
Alan David m. Frances Mary **Murphy** 12/1/1973 in Alton
M. Dean m. Elaine Ruth **Chagnon** 1/8/1977

STUART,
David Forrest m. Robin Lynn **Hamel** 8/3/1991

STULL,
Andrew Thomas m. Elizabeth Ellen **Blackadar** 6/23/1995

SWETT,
James E. m. Cherine A. **Nelson** 9/1/1980
James Edward m. Claire Marion **Deane** 6/20/1975 in Portsmouth
John Ernest m. Marion Agnes **Bierweiler** 1/24/1973 in Wolfeboro
Thomas Earl m. Donna Lynn **Walker** 8/25/1990

TAPPER,
Frederick H., III m. Kimberly L. **Shields** 1/11/1986 in Alton

TARBOX,
Robert Charles m. Kimberly Marie **Scheyer** 8/13/1989 in North Hampton

TARMEY,
Philip M. m. Barbara J. **Bickford** 11/20/1979 in Wolfeboro

TEBBETTS,
Charles H. of Sanford, ME m. Bertha F. **Dore** of New Durham 11/25/1897 in Alton; H - 33, horseman, b. Sanford, ME, s/o Frank J. Tebbetts (Sanford, ME, farmer) and Eliza J. Rollins (Sanford, ME, housewife); W - 25, housekeeper, b. Farmington, d/o Charles H. Dore (Alton, farmer) and Orrisa E. Dore (deceased)

TETREAULT,
Ryan Joseph m. Lori Ann **Chase** 10/2/1993 in Rochester

THIBEDEAU,
Morace of New Durham m. Addie Blanche **Elliott** of New Durham 10/28/1914 in Alton; H - 47, teamster, 2d, b. Shelbrook, Canada, s/o Joel Thibedeau (Canada, laborer) and Nora Brooks (Canada, housewife); W - 16, housewife, b. West Rumney, d/o Daniel W. Elliott (Rumney, teamster) and Bertha Plummer (W. Fairlee, VT, housewife)

THIEL,
Donald Charles m. Linda Jeanne **Klausmeyer** 6/27/1990 in Wolfeboro

THOMAS,
Eric J. m. Debra Rose **Moore** 7/30/1994 in Alton
Eric John of New Durham m. Patti Morgan **Wyatt** of New Durham 10/27/1996

THOMITS,
William Francis m. Beverly Carol **Vaughn** 7/31/1970 in Portsmouth

THOMPSON,
Charles Carr m. Katharine Esther **Booth** 1/12/1964
Clifton F. m. Barbara J. **Hartford** 9/26/1981
John C. of New Durham m. Julia **Otis** of Farmington 8/2/1903 in Alton Bay; H - 30, carpenter, 3d, b. Concord, s/o George W. Thompson (Dracut, iron moulder) and Annie Colby (Concord, housewife); W - 19, housewife, 2d, b. Farmington, d/o Charles Emerson (Farmington, farmer) and Vina Dolby (Hopkinton, housewife)
Lloyd G. of Farmington m. Doris E. **Leighton** of New Durham 2/7/1939 in Farmington; H - 19, shoeworker, b. Farmington, s/o John Thompson (Concord, carpenter) and Julia Emerson (Farmington, housewife); W - 18, at home, b. Farmington, d/o Fred Leighton (Farmington, stableman) and Grace Tebbetts (Milton, shoeworker)
Peter Robert m. Janice Janine **Hillsgrove** 11/1/1975
Wilfred A., Jr. m. Debbra A. **Chasse** 9/24/1994 in Rochester

THURSTON,
Albert Josiah m. Dorothy Marian **Chickering** 11/15/1952 in Hampton Falls
Bruce Alan m. Karen Star **Perkins** 8/9/1973
W. S., Jr. of New Durham m. Virginia A. **Shaw** of New Durham 9/22/1944; H - 17, laborer, b. New Durham, s/o W. S. Thurston

(Berwick, ME, pipe fitter) and Viola B. Eaton (W. Newton, MA, housewife); W - 16, at home, b. Farmington, d/o William H. Shaw (Farmington, shoemaker) and Mabel Ricker (Farmington, housewife)

Walter S. of New Durham m. Viola B. **Eaton** of New Durham 10/2/1920; H - 31, laborer, b. Berwick, ME, s/o J. W. Thurston (Effingham, farmer) and Sylvia A. Newhall (Wells, ME, housewife); W - 24, housework, b. W. Newton, MA, d/o Albert R. Eaton (NS, farmer) and Mary Woodward (England, housewife)

TLUSTY,
Michael Frank m. Jennifer Ann **Leak** 8/19/1989

TONKIN,
John F. of Dover m. Grace G. **Rosselle** of New Durham 2/8/1949 in Farmington; H - 40, claims office, 2d, b. Bristol, CT, s/o John C. Tonkin (Aura, NJ) and F. I. Saunders (CT); W - 37, shoeworker, 2d, b. Franklin, d/o Sidney R. Locke (CA) and Manil Ida Hill (NH)

TOWLE,
Charles F., Jr. of New Durham m. Henrietta **Woodman** of Alton 3/5/1898 in Wolfeboro; H - 23, brushmaker, b. New Durham, s/o Charles F. Towle (Wolfeboro) and Etta E. Witham (New Durham); W - 19, housework, b. Alton, d/o Henry D. Woodman (Alton) and Susan E. Chamberlin (Alton)

Stanley L. of Farmington m. Ruby M. **Hanchette** of New Durham 12/29/1940; H - 29, physical inst., b. New Durham, s/o Charles Towle (New Durham, brush maker) and H. Woodman (Alton, housewife); W - 24, governess, b. Brockton, MA, d/o William Hanchette (Natick, MA, painter) and Eveline Lingham (Cambridge, MA, housewife)

TOWNE,
Richard N., Jr. m. Elida E. **Brown** 8/6/1994 in Wolfeboro

TRAFTON,
Frederick O. of New Durham m. Bernice M. **Coburn** of New Durham 10/3/1917 in Rochester; H - 21, varnish maker, b. So. Berwick, ME, s/o William L. Trafton (Alfred, ME, shoemaker) and Ellen F. Young (York, ME, housewife); W - 20, b. New Durham, d/o Alonzo G. Coburn (New Durham, knifemaker) and Annie V. Adams (New Durham, housewife)

TREMBLAY,
Gary Paul m. Deborah Ann **Thibodeau** 12/30/1990

TROIANA,
Matthew E. m. Sharon E. **Bisson** 11/27/1986

TUCKER,
Raymond Douglas m. Marilyn Jean **Takesian** 9/6/1969 in Haverhill, MA

TUFTS,
Michael A. m. Brenda J. **Hayward** 11/22/1980 in Farmington

TWITCHELL,
Franklin W., Jr. m. Susan M. **Gilpatrick** 3/14/1992
Franklin W., III m. Terri L. **Parsons** 8/25/1979
Franklin Wesley, Jr. m. Nellie **Joy** 10/23/1958 in Farmington
Kenneth A. m. Heidi E. **Bedell** 8/4/1984
Kenneth Allen m. Bertha Rose **Arsenault** 9/12/1992

VACHON,
Joseph of New Durham m. Flossie **Goodrow** of New Durham 6/23/1923 in Alton; H - 23, laborer, b. Lancaster, s/o Dennis Vachon (Canada, laborer) and Florida Vachon (Canada, housewife); W - 19, housekeeper, b. No. Berwick, ME, d/o James Goodrow (Canada, laborer) and Winnie Goodrow (Somersworth, housewife)

VAILLANCOURT,
Alexander David m. Tessie Marie **Moody** 9/30/1995 in Alton Bay

VANTRUMP,
Larry Joe of New Durham m. Melissa Joy **Samoisette** of New Durham 8/22/1998

VARNEY,
Benjamin E.W. of New Durham m. Vera A. **Ketchen** of Newport 2/11/1928 in Rochester; H - 31, shoemaker, 2d, b. Farmington, s/o Albert D. Varney (Farmington, farmer) and Lulu Brackett (Lowell, MA, housewife); W - 23, school teacher, b. Newport, d/o John C. Ketchen (Berlin, Canada, merchant) and Augusta W. Blaisdell (Newport, housewife)

VENDICE,
Louis F. m. Janet M. **Nixon** 10/2/1993

VOLD,
Carl Leroy m. Ruth Adella **Chamberlin** 11/23/1961

WADEAU,
Theodore of New Durham m. Claffi **Houard** of Rochester 1/11/1892 in Rochester; H - 23, wood chopper, b. Canada, s/o Alex Wadeau (Canada, wood chopper) and Lena Gner (Canada, housewife); W - 24, housekeeper, b. Canada, d/o John Houard (Canada, farmer) and Rose Febairge (Canada, housekeeper)

WALDRON,
Samuel G. of Hyde Park, MA m. Shirley E. **Smith** of New Durham 5/21/1950; H - 33, musician, b. MA, s/o Ralph Waldron (MA) and Grace A. Gardner (MA); W - 16, at home, b. MA, d/o Edward W. Smith (NH) and Altie E. Hayes (NH)

WALKER,
Thomas A. m. Kathleen E. **Andrews** 5/17/1980

William Ernest, III m. Christine Elsa **Shorette** 8/2/1992

WALLACE,
Louis Joachim m. Maisie Ellen **Wallace** 10/14/1989

WALLINGFORD,
Harry Irving m. Ruth Rena **Berry** 7/18/1959

WALTER,
Donald Charles m. Roxann M. **Cummings** 6/24/1990

WALTON,
Craig S. of Meredith m. Catherine J. **DeBoer** of New Durham 1/30/1998

WARREN,
Mark A. m. Susan L. **Tarbox** 11/21/1986 in Rochester

WEBSTER,
William R. of New Durham m. Effie A. **Willey** of New Durham 2/10/1909; H - 28, laborer, b. Lee, s/o George Webster (farmer) and Lizzie Rogers (England); W - 16, housework, b. New Durham, d/o Edward M. Willey (New Durham, knife maker) and Mary Randall (New Durham)

WEIDMAN,
Edward Allen m. Darlene Ann **Vandermolen** 12/10/1988

WENTWORTH,
Ernest Lorin m. Sunny Ann **McKay** 10/22/1994 in Wolfeboro
Lewis A. of New Durham m. H. Irene **Nutter** of Farmington 10/11/1915 in Farmington; H - 23, farmer, b. New Durham, s/o Robert W. Wentworth (No. Barnstead, farmer) and Mabel M. Marston (Nottingham, housewife); W - 16, housework, b. Farmington, d/o J. Freeman Nutter (Gilmanton, shoemaker) and Lilla E. Babb (River Philip, NS, housewife)

WESTCOTT,
Melvin Allen m. Waneta Joyce **Cutter** 7/14/1972 in Farmington

WETHERBEE,
Russell C.C. m. Robin L. **Estabrook** 11/29/1985 in Wolfeboro Falls

WHEELER,
Charles H. of Alton m. Judith E. **Hayes** of New Durham 1/23/1895 in Laconia; H - 28, laborer, b. Ashland, MA, s/o D. E. Wheeler (Acton, MA, hotel keeper) and Angelett H. Clements (Alton, housekeeper); W - 17, housekeeper, b. New Durham, d/o Augustus W. Hayes (Alton, knife maker) and Martha E. Jewett
Charles W. of New Durham m. Freda L. **Frost** of Middleton 12/11/1998
Clair G. m. Norma R. **Smith** 1/20/1979 in Farmington
David M. m. Holly L. **Stuart** 5/14/1983 in Alton
James W. m. Cynthia M. **McNulty** 9/14/1985 in Portsmouth

WHELDEN,
Roy M., Jr. of New Durham m. Evelyn E. **Merritt** of Alton 10/26/1947 in Kittery, ME; H - 26, student, b. Cumberland, ME, s/o Roy M. Whelden (Quincy, MA, research) and Leonora Dyer (Charleston, ME, housewife); W - 29, teacher, b. Canton, PA, d/o Lymie L. Merritt (PA, coal dealer) and Pauline Brown (PA, housewife)

WHIFFEN,
James Michael m. Christina Marie **Milbury** 2/1/1975 in Rochester

WHITE,
David A. m. Juanita M. **Sykie** 2/27/1977
Duane R. m. Jeri Lynn **Southard** 9/26/1987 in Wolfeboro
Richard D. m. Tammy E. **Caskins** 10/2/1982 in Wolfeboro

WHITEHOUSE,
Harold Bruce m. Sharon Cecilia **Cronier** 7/1/1978

Nicholas of New Durham m. Maggie **Cassidy** of Boston, MA
9/25/1893; H - 21, farmer, b. Middleton, s/o Alonzo Whitehouse
and Lydia Smede; W - 21, housekeeper, b. Boston, MA, d/o
James Cassidy and Annie Cassidy

Warren P. m. Karen A. **Cronier** 8/22/1981

WILDNAUER,
David John m. Margaret Ellen **Kundert** 6/17/1995

WILKINS,
Olif M. m. Madelene H. **McKenney** 6/19/1966

WILLEY,
Edward M. of New Durham m. Mary A. **Randall** of New Durham
12/3/1887; H - 24, farmer, s/o Stephen Willey (farmer) and
Almina D. Willey; W - 16, housekeeper, d/o George F. Randall
(laborer) and Cora Randall

Henry D. of New Durham m. Gertie F. **Randall** of New Durham
10/29/1893; H - 25, blacksmith, b. New Durham, s/o John W.
Willey and Mary E. Willey; W - 21, seamstress, b. Canada, d/o
Ezekiel T. Randall and Melissa Randall

Leslie L. of New Durham m. Elizabeth **Willey** of Middleton
12/5/1921 in Farmington; H - 25, farmer, b. New Durham, s/o
Edward M. Willey (New Durham, farmer) and Mary A. Randall
(New Durham, housewife); W - 27, housekeeper, 2d, b. New
Durham, d/o Henry D. Willey (New Durham, blacksmith) and
Gertrude Randall (Canada, housewife)

Leslie L. of New Durham m. Hilda V. **Messinger** of New Durham
5/31/1924 in New Durham; H - 28, farmer, 2d, b. New Durham,
s/o Edward M. Willey (New Durham, farmer) and Mary Randall
(New Durham, housewife); W - 23, housework, b. Beverly, MA,
d/o Charles E. Messinger (NS, carpenter) and Ada Palmer (NS, at
home)

WILSON,
Craig Elliot of Westboro, MA m. Nicole Marie **Colbert** of Westboro, MA 7/6/1996

WINN,
George E. of New Durham m. Yvonne F. **Scofield** of Newmarket 2/20/1937; H - 62, farmer, 2d, b. West Lebanon, ME, s/o Caleb Winn (West Lebanon, ME, farmer) and Sarah Wentworth (West Lebanon, ME, housewife); W - 36, shoe maker, 2d, b. Thetford Mines, PQ, d/o John Cyr (Canada, retired) and Octave Therrien (Canada, housewife)

John W. of Farmington m. Isabel F. **Evans** of New Durham 10/23/1887; H - 25, bookkeeper, b. Lebanon, ME, s/o Caleb W. Winn (farmer) and Sarah Winn; W - 23, dressmaker, b. New Durham, d/o Samuel F. Evans (farmer) and Martha J. Evans

WOOD,
Kevin S. m. Charlene L. **Pelletier** 12/21/1985 in Berlin

WOODBURY,
Clarence E. of New Durham m. Doris I. **Brainard** of Plymouth 8/20/1930 in New Hampton; H - 25, laborer, b. Lanesville, MA, s/o Joseph E. Woodbury (Lanesville, MA, laborer) and Mary H. Lucas (Lanesville, MA, housework); W - 20, nurse, b. Plymouth, d/o Alvin Brainard (Holderness, trainman) and Roxie E. Stillings (Wolfeboro, housework)

WOODMAN,
Fred I. of New Durham m. Cora B. **Dorway** of Alton 6/28/1906; H - 35, laborer, b. Alton, s/o Jonathan Woodman (Alton, farmer) and Hannah P. Rollins (Alton, housewife); W - 44, housekeeper, 2d, b. Alton, d/o Freeman Smith (farmer) and Jerusha -----

WOODS,
Carlton W. m. Kathryn B. **Rousseau** 3/21/1983

WORSTER,
George O. of Farmington m. Doris M. **Burres** of New Durham 10/4/1944 in Rochester; H - 18, US Navy, 2d, b. Farmington, s/o H. H. Worster (Somersworth, mechanic) and Clara A. LeClair (Danville, housewife); W - 19, at home, b. Gilmanton I.W., d/o O. L. Burres (Gilmanton I.W., lumber jack) and Eva M. Rollins (Gilmanton I.W., housewife)

YEATON,
James E. of New Durham m. Lavina **Salter** of Everett, MA 1/26/1922 in Wolfeboro; H - 60, farmer, 2d, b. Portland, ME, s/o John Yeaton (Alfred, ME, farmer) and Susan Black (Gray, ME, housekeeper); W - 58, nurse, 2d, b. Unadilla, NY, d/o Austin Cable (Unadilla, NY, broker) and Caroline Nutter (Unadilla, NY, housekeeper)

YORK,
Clarence R. of New Durham m. Mary Anna **Dionne** of Rochester 5/29/1948 in Rochester; H - 28, woodsman, b. Gilmanton I.W., s/o Raymond York (Belmont, laborer) and Caroline F. Jones (Gilmanton Corner, at home); W - 27, domestic, b. Somersworth, d/o Louise J. Dionne (Canada, mill operator) and Anna Couture (Canada, housewife)

Fred A. of New Durham m. Lizzie B. **Gilson** of Wolfeboro 3/19/1888 in Wolfeboro; H - 27, laborer, b. New Durham, s/o Arthur York and Abigail -----; W - 16, housekeeper, b. Wolfeboro, d/o Alonzo Gilson (farmer)

George A. of New Durham m. Barbara T. **Wyatt** of Farmington 4/22/1936; H - 18, laborer, b. Belmont, s/o Raymond York (Belmont, woodturner) and Caroline Jones (Gilmanton, housekeeper); W - 18, housework, b. Barrington, d/o Ralph F. Wyatt (Farmington, laborer) and Ellen Thompson (Barrington, housekeeper)

YOUNG,
John Henry m. Shirley Mae **Edwards** 9/14/1958 in Alton

Robert Lewis m. Nancy Louise Marie **Hills** 2/21/1959 **in Concord**

ZARKA,
Joseph M., Jr. m. Sandra L. **Austin** 8/24/1985

NEW DURHAM
DEATHS

ABBOTT,
Jeanette A., d. 6/28/1990 in New Durham at 67

ACTON,
Sandra, d. 8/2/1973 in Hanover at 33

ADAMS,
Betsey E., d. 10/3/1902 in New Durham at 82/10; old age; housewife; widow; b. Haverhill
Charles, d. 4/27/1899 in New Durham at 87/2/26; heart disease; house painter; married; b. Newport; James Adams
Charles, d. 11/17/1936 in Dover at 85/0/1; painter; single; b. Lisbon; Charles Adams (Newport, VT) and Eliza Farnsworth (Haverhill)
Edgar Norman, d. 1/7/1997 in New Durham [at 93]; Alvan Adams and Emma Forbus
Sylvia M., d. 2/5/1980 in Hanover at 54
Verna M., d. 11/22/1984 in Rochester at 79

AHLIN,
William A., d. 6/6/1992 in New Durham at 64

AIKEN,
Lewis F., d. 2/19/1968 in New Durham at 86

AKERMAN,
Leslie R., d. 5/29/1905 in New Durham at 0/9/27; cholera infantum; b. East Derry; Roy L. Akerman (Barnstead) and Maud S. Huston (Derry)

ALBERT,
Norman D., d. 6/9/1992 in Dover at 57

ALLAN,
Christabel H., d. 4/29/1971 in Rochester at 59

ALLEN,
Ivory L., d. 2/1/1996 in New Durham; Ivory Allen and Nellie Lowney

AMES,
Lydia L., d. 10/21/1911 in New Durham at 43/6/3; chronic nephritis; housewife; married; b. Canada; Peter Jacques (Canada) and Victoria Grandin (Canada)
Ralph E., d. 3/26/1922 in New Durham at 0/2/21; b. Rochester; Walter Desotelle (Dover) and Marguerite Ames (Rochester)

ANDERSEN,
William E., d. 2/7/1975 in Rochester at 63

ANDERSON,
Andrew, d. 11/26/1926 at 64; burial in New Durham
George W., d. 3/19/1896 in New Durham at 50/1/25; paralysis; lumber dealer; widower; b. Raymond; George P. Anderson (Sandown) and Lucia J. Batchelder (Raymond)
Martha, d. 5/5/1927 at 75; burial in New Durham

ANDREWS,
Elizabeth, d. 11/10/1945 in New Durham at 57; cook; single; b. Cornwall, England; John Andrews (England) and Elizabeth Holman (England)

ASPINWALL,
John G., d. 8/4/1909 in New Durham at 64/9/2; myocarditis; widower; b. Dover; Daniel Aspinwall (Middleton) and Mary Perkins (Middleton)

ATHERTON,
Annie Maude, d. 4/14/1989 in New Durham at 106

ATWOOD,
Clifford K., d. 8/25/1992 in Rochester at 74
William E., d. 8/30/1986 in Rochester at 71

AYER,
Joseph T., d. 3/28/1933 in New Durham at 69/0/5; farmer; married; b. Wakefield; Joseph F. Ayer and Harriett Downs

AYERS,
Harriett S., d. 4/7/1927 in New Durham at 82/3/7; housewife; widow; b. Rochester; John R. Downs (Rochester) and Mary Shorey (East Rochester)

John S., d. 8/27/1911 in New Durham at 48/10/28; ataxia paraplegia; laborer; married; b. Portsmouth; John O. Ayers (Kittery, ME, retired) and Adeline Pettigrew (Kittery, ME)

Joseph F., d. 2/16/1919 in New Durham at 86/6/26; farmer; married; b. Kittery, ME; Joseph F. Ayers (Wakefield) and Ann Shapleigh (Portsmouth)

Mary J., d. 5/2/1905 in New Durham at 75/10/19; paralysis; housewife; widow; b. Barnstead; James Langley and Susan Drew

BABB,
Melvin E., d. 8/31/1930 in Farmington at 74/9/22; wheelwright; divorced; Samson H. Babb and Elmira Evans

BAILEY,
Carl Warren, d. 10/3/1992 in Rochester at 52

BAKER,
Amelia Florence, d. 6/9/1996 in Rochester [at 89]; Sydney Martin and Ninetta Louisa Pilcher

Anita L., d. 1/27/1996 in Rochester [at 41]; Elmer Berry and Ellen Bowden

Annie P., d. 10/30/1918 in New Durham at 36/9/8; housewife; married; b. Dover; Joseph P. Berube (Canada) and Mary F. Charette (Canada)

Karry J., d. 7/30/1977 in Rochester at 0/3-1/2

Oscar, d. 3/3/1997; b. 12/27/1900*

BALDWIN,
Earl H., d. 9/12/1986 in Rochester at 70

BARBER,
Maurice, d. 6/22/1949 in New Durham at 65; market farmer; widower;
    b. Sheffield, VT; Joseph Barber
Viotti M., d. 9/29/1946 in New Durham at 64/1/4; housewife;
    married; b. Walden, VT; Frank W. Ingalls (Walden, VT) and
    Adella Bixby (Warren)

BARNET,
John, Jr., d. 2/4/1991 in Dover at 75
Marion T., d. 6/24/1980 in New Durham at 87

BARNEY,
Joseph, d. 2/20/1994; b. 9/18/1913*

BARTLETT,
Clarence Milo, d. 3/18/1989 in Wolfeboro at 79
Gladys, d. 12/--/1972; b. 11/10/1893*
Pamela Ryan, d. 11/24/1992 in Manchester at 42

BATES,
Virginia, d. 8/10/1984 in Marblehead, MA at 67

BAXTER,
Hibbert, d. 7/28/1942 in New Durham at 60/3/9; trainman; married; b.
    Windsor, NS: Daniel Baxter (Windsor, NS) and M. E. Fergerson
    (St. John, NS)

BEAULIEU,
Joseph A., d. 11/19/1984 in Rochester at 76

BEMIS,
Florence R., d. 9/26/1919 in New Durham at 38/2; housewife;
married; b. Rochester; Charles E. Blackmar (Somersworth) and
Hannah S. Nute (Wolfeboro)

BENNER,
Wilson Clyde, d. 3/10/1975 in Manchester at 56

BENNETT,
Betsy N., d. 12/11/1910 in New Durham at 88/5/11; cerebral
hemorrhage; housewife; widow; b. Alton; Eleazer Davis (farmer)
and Polly Sanborn
Charles F., d. 6/30/1944 in New Durham at 87/10/28; retired dentist;
married; b. Dover; James Bennett (New Durham) and Betsy
Davis (Alton)
Donald, d. 12/3/1939 in New Durham at 29/6/12; carpenter; married;
b. Tuftonboro; Maurice Bennett (Tuftonboro) and Annie Kidd
(Scotland)
Edith A., d. 5/5/1964 in New Durham at 96
Edith E., d. 11/11/1932 in New Durham at 77/1/5; housewife;
married; b. Farmington; Richard Colbath (Tuftonboro) and Susan
Peavey (Tuftonboro)
George W., d. 1/20/1941 in New Durham at 81; farmer; widower; b.
Farmington; Stephen Bennett (Farmington) and Emily Leighton
(Farmington)

BERRY,
daughter, d. 6/10/1903 in New Durham at 0/0/1; exhaustion; Alberton
Berry (New Durham) and Mary Jenkins (New Durham)
stillborn son, d. 12/2/1906 in New Durham; John L. Berry (New
Durham, knife maker) and Fannie Clough (Alton)
Alberton, d. 1/30/1942 in New Durham at 75/7/15; farmer; widower;
b. New Durham; Joseph Berry (New Durham) and Betsey
Scruton (New Durham)
Almira F., d. 7/8/1915 in New Durham at 84/9/19; valv. heart disease;
housewife; widow; b. Alton; Joseph Gooch and Nancy Davis

Annie C., d. 10/10/1933 in New Durham at 76/6/17; housewife; married; b. New Durham; Charles Adams (Rumney) and Betsy Farnsworth (Oxford)

Betsey D., d. 12/27/1904 in New Durham at 74; senectus; housewife; married; b. Farmington; Miles Scruton (Farmington) and Sally Canney (Strafford)

Charles H., d. 1/5/1918 in New Durham at 85/3/6; farmer; single; b. New Durham; Benjamin Berry (New Durham) and Patience Pearl (Farmington)

Christina J., d. 9/29/1986 in New Durham at 86

Eben E., d. 10/25/1906 in New Durham at 75/0/5; heart disease; farmer; married; b. New Durham; Eben B. Berry (New Durham, farmer) and Mercy Hurd (Dover)

Georgia O., d. 10/7/1917 in New Durham at 62/8/20; school teacher; single; b. New Durham; Ezekiel H. Berry and Serence A. Hilton

Hannah J., d. 2/24/1902 in New Durham at 48/1; cancer; housewife; widow; b. New Durham; Allard Edgerly (Dover) and Anne Bunker (Middleton)

Ichabod P., d. 8/31/1900 in New Durham at 71/4/16; stone in the bladder with irritated ur'th's; farmer; married; b. New Durham; Benjamin Berry (New Durham) and Patience Pearl (Farmington)

Irving N., d. 4/28/1955 at 83

Isah P., d. 8/22/1960 in New Durham at 69

Janet C., d. 12/24/1995 in New Durham at 74

John, d. 7/18/1894 in New Durham at 69/7/4; killed by train; married

John M., Sr., d. 3/31/1982 in Rochester at 64

Joseph E., d. 4/25/1941 in Free Union, VA at 71/7/11; lumbering; widower; b. New Durham; Joseph Y. Berry (New Durham) and Betsey Scruton (Strafford)

Joseph N., d. 12/29/1981 in Rochester at 89

Joseph Y., d. 12/29/1906 in New Durham at 78/7/26; valvular dis. of heart; farmer; widower; b. Farmington; Nathaniel Berry (clergyman) and Mary C. Young

Mabel F., d. 8/16/1960 in Rochester at 65

Magene E., d. 7/27/1946 in Rochester at 79/6/12; retired; widow; b. Bridgton, ME; John Hale and Eleanor Ames

May A., d. 7/3/1932 in New Durham at 40/9/3; at home; single; b. New Durham; Willis E. Berry (New Durham) and Watie Joy (New Durham)

Myron E., d. 4/7/1942 in Farmington at 48/11/19; farmer; married; b. New Durham; Zanello D. Berry (New Durham) and Magene E. Hale (Bridgton, ME)

Myrtle Irene, d. 3/16/1951 at 58

Nina O., d. 6/26/1975 in Wolfeboro at 70

Ray H., d. 10/31/1918 in New Durham at 21/7/21; soldier; single; b. Wolfeboro; Alberton N. Berry (New Durham) and Mary A. Jenkins (New Durham)

Rosemary, d. 6/15/1902 in New Durham at --; premature birth; b. New Durham; Theodore Berry (Canada) and Rose Valley (Canada)

Roy W., d. 7/10/1968 in New Durham at 68

Serena O., d. 5/18/1903 in New Durham at 81/1/6; old age; housewife; widow; b. Deerfield; Nathan T. Hilton and Olevia F. Hill

Stephen W., d. 11/13/1897 in New Durham at 64/10/8; paralysis; farmer; married; b. Bangor, ME; Beniah Berry (Scarboro, ME) and Olive Whitney (Saco, ME)

Theodore Benjamin, d. 6/5/1976 in Dover at 74

Watie M., d. 10/23/1935 in New Durham at 72/11/8; housekeeper; widow; b. New Durham; Samuel W. Joy (New Durham) and Mary A. Evans (New Durham)

Willis E., d. 8/25/1926 in New Durham at 68/0/22; farmer; married; b. New Durham; Joseph Y. Berry (New Durham) and Betsey Scruton (Strafford)

Zanello D., d. 11/24/1931 in Rochester at 74/6/16; married; b. New Durham; Ichabod Berry and Almira T. Gooch (Alton)

BICKFORD,

Charles, d. 11/2/1894 in New Durham at 62/9; gastritis; farmer; widower; b. Epsom; Samuel Bickford (Epsom) and Lucy Seward (Watertown, MA)

Charles D., d. 4/8/1911 in New Durham at 47/4/29; pneumonia; farmer; married; Charles Bickford (Epsom, farmer) and Mary Downing (New Durham)

Eliza K., d. 2/12/1919 in New Durham at 88/2/16; housewife; widow; b. Cape Breton; Alexander King (NS) and Jane Marsh (NS)

Emma, d. 4/30/1929 in New Durham at 86; housework; widow; b. Lowell, MA; David Gile

George, d. 4/24/1902 in New Durham at 77/5; pneumonia; farmer; married; b. Epsom; Samuel W. Bickford (Epsom) and Lucy L. Leonard (Watertown, MA)

Harry, d. 3/4/1949 in Rochester at 58/9/27; mail carrier; married; b. New Durham; Charles D. Bickford and Mary Downs

Lillie M., d. 4/27/1937 in New Durham at 69/4/23; school teacher; single; b. New Durham; Charles Bickford (Epsom) and Mary Downing (New Durham)

Mary L., d. 9/11/1934 in New Durham at 70/11/2; housekeeper; widow; b. Wakefield; John R. Downs and Mary Shorey

Richard W., d. 12/10/1983 in Alton at 29

Selder Estelle, d. 2/12/1993 in New Durham at 69

BLACKMER,

Hannah, d. 7/26/1926 in New Durham at 69/3/4; housewife; widow; b. Wolfeboro; Alonzo D. Nute (Madbury) and Mary Reynolds (Wolfeboro)

BOODEY,

Ethel M., d. 1/18/1913 in New Durham at 44/2/21; cardiac dilation; housekeeper; divorced; b. Alton; Horace P. Boodey (Alton) and Abbie M. Huckins (Alton)

Horace P., d. 4/1/1930 in New Durham at 85/11/18; farmer; married; b. New Durham; Harrison Boodey (New Durham) and Tamson Ham (New Durham)

Joanna D., d. 11/24/1905 in New Durham at 91/7/13; cerebral hemorrhage; housewife; widow; b. Portland, ME; Samuel Runnals (New Durham) and Arvilla Randall (New Durham)

Natt H., d. 5/27/1912 in New Durham at 51/7/2; tuberculosis; stonecutter; divorced; b. New Durham; S. H. Boodey (New Durham, farmer) and Tamson L. Ham (New Durham)

BOODY,
Mary C., d. 2/24/1936 in New Durham at 84/6; at home; widow; b. Farmington; ----- Kilroy and Anna B. Leighton

BOOTH,
Frederick A., d. 3/1/1989 in Rochester at 72

BOUCHIE,
Walter Francis, d. 12/28/1997 in Dover; Jeffrey H. Bouchie and Laura May Boucher

BOUDEAU,
Alfred, d. 5/19/1925 in New Durham; suicide; woodchopper; single

BOWDEN,
Bailey P., d. 1/30/1986 in Wolfeboro at 66
Clydia R., d. 6/9/1965 in Rochester at 83
Max E., d. 11/18/1979 in New Durham at 64

BOYD,
Wesley J., d. 1/31/1981 in New Durham at 59

BRACKETT,
Azariah, d. 10/30/1914 in New Durham at 71/10/20; farmer; single; b. Middleton; Levi Brackett (Ossipee) and Susan Edwards (Parsonsfield, ME)
Erwin, d. 9/25/1946 in Rochester at 68/0/25; farmer; married; b. New Durham; Hiram Brackett (New Durham) and Augusta French (New Durham)
Grace E., d. 12/19/1974 in Dover at 78

Hiram, d. 9/29/1923 in New Durham at 83/10/29; farmer; married; b. Ossipee; Levi Brackett (Ossipee) and Susan Edwards (Parsonsfield, ME)

Joseph, d. 4/23/1920 in New Durham at 82/10/3; farmer; widower; b. Ossipee; Levi Brackett (Ossipee) and Susan Edwards (Parsonsfield, ME)

Mary E., d. 11/26/1918 in New Durham at 80/11/6; housewife; married; Joshua Wilkerson and Sally Adams

Nellie P., d. 4/30/1924 in New Durham at 58/3/26; shoemaker; single; b. Farmington; Hiram Brackett (Ossipee) and Augusta French (Farmington)

Roena E., d. 12/13/1888 in New Durham at 40/2/25; consumption; housewife; married; Gideon M. Randall (Eaton) and Lizzie D. Fox

Susan, d. 4/3/1904 in New Durham at 96/10/19; old age; housewife; widow; b. Limerick, ME; Abram Edwards and Mary Brimhall

Tom, d. 11/16/1914 in New Durham at 71/11/6; farmer; single; b. Middleton; Levi Brackett (Ossipee) and Susan Edwards (Parsonsfield, ME)

BRANDT,
Gertrude H., d. 11/1/1993 in Rochester at 79

BRECHU,
Walter A., d. 9/14/1958 at 67

BRISCOE,
Gladys E., d. 8/8/1969 in Rochester at 69

BROOKE,
Jack, d. 12/--/1983; b. 7/11/1918*

BROOKS,
Charles, d. 10/31/1905 in New Durham at 75/5/21; nephritis; farmer; married; b. New Durham; John Brooks (Buxton, ME) and Eliza Pearl (Farmington)

Mary R., d. 11/17/1906 in New Durham at 79/3/12; angina pectoris; housewife; widow; John C. Elkins (New Durham, stone mason) and Ascha Varney (Farmington)

Nancy Josephine, d. 9/20/1998 in New Durham at 67**

BROWN,
Albert Clarence, d. 1/7/1958 at 83

John L., d. 9/18/1889 in New Durham at 79/5; old age; farmer; married; b. Tuftonboro; John Brown (Tuftonboro)

Maud, d. 10/23/1901 in New Durham at 27; suicide by poisoning by $HgCl_2$; housewife; single; b. Coaticook, PQ

Nellie E., d. 11/30/1946 in Wolfeboro at 75/5/10; housewife; married; b. New Durham; T. E. Mitchell (New Durham) and Lydia Perkins (Middleton)

Nellie M., d. 10/10/1905 in New Durham at 1/2/23; exhaustion; single; Albert C. Brown (Waltham, MA) and Nellie Mitchell (New Durham)

BRUNO,
Anthony, d. 11/--/1983; b. 6/6/1909*

BULLIS,
Bertha M., d. 8/3/1975 in Wolfeboro at 57

BURBANK,
Ida L., d. 10/26/1930 in New Durham at 60/11/8; widow; b. Rochester; George W. Varney (Rochester)

BURLEIGH,
John, d. 8/13/1895 in New Durham at 80/7/18; gangrene; farmer; single; b. New Durham; John Burley (Litchfield) and Betsey Page (Litchfield)

BURNHAM,
Alice L., d. 9/27/1916 in New Durham at 53/6/10; housekeeper; widow; b. Ellsworth, ME; William Kelley

Sarah H., d. 1/18/1899 in New Durham at 73/9/16; bronchial
    pneumonia; housewife; widow; b. New Durham

BURRILL,
Elizabeth Nella, d. 8/15/1977 in New Durham at 69

BUTTERFIELD,
Laurie Ann, d. 5/1/1961 in New Durham at 0/3

CAMPBELL,
William, d. 3/--/1972; b. 5/28/1888*

CANN,
Oscar E., d. 12/7/1950 in Plaistow at 71/0/5; retired; widower; b. MA

CANNEY,
Caroline, d. 12/22/1945 in New Durham at 98/6/13; widow; b.
    Rochester; Downing Ham (Rochester) and Mary Clough
    (Barnstead)
Edgar E., d. 3/31/1941 in New Durham at 72/6/28; divorced; b.
    Farmington; Andrew Canney (Farmington) and Caroline Ham
    (Rochester)
Margaret J., d. 9/30/1889 in New Durham at 81/3/7; paralysis;
    housekeeper; married; b. Rochester; William Henderson (Dover)
    and Margaret Roberts (Rochester)

CARDINAL,
Carroll D., d. 12/10/1993 in Rochester at 60
Norma M., d. 1/26/1996 in Wolfeboro [at 73]; Arthur Smith and Clara
    Bover
P. Jayne, d. 12/12/1993 in Rochester at 60
Samuel N., d. 12/30/1975 in Rochester at 53

CARLIN,
Rufus, d. 1/8/1935 in New Durham at 68/0/25; laborer; single; b. Boston, MA; Dennis Carlin (Boston, MA) and Caroline Hurd (VT)

CARPENTER,
child, d. 2/5/1971 in Rochester at 0/0/0
Doris, d. 11/--/1987; b. 8/24/1921*

CHAGNON,
Richard L., d. 8/15/1967 in Somerville, MA at 41

CHAMBERL[A]IN,
child, d. 7/5/1955 at 0/0/0
child, d. 7/5/1955 at 0/0/0
child, d. 7/5/1955 at 0/0/0
A. J., d. 10/24/1907 in New Durham at 68/0/24; arteriosclerosis; housewife; married; b. Farmington; William Ricker (Farmington) and Mary Ames
Annie, d. 12/5/1914 in New Durham at 45; housewife; married; b. New Durham; Joseph F. Joy (New Durham) and Addie F. Berry (New Durham)
Augustus J., d. 9/17/1913 in New Durham at 62/4/14; uremia; farmer; married; b. New Durham; Joseph B. Chamberlain (New Durham) and Sally P. Holmes (Farmington)
Ellen Martha, d. 11/15/1951 at 58
George E., d. 3/10/1888 in New Durham at 3/0/26; tuberculosis; single; Henry E. Chamberlin (Alton) and Sadie M. Tucker (Concord)
H. G., d. 6/25/1914 in New Durham at 76/10/3; farmer; widower; b. Alton; Samuel Chamberlin (Alton) and Abigail Hayes (Farmington)
H. M., d. 3/27/1895 in New Durham at 86/9/10; old age; housewife; widow; b. Dover; Samuel W. Hayes (Dover) and Abigail Chesley (Durham)

I. S., d. 6/25/1914 in New Durham at 46/4/17; farmer; married; b. New Durham; David S. Edgerly (Alton) and Elmira Chamberlin (Alton)

J. S., d. 10/23/1907 in New Durham at 69/10/7; prostatic hypertrophy; farmer; widower; b. New Durham; D. Chamberlin (New Durham) and Hannah Berry (New Durham)

Jennie M., d. 10/3/1913 in New Durham at 15/4/5; appendicitis; student; single; b. New Durham; John B. Chamberlain (New Durham) and Annie M. Joy (New Durham)

John B., d. 9/28/1951 at 82

Jonas, d. 7/21/1924 in New Durham at 90/0/15; farmer; widower; b. New Durham; Daniel Chamberlin (New Durham) and Hannah Berry (New Durham)

Lovey, d. 7/2/1924 in New Durham at 88/1/10; teacher; single; b. New Durham; Joseph Chamberlain (New Durham) and Sally P. Holmes (Farmington)

Mary S., d. 2/23/1901 in New Durham at 70/1/20; catarrh'l pneumonia; housewife; married; b. New Durham; John Burley (Newmarket) and Betsy Page (Litchfield)

Sally P., d. 8/11/1887 in New Durham at 79/2/8; housekeeper; widow; b. Farmington; Isaac Holmes (Rochester) and Betsy Garland (Barnstead)

Samuel F., d. 10/18/1894 in New Durham at 86/7/15; peritonitis; farmer; widower; b. Alton; ----- Chamberlin (Alton) and Sarah Furber (Farmington)

Susan, d. 12/31/1903 in New Durham at 62/1/1; heart failure; housewife; married; b. Newmarket; John Speed (Newmarket) and Mary A. Burley

CHAMPAGNE,
Deborah, d. 3/11/1997; b. 9/4/1952*

CHAPINGE,
-------, d. 8/--/1894 in New Durham

CHASE,
son, d. 6/18/1922 in New Durham at 0/0/0; Fred H. Chase (Dover) and Ella B. Davis (Wells, ME)
Ella Blanche, d. 2/23/1957 at 73
Fred H., d. 6/27/1952 in Rochester at 76
Noris D., d. 9/29/1910 in New Durham at 0/4/8; gastroenteritis; single; Fred H. Chase (Dover, teamster) and Ella B. Davis (Wells, ME)
Vera A., d. 4/19/1920 in New Durham at 0/2/24; single; Fred H. Chase (Dover) and Ella B. Davis (Wells, ME)

CHESLEY,
Moses H., d. 5/4/1897 in New Durham at 79/4/28; grip and cyotitis; widower; b. New Durham; Miles Chesley (Durham) and Mary Furber (Farmington)

CHICK,
Grace E., d. 4/20/1949 in New Durham at 4/2/29; single; Ralph E. Drown and Verna Abbott
Lizzie R., d. 5/5/1887 in New Durham at 59/6/8; housekeeper; married

CHIGAS,
Vasiliki Bessie, d. 12/16/1996 in Rochester [at 81]; John Chigas and Georgia Harris

CHRISTOFORE,
William L., d. 7/15/1992 in Rochester at 80

CILLEY,
Harold G., d. 8/9/1972 in Rochester at 70

CLARK,
Charlotte A., d. 1/10/1976 in Rochester at 80

David, d. 11/27/1898 in New Durham at 66/6; kidney trouble; shoemaker; married; b. Gloucester, MA; John Clark (Gloucester, MA)

Ralph W., d. 2/18/1981 in Manchester at 92

CLARKE,
Barbara Jean, d. 3/5/1997 in Rochester [at 73]; Gordon T. Whitaker and Mae J. Magnuson

Richard L., d. 1/10/1993 in Rochester at 69

CLARMONT,
Samuel, d. 1/8/1889 in New Durham at 0/7; unknown; single; b. Franklin; Lewis Clarmont (Canada) and Victoria Truckee (VT)

CLAY,
Frank, d. 10/10/1892 in New Durham at 39/4/24; valv. disease of heart; laborer; married; b. New Durham; Charles Clay (Dover) and Abigail Willey (New Durham)

CLEAVES,
Benjamin B., d. 4/11/1966 in New Durham at 83

CLINTON,
Earl C., d. 5/16/1959 in New Durham at 20/0/25

CLOUGH,
Daniel V., d. 1/11/1899 in New Durham at 54; heart failure; shoemaker; married; b. Alton; Daniel Clough (Alton) and Sally Clough (Alton)

Eldora, d. 11/1/1918 in New Durham at 59/3/24; housewife; widow; b. Alton; Samuel L. Randall (New Durham) and Syntha Ellis (Alton)

COBURN,
Alonzo G., d. 2/16/1900 in New Durham at 41/11/3; consumption; knifemaker; married; b. New Durham; Franklin W. Coburn (Pelham) and Susan Willey (New Durham)

Ellen S., d. 11/11/1899 in New Durham at 54/11/2; acute nephritis; housewife; married; b. Bradford, MA; Manly Hardy and Rebecca Boynton

Franklin, d. 9/14/1911 in New Durham at 77/7/28; uremia; knife mfg.; married; b. Pelham; Jesse Coburn (Pelham, farmer) and Abigail Hardy (Pelham)

COLBATH,
son, d. 9/18/1887 in New Durham at 0/0/0; b. New Durham; Samuel E. Colbath (Alton) and Clara J. Hayes (New Durham)

Ellen A., d. 10/4/1910 in New Durham at 63/9/1; uremia; widow; Zachariah Boody (New Durham) and Joanna Runnells (Portland, ME)

Floyd N., d. 8/28/1980 in New Durham at 49

Francis, d. 1/7/1908 in New Durham at 64/6/4; pneumonia; farmer; married; b. Farmington; John K. Colbath (Farmington) and Hannah Leighton (Farmington)

Lauren A., d. 7/3/1917 in New Durham at 80/7/27; widower; b. Middleton; Leighton Colbath and Sarah Bickford

Robert G., d. 8/12/1987 in New Durham at 60

Vonia, d. 2/19/1937 in New Durham at 84/6/21; housekeeper; widow; b. New Durham; Hiram S. Lee and Maria W. Sumner

Willey L., d. 12/28/1922 in New Durham at 60/3/11; farmer; married; b. Middleton; Lauren Colbath (Middleton) and Elmira E. Willey (New Durham)

COLOMY,
Charles, d. 11/24/1899 in New Durham at 77/9/21; apoplexy; farmer; married; b. New Durham; Daniel Colomy and Rebecca Pinkham

Sarah, d. 10/4/1898 in New Durham at 81; old age; domestic; widow

CONNOR,
Joan P., d. 2/20/1973 in Rochester at 19

CONWAY,
John J., d. 5/23/1996 in New Durham [at 82]; John Conway and Katherine McCarthy

COOMBS,
Henry E., d. 4/6/1927 in New Durham at 65/4/23; watchman; married; b. Lynn, MA; William Coombs (Lynn, MA) and Sarah A. Brown (Lynn, MA)

COOPER,
James H., d. 10/1/1949 in New Durham at 64; herdsman; married; b. Providence, RI; Arthur Cooper and Elizabeth

CORDEAU,
Arthur E., d. 6/20/1971 in New Durham at 74

COREY,
Beatrice Evelyn, d. 11/14/1953 at 60

CORNO,
Clar, d. 2/8/1988; b. 10/13/1911*

CORRIGAN,
Edward Robert, d. 8/20/1985 in Wolfeboro at 64
Rita M., d. 11/1/1988 in Wolfeboro at 66

CORSON,
Etta, d. 6/11/1976 in Dover at 80
George A., d. 11/14/1910 in New Durham at 66/0/7; aortic regurgitation; laborer; married; William H. Corson (New Durham, farmer) and Druzilla Jones (Middleton)
Olive Gray, d. 1/20/1998 in Dover; b. 9/26/1906*

Robert, d. 7/14/1913 in New Durham at 70/9/11; gangrene of foot; farmer; single; b. New Durham; William Corson (New Durham) and ----- (Middleton)

Willis R., d. 1/5/1964 in Rochester at 82

CRAFTS,
Walter M., d. 9/22/1897 in New Durham at 3/3/1; cholera infantum; b. Alton; William G. Crafts (Taunton, MA) and Florence A. Moody (St. Albans, ME)

CRESS,
Everett R., d. 7/8/1974 in Wolfeboro at 60

CRUCIUS,
Mary, d. 7/23/1954 at 5/2/25

CULLIMORE,
William Blake, d. 12/2/1995 in New Durham at 57

CUMMINGS,
Harry, d. 1/10/1998; b. 7/28/1937*

CURTICE,
Elizabeth R., d. 12/31/1930 in New Durham at 87/5/18; widow; b. Isle of Wight, England; William Rogers (London, England) and Catherine Barrett (Bath, England)

CURTIN,
Fred T., d. 7/11/1987 in Rochester at 63

CURTIS,
Austin, d. 10/--/1987; b. 5/10/1897*
Winifred, d. 11/4/1987; b. 12/21/1899*

CUTTER,
Carroll Elwin, d. 12/23/1997 in New Durham [at 48]; Frank M. Cutter, Sr. and Marion Nelson

DADURA,
Edward, d. 3/27/1992; b. 7/6/1911*
Michaelena, d. 12/8/1988 in New Durham at 72

DAME,
Alonzo, d. 3/5/1918 in New Durham at 65/5/19; farmer; widower; b. Barrington
Etta F., d. 2/1/1912 in New Durham at 59/3/18; paraplegia; housewife; married; b. Farmington; Jeremiah French and Mary Hodgdon

DANIELS,
Mary E., d. 7/16/1981 in New Durham at 63

DAVIS,
Annie Darrow, d. 10/26/1991 in New Durham at 93
Betsey, d. 4/26/1898 in New Durham at 75/3/7; old age; housewife; married; b. Alton; Isaac Berry (Strafford) and Hannah Berry (Strafford)
Grace T., d. 7/13/1982 in New Durham at 76
Helen Birchall, d. 4/20/1961 in Rochester at 72
Helen E., d. 7/7/1928 in New Durham at 68/11/30; widow; b. Hopkinton; George Tucker (Hopkinton) and Lucinda Giles (Hopkinton)
Irving E., d. 9/10/1983 in Rochester at 85
John, d. 4/5/1906 in New Durham at 79/1/24; acute bronchitis; farmer; married; b. New Durham; John Davis (farmer) and Lydia Canney
John B., d. 10/27/1904 in New Durham at 73/5/3; cerebral apoplexy; farmer; widower; b. New Durham; Stephen T. Davis (New Durham) and Nancy Bickford (New Durham)

Joseph C., d. 11/1/1899 in New Durham at 86/6/6; old age; farmer; widower; b. New Durham; John Davis (Kittery, ME) and Lydia Canney (Farmington)

Marie L., d. 4/10/1941 in New Durham at 5/2/21; single; b. Warwick, RI; Maurice Davis (Alton) and Marie Light (Oldtown, ME)

Maurice E., d. 6/6/1961 in Wolfeboro at 71

Melissa A., d. 9/24/1922 in New Durham at 74/11/26; widow; b. Wells, ME; Jeremiah Williams (Wells, ME) and Mary Brown (Wells, ME)

Proctor L., d. 12/22/1998 in Rochester

Rae Pommer, d. 1/30/1997 in Manchester [at 80]; Bruno Pommer and Olga Christine Steffensen

Rosetta M., d. 3/26/1904 in New Durham at 66/10/15; pneumonia; housewife; married; James Goodwin (Wells, ME) and Mary Furbush (Wells, ME)

DAVOLL,
Harold, d. 12/12/1966 in New Durham at 65

DESPRE,
Francis X., d. 7/11/1965 in New Durham at 74

DILLMAN,
Theresa M., d. 2/27/1994 in New Durham at 76

DIMOND,
Hazel, d. 7/16/1940 in Wolfeboro at 41/0/16; housewife; married; b. Wolcott, VT; William Carpenter and A. Richardson

DION,
Kenneth R., d. 12/3/1978 in Rochester at 64

DIPALMA,
Albert Anthony, d. 1/29/1998 in Manchester; b. 11/28/1919*

DODGE,
Martha, d. 2/24/1901 in New Durham at 79; old age
William R., d. 8/18/1961 in New Durham at 61

DOLBY,
Hannah D., d. 11/5/1903 in New Durham at 95/6/8; old age; housewife; married; b. Rochester; Henry Drown (Rochester) and Isabella Morrison

Isaac, d. 1/22/1904 in New Durham at 92/8/17; old age; farmer; widower; b. Warner; Israel Dolby (Candia) and Ruth Eastman (Henniker)

DOLLIVER,
Rosa L., d. 9/2/1949 in Concord at 78; housewife; widow; b. Lunenburg, VT; Arthur Wright and Ellen M. Harris

DORE,
Etta A., d. 2/8/1908 in New Durham at 46/9/24; pneumonia; housewife; married; b. New Durham; John B. Davis (New Durham) and Rosetta Goodwin (Wells, ME)

Eugene, d. 1/27/1939 in Farmington at 86/8/21; farmer; widower; b. Alton; Joseph Dore and Angeline Hill

Ira L., d. 9/26/1917 in New Durham at 59/3; engineer; widower; b. Alton; Thomas Dore (Alton) and Nancy Wadleigh (Alton)

Justin, d. 8/23/1913 in New Durham at 62/1/29; hemorrhage of bowels; farmer; married; b. Alton; Thomas L. Dore (Alton) and Nancy Wadleigh (Gilford)

Lizzie E., d. 2/16/1908 in New Durham at 48/4/25; pneumonia; housewife; divorced; b. New Durham; John B. Davis (New Durham) and Rosetta Goodwin (Wells, ME)

DORR,
John F., d. 12/27/1911 in New Durham at 84/5; heart disease; farmer; married; b. Milton; George Dorr (Milton)

Mary A., d. 4/22/1887 in New Durham at 63/3/10; housekeeper; married

DOW,
Lorenzo, d. 1/20/1899 in New Durham at 63/2; paralysis; laborer; b. New Durham

DOWNING,
Caroline, d. 5/14/1921 in New Durham at 80/5/5; housekeeper; widow; b. Wakefield
David P., d. 11/15/1913 in New Durham at 82/2/29; apoplexy cerebral; farmer; married; b. Holderness; Royal Downing (Limerick, ME) and Fannie Prescott (Campton)
Ernest, d. 2/--/1978; b. 4/19/1896*
Nancy, d. 12/9/1899 in New Durham at 93/7/9; old age; housewife; widow; b. New Durham; Samuel Willey (New Durham) and Betsey Bennett (Alton)

DOYLE,
Maria Frances, d. 6/6/1998 in New Durham

DRAPEAU,
Mildred D., d. 7/3/1971 in New Durham at 61

DREW,
Annie, d. 11/2/1931 in New Durham at 92/5/13; widow; b. PEI
Charles A., d. 4/18/1931 in New Durham at 44/4/5; laborer; married; b. Wakefield; James Drew and Clara Glidden
Gertrude, d. 3/1/1986 in Wolfeboro at 86
John Woodbury, d. 11/6/1961 in New Durham at 90
Josie, d. 3/8/1921 in New Durham at 58/8/2; housekeeper; divorced; b. Gilmanton; ----- Drew and Electa Rollins (Alton)
Wilbur J., d. 9/3/1987 in Rochester at 64
William P., d. 6/18/1985 in Wolfeboro at 86

DREYER,
Ruth, d. 10/--/1980; b. 5/27/1893*

DUMAS,
son, d. 1/16/1893 in New Durham at --; b. New Durham; Joseph Dumas (Canada) and M. Guilmette (Canada)

DURGIN,
Hannah, d. 3/16/1891 in New Durham at 77/1/17; erysipelas; housekeeper; widow; Aaron Varney (Alton)

James, d. 6/13/1889 in New Durham at 72/10; heart disease; farmer; married; b. Alton; John Durgin (Alton) and Sarah Durgin (Alton)

James W., d. 11/9/1911 in New Durham at 71/10/19; heart disease; farmer; married; b. New Durham; Chase Durgin (farmer) and Ann Davis

DURKEE,
Ralph Irving, d. 2/29/1996 in New Durham [at 69]; Ralph Durkee and Doris Carr

DYER,
Francis Everett, Sr., d. 1/19/1979 in White River Junction, VT at 84
Jeanne M., d. 8/12/1975 in New Durham at 76

EATON,
A. R., d. 12/5/1914 in New Durham at 62/6/17; farmer; married; b. NS; Elisha Eaton (NS) and Mary Beckwith (NS)

Mary A., d. 3/21/1936 in New Durham at 73/0/25; at home; widow; b. Paignton, England; James Woodward (Paignton, England) and Maria Fuge (Paignton, England)

EDDY,
John, d. 4/--/1969; b. 1/7/1880*

EDGERLY,
daughter, d. 8/8/1906 in New Durham at 0/0/1; premature birth; Charles Edgerly (Dover, laborer) and Minnie Colomy (New Durham)

Atilla J., d. 3/23/1888 in New Durham at 51/6/15; consumption; married

Charles W., d. 2/16/1920 in New Durham at 70/11/6; farmer; widower; b. Dover

Charles W., d. 6/14/1971 in Laconia at 67

David L., d. 9/2/1891 in New Durham at 73/4/15; cerebral apoplexy; preacher; widower; b. Alton; Jeremiah Edgerly (Old Durham) and Betsey Leighton

Earl, d. 6/29/1908 in New Durham at 0/4/6; cholera infantum; b. New Durham; Grover Tuttle (New Durham) and Annie M. Edgerly (New Durham)

Earle M., d. 10/6/1970 in New Durham at 83

Fred E., d. 5/7/1912 in New Durham at 18/9/27; unknown; at home; single; b. New Durham; Charles W. Edgerly (Dover, farmer) and Minnie Colomy (New Durham)

George H., d. 4/17/1892 in New Durham at 47; pneumonia; laborer; married; b. New Durham; Shadrach A. Edgerly (New Durham) and Julia A. Bunker (New Durham)

Helen, d. 9/21/1898 in New Durham at 0/2; cholera infantum; b. New Durham; Charles Edgerly (Dover) and Minnie B. Colomy (New Durham)

Hiram W., d. 9/18/1900 in New Durham at 86/0/10; old age; blacksmith; widower; b. New Durham

Julia A., d. 3/31/1887 in New Durham at 77; housekeeper; married

Mary, d. 11/9/1893 in New Durham at 73; old age; single; John Edgerly and Ida M. Rines

Minnie, d. 8/11/1906 in New Durham at 44; chronic nephritis; housewife; married; b. New Durham; Abram Colomy and Sarah Twombly

Sarah E., d. 9/21/1895 in New Durham at 75/9/14; paralysis; housewife; married; b. Barrington; Levi Evans (Strafford) and Abigail Caswell (Northwood)

Shedrach A., d. 5/6/1893 in New Durham at 72/0/16; conges. of liver; married; b. New Durham; John Edgerly

EDWARDS,
Anna, d. 2/--/1978; b. 12/1/1888*
Doris C., d. 2/21/1941 in New Durham at 24/5/4; office asst.; single; b. Wolfeboro; Stanley Andrews (Farmington) and Jessie Kimball (Farmington)

ELDRIDGE,
Dorothy McKenna, d. 10/14/1974 in Dover at 73

ELKINS,
John C., d. 5/25/1892 in New Durham at 25/6/24; brain fever; shoe finisher; single; b. Newburyport, MA; Amasa V. Elkins (Farmington) and Lydia A. Downs (Lebanon, ME)

ELLIS,
Clarrissa J., d. 12/22/1888 in New Durham at 56/3/13; heart disease; married; b. Farmington; Joshua Tebbetts (Rochester) and Elizabeth P. Stevens (Farmington)
Daniel E., d. 5/20/1992 in New Durham at 87

ELLISON,
Arthur Edward, d. 9/21/1979 in Rochester at 89
Gertrude E., d. 6/25/1983 in Dover at 84
Harry B., d. 1/7/1971 in Manchester at 77
Stewart R., d. 12/1/1996 in New Durham [at 74]; Arthur Ellison and Carrie Cromb

EMERSON,
Frank, d. 5/21/1914 in New Durham at 77/0/7; farmer; divorced; b. Farmington; Joseph Emerson (Farmington) and Julia A. George (Barnstead)
Sophia, d. 7/21/1913 in New Durham at 69; chronic interstitial nephritis; housekeeper; married; b. Biddeford, ME; Andrew Goodrich (Biddeford, ME) and ----- (Hollis, ME)

EMERY,
Arthur T., d. 8/7/1951 at 24
George E., d. 7/2/1959 in Rochester at 60/7/3
Harriet L., d. 7/10/1909 in New Durham at 84/3/24; old age; widow;
    b. Cambridgeport, VT; George Phelps (Hartford, CT) and Lucy
    Wooley (Cambridgeport, VT)
Roger L., Sr., d. 5/15/1979 in Portsmouth at 76

ENTWISTLE,
Mary B., d. 4/19/1934 in New Durham at 78/10/8; widow; b.
    England; Ralph Briggs (England) and Dorothy Cranshaw
    (England)

EVANS,
Elizabeth H., d. 9/1/1896 in New Durham at 61/5/6; shock;
    housewife; married; b. Barrington; Daniel D. Howe and Hannah
    Stockbridge (Alton)
Loiza, d. 4/3/1899 in New Durham at 88/2/26; old age; widow; b.
    New Durham; Stephen Nute and Rebecca Perkins
Phoebe L., d. 2/1/1892 in New Durham at 85/9/23; influenza; widow;
    John Durgin and Sarah Durgin
Samuel F., d. 6/23/1919 in New Durham at 76/1/2; farmer; married; b.
    New Durham; Ezra Evans (New Durham) and Belinda York
    (New Durham)
Ziza, d. 11/6/1891 in New Durham at 87/11/3; consumption; farmer;
    married; b. New Durham; Hanson Evans (New Durham) and
    Martha Horne (Farmington)

FAGAN,
Patricia Ann, d. 8/13/1957 at 0/1/23

FAIR,
Lawrence H., d. 10/24/1990 in Rochester at 63

FAIRBANKS,
Alvin O., d. 5/26/1934 in New Durham at 61/4/5; retired; married; b. Hopkinton, MA; Oberlin Fairbanks (MA) and Harriett Smith (Holliston, MA)
Ida, d. 1/5/1944 in Norwich, CT at 70/1/13; housewife; widow; b. Barton, NS; W. Lambertson (NS) and Louisa Veness (NS)

FAIRCHILD,
Clarence, d. 4/12/1982 in Farmington at 83
Olive, d. 2/23/1949 in New Durham at 48; housewife; married; b. Kent, England; Alfred Jarvis and Kate Goodger

FALLON,
John, d. 5/20/1914 in New Durham at 80/9/2; retired; single; b. Sawyerville, PQ; Owen Fallon (Ireland) and Mary Gray (Ireland)

FAUCETT,
Anna E., d. 6/29/1936 in New Durham at 76/8/19; at home; single; b. Walpole, MA; William Faucett (St. Johns, NB) and Eliza Barry (Ireland)
Frederick, d. 1/6/1940 in New Durham at 76; laborer; b. Walpole, MA; William Faucett (St. Johns, NB) and Eliza Barry (Ireland)

FESMIRE,
Dortha F., d. 1/17/1997 in New Durham; Chester H. Worthington and Ida Jones

FESSEL,
Einer S., d. 9/19/1977 in New Durham at 86
Elida A., d. 2/13/1987 in New Durham at 100

FLEISCHER,
William E., d. 7/21/1977 in New Durham at 86

FLETCHER,
Donald, d. 7/--/1972; b. 1/27/1897*

FLYNN,
John, d. 9/6/1928 in New Durham at 67/10/2; farmer; widower; b. Guildhall, VT; Cornelius Flynn (Ireland) and Mandana Booth (VT)

FOGG,
John A., d. 7/7/1976 in Wolfeboro at 75

FORD,
Adam W., d. 1/12/1998 in Rochester
Linwood O., d. 1/27/1953 in Rochester at 28 mins.

FORSEY,
Daniel, d. 6/--/1967; b. 12/16/1885*

FOSTER,
Josephine S., d. 4/5/1936 in New Durham at 20/3/7; at home; divorced; b. Farmington, ME; Walter H. Smith (Farmington, ME) and Florence Thurston (Wells, ME)

FOWLER,
Laura P., d. 11/20/1894 in New Durham at 38/9; heart disease; dressmaker; married; b. New Durham; John L. Gleason (Shirley, MA) and Almira A. Watson (Alton)

FRENCH,
child, d. 6/21/1900 in New Durham at 0/7/15; b. New Durham; Alden C. French (Farmington) and Laurentina Runnals (New Durham)
Minnie P., d. 10/31/1982 in New Durham at 80
Rebecca, d. 4/22/1887 in New Durham at 96/9/2; housekeeper; widow; b. New Durham; Stephen Meader (Durham) and Rosy Kimball (Barrington)
Sara, d. 7/2/1989; b. 7/7/1908*

FROST,
Eben, d. 8/5/1993 in Wolfeboro at 84

GAGNE,
Laureat Joseph, d. 4/9/1989 in Dover at 67

GARDNER,
Rita, d. 9/28/1964 in Laconia at 9

GATTO,
Joseph, d. 4/8/1973 in New Durham at 67

GAUDETTE,
Arthur J., d. 4/22/1974 in New Durham at 31

GEARY,
Anthony William, d. 6/4/1963 in Wolfeboro at 72

GERRISH,
George W., d. 9/5/1920 in New Durham at 65/6/6; carpenter; married; b. Milton; Hiram Gerrish (Dover) and Mary A. Tuttle (Middleton)
Isabel, d. 10/29/1941 in New Durham at 83/3; widow; b. Alton; Alvah Ellis (Alton) and Lydia Glidden (Alton)
John J., d. 9/21/1953 in Rochester at 75

GIGLIOTTI,
Louis J., d. 6/3/1974 in New Durham at 49

GILE,
son, d. 9/26/1894 in New Durham at 0/4/10; cholera infantum; b. Strafford; Thomas Gile (So. Hampton) and Mattie Babb (Strafford)
Lucinda F., d. 11/22/1900 in New Durham at 76/10/18; diabetes; housewife; widow; b. Raymond; Jeremiah Edgerly and Betsey Leighton

GILES,
Oscar A., d. 7/14/1947 in Rochester at 69/0/13; carpenter; divorced; b. Gilmanton; Reuben Giles (Chichester) and Abbie S. Daniels (Sanbornton)

GILMAN,
Erwin, d. 6/--/1970; b. 1/23/1899*
Karen, d. 6/--/1985; b. 9/29/1889*

GLEASON,
Almira A., d. 1/5/1901 in New Durham at 80/11/21; pneumonia; housewife; widow; b. Alton; Joseph Watson (Alton) and Betsy Garland (Alton)
Benjamin F., d. 8/20/1933 in New Durham at 71/10/22; farmer; widower; b. Oakland, ME; Benjamin Gleason (Canaan, ME) and Caroline McIntire (Bingham, ME)
Helen L., d. 4/13/1930 in Cambridge, MA at 78/4/1; widow; b. Methuen, MA; Zebediah Haynes (Waltham, MA) and Sarah Moody (Camden, ME)
John L., d. 1/27/1894 in New Durham at 79; heart disease; farmer; married; b. Shirley, MA
John O., d. 9/20/1935 in New Durham at 88/4/7; farmer; single; b. Alton; John L. Gleason (Shirley, MA) and Almyra A. Watson (Alton)
William J., d. 1/7/1896 in New Durham at 46/7; apoplexy; farmer; married; b. New Durham; John L. Gleason (Shirley, MA) and Elmira A. Watson (Alton)

GLIDDEN,
son, d. 1/27/1898 in New Durham at 0/0/2; b. New Durham; James O. Glidden (Gilford) and Ida Berry (New Durham)
Georgie Ellen, d. 4/9/1898 in New Durham at 5/10/21; pneumonia; b. New Durham; George Z. Glidden (Gilford) and Lula F. Ricker (Milton)

Hannah E., d. 6/16/1913 in New Durham at 76/1/15; herniplegia; housekeeper; married; b. Alton; Ziza Evans (New Durham) and Louisa Nute (Alton)

Herman, d. 10/1/1915 in New Durham at 0/3; malnutrition; single; b. Laconia; Herman Glidden (S. Tamworth, ME) and Myrtle Flanders (Windsor, VT)

Ida B. [Mrs. James O.], d. 1/26/1898 in New Durham at 40/1/12; heart disease; housewife; married; b. New Durham; Eben E. Berry (New Durham) and Lucy M. Chesley (New Durham)

John F., d. 12/31/1908 in New Durham at 50/4/9; pneumonia; farmer; married; b. New Durham; Joseph Glidden and Hannah Evans

Joseph F., d. 8/20/1913 in New Durham at 81/4/8; valv. disease of heart; farmer; widower; b. Alton; Joseph Glidden (Alton) and ---- Buzzell (Alton)

Lura, d. 8/15/1905 in New Durham at 32; chronic mania; single; b. New Durham; Joseph F. Glidden and Hannah Evans

Mary J., d. 5/18/1926 in New Durham at 80/0/11; housewife; married; b. New Durham; William Corson (New Durham) and Drusilla Jones (Middleton)

Sam I., d. 10/29/1901 in New Durham at 33; not known; shoemaker; married; b. Alton; Hen'r J. Glidden (Alton) and Maria Kimball (Wolfeboro)

GOLLER,
Frederick G., d. 5/19/1975 in Rochester at 62

GOOCH,
John M., d. 2/22/1923 in New Durham at 89/6/17; farmer; married; b. Alton; Joseph Gooch and Nancy N. Davis (Lee)

GOODRICH,
Nancy H., d. 11/14/1892 in New Durham at 81/3; old age; widow

GOODROW,
Andrew, d. 7/9/1987 in Laconia at 85
Charles A., d. 12/23/1997; b. 10/29/1930*

Middie, d. 10/4/1967 in Wolfeboro at 66
Ruth M., d. 10/25/1973 in Wolfeboro at 59

GOODWIN,
Edward R., d. 8/8/1965 in New Durham at 74
Minnie F., d. 2/16/1961 in New Durham at 72

GOSS,
John W., Jr., d. 9/18/1998 in Rochester at 76**

GOULD,
Florence M., d. 8/16/1923 in New Durham at 27/8/19; housewife; married; b. New Durham; Charles Edgerly (Dover) and Minnie Colomy (Milton)
Gordon D., d. 5/24/1970 in New Durham at 65
Helen R., d. 8/21/1980 in Rochester at 77
Maud S., d. 3/2/1927 in New Durham at 49/10/15; housewife; married; b. New Durham; Franklin Coburn (Pelham) and Judith Willey (New Durham)

GOYETTE,
Arthur, d. 11/--/1981; b. 1/24/1902*

GRASSIA,
Harriet H., d. 4/10/1990 in Rochester at 80

GRATTON,
John T., d. 5/27/1917 in New Durham at 65; laborer; widower; b. England

GRAY,
Betsey F., d. 12/2/1906 in New Durham at 45/11/20; tuberculosis; single; Wendell S. Gray (New Durham, farmer) and Hannah E. Foss (Strafford)
Frank P., d. 11/25/1980 in Rochester at 66
George W., d. 6/4/1978 in Rochester at 67

Hannah E., d. 10/4/1907 in New Durham at 74/11/26; cancer; housewife; widow; b. Strafford; Moses Foss (Strafford) and Betsey Foss (Strafford)

Harry Lorenzo, d. 4/13/1951 at 76/2/4

Joseph Peter, d. 6/3/1956 at 3

Lavina, d. 9/1/1894 in New Durham at 77/5/5; paralysis; farmer; married; b. Jackson; John Perkins and Hannah Hall

Mildred V., d. 6/21/1975 in New Durham at 79

Samuel J., d. 12/27/1960 in New Durham at 69

Sarah A., d. 9/18/1934 in New Durham at 77/5/17; housekeeper; single; b. New Durham; Solomon F. Gray (Strafford) and Levina Perkins (Jackson)

Wendell S., d. 4/27/1897 in New Durham at 69/8/11; pneumonia; farmer; married; b. New Durham; Henry Gray and Dolly Otis

William A., d. 8/22/1976 in Laconia at 60

GREELEY,
Susie B., d. 7/20/1908 in New Durham at 19/10/27; pulmonary phthisis; teacher; single; b. Hampden, ME; S. D. Greeley (Swanville, ME) and Jennie Nickerson (Swanville, ME)

GREGOIRE,
John R., d. 8/8/1998 at 69**

GRENIER,
Elizabeth B., d. 9/4/1996 in Rochester [at 66]; Albert L. Langley and Mabel Hoyt

Raymond J., d. 11/25/1981 in Rochester at 76

Wilfred, Jr., d. 4/19/1929 in New Durham at 0/0/0; b. New Durham; Wilfred Grenier (Rochester) and Nettie Chesley (Farmington)

GRISENTHWAITE,
Thomas, d. 2/13/1935 in New Durham at 78/5/29; retired; widower; b. England

GROSJEAN,
Arthur Allen, d. 6/12/1967 in Rochester at 83

GUAY,
Anna, d. 4/4/1997; b. 4/11/1921*

GUSTARTIS,
John M., d. 5/30/1987 in Rochester at 73

HADLEY,
John L., d. 12/3/1906 in New Durham at 80; apoplexy; laborer; widower; b. Holderness; Jeremiah Hadley and Sally Piper

HAINES,
Harriet Belle, d. 7/22/1964 in Dover at 75

HALE,
Corie E., d. 10/1/1912 in New Durham at 57/4/11; cerebral hemorrhage; shoe operator; married; b. Lee, ME; John R. Hale (farmer) and Eleanor Ames

Crystal V., d. 9/23/1893 in New Durham at 0/1/29; heart disease; b. New Durham; Corie E. Hale (Lee, ME) and Clarissa Jones (Rochester)

Edgar Earl, d. 7/18/1891 in New Durham at 4 hours; heart failure; b. New Durham; Corie E. Hale (Lee, ME) and Ida M. Rines (Rochester)

Hazel, d. 9/12/1892 in New Durham at 0/0/4; debility; b. New Durham; Corie E. Hale (Lee, ME) and Ida M. Rines (New Durham)

John, d. 3/12/1898 in New Durham at --; millities cerebri; farmer; widower; Charles Hale (Waterford, ME) and Sarah Ricker (E. Rochester)

HALL,
Adrian Elmer, d. 5/16/1951 at 69/6/21

HALLER,
Walter, d. 4/25/1959 in Wolfeboro at 68/0/28

HAM,
Gertrude, d. 8/16/1907 in New Durham at 35; tuberculosis; housewife; married; b. Canada; Ezekiel Randall and Melissa Towle

Penuel C., d. 3/12/1904 in New Durham at 80/11/29; shock; farmer; widower; b. New Durham; Nathaniel Ham and Clarissa Chamberlin

HAMILTON,
John, d. 11/20/1950 in New Durham at 72; retired; married; b. MA; Albert Hamilton and Agnes G. Phillips

HAMMOND,
Clara R., d. 4/4/1979 in New Durham at 79
Florence, d. 8/22/1973 in Wolfeboro at 73
Paul R., d. 9/17/1981 in Rochester at 78

HANBURY,
Evan E., d. 5/22/1965 in Concord at 85

HANCOCK,
Alexander, d. 12/28/1891 in New Durham at 25/0/2; pneumonia; teamster; single; b. VA

Francis Leroy, d. 12/13/1997 in Rochester [at 47]; Ellison Edward Hancock, Sr. and Florence V. Lapanne

Frank E., Sr., d. 6/20/1972 in Rochester at 76
Hazel, d. 1/--/1983; b. 10/30/1898*

HANSON,
Betsy, d. 9/21/1920 in New Durham at 77/7/28; housekeeper; widow; b. Waterboro, ME; Benjamin Smith and Susan Smith

John S., d. 3/13/1907 in New Durham at 69/9/13; heart failure; farmer; married; b. Waterboro, ME; Jonathan Hanson (Waterboro, ME) and Mary Bean (Waterboro, ME)

HARDING,
Gladys M., d. 12/14/1910 in New Durham at 0/3/6; pneumonia; single; b. New Durham; Joseph D. Harding (NS, farmer) and Mary A. Trafton (ME)
Ida P., d. 8/4/1906 in New Durham at 51/4/8; inflam. of caecum; housewife; married; b. Farmington; Daniel Pearl (Milton, farmer) and Lydia B. Jones (New Durham)
Joseph D., d. 4/29/1916 in New Durham at 55/2/7; farmer; married; b. NB

HARRIS,
Ruth Claire, d. 12/12/1992 in New Durham at 69

HARVEY,
Sheldon, d. 4/10/1989; b. 12/18/1905*

HASKINS,
Horace W., d. 2/13/1970 in New Durham at 57

HAWLEY,
infant son, d. 9/6/1907 in New Durham at 0/0/1; defective heart; Henry A. Hawley (Jeffersonville, VT, merchant) and Gertrude Avery (Newbury, VT)

HAYES,
daughter, d. 9/19/1925 in New Durham at 0/0/0; strangulation; b. New Durham; Everett W. Hayes (New Durham) and Rosaria Grenier (Rochester)
Abbie E., d. 2/23/1946 in New Durham at 79/8/17; retired; widow; b. East Kingston; George W. Swett and Martha E. Carter
Abbot N., d. 8/14/1969 in New Durham at 61

Augustus, d. 12/18/1926 in New Durham at 71/9/15; knife mfgr.; married; b. Alton; Samuel Hayes and Mary Whitehouse

Bernice T., d. 5/10/1929 in New Durham at 31/10/12; married; b. New Durham; Alonzo G. Coburn (Pelham) and Annie V. Adams (Farmington)

Bessie E., d. 3/7/1959 in Dover at 72/10/24

Clara E., d. 1/14/1897 in New Durham at 28/5/10; consumption; housekeeper; married; b. East Kingston; George Swett (East Kingston) and Martha A. Carter (East Kingston)

Clarence, d. 1/13/1946 in Windsor, VT at 58/5/26; married; b. New Durham; Seth W. Hayes (Alton) and Abbie E. Swett (East Kingston)

Edith, d. 3/16/1995 in Rochester at 83

Elihu, d. 11/21/1889 in New Durham at 73/9/4; pneumonia; farmer; married; b. New Durham; Reuben Hayes (Madbury) and Patience Tash (New Durham)

Emma J., d. 1/16/1929 in New Durham at 77/6/26; housewife; widow; b. Tuftonboro; Isaac Laurens

Ernest W., d. 6/23/1972 in Rochester at 63

Ethel E., d. 11/25/1892 in New Durham at 0/0/8; canker; b. New Durham; George L. Hayes and Clara E. Swett

Everett W., d. 5/8/1966 in New Durham at 67

George L., d. 3/2/1934 in New Durham at 70/2/25; retired; widower; b. Alton; Samuel Hayes (New Durham) and Mary Whitehouse (Middleton)

Grover C., d. 10/11/1946 in New Durham at 61/7/7; retired; married; b. New Durham; Seth W. Hayes (Alton) and Abbie E. Swett (East Kingston)

Harold Antonio, d. 3/22/1998 in New Durham

Heber C., d. 7/27/1950 in New Durham at 86; retired; widower; b. NB; Charles Hayes and Mary Hallett

James F., d. 1/14/1891 in New Durham at 47/3; killed by accident; farmer; married; ----- (VT)

John W., d. 12/26/1969 in New Durham at 48

Margaret E., d. 2/24/1920 in New Durham at 8/5/2; schoolgirl; single; b. New Durham; Seth W. Hayes (Alton) and Abbie E. Swett (East Kingston)

Martha E., d. 2/23/1891 in New Durham at 35/0/14; consumption; housekeeper; married; b. Portland, ME

Maurice Freeman, d. 6/12/1961 in Manchester at 71

Mrs. John F., d. 7/23/1898 in New Durham at 68/11/3; old age; housewife; married; b. Milton; Timothy Ricker and Laura Ricker

Robert L., d. 1/6/1938 in New Durham at 6/2/22; single; b. New Durham; Everett W. Hayes (New Durham) and Rosaria Grenier (Rochester)

Rosaria M., d. 8/24/1987 in New Durham at 86

Rosemary, d. 1/7/1950 in Rochester at --; b. Rochester; Warren A. Hayes (New Durham) and Virginia L. Wyatt (Farmington)

Sarah E., d. 7/27/1893 in New Durham at 51/6/16; uremia; widow; b. Middleton; Winthrop Colbath (New Durham) and ----- (Middleton)

Seth W., d. 3/19/1927 in New Durham at 66/11/7; mail carrier; married; b. Alton; Samuel Hayes (New Durham) and Mary Whitehouse (Middleton)

Virginia L., d. 9/20/1973 in New Durham at 48

HAYNES,
Robert C., d. 7/16/1972 in New Durham at 18

HEALEY,
Tina Marie, d. 3/13/1963 in New Durham at 1

HERSOM,
Edith N., d. 6/10/1984 in Rochester at 74
Richard H., d. 6/8/1993 in Exeter at 86

HILL,
Earl A., d. 1/3/1982 in Rochester at 82

Earline M., d. 10/22/1928 in New Durham at 1/8/3; b. Farmington; Earl A. Hill (New Durham) and Effie M. Thurston (Berwick, ME)

Effie J., d. 4/9/1944 in New Durham at 79/3/16; housewife; married; b. Barnstead; A. J. Wentworth (Wakefield) and J. E. Littlefield (Barnstead)

Effie M., d. 6/20/1930 in New Durham at 39/1/10; housework; married; b. Brunswick, ME; Josiah W. Thurston (Effingham) and Sylvia Newhall (Wells, ME)

Hervey, d. 1/2/1925 in New Durham at 54; paralysis; farmer; single; b. New Durham; Joseph Hill

Leslie J., d. 2/25/1983 in Rochester at 87

Maria W., d. 4/2/1900 in New Durham at 68/2/12; grippe; housewife; married; b. New Durham; William Sumner and Mary Simpson

Sylvester J., d. 5/17/1950 in New Durham at 82; farmer; widower; b. New Durham; Joseph Hill and Myra Sumner

HILLSGROVE,
Harry G., d. 7/1/1987 in New Durham at 62
Harry J., d. 3/9/1966 in Dover at 72

HODGES,
Brenda, d. 1/8/1953 at 0/6/29

HOLMES,
Robert C., d. 1/5/1988 in New Durham at 64

HORNE,
Abigail T., d. 4/1/1889 in New Durham at 68; pneumonia; housewife; married; b. Gilmanton; Nehemiah Marsh

Daisy M., d. 10/12/1909 in New Durham at 1/6/19; cholera infantum; b. Farmington; Frank O. Horne (Rochester) and Elsie Varney (Milton)

Mildred D., d. 9/25/1980 in New Durham at 76

Susan, d. 7/21/1889 in New Durham at 66/9/4; malignant growth about the liver; housewife; married

HOUSSEN,
Ahmed, d. 6/15/1963 in Rochester at 81

HOWARD,
Fred W., d. 11/11/1921 in New Durham at 25/0/25; farmer; married; b. Derry; Fred J. Howard (Alton) and Grace Amizene (Durham)

HUME,
Herbert J., d. 1/20/1998 in Alton at 54**

HUPE,
Mary, d. 7/13/1895 in New Durham at 0/5; pephistis; b. Wolfeboro; Octave Hupe (Quebec) and Adel Graven

HURD,
Carlos W., d. 8/21/1915 in New Durham at 74/9/1; valv. heart disease; engineer; married; b. Newport; Hial Hurd (Newport) and Beulah Sargent (Sutton, VT)
Clara A., d. 12/10/1917 in New Durham at 79/8/20; housekeeper; widow; b. Canterbury; Elijah W. Hurd and Sarah Randlett
Clarence P., d. 1/15/1899 in New Durham at 0/9/15; marasmus; b. Milton Mills; Arthur Hurd (Lebanon, ME) and Lizzie M. Webber (Milton)

HUSSEY,
Christine P., d. 12/9/1998 in Portsmouth
Kenneth R., Jr., d. 7/13/1995 in Alton at 62
Wilfred D., d. 9/18/1989 in Colebrook at 51

INGHAM,
Charles, d. 8/--/1980; b. 9/6/1920*

ISAACSON,
Dorothy, d. 3/--/1987; b. 6/16/1921*

JACKLIN,
Harry L., d. 2/27/1981 in Rochester at 63

JACOBSMEYER,
Priscilla, d. 7/26/1983 in New Durham at 79

JACOBUS,
Mildred A., d. 2/8/1989 in New Durham at 89

JARVIS,
Kate, d. 4/17/1960 in Rochester at 90

JENKINS,
William P., d. 3/26/1906 in New Durham at 69/11/23; shock; farmer; married; b. New Durham; Elijah Jenkins (New Durham, farmer) and Abigail B. Drew (Alton)

JENNINGS,
Gladys, d. 3/4/1996; b. 5/31/1918*
Irving E., d. 11/15/1976 in New Durham at 76

JEWELL,
Ellen M., d. 6/28/1968 in Rochester at 75
Ernest C., d. 1/10/1977 in Rochester at 87
George, d. 11/--/1971; b. 10/12/1887*

JOHNSON,
Barbara, d. 7/6/1995 in Rochester at 82
Eric Gustav, d. 9/15/1996 in New Durham [at 83]; Johan Johnson and Elizabeth Svensson

JOHNSTON,
A. Jennie, d. 10/24/1966 in New Durham at 96
Edward, d. 10/17/1939 in Dover at 53/0/22; deputy sheriff; married; Charles Johnston and M. Johnston

JONES,
George A., d. 2/13/1931 in New Durham at 72/7/5; laborer; married; b. Gilmanton; Phillip Jones and Lucretia Baker

George F., d. 4/21/1909 in New Durham at 68/7/5; pneumonia; retired; widower; b. New Durham; John L. Jones and Nancy Chamberlain

Howard S., d. 7/24/1896 in New Durham at 46/10/24; ulceration of bowels; farmer; married; b. Farmington; Howard S. Jones and Susan R. Peavey

Jennie E., d. 2/18/1908 in New Durham at 62/10/8; carcinoma; housewife; married; b. New Durham; Maj. George D. Savage (New Durham) and Hannah Lang (Brookfield)

JORDAN,
Lisa Ann, d. 9/15/1965 in New Durham at 0/6

JORDON,
Charles E., d. 11/24/1947 in New Durham at 80/7/29; farmer; single; b. Farmington; Frank Jordon and Lydia Jordon

JOY,
Arlene, d. 3/27/1929 in Rochester at 0/0/19; b. Rochester; Arthur Joy (New Durham) and Elsie Cilley (Nottingham)

Arthur A., Sr., d. 5/27/1982 in New Durham at 79

Joseph F., d. 6/13/1912 in New Durham at 74/0/28; suicide; minister; widower; b. New Durham; Samuel Joy (farmer) and Watie Pettigrew

Mary A., d. 6/21/1920 in New Durham at 87/0/18; housewife; widow; b. New Durham; Ezra Evans and Sallie Clough

Mary E., d. 6/12/1935 in New Durham at 71/3/3; at home; widow; b. New Durham; Joseph Y. Berry (New Durham) and Betsey Scruton (Strafford)

Robert A., d. 11/5/1998 in New Durham

Samuel O., d. 8/22/1934 in New Durham at 74/11/20; farmer;
  married; b. New Durham; Samuel W. Joy (New Durham) and
  Mary A. Evans (New Durham)
Samuel O., III, d. 9/10/1989 in Rochester at 59
Samuel W., d. 1/23/1906 in New Durham at 71/6/21; tuberculosis;
  farmer; married; b. New Durham; Samuel Joy (New Durham,
  farmer) and Watie Pettigrew (New Durham)

KAYLOR,
Thomas, d. 10/--/1978; b. 3/9/1903*

KELLERHOUSE,
George H., d. 6/23/1984 in Rochester at 70

KELLY,
Leonard J., d. 5/28/1990 in New Durham at 67

KEMPTON,
Anna, d. 1/22/1937 in Rochester at 78/10/21; widow; b. Peabody,
  MA; Joseph MacLain (NB) and Susan Parker (NB)
Harry D., d. 8/4/1937 in Dover at 37/2/5; laborer; divorced; b.
  Andover, MA; Bert Kempton (Winchester) and Charlotte
  Hazzard (Warren, MA)

KENNEDY,
Norwood P., d. 10/9/1998 in New Durham at 82**

KE[N]NISTON,
child, d. 3/6/1940 in New Durham at 0/0/0; Elmer Keniston
  (Newmarket) and Georgia Hill (Hill)
Elmer Joseph, Sr., d. 6/18/1956 at 53

KIMBALL,
Chester A., d. 5/15/1980 in Laconia at 65
Helen M., d. 12/31/1979 in New Durham at 59
Mary Adeline, d. 6/12/1963 in Wolfeboro at 0/0/8

KING,
Frank L., d. 4/26/1978 in Rochester at 67

KIRKLAND,
Dorcas A., d. 9/25/1968 in Wolfeboro at 70
Hugh, d. 11/--/1970; b. 6/6/1895*

KNEELAND,
Etta G., d. 11/16/1889 in New Durham at 22/3/15; chronic albuminuria; housewife; married; b. Milton; John H. Young (Farmington) and Melissa Downing (Holderness)
Harriet M., d. 10/19/1901 in New Durham at 23/1; anemia and ulcer of stomach; single; b. Cambridgeport, MA; Daniel Kneeland (Cambridgeport, MA) and Harriet A. Semple (Ireland)

LADD,
Elbridge, d. 3/3/1900 in New Durham at 33/2/17; pneumonia; laborer; married; b. Moultonboro; George C. Ladd (VT) and Emma J. Fogg (Moultonboro)

LAGASSE,
Raymond, d. 12/6/1990; b. 11/9/1911*

LAMBERTSON,
G., d. 2/15/1941 in New Durham at 65/3/1; wood turner; married; b. Barton, NS; W. Lambertson (Barton, NS) and Louisa Viness (NB)

LAMOREUAX,
Jennie M., d. 6/16/1987 in Hanover at 68
Robert F., d. 1/19/1974 in New Durham at 52

LANCE,
Anthony Franklin, d. 3/30/1998 in New Durham at 12**

LANEY,
George E., d. 5/27/1949 in Rochester at 59/8/25; sawmill worker;
married; b. Skowhegan, ME; H. Laney and Celina Roderique

LANGLEY,
Fred A., d. 10/9/1948 in Wolfeboro at 74/5/2; farmer; widower; b.
New Durham; Samuel Langley (New Durham) and Frances
Perkins (New Durham)
George H., d. 5/29/1933 in New Durham at --; laborer; single;
Thomas Langley (Barnstead) and Nellie T. Hayes (New Durham)
Ray, d. 1/20/1988; b. 6/8/1904*
Ronald G., d. 4/29/1994 in Rochester at 59

LARRABEE,
Erwin H., d. 11/13/1997 in Rochester [at 83]; Herbert Larrabee and
Ruth Graves

LAWRENCE,
Lydia Jane, d. 3/26/1961 in New Durham at 74

LEARY,
Donald E., d. 6/18/1922 in New Durham at 0/0/1; b. New Durham;
Frank G. Leary (Merrimac, MA) and Marcia E. Lowell (Lebanon,
ME)
Frank G., d. 8/18/1969 in New Durham at 77

LEAVITT,
Maurice, Sr., d. 2/20/1983 in Salem, MA at 70

LEE,
Edward M., d. 9/28/1914 in New Durham at 72/6/2; farmer; married;
b. Moultonboro; Nathan Lee (Moultonboro) and Eliza M. Brown
(Moultonboro)
Lillian, d. 1/14/1935 in New Durham at 70/3/24; housewife; married;
b. Stark; Mark Miner

LE FOE,
Edward, d. 3/10/1915 in New Durham at 40; accidental drowning; woodchopper; single

LEIGHTON,
George F., d. 1/6/1887 in New Durham at 56; shoemaker; married; b. Farmington; Richard Leighton (Alton) and Rachel Kimball

LEIMEAUX,
son, d. 10/24/1892 in New Durham at 0/1/1; brain trouble; M. Leimeaux

LEMAY,
Catherine M., d. 3/14/1977 in Rochester at 49

LEROUX,
Esdres, d. 2/20/1916 in New Durham at 9; single; b. Doned, Canada; Thomas Leroux (Doned, Canada) and Mary Gen (Canada)

LESSARD,
Edgar, d. 1/7/1990; b. 8/8/1922*

LEWIS,
William I., d. 12/11/1968 in New Durham at 69

LIBBEY,
Clara S., d. 3/1/1887 in New Durham at 59/5/15; housekeeper; married; b. Alton
Isaac C., d. 11/22/1889 in New Durham at 68/0/14; chronic peritonitis; farmer; married; b. New Durham

LIBERI,
Bertha, d. 8/--/1986; b. 2/9/1903*

LIEBERMAN,
Melvin, d. 12/8/1987 in Rochester at 63

LINDNER,
Pauline M., d. 2/7/1992 in Rochester at 64

LITTLEFIELD,
Victoria, d. 12/3/1917 in New Durham at 75; b. Eaton

LOCKHART,
Agnes G., d. 1/28/1971 in New Durham at 71

LORD,
Hiram A., d. 6/15/1925 in New Durham at 63/4/5; cer. hemorrhage; sawyer; divorced; b. Acton, ME; Andrew J. Lord (Acton, ME) and Hattie Moodey (Newfield, ME)

LORING,
Auralie E., d. 3/18/1971 in New Durham at 55
Jennie L., d. 1/31/1963 in New Durham at 84
Ruby F., d. 5/14/1955 at 58

LOWELL,
Abner, d. 9/17/1894 in New Durham at 76/1; accident; laborer; widower; b. Newburyport, MA
Fred C., d. 12/23/1927 in New Durham at 0/0/23; b. Rochester; Fred C. Lowell (Lebanon, ME) and Marjorie Ryan (Kennebunk, ME)
Philemon S., d. 6/29/1937 in New Durham at 64/0/28; sawyer; widower; b. Hiram, ME; James A. Lowell (Hiram, ME) and Joanna Parker (Hiram, ME)
Sherwood A., d. 3/3/1934 in New Durham at 0/0/21; single; b. New Durham; Fred C. Lowell (Lebanon, ME) and Marjorie Ryan (Kennebunk, ME)

LOZZI,
Donald M., d. 8/10/1972 in New Durham at 13
Paul, d. 8/10/1972 in New Durham at 3

LUCAS,
Sarah F., d. 12/14/1892 in New Durham at 70/10; Brights dis.; widow; b. New Durham; John Chesley and Lucy Coleman

MACKAY,
Mae B., d. 3/1/1988 in Rochester at 84
Robert, d. 2/6/1980 in Rochester at 81

MACLENNAN,
Hugh R., d. 6/6/1986 in Wolfeboro at 78

MAGGIORE,
stillborn son, d. 5/17/1913; b. New Durham; Joseph Maggiore (Italy) and Rosia Maggiore (Italy)
stillborn son, d. 2/2/1915; b. New Durham; Joseph Maggorie (sic) (Italy) and Rose Spatafore (Italy)

MANIS,
George D., d. 4/19/1968 in Farmington at 52

MANNINEN,
Eino, d. 6/27/1989 in New Durham at 75

MARCH,
Walter C., d. 3/13/1961 in Wolfeboro at 49
Winifred J., d. 3/15/1990 in Rochester at 83

MARCOTTE,
Marion, d. 5/24/1893 in New Durham at 0/0/11; teething

MARSHALL,
David Oscar, d. 1/23/1956 at 0/0/5

MASON,
Sally W., d. 2/25/1888 in New Durham at 75/6; old age; housekeeper; widow; b. Ossipee

MASSEY,
Kenneth Paul, d. 8/22/1997 in Manchester; William H. Massey and Barbara Young

MAY,
Charles H., d. 6/2/1914 in New Durham at 55/3/4; wood turner; married; b. Fitchburg, MA; James May (Peabody, MA) and Mary A. Porter (Glasgow, Scotland)

McCOY,
John, d. 2/11/1994; b. 8/1/1914*

McGRATH,
John F., d. 1/23/1924 in New Durham at 30/0/5; workman; single; b. Lynn, MA; Thomas McGrath (Ireland) and Margaret O'Connell (Ireland)

McGREEVY,
Mary A., d. 8/14/1982 in New Durham at 23

McKEEN,
stillborn daughter, d. 11/3/1909 in New Durham; James McKeen (New Durham) and Flora M. Towle (New Durham)
Donald M., d. 7/31/1981 in Wolfeboro at 70
Flora M., d. 12/6/1938 in New Durham at 61/5/4; housewife; married; b. New Durham; William A. Towle (Stanstead, PQ) and Mary J. King (Dover)
James, d. 2/25/1892 in New Durham at 47/1/14; malarial poisoning and disease of stomach; farmer; married; b. Fryeburg, ME; James McKeen (Fryeburg, ME) and Mary McDaniel (Lowell, ME)
James F., d. 8/28/1944 in New Durham at 68/11/28; retired; widower; b. New Durham; James McKeen (Fryeburg, ME) and Mary A. Smith (Gorham, ME)
Mary A., d. 3/11/1922 in New Durham at 83/4/7; retired; widow; b. Gorham, ME; William Smith and Mary Dunn

McNEILL,
Beatrice A., d. 1/26/1978 in Rochester at 87

McPHEE,
John, d. 1/18/1959 in Alton at 95/5/16

MEAD,
Annie A., d. 12/23/1923 in New Durham at 79/3/25; housewife; married; b. New Durham; Lewis R. Sumner (Rochester) and Polly J. Berry (New Durham)

MEADER,
Harry D., d. 4/9/1979 in Wolfeboro at 61

MEINELT,
Margaret, d. 3/6/1977 in Rochester at 91
William E., d. 1/16/1964 in New Durham at 76

MELCHER,
Martha P., d. 11/3/1968 in New Durham at 87

MELDRUM,
William A., d. 3/22/1927 in New Durham at 94/3/14; flax sorter; widower; b. Scotland; William Meldrum (Scotland)

MILES,
Edith M., d. 10/1/1974 in Exeter at 81

MILLER,
son, d. 8/14/1907 in New Durham at 0/0/6; rupture cord navel; b. New Durham; Richard Miller (New Durham, farmer) and Eda O. Joy (New Durham)
Annie M., d. 2/24/1966 in Rochester at 78
Carrie, d. 11/--/1968; b. 3/2/1872*

Edith J., d. 2/9/1950 in Rochester at 77/6/1; housewife; married; b. New Durham; Joseph Joy (New Durham) and Addie Berry (New Durham)

Ella J., d. 2/3/1944 in New Durham at 88/5/27; at home; widow; b. Alton; Freeman Glidden and Hannah Evans

George Russell, d. 10/18/1989 in New Durham at 71

Grover C., d. 8/26/1967 in Rochester at 80

James, d. 3/4/1963 in Concord at 85

James A., d. 5/29/1910 in New Durham at 76/7/7; cancer of liver; farmer; married; b. New Durham; Richard Miller (Acton, ME, farmer) and Pauline Buzzell

Lester J., d. 1/4/1911 in New Durham at 0/0/20; gastroenteritis; b. New Durham; Richard Miller (New Durham, farmer) and Eda O. Joy (New Durham)

Lydia O.A., d. 1/28/1915 in New Durham at 66/9/8; locomotor ataxia; nurse; widow; b. Newport; Hial Hurd (Newport) and Beulah Sargent (Sutton, VT)

Mary E., d. 1/31/1917 in New Durham at 66/10/15; housewife; married; b. New Durham; Levi Brackett and Susan Edwards

Richard, d. 3/16/1915 in New Durham at 0/0/12; submuc'us hem'ge; single; b. New Durham; Richard Miller (New Durham) and Eda O. Joy (New Durham)

Richard, d. 1/20/1967 in Rochester at 85

Russell R., d. 2/25/1938 in Farmington at 92/3/16; farmer; widower; b. New Durham; Richard Miller (Milton) and Pauline Buzzell (Acton, ME)

Walter H., d. 1/29/1954 at 79

MILLS,
Raymond W., d. 8/30/1968 in Hanover at 62

MINKHEIM,
Robert, d. 10/15/1958 at 0/2/7

MITCHELL,
Betsey, d. 2/20/1898 in New Durham at 91/4; apoplexy; housekeeper; single; b. New Durham
Eunice, d. 2/25/1898 in New Durham at 85; general debility; housekeeper; single; b. New Durham
Sally, d. 12/8/1891 in New Durham at 83; old age; housewife; widow; b. Brookfield; Joseph Drew and Susan Hill (Newfield, ME)
Samuel, d. 4/20/1889 in New Durham at 78/11/4; suicide by hanging; farmer; married; b. New Durham; Samuel Mitchell and Betsy Edgerly
Thomas E., d. 3/11/1905 in New Durham at 73/8/6; pneumonia; farmer; married; b. New Durham; William P. Mitchell (New Durham) and Lydia Libby

MOISAN,
Josephine M., d. 12/24/1967 in Rochester at 84

MOISON,
stillborn son, d. 3/26/1913 in New Durham; Fred Moison (Quebec) and Clara Boucher (New Durham)

MONCHAMP,
Louis Mellasippe, d. 2/26/1963 in Manchester at 71

MOONEY,
Michael William, d. 10/25/1986 in New Durham at 29

MOORE,
George Albert, Sr., d. 12/20/1994 in Rochester at 68
Raymond, d. 4/23/1938 in Gilford at 37/10/24; shoe treer; single; b. So. Berwick, ME; Lillian Howard

MORAHAN,
Kevin H., d. 12/14/1979 in Concord at 27

MORRISON,
William R., d. 6/12/1990 in New Durham at 64

MORSE,
Jane, d. 9/1/1909 in New Durham at 73/7/29; nephritis; housekeeper; widow; b. Gilford; Daniel Grant (Gilford) and Sarah A. Blaisdell (Gilford)
Sarah, d. 12/7/1908 in New Durham at 71/4/14; valv. disease of heart; housework

MOULTON,
Edward E., d. 4/10/1979 in Rochester at 92
Frank L., d. 3/5/1964 in Wolfeboro at 74
Mabel, d. 12/9/1916 in New Durham at 39/1/15; housework; married; b. Rockport, MA; Stephen Poole and Minnie Carleton
Theodore F., d. 5/15/1989 in New Durham at 62

MURRAY,
Rachel Jean, d. 9/7/1996 in Rochester [at 73]; Stanley W. Snelling and Ada Jane Lander

MYATT,
Isabel L., d. 7/8/1974 in Lawrence, MA at 48

NASH,
Marguerite, d. 12/--/1980; b. 7/31/1898*

NEAL,
Horace U., d. 4/8/1956 at 90
Susan M., d. 1/20/1957 at 81

NEHRING,
Viva, d. 8/30/1997; b. 9/8/1920*
William H., d. 8/31/1995 in Rochester at 80

NEWCOMBE,
Deborah Ellen, d. 3/11/1997 in New Durham [at 44]; Hovey Benson Clock and Mildred Mabel Fuller

NICHOLS,
Allura C., d. 10/27/1972 in Wolfeboro at 65
James, d. 2/1/1971 in Center Harbor at 84

NICHOLSON,
Norman, d. 9/1/1988 in New Durham at 89
Violet Jane, d. 7/27/1996 in Wolfeboro; Samuel W. Rumson and Ann E. Pike

NICKERSON,
Leroy, d. 7/11/1971 in Hanover at 56
Margaret, d. 1/18/1938 in New Durham at 67/5/20; housewife; widow; b. New Durham; Charles Harris (Methuen, MA) and Martha A. Carley (Prospect, ME)
Violet E., d. 11/21/1975 in Wolfeboro at 60

NIXON,
Robert, d. 9/--/1979; b. 8/15/1888*
Robert A., d. 8/23/1996 in New Durham [at 83]; Robert Nixon and Mabel Kinnear

NORTHRIDGE,
Howard Wilbur, d. 12/5/1980 in Manchester at 75

NUTTER,
Frank H., d. 11/26/1965 in Dover at 74
Harry W., d. 12/16/1983 in Concord at 72
Mary Ann, d. 3/25/1906 in New Durham at 79/3/20; organic dis. of heart; widow; b. Alton; Jethro Nutter (Barnstead, farmer) and Lydia Kimball (Alton)

Phoebe A., d. 3/16/1925 in New Durham at 73/5/13; cook; widow; b. Milton; Hazen Duntley (Bow, VT) and Phoebe Leighton (Farmington)
Vaughn A., d. 4/14/1992 in Rochester at 74

NYLAND,
Clarence, d. 7/14/1996; b. 3/29/1914*
Jean, d. 8/29/1955 at 67
Mary H., d. 1/7/1998 in Rochester

NYLUND,
Clarence, d. 7/14/1996 in New Durham; Andrew Nylund and Naomi Sundblom

OBAN,
Clayton, d. 5/15/1992; b. 10/23/1919*

O'DONNELL,
William, d. 10/31/1940 in New Durham at 71/9/28; retired; married; b. Ireland; Phillip O'Donnell (Ireland) and Mary Franklin (Ireland)

OIKLE,
John Allen, d. 10/26/1962 in New Durham at 78
Mabel L., d. 8/15/1965 in New Durham at 83

OLIVER,
Harvey A., d. 10/4/1965 in Rochester at 83
Nellie J., d. 11/20/1988 in Rochester at 99

O'NEIL,
Howard, d. 3/--/1981; b. 10/4/1927*

OTIS,
John, d. 12/24/1932 in New Durham at 67/11/27; carpenter; widower;
    b. Rochester; John Otis (Rochester) and Mary Howard
    (Rochester)
Nella M., d. 11/29/1930 in New Durham at 50/3/0; housewife;
    married; b. Farmington; George Henderson (Farmington) and
    Lewasha Downs (Farmington)

OUTWATER,
Howard T., d. 6/25/1961 in Rochester at 70

OVERMAN,
Mary Helen, d. 4/26/1964 in York, ME at 54

PAGE,
Robert F., d. 10/17/1995 in Wolfeboro at 52

PARSHLEY,
Charles E., d. 2/14/1930 in New Durham at 70/10/0; retired; widower;
    b. Strafford; Stephen Parshley (Strafford) and Mary Fogg
    (Strafford)
Gracia, d. 7/--/1973; b. 7/31/1909*
James H., d. 7/27/1981 in Rochester at 71

PATCH,
Russell Everett, d. 2/8/1997 in Rochester [at 58]; Everett L. Patch and
    Marjorie O. Edwards

PATTERSON,
William, d. 9/8/1942 in Farmington at 58/7/8; wire b. worker; single;
    b. Boston, MA

PEARSON,
Welton, d. 5/--/1986; b. 2/16/1911*

PEAVEY,
Henry K., d. 8/18/1894 in New Durham at 35/10/5; consumption; shoemaker; married; b. Farmington; Knight Peavey (Farmington) and Mary A. Beal (CT)
Josephine L., d. 9/14/1888 in New Durham at 25/3/3; typhoid fever; housework; single
William, d. 9/28/1938 in New Durham at 87/1/8; farmer; married; b. Alton

PECK,
Amybelle I., d. 9/27/1946 in New Durham at 69/3/4; housewife; widow; b. British Isles; Charles Cook and Louisa Andrews (England)

PERKINS,
B. F., d. 1/4/1889 in New Durham at 39; inflammation of stomach and bowels; farmer; single; b. New Durham; B. C. Perkins (New Durham) and Olive Deland (New Durham)
Benjamin C., d. 3/29/1893 in New Durham at 75; liver and kidney; married; b. New Durham; Z. C. Perkins (New Durham) and Betsey Caverly (New Durham)
Emma F., d. 1/23/1888 in New Durham at 12/10/24; dropsy; single
Harriet A., d. 8/5/1889 in New Durham at 59/6/23; congestion of lungs and dropsy; housewife; married; b. Middleton; Alfred Garland (Rochester) and Abigail Horne (Middleton)
John D., d. 4/29/1896 in New Durham at 73/4/11; oronic nephritis; farmer; widower; b. New Durham; James Perkins and Polly Davis
Mary O., d. 7/23/1922 in New Durham at 62/3/3; housewife; married; b. Washington, VT; Joseph Brackett
Olive P., d. 7/17/1904 in New Durham at 83/7; housewife; widow
Sadie M., d. 9/16/1911 in New Durham at 33/2/23; tuberculosis; housewife; married; b. New Durham; Thomas Mitchell (New Durham, farmer) and Lydia A. Perkins (Middleton)
Sarah H., d. 10/14/1887 in New Durham at 65/6/4; housekeeper; single

Thirza Beatrice, d. 9/16/1993 in New Durham at 78

PERRY,
Arthur C., d. 8/13/1963 in New Durham at 76

PETERSON,
Ellen O., d. 7/19/1967 in New Durham at 86
Ethel, d. 7/6/1983 in Dover at 59

PHILLIPS,
Lawrence J., d. 6/18/1969 in Rochester at 68

PICKERING,
Jane, d. 10/23/1892 in New Durham at 90/10/27; old age; widow

PICQUETT,
Mary W., d. 4/23/1962 in New Durham at 87

PIERCE,
Debra A., d. 5/15/1984 in New Durham at 25

PIKE,
Cecil M., d. 11/8/1971 in New Durham at 69

PINKHAM,
Abbie J., d. 9/22/1919 in New Durham at 83/8/13; housewife; widow; b. Barrington; David How and Annie Stockbridge
Eva M., d. 10/7/1935 in New Durham at 58/10/26; housewife; married; b. Farmington; Stephen W. Berry (Bangor, ME) and Hannah J. Edgerly (Middleton)
Fred, d. 2/25/1946 in New Durham at 81/1/22; retired; widower; b. Farmington; John Pinkham and Eliza Pinkham
Merl Clifton, d. 9/26/1891 in New Durham at 0/6/10; cholera infantum; b. New Durham; Kingman Pinkham (Rochester) and Nettie H. Furber (Alton)

Sarah A.T., d. 3/1/1888 in New Durham at 64/5/2; typhoid pneumonia; housewife; married; b. New Durham; William S. Sumner and Sarah Tebbetts (Rochester)

William H., d. 7/12/1889 in New Durham at 44/1/11; phthisis pulmenalis; farmer; married; b. Rochester; Willis R. Pinkham (New Durham) and Martha Gray (New Durham)

PLACE,
Stanley L., d. 9/12/1997 in New Durham [at 84]; Percy Place and Freena Lover

PLANTE,
Joanne Marie, d. 2/5/1962 in New Durham at 1
Katherine Ann, d. 5/16/1960 in Wolfeboro

PLUDE,
Jene, d. 4/28/1930 in New Durham at 0/7/11; single; b. Rochester; Oliver Plude (Canada) and Alma Dyar (Gonic)

PLUMMER,
Sarah E., d. 5/20/1918 in New Durham at 81/0/4; housekeeper; widow; b. New Durham; Daniel Colomy and Rebecca Pinkham (New Durham)

POMMER,
Olga C., d. 11/15/1981 in New Durham at 90

PRESBY,
Jennie C., d. 7/31/1981 in New Durham at 88

PROCTOR,
Katherine, d. 6/2/1934 in New Durham at 82/0/10; housekeeper; widow; b. Westfield, NJ; William Rogers (London, England) and Catherine Barrett (Wells, England)

PULLIAM,
Robert C., d. 5/27/1990 in Rochester at 39

QUALEY,
Martha, d. 3/3/1970 in Farmington at 92
Thomas A., d. 5/29/1951 at 80

QUIRK,
John, d. 3/--/1980; b. 8/2/1936*

RAMSEY,
Herbert A., d. 12/13/1989 in Rochester at 71

RAND,
Dona, d. 9/17/1973 in New Durham at 66
Florence Evelyn, d. 2/12/1998 at 88**
Jacob P., d. 8/11/1952 in Alton at 77

RANDALL,
Andrew D., d. 1/27/1892 in New Durham at 67/8/10; influenza; farmer; widower; b. New Durham; James Randall and Hannah Ducoin
Benjamin W., d. 12/26/1908 in New Durham at 59/0/16; typhoid fever; farmer; married; b. New Durham; Smith Randall (New Durham)
Betsey, d. 5/6/1905 in New Durham at 98; old age; widow
Charles A., d. 2/19/1924 in New Durham at 73/8/10; farmer; married; b. New Durham; Peter Randall (New Durham) and Betsey Willey (New Durham)
Charles H., d. 2/10/1974 in New Durham at 92
Charles H., Jr., d. 6/12/1967 in New Durham at 41
Cheryl Darlene, d. 5/17/1956 at 0/0/1
Cora S., d. 3/21/1917 in New Durham at 64/2/21; retired; widow; b. Alton; Eben Ellis (Rochester) and Mary Watson (Gilmanton)
Ezekiel T., d. 4/2/1901 in New Durham at 62/4; heart disease; farmer; married; b. New Durham; James Randall and Hannah Ducoin

Martha J., d. 8/18/1931 in New Durham at 75/9/26; home; widow; b. Gilmanton; Jonathan Woodman and Hannah Rollins

Mary M., d. 5/17/1907 in New Durham at 68/7/11; heart failure; housewife; widow; b. Wolfeboro; William Towle (Alton) and Ruth Doe (Farmington)

Mildred, d. 12/30/1911 in New Durham at 14/0/5; pneumonia; at home; single; b. New Durham; Charles A. Randall (New Durham, farmer) and Martha Woodman (Gilmanton)

Moses, d. 11/5/1896 in New Durham at 73/4; cancer; farmer; widower; b. Rochester; James Randall (Rochester) and Hannah Durgin (New Durham)

Robert J., d. 8/8/1990 in Wolfeboro at 72

Ruth M., d. 8/2/1976 in Rochester at 71

Samuel Erwin, Jr., d. 5/16/1956 at 0/0/1

W. S., d. 1/27/1889 in New Durham at 83/7/24; erysipelas; blacksmith; married; b. New Durham; Benjamin W. Randall (New Durham) and Sarah Parsons (Wiscasset, ME)

Willie E., d. 3/10/1914 in New Durham at 33/1/20; married; b. Rochester; George F. Randall (New Durham) and Cora S. Ellis (Farmington)

REED,

Bettyann A., d. 8/22/1998 in Rochester at 63**

George W., d. 3/28/1900 in New Durham at 77/10/7; malignant tumor; farmer; widower; Benjamin Reed and Eliza Holmes (Farmington)

REINHAGEN,

Robert C., d. 1/16/1998 in FL; b. 2/8/1921*

RHINES [see also Rines],

Alvah H., d. 4/2/1923 in New Durham at 66/6/22; shoemaker; married; b. New Durham; Alvah C. Rhines (New Durham) and Lydia French

Evelyn A., d. 10/12/1922 in New Durham at 16/2/28; single; b. New Durham; Herman Rhines (New Durham) and Lucy B. Dow (Dorchester)

Gracie J., d. 8/22/1929 in New Durham at 52/11/9; housekeeper; divorced; b. New Durham; Joseph F. Joy (New Durham) and Addie F. Berry (New Durham)

RHOADES,
Earl James, d. 10/8/1996 in Dover [at 83]; William G. Rhoades and Ida Mitchell

RICE,
Kenneth, d. 9/2/1988; b. 10/25/1917*

Laura A., d. 5/23/1906 in New Durham at 47/7/14; hysteric hemiplegia; married; b. Barnstead; Joshua W. Ayers (Barnstead, farmer) and Mary Langley (Barnstead)

RICHARDS,
Cora P., d. 5/18/1971 in Wolfeboro at 91
William E., d. 2/1/1968 in Dover at 83

RICHARDSON,
Ralph E., d. 10/20/1972 in Rochester at 75

RICKER,
Charles H., d. 6/13/1901 in New Durham at 51/11/2; cerebral hemorrhage; merchant; married; b. Barrington; Ira S. Ricker (Dover) and Mary E. Hall (Barrington)

Charles H., d. 11/19/1913 in New Durham at 57; cerebral hemorrhage; clerk; married; b. Wolfeboro; Augustus Ricker (Wolfeboro) and Nancy Coleworth (Wolfeboro)

Daniel H., d. 3/18/1901 in New Durham at 43/6/12; sola pneumonia; laborer; single; b. New Durham; Ira S. Ricker (Dover) and Mary E. Hall (Barrington)

Florence D., d. 4/10/1979 in Dover at 92

Ira S., d. 9/18/1896 in New Durham at 72/0/26; gastritis; station agent; married; b. Dover; John H. Ricker (Dover) and Eliza Corson (Lebanon, ME)

James M., d. 5/8/1899 in New Durham at 62/3/6; chronic diarrhea; farmer; married; b. New Durham; William Ricker (Newfield, ME) and Lucy Whitten (Newfield, ME)

John, Jr., d. 11/14/1976 in New Durham at 60

John H., Sr., d. 11/11/1960 in Rochester at 80

Leslie W., d. 1/15/1932 in New Durham at 71/6/19; retired; widower; b. New Durham; Ira S. Ricker (Barrington) and Mary E. Hall (Dover)

Wendella, d. 11/1/1927 in New Durham at 59/4/12; housewife; married; b. New Durham; John F. Tash (New Durham) and Almira B. Ham (Alton)

RIDDLE,

Wilbur, d. 3/12/1940 in New Durham at 72/5/25; laborer; widower; b. Grafton; Andrew Riddle (Grafton) and Janette Martin (Grafton)

RINES [see also Rhines],

Addie L., d. 8/9/1894 in New Durham at 32/6/9; consumption; dressmaker; married; b. New Durham; Alvah C. Rines (New Durham) and Lydia L. French (New Durham)

Albert A., d. 11/2/1978 in Alton at 78

Alonzo, d. 2/23/1927 in New Durham at 85/10/14; farmer; widower; b. New Durham; Henry Rines (New Durham)

Alphonzo, d. 3/29/1899 in New Durham at 50/9/12; cancer; farmer; single; Henry Rines

Alvah C., d. 2/27/1904 in New Durham at 75/7/2; cerebral hemorrhage; farmer; married; b. Alton; Henry Rines and Mary Babb

Angie S., d. 3/17/1899 in New Durham at 39/10/29; peritonitis; housewife; married; b. Limerick, ME; John Brown (Limerick, ME) and Hannah Brown (Limerick, ME)

Charles H., d. 2/4/1915 in New Durham at 84; cancer; farmer; married; b. Alton; Charles H. Rines (Alton) and Mary H. Babb (New Durham)

Dora May, d. 4/6/1913 in New Durham at 31/4/0; pneumonia; housekeeper; married; b. Freedom; Ai Berry and Emma Giles

Myrtie M., d. 11/3/1888 in New Durham at 10/11/3; inflammation of brain; single; b. New Durham; Alphonso Rines (New Durham) and Nellie M. Davis

Vivian F., d. 9/14/1895 in New Durham at 1/11; pertussis; b. New Durham; Irving Rines (New Durham) and Angie Brown (Limerick, ME)

Winnie I., d. 4/3/1892 in New Durham at 27/3/27; consumption; housekeeper; married; b. Canada; William H. Morrell (Tuftonboro) and Susan E. Brown (Moultonboro)

RING,
Gloria J., d. 1/13/1947 in Wolfeboro at 1/7/11; single; b. New Durham; Ernest E. Ring (Belmont) and Ethel Shaw (Farmington)

ROBBINS,
Bessie M., d. 6/15/1953 at 72

ROBERTS,
Eliza A., d. 3/16/1916 in New Durham at 86/11/21; housewife; widow; b. Brighton, ME; Isaac Lord (Acton, ME) and Eliza Hussey (Acton, ME)

Ephraim K., d. 1/2/1908 in New Durham at 81/8/14; cerebral sclerosis; farmer; married; b. Farmington; Hanson Roberts (Farmington) and Eleanor Kimball (Farmington)

ROBINSON,
Diane Lee, d. 6/7/1977 in New Durham at 31

George H., d. 3/12/1902 in New Durham at 54/4/22; consumption; baker; married; b. Kingston; Jonathan Robinson (Gilmanton) and Harriet W. York (Gilmanton)

George W., d. 8/7/1966 in New Durham at 82

ROGERS,
George J., Jr., d. 6/3/1984 in Rochester at 71
Lucien D., d. 1/16/1983 in New Durham at 91

ROHAN,
George F., d. 2/4/1912 in New Durham at 51/11/4; tuberculosis; knifemaker; married; b. Northampton, MA; Thomas Rohan (Ireland) and Margaret Cairus (Ireland)
Helen M., d. 9/28/1894 in New Durham at 0/5/7; cholera infantum; b. New Durham; George H. Rohan (Northampton, MA) and Josephine Rohan (PEI)
Leon W., d. 1/26/1911 in New Durham at 18/7/4; phthisis pulmonis; laborer; single; b. New Durham; George F. Rohan (Northampton, MA, knife maker) and Josephine Galbreith (PEI)

ROLLINS,
Addie F., d. 1/10/1919 in New Durham at 25/9/29; school teacher; married; b. Alton; Frank E. Morse (Alton) and Dora V. Lamper (Alton)
Doris M., d. 8/7/1988 in New Durham at 85
Harold E., d. 6/3/1969 in New Durham at 73
Herman S., d. 4/30/1887 in New Durham at 20/11/14; shoemaker; single; b. New Durham; Cyrus C. Rollins
Solomon P., d. 12/25/1903 in New Durham at 64/5/19; ep'h'la int. maxillary; farmer; married; b. Alton; John Rollins (Alton) and Polly Perkins (Middleton)

ROSS,
Helen, d. 6/--/1987; b. 6/11/1892*

ROTHERMEL,
Raymond H., d. 9/24/1998 in New Durham at 42**

ROULEAU,
Della, d. 11/21/1923 in New Durham at 13/11/5; student; single; b. Lynn, MA; Alfred C. Rouleau (Canada) and Matilda Dupois (Canada)

ROUSSEAU,
Leon J., d. 7/14/1992 in New Durham at 40

ROYAL,
stillborn son, d. 4/26/1925 in New Durham; Ulmer L. Royal (Ellsworth, ME) and Bessie May

ROYCE,
Charles John, d. 12/12/1997 in Dover; Henry Royce and Amanda Goulette
Mildred F., d. 7/9/1969 in Dover at 57

RUITER,
Sharon Ann, d. 1/28/1953 at 0/7/8

RUNNALS,
Caleb R., d. 8/13/1907 in New Durham at 75/5/29; septicemia; farmer; married; b. New Durham; Samuel Runnals (New Durham) and Eliza Ricker (New Durham)
Eliza, d. 3/21/1889 in New Durham at 84/0/6; old age; housewife; married; b. New Durham; Caleb Ricker and Darkes Horne
Lydia A., d. 3/29/1911 in New Durham at 68/8/27; pneumonia; housewife; widow; Benjamin Savage (farmer) and Lois Davis

RUSSELL,
Chester, d. 11/16/1939 in New Durham at 47/2/22; shoeworker; married; b. Middleton, MA; Frank Russell (Middleton, MA) and Nellie Wells
Herman, d. 7/20/1926 at 21/8/22; burial in New Durham

SABDS,
Hattie I., d. 7/26/1954 at 88/8

SAMPSON,
Joseph N., d. 1/10/1901 in New Durham at 52/1/23; heart failure; farmer; married; b. New Durham; Ivory P. Sampson and Mary French

Mary M., d. 8/17/1895 in New Durham at 74/11/19; heart disease; housewife; married; b. Farmington; Joseph G. French (Farmington) and Rebekah Meader (Durham)

SAMUELS,
Carol, d. 4/--/1984; b. 12/25/1931*

SATTERWHITE,
B., (female), d. 10/2/1949 in Wolfeboro at 52; at home; single; b. Hewlett, VA; F. D. Satterwhite and Viva Waldron

SAUCIER,
Louis A., d. 2/11/1991 in Dover at 69

SCHAEFER,
Frank, d. 7/9/1940 in New Durham at 74/7/15; retired; widower; b. Springfield, OH; Michael Schaefer (Germany) and M. Honefanger (Germany)

SCHMIDT,
Edward G., d. 7/27/1974 in New Durham at 32

SCOTT,
Roy N., d. 11/21/1968 in New Durham at 77

SCRIPTURE,
Owen I., d. 8/5/1985 in Rochester at 65

SCRUTON,
Lovey T., d. 1/7/1902 in New Durham at 72/4/19; cardiac dilation; dressmaker; widow; b. Farmington; John E. Elkins (New Durham) and Achsah Varney (Farmington)
Norma C., d. 9/25/1947 in Rochester at 30/0/25; housewife; married; b. New Durham; Floyd P. Coburn (New Durham) and Ethel E. Hayes (New Durham)

SEARLES,
Walter J., d. 2/28/1973 in New Durham at 70

SHAW,
Ruby, d. 10/--/1989; b. 10/4/1904*
William Henry, d. 5/18/1951 at 74

SHEDD,
Millie F., d. 7/26/1889 in New Durham at 22/5/22; consumption; shoe stitcher; single; b. Westford, MA; William H. Shedd and Eliza P. Abbott (Boston, MA)

SHIELDS,
Darren K., d. 10/29/1988 in New Durham at 22

SHIRLEY,
John C., d. 1/11/1956 at 89

SHOREY,
Samuel A., d. 11/24/1952 in Rochester at 71

SHUMWAY,
Craig B., d. 9/15/1991 in New Durham at 13

SILVESTRI,
Dorothy L., d. 1/6/1983 in New Durham at 56

SIMONDS,
Ruby B., d. 5/8/1986 in New Durham at 77

SIMPSON,
Effie L., d. 8/18/1954 at 71

SKANE,
Herbert J., d. 4/29/1976 in New Durham at 69

SKIDMORE,
Kathleen Elizabeth, d. 9/28/1959 in New Durham at 4/0/29

SLACK,
Origen F., d. 7/17/1919 in New Durham at 83/11/14; **farmer; married;**
   b. Washington, VT; Silas Slack (CT) and Mary Cummings (Washington, VT)

SMITH,
Alfred, d. 2/23/1974 in Rochester at 65
Alfred W., d. 2/25/1978 in New Durham at 46
Altie H., d. 5/31/1985 in Rochester at 83
Axel, d. 1/30/1926 in New Durham at 65/7/8; **cornice maker; married;**
   b. Sweden
Charles W., Sr., d. 6/15/1970 in Rochester at 63
Clifford Austin, d. 7/12/1961 in Manchester at 63
Diamon, d. 3/15/1907 in New Durham at 55; influenza; single; b.
   Waterboro, ME; Benjamin Smith (Waterboro, ME) **and Susan**
   Smith (Waterboro, ME)
Edward W., d. 12/4/1971 in Wolfeboro at 69
Ellis W., d. 5/28/1970 in Wolfeboro at 92
Elmer C., d. 12/2/1985 in Rochester at 68
Grace Isabelle, d. 10/25/1991 in Rochester at 77
Marion M., d. 4/24/1978 in Wolfeboro at 81
Ruth C., d. 12/30/1961 in New Durham at 5
Steven A., d. 10/19/1979 in Alton at 28
William, d. 2/1/1952 at 69

SPEAD,
Mary A., d. 4/23/1887 in New Durham at 78; housekeeper; widow; b. Newmarket

SPENCER,
Howell A., d. 5/24/1937 in New Durham at 35/6/2; electrician; married; b. Berwick, ME; Oscar Spencer (Berwick, ME) and Charlotte Lowell (So. Berwick, ME)

SPONGBERG,
Alvida Sophia, d. 6/22/1952 at 82

STANSFIELD,
George W., d. 2/4/1983 in West Palm Beach, FL at 66

STANTON,
Abigail, d. 3/12/1887 in New Durham at 83/8/22; housekeeper; widow; b. Alton; Israel Hayes (Strafford) and Louise Emerson (Madbury)
George Hill, Jr., d. 1/26/1998 in New Durham; b. 4/23/1919*
Sarah E., d. 6/4/1888 in New Durham at 51/2/17; single; b. New Durham; Ephraim Stanton (Strafford) and Abigail Hayes (Alton)

STAPLES,
Barbara L., d. 10/21/1953 at 22
Charles F., d. 1/25/1966 in New Durham at 62
Doris S., d. 1/25/1966 in New Durham at 55

STEVENS,
Betsey, d. 5/1/1888 in New Durham at 92/6/10; old age; married
Hale, d. 10/23/1887 in New Durham at 87/4/28; farmer; married; Durrell Stevens (Lee) and Nancy Hill (Lee)
Hale, d. 6/13/1891 in New Durham at 92/8; old age; widower
Nancy H., d. 1/15/1917 in New Durham at 83/11/19; school teacher; single; b. Alton; Hale Stevens (New Durham) and Sarah E. Buzzell

STIMPSON,
Norma D., d. 10/13/1973 in Wolfeboro at 43

STOCK,
daughter, d. 11/25/1926 in New Durham at 0/0/1; Hubert Stock and Eva Jones (Gilmanton)

SUMNER,
Lewis, d. 6/29/1906 in New Durham at 89/6/2; old age; farmer; widower; b. Farmington; Will S. Sumner (Farmington) and Sarah Tebbitts

Polly J., d. 11/22/1902 in New Durham at 85/8/12; old age; housewife; married; b. Rochester; Jethro Berry (New Durham) and Polly Berry (New Durham)

Selinda, d. 5/23/1907 in New Durham at 79/7/26; heart disease; housekeeper; single; b. New Durham; W. S. Sumner and Sarah Tibbetts

William S., d. 7/10/1905 in New Durham at 68/5/19; heart failure; farmer; married; b. New Durham; William S. Sumner and Sarah H. Tibbetts (Rochester)

SWETT,
Fern, d. 10/4/1959 in Concord at 72/11/19

TASH,
Almira B., d. 1/15/1906 in New Durham at 75/3; cerebral hemorrhage; housewife; widow; b. Alton; Nathaniel Ham (Barrington, farmer) and Clarissa Chamberlin (New Durham)

John F., d. 8/2/1888 in New Durham at 66/6/10; bilious fever; farmer; married; William Tash (New Durham) and Nancy Folsom

John N., d. 6/26/1932 in New Durham at 66/2/29; farmer; married; b. New Durham; John F. Tash (New Durham) and Almira B. Ham (New Durham)

Mattie, d. 12/21/1908 in New Durham at 54/5/4; paralysis; shoe stitcher; single; b. New Durham; John F. Tash (New Durham) and Almira B. Ham (Alton)

TAYLOR,
Celina, d. 7/17/1988 in Rochester at 75
Dorothy E., d. 6/13/1993 in Rochester at 73
Stanley M., d. 12/21/1986 in Rochester at 77

TEBBETTS,
Baalis B., d. 1/25/1903 in New Durham at 78/3/16; la grippe; farmer; widower; b. Farmington; Joshua Tebbets (Rochester) and Elizabeth Stevens (Farmington)
Donald R., d. 7/21/1987 in Rochester at 73
Orrin E., d. 2/10/1935 in New Durham at 76/10/9; retired; widower; b. New Durham; Silas Tebbetts (Farmington) and Lois Grace (New Durham)
Sarah N., d. 12/11/1909 in New Durham at 50/0/16; natural causes; shoe stitcher; married; b. New Durham; Joseph Hill (Wenham, MA) and Maria Sumner (New Durham)
Silas C., d. 12/23/1895 in New Durham at 74; influenza; farmer; married; Joshua Tebbetts (Farmington) and Elizabeth Stevens

THOMPSON,
Leon P., d. 10/30/1896 in New Durham at 17/1/10; gastritis; laborer; single; b. Concord; George W. Thompson (Dracut, MA) and Anna A. Colby (Pembroke)

THORNTON,
William Gordon, d. 4/16/1951 at 37

THURSTON,
Clara, d. 9/27/1944 in New Durham at 66/11/27; housewife; married; b. Chelsea, MA; Dennis Carlin (East Kingston) and Caroline Hurd (Newport)
Clarence, d. 1/6/1924 in New Durham at 21/11/3; farmer; single ; b. Effingham; Martin Thurston (Brownfield, ME) and Clara M. Carlin (Chelsea, MA)
Josiah, d. 6/22/1948 in New Durham at 84/1/17; farmer; married; b. Effingham; Joseph Thurston and Esther Drew

Martin, d. 2/29/1948 in Wolfeboro at 75/6/6; laborer; widower
Sylvia Ann, d. 1/4/1952 at 87
Walter, d. 7/6/1945 in New Durham at 55/9/18; navy yard; married; b. Berwick, ME; J. W. Thurston (Effingham) and Sylvia Newhall (Wells, ME)
William J., d. 5/11/1928 in New Durham at 35/0/0; farmer; single; b. No. Berwick, ME; Josiah Thurston (Effingham) and Sylvia A. Newhall (Wells, ME)

TIBBETTS,
Alma J., d. 9/11/1887 in New Durham at 25/4/11; dressmaker; married; Frank W. Coburn
Eva L., d. 4/28/1977 in Rochester at 67
Levi, d. 5/9/1887 in New Durham at 85/8/24; laborer
Nelson S., d. 5/30/1979 in Portsmouth at 89

TOBEY,
Edward E., d. 8/17/1953 in Wolfeboro at 85
Grace L., d. 12/20/1946 in New Durham at 80/2/16; housewife; married; b. Sweden, ME; James McKeen (Fryeburg, ME) and Mary A. Smith (Gorham, ME)

TOWLE,
Charles F., d. 12/6/1898 in New Durham at 71/11; paralysis; shoemaker; married; b. Wolfeboro; William Towle and Ruth Dow
Ezekiel B., d. 11/30/1897 in New Durham at 65/7/8; paralysis; shoemaker; married; b. Wolfeboro; William Towle (Alton) and Ruth L. Dow (Kensington)
Floyd, d. 12/--/1985; b. 7/27/1898*
Lillian M., d. 7/15/1889 in New Durham at 15/1/5; valv. disease of heart; single; b. New Durham; William A. Towle (Wolfeboro) and Mary J. King (Trimrick, PEI)
Lucine, d. 3/15/1939 in New Durham at 0/3/16; single; b. New Durham; Warren Towle (Pittsburg) and L. Hutchinson (Vinal Haven, ME)

Mary Jane, d. 12/20/1915 in New Durham at 70/3/7; cancer of liver; housewife; widow; b. Canada; Josiah King

William A., d. 12/5/1914 in New Durham at 79/5/26; farmer; married; b. Wolfeboro; William Towle (Alton) and Ruth Dor (Kingston)

TRAFTON,
Edward F., d. 11/16/1987 in Dover at 89

Mary A., d. 8/12/1912 in New Durham at 68/8/7; cancer; housewife; married; b. Hartford, ME; Mark Jose (Saco, ME, farmer) and Roxanna Soule (Hartford, ME)

William, d. 6/1/1917 in New Durham at 70/9/18; clergyman; widower; b. Acton, ME; Hezekiah Trafton and Mary Edgerly

TRANCEE,
Mary P., d. 4/26/1893 in New Durham at 60; paralysis; married; b. Canada

TRASK,
Ralph C., d. 9/2/1978 in Rochester at 86

TROWBRIDGE,
J. T., d. 4/11/1949 in New Durham at 65; farmer; married; b. Newfoundland; S. Trowbridge and Elmira Reed

John, d. 6/17/1947 in Wolfeboro at 15/7/1; student; single; b. Beverly, MA; J. T. Trowbridge (Newfoundland) and Lillian Gleason (Dorchester, MA)

TUCKER,
Burton A., d. 1/15/1986 in New Durham at 80

Hilda, d. 4/--/1994; b. 8/31/1913*

TUFTS,
Virginia, d. 10/--/1983; b. 1/22/1911*

TURCOTTE,
child, d. 12/2/1937 in New Durham at 0/0/0; b. New Durham; Thomas Turcotte (Berry, Canada) and Leona Marcou (Walden, VT)
Thomas, d. 12/5/1940 in New Durham at 49/5/20; laborer; married; b. Canada; Philias Turcotte and E. Turcotte

TURTIAINEN,
Hilma K., d. 2/5/1991 in New Durham at 96

TUTTLE,
Curtis E., d. 4/28/1909 in New Durham at 6/1/4; typhoid fever; single; b. New Durham; William B. Tuttle (Middleton) and Mazina Colomy (New Durham)
James A., d. 7/20/1929 in New Durham at 1/3/1; b. New Durham; Clarence E. Tuttle (New Durham) and Mary Patch (Alton)
Mazina, d. 3/3/1903 in New Durham at 35; gastroenteritis; housewife; married; b. New Durham; Abram Colomy
Nehemiah D., d. 3/6/1896 in New Durham at 2/2; whooping cough; b. New Durham; William B. Tuttle (Middleton) and Minnie M. Colomy (New Durham)
W. B., d. 11/22/1912 in New Durham at 70/0/0; nephritis; laborer; widower; b. Middleton; Stephen Tuttle (Middleton, farmer)

TWITCHELL,
Nellie J., d. 2/12/1987 in Rochester at 52
Steven M., d. 12/29/1966 in Rochester at 0/0/0

TWOMBLY,
Lydia M., d. 1/22/1897 in New Durham at 75/4/4; cancer; housekeeper; widow; b. Rochester; Israel Varney (Rochester) and Sarah Knowles (Rochester)

URQUHART,
Glen A., d. 6/28/1986 in New Durham at 33

VACHON,
Florence, d. 9/30/1923 in New Durham at 19/10/27; housewife; married; b. No. Berwick; James Goodrow (Canada) and Vinnie Goodrow (Somersworth)

VALLEY,
son, d. 3/18/1898 in New Durham at --; premature birth; b. New Durham; Lewis Valley (Canada)
Maurice E., d. 3/27/1974 in New Durham at 49
Rosemy, d. 3/13/1898 in New Durham at 0/7/12; con. hydrosephalus; b. Wolfeboro; Lewis Valley (Canada) and Elize Champer (Canada)

VALLIE [see also Valley],
son, d. 4/4/1899 in New Durham at 0/0/7; premature birth; b. New Durham; Lewis Vallie (Canada) and Lizzie Lambien (Canada)

VARNEY,
Carl St.C., d. 10/30/1895 in New Durham at 16/9/23; typhoid fever; single; b. Alton; Elihu Varney (Alton) and Ellen E. Roberts (Rollinsford)
Eleanor F., d. 3/27/1900 in New Durham at 1/10/21; lobular pneumonia; b. New Durham; Thomas S. Varney (Alton) and Sarah E. Varney (Chelsea, MA)
Mildred E., d. 9/3/1922 in New Durham at --; b. New Durham; Benjamin Varney (Farmington) and Esther Thompson (New Durham)
Sarah E., d. 6/9/1898 in New Durham at 22/10/22; cerebral hem.; housewife; married; b. Chelsea, MA; L. B. Tenney (Plymouth) and Florence King

VIEIRA,
Robert P., d. 1/13/1979 in Rochester at 41

VIGENT,
Carl N., d. 4/24/1948 in New Durham at 64/4/3; laborer; divorced; b. VT; Noah Vigent and Alma Clarke

VIGNEAULT,
Constance Ida, d. 3/27/1997 in Rochester [at 66]; Phillippe Romeo Beaudet and Jeannette M. Biron

WALDRON,
son, d. 12/3/1935 in New Durham at 0/0/0; b. New Durham; Robert Waldron (Farmington) and Evelyn Pinkham (No. Lebanon, ME)
son, d. 12/3/1935 in New Durham at 0/0/0; b. New Durham; Robert Waldron (Farmington) and Evelyn Pinkham (No. Lebanon, ME)

WALKER,
David Richardson, d. 6/19/1992 in New Durham at 64
Emma F., d. 1/28/1942 in New Durham at 88/11/10; housewife; widow; b. Charlestown, MA; Daniel Burnham (New Durham) and Sarah H. Dow (New Durham)
Grace N., d. 4/15/1908 in New Durham at 19/11/8; tubercular meningitis; domestic; single; b. New Durham; John M. Walker (Farmington) and Emma Burnham (Charlestown, MA)
John N., d. 6/13/1896 in New Durham at 72; cystitis; farmer; married; b. Farmington; John R. Walker and Abra Nute
Joseph F., d. 5/31/1969 in Rochester at 101

WALLACE,
Dora, d. 2/27/1932 in New Durham at 69/7/8; housewife; married; b. Middleton; Joseph L. Perkins (Middleton) and Sarah Perkins (Dover)

WALLINGFORD,
Betsey J., d. 9/1/1901 in New Durham at 63; consumption; housewife; married; b. Rochester; ----- Ricker

WARBURTON,
Charles E., d. 3/22/1970 in New Durham at 67

WATERMAN,
William R., d. 10/29/1986 in New Durham at 56

WATSON,
Gertrude B., d. 2/20/1955 at 77
Raymond A., d. 10/26/1954 at 0/11/22

WEAVER,
George C., d. 9/23/1987 in Dover at 59

WEEKS,
Anna E., d. 12/18/1972 in Wolfeboro at 82
Nancy J., d. 6/13/1911 in New Durham at 79/6/11; senility; retired; widow; Samuel Joy (New Durham, farmer) and Matie Pettigrew (New Durham)
Raymond A., d. 5/28/1967 in Wolfeboro at 76
Sarah A., d. 8/22/1896 in New Durham at 53/1/22; apoplexy; housework; married; b. Farmington

WEIGHTMAN,
Helen M., d. 2/13/1972 in New Durham at 65

WELCH,
Mary E., d. 12/28/1934 in Rochester at 70/5/13; housewife; married; b. Richmond, NS; Joseph Brown (Scotland) and Dolly E. Morris

WENTWORTH,
Ambrose J., d. 12/20/1889 in New Durham at 63/1/4; cystitis; farmer; married; b. Wakefield; J. S. Wentworth (Wakefield) and Martha A. Wentworth (Somersworth)
Arnette, d. 3/8/1926 at 66/9/0; housekeeper; married; b. Alton; Augustus Ricker (Wakefield) and Nancy J. Colbath (Middleton); burial in New Durham

Benjamin, d. 6/15/1926 in New Durham at 78/11/18; farmer; married; b. Farmington; David Wentworth (Milton) and Charlotte Corson (Milton)

Elvira, d. 9/25/1920 in New Durham at 87/1/19; housekeeper; widow; b. Barnstead; Obadiah Littlefield (Strafford) and Susan Miles (Gilmanton)

Ethelda Mae, d. 2/12/1998 in Dover; b. 5/10/1926*

Irene M., d. 7/22/1985 in Waltham, MA at 85

Mabel, d. 3/6/1934 in New Durham at 78/11/19; widow; b. Nottingham; Frank Marston and ----- McCoy

Moses L., d. 1/4/1904 in New Durham at 73/10/7; heart disease; farmer; married; b. Lebanon, ME; William Wentworth (Lebanon, ME) and Ann Legro (Lebanon, ME)

N. I., d. 2/15/1941 in New Durham at 80/3/23; housewife; widow; b. So. Berwick, ME; Charles Durgin (So. Berwick, ME) and Mary Gould (Stratham)

Nettie E., d. 10/4/1932 in New Durham at 69/2/16; housekeeper; widow; b. Lebanon, ME; Moses L. Wentworth (Lebanon, ME) and Sophronia Copp (Lebanon, ME)

Robert W., d. 9/18/1931 in New Durham at 70/2/4; farmer; married; b. Barnstead; Ambrose J. Wentworth and Jane E. Littlefield

Sophia, d. 12/29/1908 in New Durham at 73/3/15; cerebral degeneration; housewife; widow; b. W. Lebanon, ME; Isaac Copp (W. Lebanon, ME) and Betsy Wentworth (W. Lebanon, ME)

WHEELER,
James W., d. 8/21/1998 in New Durham at 40**
Margaret J., d. 6/30/1986 in New Durham at 62
Mildred T., d. 10/14/1992 in New Durham at 58
Russell T., d. 10/31/1985 in Rochester at 58

WHELDEN,
Leonora Dyer, d. 5/31/1962 in Wolfeboro at 70
Roy M., Sr., d. 1/29/1969 in Concord at 76

WHELLER,
Clair G., d. 1/29/1994 in Rochester at 55

WHITE,
Anna M., d. 10/31/1976 in Wolfeboro at 70

WHITNEY,
Harold E., d. 4/30/1974 in Wolfeboro at 71

WIGGIN,
George E., d. 2/19/1916 in New Durham at 57/5/25; farmer; married; b. Farmington; Stephen Wiggin (Moultonboro) and Lydia Foss (Strafford)

WILKES,
George T., d. 5/6/1937 in New Durham at 72/7/21; retired engineer; married; b. Thompson, CT

WILKINS,
Olif M., d. 5/26/1972 in New Durham at 64

WILLETT,
Bessie W., d. 7/22/1962 in New Durham at 83
Joseph, d. 8/6/1916 in New Durham at 53/7
Lloyd J., d. 2/14/1908 in New Durham at 0/6/14; organic heart disease; b. New Durham; Joseph Willett (Canada, laborer) and Bessie J. Ayers (New Durham)

WILLEY,
son, d. 12/8/1887 in New Durham at 0/0/0; b. New Durham; Charles F. Willey (New Durham) and Minnie F. Willey (Natick, MA)
son, d. 10/5/1891 in New Durham at 0/0/18; premature birth; b. New Durham; Edward Willey (New Durham) and Mary Randall (New Durham)
Albert I., d. 4/22/1964 in Laconia at 93

Almina D., d. 1/8/1931 in New Durham at 89/3/20; widow; b. Belgrade, ME; Isaac Willey (New Durham) and Louisa Bickford (Belgrade, ME)

Annie M., d. 10/22/1952 in Wakefield at 84

Edward M., d. 1/15/1951 at 87/3/14

Elizabeth, d. 3/23/1922 in New Durham at 27/5/5; housewife; married; b. New Durham; Henry Willey (New Durham) and Gertrude Randall (New Durham)

Ellen P., d. 7/12/1932 in New Durham at 79/10/23; housekeeper; widow; b. New Durham; Silas Tibbets (Farmington) and Lois Grace (New Durham)

George E., d. 1/7/1959 in New Durham at 70/9/7

George I., d. 2/3/1926 in New Durham at 71/8/12; farmer; single; Isaac Willey and Lovisa Bickford

Isaac S., d. 5/24/1895 in New Durham at 83; septicemia; farmer; married

Jennie M., d. 5/17/1930 in Rochester at 71/9/10; housework; widow; b. Natick, MA; Woodbury Keneson (NH) and Mary Penney

John, d. 1/10/1891 in New Durham at 86/4/25; consumption; farmer; widower; b. New Durham; Bartholomew Willey (New Durham) and Dolley Rankin (Milton)

John M., d. 7/5/1901 in New Durham at 58/5/1; nephritis; farmer; widower; b. New Durham; Alfred Willey and Mary Miller

John W., d. 5/5/1904 in New Durham at 61/11/14; farmer; married

Leslie L., d. 1/21/1935 in Rochester at 38/8/30; laborer; married; b. New Durham; Edward M. Willey (New Durham) and Mary A. Randall (New Durham)

Lovisa, d. 3/29/1912 in New Durham at 92/9/21; heart failure; housewife; widow; b. Dearborn, ME; William Bickford and Polly Burdon

Lyman A., d. 4/18/1916 in New Durham at 59/3/24; stock fitter; married; b. New Durham; Stephen Willey (New Durham) and Almira Willey (Belgrade, ME)

Mary A., d. 11/30/1923 in New Durham at 52/1/18; housewife; married; b. New Durham; Frank Randall (New Durham) and Cora Ellis

Mary E., d. 11/14/1898 in New Durham at 56/1/4; Brights dis.; invalid; married; b. New Durham; Chase Durgin (New Durham) and Fannie Davis (New Durham)

Mary F., d. 2/4/1892 in New Durham at 80/8/9; consumption; housekeeper; widow; b. Milton; Henry Miller (Milton) and Mary Rines (Milton)

Reuel W., d. 6/6/1905 in New Durham at 78/9/9; cancer of leg; farmer; widower; b. New Durham; Joseph Willey (New Durham) and Martha Stevens (Belgrade, ME)

Stephen, d. 8/19/1915 in New Durham at 88/7/15; arteriosclerosis; farmer; widower; b. New Durham; John Willey and Lovey Watson (Alton)

WINN,

Caleb W., d. 1/18/1909 in New Durham at 73/9/6; chronic uremia; farmer; married; b. Lebanon, ME; Jotham Winn and Mary Wentworth

David B., d. 3/21/1909 in New Durham at 11/0/8; pneumonia; single; b. Farmington; George E. Winn (Lebanon, ME) and Helen Barker (Farmington)

George E., d. 3/22/1955 at 80

Helen B., d. 8/23/1929 in New Durham at 55/3/9; housewife; married; b. Farmington; John H. Barker (Wolfeboro) and Ella T. Leighton (Farmington)

Sarah, d. 6/25/1915 in New Durham at 76/10/19; chronic myocarditis; retired; widow; b. Lebanon, ME

WITHAM,

Jerome B., d. 12/2/1897 in New Durham at 66/6/7; paralysis; farmer; married; b. New Durham; Moses Witham and Lydia Ducois (New Durham)

Mellissa, d. 10/12/1909 in New Durham at 70/5/7; acute dysentery; housekeeper; widow; b. Holderness; Royal Downing (Holderness) and Fanny Prescott (Holderness)

WOODARD,
Audris, d. 9/19/1945 in New Durham at 33/3/3; housewife; married; b. Wolcott, VT; Lewis Aiken (Woodbury, VT) and Bernice Alger (Lowell, VT)

WOODMAN,
Albert, d. 6/17/1919 in New Durham at 71/4/27; farmer; single; b. Alton; Jonathan Woodman (Alton) and Hannah Rollins (Alton)
Hannah, d. 4/15/1915 in New Durham at 83/7/23; chron. int. nephritis; housewife; widow; b. Alton; John Rollins and Polly Perkins (Middleton)
Henry, d. 12/1/1918 in New Durham at 64/11/3; farmer; widower; b. Alton; Jonathan Woodman (Alton) and Hannah Woodman (Alton)

WOODSIDE,
William C., d. 9/4/1986 in Rochester at 68

WOODSUM,
Mary A., d. 10/28/1904 in New Durham at 79/11/11; senectus; housewife; widow; b. Pelham; Jesse Coburn and Abigail Hardy

WOODWARD,
Bert Otis, d. 7/24/1937 in New Durham at 58/10/5; stone sawyer; married; b. Franklin Falls; George E. Woodward (Northfield, VT) and Sarah Brown (Boscawen)

WRIGHT,
Bertha A., d. 5/24/1936 in New Durham at 50/10/20; housekeeper; single; b. New Durham; Frank I. Wright (Milton) and Abbie C. Jenkins (New Durham)

WYATT,
Ruth L., d. 12/1/1967 in Wolfeboro at 75
William C., d. 12/24/1980 in Rochester at 86

YEATON,
Hattie, d. 8/8/1920 in New Durham at 65/2; housewife; married; b. Ireland; Michael Hogan (Ireland) and ----- McCarthy (Ireland)
William A., d. 11/8/1923 in New Durham at 61/7/8; B and M. engineer; married; b. Seabrook; Joseph Yeaton and Anna G. Greene

YORK,
George A., d. 3/20/1910 in New Durham at 20/9/19; pneumonia; laborer; single; b. Farmington; Wells York (Pittsfield, laborer) and Lizzie Jordan
Mary A., d. 1/20/1969 in Rochester at 48
Mary C., d. 11/9/1937 in New Durham at 87/9/22; at home; divorced; b. Rochester; Edward Ellis (Alton) and Mary Watson

YOUNG,
Ala'da W., d. 7/7/1894 in New Durham at 64/11/15; apoplexy; laborer; widower; b. Farmington; Jonathan Young (Lebanon, ME) and Alice Peavey (Milton)
Edwin R., d. 7/29/1914 in New Durham at 66/7/20; farmer; married; b. Barrington; Jonathan Young (NH) and Sophia (NH)
Effie A., d. 12/18/1956 at 79
Fred S., d. 3/22/1938 in New Durham at 1/3/14; single; b. New Durham; Herman F. Young (Middleton) and Nellie A. Fogg (Gilmanton)
Herman F., Sr., d. 7/29/1976 in Rochester at 64
Josiah B., d. 9/17/1894 in New Durham at 73/0/1; accident; laborer; widower; b. Alton
Lewis F., d. 8/24/1935 in New Durham at 68/11/7; farmer; married; b. Middleton; John H. Young (Tuftonboro) and Eliza M. Clark (Middleton)
Perley, d. 7/23/1967 in Wolfeboro at 69

ZINS,
Alfred J., d. 11/21/1988 in New Durham at 68

MIDDLETON BIRTHS

ADAMS,
Beatrice A., b. 4/11/1924; fourth; Horace Adams (lumberman, Atkinson) and Sarah S. Page (Hampstead)
Myles Kelly, b. 11/22/1988; Jeffrey Adams and Eileen Streeter

ALLARD,
Charlotte Lynn, b. 10/7/1998; Charles S. Allard and Tammy Lynn Seale
Paul Smith, b. 6/9/1997; Charles S. Allard and Tanmy L. Seale

ALLFREY,
Katie Lynn, b. 2/16/1986; Frederic Allfrey and Kathleen Peterson

AMMANN,
Amanda Lynn, b. 3/18/1986; George Ammann and Robin Ferro

ANDERSON,
Rebecca May, b. 5/31/1990; Hames L. Anderson and Betty S. Eaton

ANZALONE,
Christopher Vincent, b. 1/22/1985 in Rochester; John Anzalone and Sharon Penny

AUSTIN,
Joshua Noah, b. 9/28/1998; Barry D. Austin and Linda Lee Green

BADGER,
Jeremiah Thomas, b. 6/9/1997; Edward F. Badger III and Sheila M. Buckley
Michael A., b. 6/24/1987; Edward Badger and Sheila Buckley

BAKER,
Courtney, b. 4/5/1990; Kenneth E. Baker and Violet Buckland

BALDWIN,
Leonard R., b. 6/29/1957; Richard Baldwin and Gail Tufts

Shelly Lee, b. 11/27/1961; Richard E. Baldwin and Gail A. Tufts

BARKER,
Benjamin Burgess, b. 5/10/1989; John Barker and Teena Seale

BATES,
Kathelyn Talia, b. 6/23/1991; Robert A. Bates and Jo-Ann A. Bates

BEAN,
Jeffery Douglas, b. 7/24/1976; John and Edith Darlene Bean
Michelle Rene, b. 7/4/1978; John Irving Bean and Edith Darlene Doane

BELANGER,
Ryan Perry, b. 2/6/1991; Perry H. Belanger and Concetta L. Stracuzzi

BELL,
Edwin F., b. 10/20/1960; Robert L. Bell and Elizabeth J. Worden
Regina A., b. 6/14/1959; Robert L. Bell and Elizabeth J. Worden

BERRY,
Alvin F., III, b. 9/3/1987; Alvin Berry, Jr. and Patricia Hartley
John Hartley, b. 2/2/1990; Alvin F. Berry, Jr. and Patricia D. Hartley

BIGLOW,
Jessica M., b. 9/18/1977; Donald R. Biglow and Marianne Archer

BISHOP,
Richard C., Jr., b. 6/1/1948 in Rochester; second; Richard C. Bishop (laborer, Lynn, MA) and Ruby I. Regan (Lynn, MA)

BLIDBERG,
Nicholas Jessie, b. 4/11/1995; Walter D. Blidberg, Sr. and Debra T. Nasuti
Walter David, Jr., b. 5/3/1992; Walter D. Blidberg and Debra T. Nasuti

BOLDUC,
Jessie M., b. 6/9/1987; Michael Bolduc and Heidi Bradburn
Keith Richard, b. 3/2/1989; Michael Bolduc and Heidi Bradburn

BOLLES,
Paul Alvin, b. 9/1/1941; first; Clifford Roy Bolles (mason's helper, Belfast, ME) and Helen Mabel Eastman (Middleton)

BOUCHER,
Roger Gerard, Jr., b. 12/22/1991; Roger G. Boucher and Marjorie H. Boucher
Shayna Leigh, b. 5/17/1996; Roger G. Boucher, Sr. and Marjorie H. Harwood

BOWDEN,
Matthew Glen, b. 2/16/1996; Donald A. Bowden and Andrea J. Urquhart

BOWLES,
Norman Edward, b. 7/8/1947 in Rochester; first; Norman Franklin Bowles (mill worker, Rochester) and Carlyne Pauline Cook (Union)
Vincent W., b. 8/26/1950 in Rochester; fourth; Carlyle G. Bowles (truck driver, NH) and Martha R. Hill (NH)

BOWLEY,
Roger Edward, b. 11/10/1980; Norman A. Bowley and Georgia D. Perkins

BRADFORD,
Caroline B., b. 6/22/1906; second; Baury deB. Bradford (electrician, 25, Kittery, ME) and Annie V. Lawrence (21, Exeter); residence - Boston, MA
Robert Forbes, b. 8/6/1912; fourth; Banry B. Bradford (ele. engineer, 31, Kittery, ME) and Annie V. Lawrence (27, Exeter)

BRANNAN,
Bonnie Lee, b. 6/30/1960; Gerard E. Brannan and Elizabeth Cassell
Donna M., b. 5/18/1959; Gerard E. Brannan and Elizabeth A. Cassell
Francis Joseph, b. 8/15/1936; second; Norbert Brannan (war veteran, East Boston, MA) and Rose Tufts (Middleton)
George P., Jr., b. 1/14/1964; George P. Brannan and Judith Young
George Paul, b. 7/19/1937 in Rochester; third; Norbert Brannan (veteran, East Boston, MA) and Rosy Tufts (Middleton)
Gregory Nicholas, b. 11/28/1994; George Brannan, Jr. and Adrienne L. Thomas
Guard Edward, b. 4/26/1939 in Rochester; fourth; Norbert Brannan (veteran, East Boston, MA) and Ruby Tufts (Middleton)
Thomas V., b. 10/22/1934 in Rochester; first; Norbert Brannan (East Boston, MA) and Ruby Tufts (Middleton)

BREWER,
Catherine E., b. 6/7/1949 in Rochester; first; James W. Brewer (lumberman, NH) and Louise A. Herr (MA)
James W., Jr., b. 8/24/1950 in Rochester; second; James W. Brewer (woodsman, NH) and Louise Ann Herr (MA)
John L., b. 8/31/1954 in Rochester; Aaron W. Brewer and Lillian A. Basworth

BREWSTER,
Heather Noel, b. 3/30/1989; Steve Brewster and Stacy Goff

BROOKS,
Angel, b. 6/28/1979; Theodore Brooks, Sr. and Gail Gorton
Bonnie Lyn, b. 5/29/1967; Louis W. Brooks and Mary L. Fifield
Gary F., b. 2/28/1956 in Rochester; Carlyle G. Brooks and Martha Hill
George M., b. 10/24/1954 in Rochester; Carlyle G. Brooks and Martha K. Hill
James Elmer, b. 10/11/1953 in Rochester; Carlyle Gordon Brooks (Rochester) and Martha Kimball Hill (Wakefield)

Louis Waldo, b. 5/14/1947 in Rochester; first; Carlyle Gordon Brooks (planer, Rochester) and Martha Kimball Hill (Wakefield)
Samuel C., b. 4/1/1948 in Rochester; second; Carlyle G. Brooks (planer, Rochester) and Martha K. Hill (Wakefield)
Sandra D., b. 6/13/1952 in Rochester; fifth; Carlyle Brooks (woodsman, Rochester) and Martha K. Hill (Wakefield)
Terrie Lee, b. 2/23/1957; Carlyle Brooks and Martha Hill
Theodore C., b. 2/17/1949 in Rochester; third; Carlyle G. Brooks (oil company, NH) and Martha K. Hill (NH)
Vincent E., b. 7/8/1965; Louis Brooks and Mary Fifield

BROWN,
James G., b. 7/6/1956 in Rochester; William A. Brown and June Tufts
Kelly Jean, b. 5/21/1978; James Gordon Brown and Jean Anne Merrill
Kendra Lee, b. 9/10/1980; James G. Brown and Jean A. Merrill
Natalie Lee, b. 6/9/1945 in Rochester; second; William A. Brown (lineman, New Durham) and June Tufts (Middleton)
Wanda Irene, b. 10/6/1951 in Rochester; third; William A. Brown (lineman, New Durham) and June S. Tufts (Middleton)
Wendell M., b. 7/31/1955 in Rochester; William A. Brown and June S. Tufts
William Alfred, Jr., b. 7/28/1943 in Rochester; first; William Alfred Brown (lineman, New Durham) and June St. Clair Tufts (Middleton)

BRUEDLE,
Suzanne Marie, b. 2/20/1980; Robert William Bruedle and Sandra May Emery

BRYANT,
Kierstin Marie, b. 7/4/1998; Travis Bryant and Kelly J. Brown

BULLIS,
Jean Elizabeth, b. 12/2/1945 in Rochester; second; Eric A. Bullis, Jr. (truck driver, Haverhill, MA) and E. Edna Eastman (Middleton)

Richard Addison, b. 4/26/1943 in Rochester; first; Eric Addison Bullis, Jr. (mill employee, Haverhill, MA) and Elizabeth Edna Eastman (Middleton)

Stewart W., b. 6/21/1934 in Rochester; eighth; Eric A. Bullis (shoeworker, Westminster, MA) and Viola F. Griffin (Haverhill, MA)

BURLEIGH,
son [Ray], b. 9/11/1896; fifth; Harry A. Burleigh (shoemaker, 29, Portsmouth) and Estella M. Tuttle (38, Middleton)

son, b. 5/24/1900; sixth; Harry A. Burleigh (shoemaker, 33, Portsmouth) and Estella M. Tuttle (40, Middleton)

BURNHAM,
Donald Edwin, b. 7/6/1934 in Rochester; third; Nelson Burnham (mill employee, NB) and Doris Moore (Lebanon)

BURNS,
James William, b. 10/13/1945 in Rochester; second; George William Burns (electrician, RI) and Emma F. Tufts (Middleton)

BURROWS,
daughter [Bessie], b. 11/25/1902; third; David Burrows, Jr. (farmer, 41, Middleton) and Mina Pinkham (29, Middleton)

son [John A.], b. 10/25/1910; fifth; David E. Burrows (farmer, 50, Middleton) and Mina E. Pinkham (37, Middleton)

Andrew John, b. 10/4/1980; Richard A. Burrows and Kim W. Dixon

Arthur J., b. 4/22/1958; John A. Burrows and Millie A. Pervere

Faith Jeannette Kim, b. 5/27/1985 in Wolfeboro; Richard Burrows and Kim Dixon

Helen R., b. 4/14/1905; fourth; David E. Burrows (farmer, 43, Middleton) and Mina E. Pinkham (32, Milton)

Judith Ann, b. 9/1/1948 in Rochester; second; George D. Burrows (shoe shop, Middleton) and Janet M. Bullis (Haverhill, MA)

Keith Michael, b. 9/21/1991; Arthur J. Burrows and Brenda L. Doe

Laura Agnes, b. 7/21/1898; second; David Burrows (farmer, 34, Middleton) and Mina Pinkham (23, Middleton)
Lorraine Mary, b. 3/30/1951 in Rochester; first; John A. Burrows (lumber, Middleton) and Millie A. Pervere (East Stratford)
Mark C., b. 8/5/1894; first; David Burrows (farmer, 32, Middleton) and Mina Pinkham (21, Middleton)
Paul A., b. 8/6/1952 in Rochester; second; John A. Burrows (sawmill, Middleton) and Millie A. Pervere (No. Strafford)
Richard A., b. 7/29/1960; John A. Burrows and Millie A. Pervere

BUTLER,

Brian Curtis, b. 12/7/1961; Kenneth A. Butler and Catherine V. Buchanan
Kenneth Allen, b. 1/5/1943; second; Clifford Roy Butler (laborer, Belfast, ME) and Helen Mabel Eastman (Middleton)
Phyllis A., b. 6/26/1964; Kenneth Butler and Catherine V. Buchanan
Randolph Keith, b. 3/16/1963; Kenneth Butler and Catherine Vera Buchanan
Wayne Edward, b. 11/17/1948 in Rochester; fourth; Clifford Butler (laborer, Belfast, ME) and Helen Eastman (Middleton)

CAMERON,

Brenda L., b. 9/30/1964; Lawrence C. Cameron and Katheryne B. Richards
Colby Steven, b. 1/3/1991; Steve S. Cameron and Darlene T. Smith
Debra Lynn, b. 4/19/1961; Lawrence Cameron and Kathryne B. Richard
Donna Jean, b. 9/12/1958; Lawrence C. Cameron and Kathryne B. Richards

CANN,
Crystal Marie, b. 10/23/1989; Robert Cann and Janice Ela

CAPLETTE,
Jacob Wayne, b. 9/28/1995; Alan R. Caplette and Lisa M. Shannon
Joshua Alan, b. 9/21/1992; Alan R. Caplette and Lisa M. Shannon

Kaitlyn Marie, b. 4/15/1997; Alan R. Caplette and Lisa M. Shannon

CARDINAL,
Erric Mack, b. 3/21/1926; third; John Cardinal, Jr. (lumberman, Epping) and Helen Burrows (Middleton); residence - Alton

CARNEY,
Thomas Joseph, b. 4/17/1986; Thomas Carney and Tracy Wadsworth

CARON,
Adam Clayton, b. 9/22/1978; Stephen Michael Caron and Marie Anne Lehoullier

CARR,
Patrick Coty, b. 8/12/1991; Scott J. Carr and Vickie M. Goslin
Zachary Webber, b. 3/2/1994; Scott J. Carr and Vickie May Goslin

CASAVANT,
Mary Jane, b. 7/23/1939; second; Joseph Casavant (shoe worker, Middleton) and M. Dorothy Fossett (Boston, MA)

CATHCART,
Paul Burton, b. 8/2/1940; second; Hubert Roland Cathcart (leatherboard, Farmington) and Pauline May Lany (Alton)

CHAPMAN,
Eliza, b. 11/11/1898; sixth; Willie A. Chapman (night watchman, 33, Dover) and Amelia Battersby (30, New York, NY)

CHESLEY,
Anne Jean, b. 4/8/1979; Gary Chesley and Dorothy C. Sindorf
Jamie Lynn, b. 3/23/1976; James M. Chesley and Debra L. Frost
Matthew John, b. 4/19/1979; James Chesley and Debra Frost
Michael A., b. 3/10/1977; James M. Chesley and Debra L. Frost

COLBATH,
Ricky E., b. 5/3/1955 in Rochester; Richard P. Colbath and Virginia Stevens

COMMONS,
Laura Ashley, b. 11/20/1996; Peter K. Commons and Beth Jane Carver

CONNELL,
Roane Lisa, b. 9/2/1979; Robert F. Connell and Diane M. Ball

COOK,
daughter [Helen M.], b. 8/5/1887; third; D. Smith Cook (farmer, 32, Middleton) and Lucy A. Hill (38, Middleton)
son [Clarence E.], b. 12/26/1905; third; Edwin Cook (mill operative, 38, Middleton) and Ena M. Jones (25, Middleton)
daughter, b. 5/27/1929; third; Clarence Cook (laborer, Middleton) and Pauline Tufts (Middleton)
Charles Linwood, b. 2/14/1907; fourth; Edwin Cook (laborer, 39, Middleton) and Ennie M. Jones (26, Middleton)
Eva May, b. 8/14/1901; first; Edward Cook (farmer, 34, Middleton) and Eunice May Jones (21, Middleton)
Flora, b. 3/7/1903; Edwin Cook (farmer, Middleton) and Enni M. Jones (Middleton)
George Harry, b. 9/25/1938 in Rochester; third; Charles L. Cook (beaterman, Middleton) and Dorothy E. Poore (Landaff)
Kenneth, b. 6/8/1915; second; Fred R. Cook (farmer, 31, Middleton) and Ella F. Moulton (23, York, ME)
Michael Robert, Jr., b. 9/3/1996; Michael R. Cook and Lisa M. Chartier
Norman Edward, b. 7/26/1926; first; Clarence E. Cook (mill hand, Middleton) and Pauline D. Tufts (Middleton)

COOLIDGE,
Tiffany Marie, b. 6/18/1989; Harland Coolidge, Jr. and Cassandra DiPrizio

COPE,
David P., b. 5/11/1954 in Rochester; Daniel P. Cope and Kathleen C. Peters

CORBETT,
Sarah Ashley, b. 7/2/1985 in Wolfeboro; Richard Corbett and Cheryl Haramut

CREMMEN,
Collene Janet, b. 4/14/1988; Daniel Cremmen and Darlene Wade

CUNNINGHAM,
David Michael, b. 10/3/1970; Harvey J. Cunningham and Sharon Lee Grace

CURRIER,
Samuel Victor, b. 11/2/1986; Samuel Currier and Vickie Patch

DADURA,
Morgan Carol Fuller, b. 6/29/1984

DALY,
Keith A., b. 6/1/1973; James C. Daly and Susan H. Stodder

DAME,
Daniel Oscar, b. 6/27/1898; first; Daniel C. Dame (weaver, 25, Portsmouth) and Minnie M. Smith (18, Farmington)

DAMON,
Marsha Elaine, b. 7/14/1978; James Robert Damon and Kathie Elaine Nason
Philip James, b. 7/14/1978; James Robert Damon and Kathie Elaine Nason

DAVENPORT,
Michael William, b. 11/17/1989; Michael Davenport and Charlotte May

DEBROUX,
Travis Adam, b. 9/4/1979; Guy A. DeBroux and Jennifer G. Lee

DECHANIO,
Lester E., b. 3/23/1938 in Rochester; first; Raymond Dechanio (clerk, Sanbornville) and Addie C. Kimball (Alfred, ME)

DEVENEAU,
Althea Frances, b. 3/27/1946 in Rochester; second; Frederick Deveneau (ship fitter, San Francisco, CA) and Nellie F. Gregson (San Francisco, CA); residence - Union

DIGIOVANNI,
Cody James, b. 1/13/1988; Steven DiGiovanni, Jr. and Jill Power

DIMOCK,
Jenna K., b. 1/16/1987; Jeffrey Dimock and Gina Lewis

DION,
Dawn M., b. 10/11/1973; Leo V. Dion and Wanda M. Soucy

DIPRIZIO,
Albert C., b. 3/14/1949 in Rochester; first; John H. DiPrizio (manager, Middleton) and Enid M. Lowd (ME)
Alvino Charles, b. 3/15/1928; fifth; Charles DiPrizio (farmer, Italy) and Louisa Barletta (Italy)
Anthony V., b. 1/15/1937; eighth; Charles DiPrizio (builder, Italy) and Louise Barletta (Italy)
Carmen John, b. 12/13/1953; John DiPrizio and Enid M. Lowd
Cassandra Mara, b. 2/25/1971; Charles C. DiPrizio and Earleen S. Dodier

Charles, b. 10/15/1932; seventh; Charles DiPrizio (stone mason, Italy) and Louise Barletta (Italy)

Curt C., b. 3/7/1973; Charles Constandino DiPrizio and Earleen S. Dodier

Edward C., b. 7/20/1960; Charles DiPrizio, Jr. and Sonia D. Hector

Eleanor L., b. 10/12/1930; sixth; Charles DiPrizio (stone mason, Italy) and Louisa Barletta (Italy)

James J., b. 10/14/1955 in Rochester; Alvino C. DiPrizio and Rosemarie T. Long

James John, Jr., b. 3/1/1984

Jean Marie, b. 11/15/1954 in Rochester; Alvino C. DiPrizio and Rosemarie T. Long

Jessica, b. 6/28/1986; James DiPrizio and Shirley Murphy

Joanne Marie, b. 6/10/1963; Alvino Charles DiPrizio and Rosemarie Theresa Long

John D., b. 9/22/1922; third; Charles D'Prizio (farmer, Naples, Italy) and Louise Berrletto (Naples, Italy)

Jonathan Charles, b. 8/21/1980; Joseph C. DiPrizio and Kimberly A. LeFavour

Joseph C., b. 10/14/1955 in Rochester; Alvino C. DiPrizio and Rosemarie T. Long

Joseph Charles, Jr., b. 8/1/1978; Joseph C. DiPrizio and Kimberly Lefavor

Karen Marie, b. 5/2/1978; James John DiPrizio and Shirley Jean Murphy

Kathy Jean, b. 9/30/1979; James J. DiPrizio and Shirley J. Murphy

Prisco N., b. 7/21/1924; fourth; Charles M. D'Prizio (farmer, Italy) and Louisa Barletta (Italy)

Ryan George, b. 9/11/1976; Carmen and Joyce DiPrizio

Signe Louise, b. 4/2/1971; Charles DiPrizio, Jr. and Sonia D. Hector

Tania Michelle, b. 9/18/1972; Michael A. DiPrizio and Maria C. Ianniciello

Timothy Michael, b. 12/12/1962; Charles DiPrizio, Jr. and Sonia Dolores Hector

DIXON,
Justin Robert, b. 10/24/1986; Kelly Dixon and Tami Dow
Kevin David, b. 2/16/1984
Michelle Ruth, b. 5/6/1969 in Rochester; Wilbur J. and Jeannette M. Dixon

DOOLEY,
Cecelia M., b. 2/3/1987; Paul Dooley and Rosemarie Marshall

DOW,
Brenda Lee, b. 7/2/1957; Robert Dow and Joan Tufts
Randy Myron, b. 9/4/1967; Robert E. Dow and Joan L. Tufts
Tami L., b. 6/14/1964; Robert E. Dow and Joan L. Tufts
Wayne E., b. 1/7/1959; Robert E. Dow and Joan L. Tufts

DOWNS,
Sara Ann, b. 7/1/1949 in Rochester; first; Fred W. Downs (knife factory, NH) and Virginia A. Stevens (NH)

DREW,
son [Robert B.], b. 7/25/1904; second; Ellsworth Drew (farmer, 35, Eaton) and Flora Bryant (28, Freedom)
Candy Lee, b. 10/25/1960; Forrest W. Drew and Linda D. Stevens
Elmer E., b. 11/17/1912; third; Ellsworth Drew (farmer, 42, Eaton) and Flora Bryant (36, Freedom)
John J., b. 12/18/1893; eighth; Horace Drew (farmer, 43, Eaton) and Maggie E. Walker (39, Ireland)
Kathy Lynn, b. 8/3/1958; Forrest W. Drew and Linda O. Stevens
Lisa Ann, b. 3/15/1963; Forrest Warren Drew and Linda Ora Stevens
Lucenda M., b. 10/10/1902; first; Ellsworth Drew (farmer, 32, Eaton) and Flora M. Bryant (26, Freedom)

DUCHANLIN,
Cora, b. 5/11/1902; first; Moses Duchanlin (laborer, 27, Canada) and Mary Welch (17, Camden)

DUNLOP,
Eva May, b. 4/30/1909; sixth; Thomas Dunlop (46, St. Johns, NB) and Mary E. Claven (36, Vanceboro, ME)

DUPREY,
Diana Lynn, b. 1/14/1966; Louis W. Duprey and Paula A. Vachon
Donald W., b. 8/12/1964; Louis W. Duprey and Paula A. Vachon
Lynda K., b. 4/3/1949 in Rochester; second; Wilfred J. Duprey (shoe shop, MA) and Clare M. Cochrane (MA)

DURKEE,
Julie Mae, b. 7/14/1957; Donald Durkee and Lorraine Benton

EASTMAN,
daughter, b. 4/28/1909; first; Charles F. Eastman (farmer, 26, Milton) and Mary A. Tufts (18, Middleton)
daughter, b. 4/2/1914; fourth; Charles F. Eastman (farmer, 34, Milton) and Mary A. Tufts (24, Middleton)
son [Loyde R.], b. 7/22/1916; sixth; Charles F. Eastman (farmer, 33, Milton) and Mary A. Tufts (26, Middleton)
son [John], b. 8/19/1919; ninth; Charles F. Eastman (farmer, Milton) and Mary A. Tufts (Middleton)
daughter, b. 10/29/1921; tenth; Charles F. Eastman (farmer, Middleton) and Mary A. Tufts (Middleton)
daughter, b. 3/6/1923; eleventh; Charles E. Eastman (farmer, Middleton) and Mary A. Tufts (Middleton)
Bertha May, b. 9/5/1917; seventh; Charles F. Eastman (farmer, 34, Middleton) and Mary A. Tufts (27, Middleton)
Dorothy, b. 9/21/1911; third; Charles F. Eastman (farmer, 28, Milton) and Mary A. Tufts (21, Middleton)
Harry Hanson, b. 7/22/1946 in Rochester; first; Harry Eastman (truck driver, Middleton) and Evelyn Holman (Lexington, MA)
Jo-Ann Enola, b. 1/22/1943 in Rochester; second; Waldo Hill (molder) and Anna Beryl Eastman (Middleton)
Joyce Elaine, b. 10/6/1943 in Rochester; first; Rene Maxfield (shoe shop) and Ruth Ellen Eastman (Middleton)

Leo P., b. 10/28/1910; second; Charles F. Eastman (farmer, 27, Milton) and Mary A. Tufts (20, Middleton)

Nancy Lee, b. 6/29/1945 in Rochester; second; Ruth E. Eastman (Middleton)

Phyllis Audrey, b. 7/30/1947 in Rochester; second; Harry Hanson Eastman (lumberman, Middleton) and Evelyn May Holman (Lexington, MA)

Ruth E., b. 8/2/1918; eighth; Charles F. Eastman (farmer, Milton) and Mary A. Tufts (Middleton)

EDGERLY,
Pearl I., b. 7/10/1956 in Rochester; Chester G. Edgerly and Ethel Hale
Raymond C., b. 7/28/1958; Chester G. Edgerly and Ethel E. Hale

ELLINGWOOD,
Michelle L., b. 9/15/1974; Maynard and Margaret Ellingwood

ELLIOTT,
daughter [Blanche I.], b. 8/25/1909; twelfth; Frank H. Elliott (teamster, 31, Stoneham, MA) and Minnie Graton (34, Manchester)

George Everett, b. 4/19/1908; eleventh; Frank H. Elliott (woodsman, 31, Stoneham, MA) and Minnie Graton (33, Manchester)

EMERSON,
Tina Marie, b. 8/29/1973; Harold A. Emerson and Carol J. Ellingwood

EMERY,
Kristin Ann, b. 6/16/1992; John P. Emery and Cathy A. Ledoux

ESTES,
Caitlin Christine, b. 12/1/1988; Richard Estes and Patricia Theberge

EVANS,
Jordan Dean, b. 1/26/1996; John D. Evans and Susan A. Jones

EVENS,
Robert C., b. 2/22/1893; first; Charles W. Evens (teamster, 24, Alton) and Alice A. Tibbetts (17, Rochester)

FRANCIS,
Peter John, b. 8/13/1980; Richard B. Francis and Anne M. Duston

FRANKLIN,
Crystal Angeline, b. 9/4/1984

FULLER,
Matthew Myron, b. 3/14/1980; Peter T. Fuller and Christine M. Olshewsky

GAGNON,
Kelly Rosaria, b. 11/12/1996; Kenneth H. Gagnon and Bonnie E. Parker
Matthew H., b. 10/3/1987; Kenneth Gagnon and Bonnie Parker
Steven Curris, b. 7/28/1989; Kenneth Gagnon and Bonnie Parker

GARRETT,
Sara Gwen, b. 11/16/1990; Gery D. Garrett and Valerie J. Smith

GARSIDE,
daughter, b. 12/8/1912; seventh; William E. Garside (RR employee, 33, Southbridge, MA) and Sarah E. Dopheney (33, Dover, NH)

GIBSON,
Emily May, b. 11/24/1996; David N. Gibson and Dory Jane Megee

GILMORE,
daughter, b. 8/26/1905; second; Frank S. Gilmore (mill operative, 40, Milton) and Clara E. Tuttle (28, Farmington)

GLIDDEN,
Matthew Scott, b. 2/28/1985 in Rochester; Danny Glidden and Jean Stanley
Trace Amber, b. 6/13/1966; David O. Glidden and Natalie L. Brown

GOODWIN,
Justin Keith, b. 8/23/1988; Keith Goodwin and Rhonda Drew
Kristen Ann, b. 2/21/1985 in Rochester; Keith Goodwin and Rhonda Drew

GORTON,
Jacob Thaddeus, b. 11/9/1993; Stephen J. Gorton and Kristin M. Gorton
Jared Azarius, b. 2/28/1997; Stephen J. Gorton and Kristin M. Gorton

GRACE,
son, b. 5/17/1925; fourth; Joseph L. Grace (farmer, NH) and Lodema L. Cates (NH)
Donald Lee, b. 6/18/1949 in Rochester; second; Joseph Grace (lumberman, NH) and Norma M. Adams (ME)

GUSTAFSON,
Joshua David, b. 5/8/1994; Eric C. Gustafson and Kim L. Laporte
Zachary James, b. 12/20/1997; Eric C. Gustafson and Kim L. Laporte

HALEY,
Brandee Jean, b. 10/23/1988; William Haley and Helen Shave

HANCHETT,
Christopher A., b. 7/12/1974; Larry and Linda Hanchette (sic)
Nicholas R., b. 1/12/1977; Larry A. Hanchett and Linda D. Tripp
Robert Christopher, b. 10/1/1996; Christopher A. Hanchett and Stephanie A. Martin

HARMON,
Gordon J., b. 6/19/1958; John F. Harmon and Thelma E. Meserve

HARTFORD,
stillborn daughter, b. 4/25/1906; first; Alonzo G. Hartford (fireman, 35, E. Rochester) and Maud M. Tibbetts (28, Haverhill, MA); residence - Lebanon, ME

Earle Leroy, b. 6/16/1908; third; Alonzo G. Hartford (fireman, 37, East Rochester) and Maud M. Tibbetts (30, Haverhill, MA); residence - Lebanon, ME

Effie Lenora, b. 6/16/1908; second; Alonzo G. Hartford (fireman, 37, East Rochester) and Maud M. Tibbetts (30, Haverhill, MA); residence - Lebanon, ME

Wilfred Alonzo, b. 7/4/1909; fourth; Alonzo G. Hartford (stationary fireman, 39, E. Rochester) and Maude M. Tibbetts (31, Haverhill, MA); residence - Lebanon, ME

HARTLEY,
daughter, b. 5/4/1907; Frances Hartley (27, Exeter)

HASKINS,
Mary E., b. 12/24/1958; Horace Haskins and Sadie J. Goodwin

Shirley E., b. 8/23/1952 in Rochester; third; Horace Haskins (woodsman, MA) and Sadie J. Goodwin (Barnstead)

Theresa A., b. 6/20/1948 in Rochester; first; Horace W. Haskins (woodsman, Worcester, MA) and Sadie J. Goodwin (Barnstead)

William Clifton, b. 6/5/1950 in Rochester; second; Horace W. Haskins (woodsman, MA) and Sadie J. Goodwin (NH)

HASTINGS,
Tammy Lyn, b. 2/8/1970; Everett Allen Hastings and Georgianna Tufts

HATFIELD,
Brandon Scott, b. 10/31/1988; Timothy Hatfield and Karyn Osbourne

HEBERT,
William M., b. 6/12/1987; Roger Hebert and Susan Turner

HEON,
Steven Craig, b. 7/24/1972; Martin R. Heon, Jr. and Rachel Y. Gagnon

HERBERT,
Jacob Jeffrey, b. 10/17/1990; Scott W. Herbert and Laura J. Collocci
Katelyn Marie, b. 5/5/1993; Scott W. Herbert and Laura J. Collucci

HILL,
Brenda Joyce, b. 11/12/1963; Alfred James Hill and Dorothy Ardelle Smith
Craig, b. 8/26/1959; Alfred J. Hill and Dorothy A. Smith
David James, b. 2/9/1993; James E. Hill and Tracye L. Brewer
Elaine Dawn, b. 3/30/1962 in Rochester; Alfred J. Hill and Dorothy A. Smith
Penny Lee, b. 12/15/1960; Alfred J. Hill and Dorothy A. Smith
Shane Allen, b. 8/16/1996; James E. Hill and Tracye Lynn Brewer
Thomas W., b. 11/25/1973; Alfred J. Hill and Dorothy A. Smith
Tyler Craig, b. 7/3/1998; James E. Hill and Trayce L. Brewer

HIOS,
Mathew Noel, b. 12/27/1991; Ronald P. Hios and Edith I. Gauthier

HOLLAND,
Kylee Marie, b. 7/16/1996; Robert J. Holland and Stephanie L. Holland

HUNTER,
Nicole Lynn, b. 12/8/1986; Rockie Hunter and Darlene Allen
Rocky Allen, b. 12/19/1988; Rockie Hunter and Darlene Allen

HUSSEY,
Matthew Charles, b. 1/28/1994; James M. Hussey, Sr. and Bonnie L. Coffin

JACQUES,
Lindsey Taylor, b. 9/6/1991; Richard A. Jacques, Jr. and Joyce A. Kazlauskas

JENCKES,
Scott Fitzgerald, b. 3/16/1995; Kevin M. Jenckes and Helen S. Fitzgerald

JENNESS,
daughter, b. 11/19/1928; third; Elmer E. Jenness (in leather b'd mill, Rochester) and Lucinda Drew (Middleton)
Alden Gerard, b. 4/14/1925; second; Elmer E. Jenness (farmer, Rochester) and Lucinda M. Drew (Middleton)
Clarence E., b. 5/7/1923; first; Elmer E. Jenness (mill hand, Rochester) and Lucindia M. Drew (Middleton)
Freda Lucinda, b. 2/11/1931; fourth; Elmer E. Jenness (leather board mill, Rochester) and Lucinda M. Drew (Middleton)

JOHNSON,
Brooke L., b. 6/16/1979; Bradford F. Johnson and Darlene A. LaBranche
Delilah R., b. 4/30/1987; Daniel Johnson and Suzanne Knapp
Kendra R., d. 2/20/1985 in Dover; Bradford Johnson and Darlene LaBranche
Myles B., b. 6/4/1987; Bradford Johnson and Darlene LaBranche

JOY,
Nelson Marsh, b. 11/20/1907; second; Frank D. Joy (laborer, 25, So. Berwick, ME) and Alice P. Kimball (20, Middleton); residence - Union
Stephen K., b. 11/26/1996; Philip Joy and Ann Patch

JUNE,
Andrew Josef, b. 10/21/1990; Charles W. June and Melanie J. Sroka
Kristie Molly, b. 11/30/1996; Charles W. June and Melanie J. Sroka

KEEGAN,
Cole Robert, b. 7/29/1994; James R. Keegan, Jr. and Roxanne A. Tufts
Kelsey Elizabeth, b. 5/11/1990; James R. Keegan, Jr. and Roxanne A. Tufts-Keegan

KELLEY,
Charlotte Effie, b. 8/9/1915; third; Chester A. Kelley (mill hand, 26, Allenstown) and Ada Kelley (24, Lynn, MA)

KIMBALL,
stillborn daughter, b. 2/24/1898; eighth; George Kimball (mill hand, 42, Middleton) and Eliza Hanscom (43, Dover)
Almer B., b. 2/15/1896; seventh; George W. Kimball (millhand, 40, Middleton) and Eliza S. Hanscomb (42, Dover)
Anna E., b. 7/22/1924; first; Elmer Kimball (mill hand, Middleton) and Margaret Wentworth (Milton)
David Leon, b. 2/9/1946 in Rochester; first; Alphonzo Kimball (shoe shop, Alfred, ME) and Priscilla Tufts (Middleton)
Elmer R., b. 1/29/1906; first; Oscar Kimball (brakeman, 23, Middleton) and Florence Runnells (22, Cherry Valley, MA); residence - Wakefield
Ethel, b. 1/25/1893; fifth; Frank E. Kimball (mill hand, 32, Parsonsfield, ME) and Annie Patch (23, Newfield, ME)
Viola, b. 3/22/1900; ninth; George Kimball (mill hand, 44, Middleton) and Eliza Hanscom (45, Dover)

KINNEY,
Carol Eva, b. 6/15/1947 in Rochester; second; Walter Vidito Kinney (lumberman, Westfield) and Virginia Frances Tufts (Middleton)

KINSLEY,
Tyler Brandon, b. 3/9/1995; Walter R. Kinsley and Jamie L. Glidden

KNIGHT,
Brittany Ann, b. 12/17/1992; Arthur C. Knight and Diane C. Burke

Catherine Barbara, b. 12/17/1992; Arthur C. Knight and Diane C. Burke

KNOWLES,
Joseph F., b. 3/6/1903; Charles Knowles (farmer, Middleton) and Bessie I. Keyes (No. Conway)

KUEHL,
Erik Christopher, b. 11/20/1991; Christopher W. Kuehl and Sheila Kuehl
Maria Christina, b. 10/18/1992; Christopher W. Kuehl and Sheila Alequin

LABRECQUE,
Ina May, b. 12/18/1949 in Rochester; first; Franklin D. LaBrecque (truck driver, NH) and Gloria M. Tufts (Sanford, ME); residence - Farmington
Jessie L., b. 12/20/1977; Michael G. LaBrecque and Valerie J. Michaud
Joslyn Kate, b. 3/13/1980; Michael G. LaBrecque and Valerie J. Michaud

LANCEY,
Jacob Andrew, b. 6/21/1989; Keith Lancey and Brenda Harriman

LANEY,
Russell K., b. 8/17/1954 in Rochester; Frank T. Laney and Priscilla E. Webster
Stephen G., b. 10/14/1955 in Rochester; Frank T. Laney and Priscilla Webster

LANG,
Casey Michelle, b. 2/1/1995; Robert J. Lang and Michelle L. Carter

LANGLEY,
Adam Wayne, b. 6/15/1991; Ricky E. Langley and Laurie E. Gowen

Ashley Rose, b. 6/15/1991; Ricky E. Langley and Laurie E. Gowen
Kevin Alan, b. 4/9/1986; Wallace Langley and Susan Carlson

LAPIERRE,
Christine M., b. 4/3/1974; Richard and Linda LaPierre
Cynthia Ann, b. 2/21/1963; Robert Louis-Dennis Lapierre and Carolyn Ann Wilkinson
Dennis F., b. 11/18/1968; Robert LaPierre and Carolyn Wilkinson
James E., b. 8/11/1975; Robert D. LaPierre and Carolyn Wilkinson
Jennifer A., b. 5/16/1973; Robert L.D. LaPierre and Carolyn A. Wilkinson
Jeffrey A., b. 5/16/1973; Robert L.D. LaPierre and Carolyn A. Wilkinson
Richard Ralph, b. 2/15/1976; Mr. and Mrs. Richard LaPierre
Robert Louis, b. 12/28/1961; Robert L. LaPierre and Carolyn A. Wilkinson
Timothy Edward, b. 7/9/1978; Robert Louis Dennis LaPierre and Carolyn Ann Wilkinson
Timothy Scott, b. 12/18/1979; Richard R. LaPierre and Linda S. Luongo

LASHAW,
son, b. 6/9/1887; fourth; Thomas Lashaw (laborer, 27, Canada) and Emma Orsennette (23, Canada)

LAVERTUE,
Stephen J., b. 11/11/1957; John Lavertue and Phyllis Morrill

LEAVITT,
daughter, b. 10/29/1914; second; Ralph Leavitt (teamster, 25, Wolfeboro) and Iva Whitehouse (23, Farmington); residence - Ossipee

LECLAIR,
Scott M., b. 7/23/1968; John Leclair and Kathleen Allfrey

LEIGHTON,
son, b. 12/20/1888; fifth; Charles H. Leighton (farmer, 46, Middleton) and Lucy A. Drew (36, Eaton)
son [Presco F.], b. 5/9/1899; fifth; Walter F. Leighton (carpenter, 35, Middleton) and Elizabeth S. Drew (25, Middleton)
stillborn daughter, b. 5/19/1901; third; James P. Leighton (farmer, 26, Middleton) and Etta M. Young (35, Middleton)
son, b. 11/20/1929; fifth; Presco Leighton (laborer, Middleton) and Gladys Russell (Danvers, MA)
Albert Roy, b. 9/3/1932; seventh; Presco Leighton (laborer, Middleton) and Gladys Russell (Danvers, MA)
Annie Isabelle, b. 8/15/1897; fourth; Walter F. Leighton (carpenter, 33, Middleton) and Elizabeth Drew (23, Middleton)
Bennie William, b. 12/31/1937 in Wolfeboro; fourth; William Leighton (laborer, Middleton) and Leona Grace (Tamworth)
Beulah Marjorie, b. 6/15/1936; third; William T. Leighton (laborer, Middleton) and Leona Grace (Tamworth)
Delwin H., b. 12/24/1895; third; Walter F. Leighton (carpenter, 30, Middleton) and Elizabeth S. Drew (21, Middleton)
Edwin P., b. 11/11/1924; second; Presco F. Leighton (laborer, Middleton) and Gladys E. Russell (Danvers, MA)
Eleanor Margaret, b. 7/12/1936 in Union; eighth; Presco Leighton (laborer, Middleton) and Gladys Russell (Danvers, MA)
Herbert F., b. 9/14/1930; sixth; Presco Leighton (woodsman, Middleton) and Gladys Russell (Danvers, MA)
Leo S., b. 5/15/1897; third; Charles H. Leighton (saw mill hand, -8, Meadville, PA) and Carry V. Guilford (26, Portlan, ME)
Mabel Rose, b. 6/27/1932; first; William T. Leighton (laborer, Middleton) and Leona M. Grace (Tamworth)
Madeline, b. 3/8/1903; Walter F. Leighton (carpenter, Middleton) and Elizabeth Drew (Middleton)
Molly Rosmond, b. 6/27/1939 in Rochester; fourth; William Leighton (mechanic, Middleton) and Leona Grace (Tamworth)
Rodney Willis, b. 8/9/1934; second; William T. Leighton (laborer, Middleton) and Leona M. Grace (Tamworth)

Violet M., b. 3/22/1905; eighth; Walter F. Leighton (carpenter, 39, Middleton) and Elizabeth Drew (31, Middleton)

W. F., b. 2/8/1901; sixth; Walter F. Leighton (carpenter, 36, Middleton) and Elizabeth S. Drew (27, Middleton)

LEPENE,
Anne K., b. 2/24/1964; Donald Lepene and Patricia Stevens
Danny A., b. 7/20/1958; Donald M. Lepene and Patricia A. Stevens
James L., b. 6/19/1960; Donald M. Lepene and Patricia Stevens
Patric Donald, b. 12/23/1979; Danny A. Lepene and Debra M. Gray

LESSARD,
son, b. 10/26/1927; fourth; Delphis Lessard (laborer, Canada) and Edith M. Lessard (Somersworth)
Brian Roger, b. 10/15/1958; Roger L. Lessard and Charlotte M. Stevens
Debra-Rae Mary, b. 11/14/1995; Kelly F. Lessard and Lori L. Harvey
Forrest George, b. 5/16/1922; first; Delphise Lessard (mill hand, Canada) and Edith M. Gage (Somersworth)
Margaret E., b. 5/5/1954 in Rochester; Roger L. Lessard and Charlotte M. Stevens
Robert D., b. 4/4/1924; second; Joseph D. Lessard (laborer, NH) and Edith M. Gage (NH)
Roger Leslie, b. 12/4/1925; third; Delphis Lessard (mill hand, Canada) and Edith M. Gage (Somersworth)
Saph Spencer, b. 3/7/1988; Brian Lessard and Wanda Walbridge
Sue Ellen, b. 4/19/1967; Robert L. Lessard and Charlotte M. Stevens

LONTINE,
Jessica Jade, b. 2/24/1989; Gary Lontine and Nan Spencer

LUNEAU,
Amy Dawn, b. 1/8/1978; Michael Alan Luneau and Sharon Cathrine Alexander

LUONGO,
Jennifer Lynne, b. 10/3/1980; James E. Luongo and Lori M. Pikr

LUTHANEN,
Donn Stephen, b. 7/20/1976; Kenneth and Marie Luthanen

LYNCH,
Kelly Marie, b. 3/26/1977; John R. Lynch and Marie L. McCarthy

MACDONALD,
Charles Robert, III, b. 7/1/1993; Charles R. MacDonald, Jr. and Lucie M. Fecteau
Rebecca Marie, b. 1/2/1991; Charles R. MacDonald and Lucie M. Fecteau

MARQUIS,
Megan Lynn, b. 2/14/1997; Scott P. Marquis and Darlene M. Bruedle

MAXWELL,
Samantha Adams, b. 9/1/1989; James Maxwell and Robin Harwood

McLENDON,
Carla Lauren, b. 7/10/1991; Carl McLendon and Susan D. Henderson
Erin Johannah, b. 4/15/1989; Carl McLendon and Susan Henderson

McQUEEN,
John William, b. 10/16/1938 in Rochester; seventh; David A. McQueen (wood dealer, Revere, MA) and Mary L. McHugh (Dorchester, MA)

McPHERSON,
Chloe Paige, b. 11/21/1995; Jeffrey B. McPherson and Samantha G. Jones
Jacob Robert, b. 5/24/1998; Jeffrey B. McPherson and Samantha G. Jones
Jeffrey R., b. 2/13/1975; Russell E. McPherson and Dianne H. Lowell

MELANSON,
Joseph Frank, b. 11/16/1989; Leonard Melanson and Jeanne Smith

MILLER,
Ronald H., b. 7/25/1932; first; Horace W. Miller (tile setter, Washington, DC) and Vera Heather (Medford, MA)
Sedgeley M., b. 3/8/1921; second; John H. Miller (cook, Farmington) and Lois G. Hatch (Simon, ME)

MILLS,
Darold W., Jr., b. 11/18/1973; Darold W. Mills and Wanda I. Brown
Derwood Stanton, b. 6/23/1971; Darold W. Mills and Wanda I. Brown
Garett Leon, b. 3/17/1980; Darold W. Mills and Wanda I. Brown

MOODY,
Eric Jeremy, b. 7/31/1995; Craig A. Moody and Elena Tavoularis
Job, b. 10/16/1984

MOONEY,
Benjamin W., b. 7/5/1918; first; Benjamin W. Mooney (farmer, Somerville, MA) and Marion Helen Knowles (Milton)
Dorothy L., b. 8/30/1919; second; Benjamin W. Mooney (farmer, Somerville, MA) and Marion H. Knowles (Milton)
Norma Roberta, b. 9/20/1921; fourth; Benjamin W. Mooney (farmer, Somerville, MA) and Marion H. Knowles (Milton)

MOORE,
Gladys S., b. 4/17/1903; Eli S. Moore (farmer, Middleton) and Ethel I. Wentworth (Lynn, MA)
Myrtle J., b. 6/2/1898; first; Eli S. Moore (farmer, 30, Middleton) and Ethel Wentworth (25, Lynn, MA)
Roland R.E., b. 10/6/1911; third; Eli S. Moore (farmer, 43, Middleton) and Ethel I. Wentworth (38, Lynn, MA)

MORELAND,
Gabriel J., b. 3/21/1977; Merrin J. Moreland and Polyne A. Masaitis

MOULTON,
daughter [Eva E.], b. 7/25/1907; third; Justin Moulton (farmer, 30, NH) and Flora Howard (23, NH)
daughter, b. 6/20/1908; sixth; Chester A. Moulton (farmer, 29, Farmington) and Edith M. Ham (28, Farmington)
Alden L., b. 3/17/1929; third; Fred A. Moulton (laborer, Middleton) and Vivian E. Grace (Tamworth)
Frederick Elroy, b. 7/28/1922; first; Edith B. Moulton (New Durham)
Stacey Ann, b. 7/29/1986; Mark Moulton and Donna Smith
Theodore F., b. 10/28/1926; second; Frederick A. Moulton (laborer, Middleton) and Evelyn V. Grace (Tamworth)

MULLEN,
Thomas Francis, b. 3/9/1997; Thomas R. Mullen, Jr. and Joan Marie Cicolini

MYERS,
Brandy Leo, b. 3/24/1984

NEAL,
Rachael E., b. 11/14/1987; Daniel Neal and Mary Kimball

NELSON,
son, b. 1/19/1913; second; Ernest G. Nelson (woodsman, 26, Effingham) and Elizabeth Patterson (28, Boston, MA)
Ryan Eric, b. 12/30/1988; Eric Nelson and Lauren Carozzo
Tyler Ernest, b. 7/31/1990; Eric S. Nelson and Lauren A. Nelson

NEWTON,
Shanel Newell, b. 12/8/1991; Dennis J. Newton and Cynthia D. Newton

NICHOLS,
Jennifer K., b. 11/7/1977; Dennis E. Nichols and Deborah A. Taylor

O'KEEFE,
Mariah Kendall, b. 5/11/1990; Owen M. O'Keefe and Laurianne M. Couture

OLEWINE,
Timothy Andrew, b. 5/17/1998; Dwight Olewine and Nary Olewine

PACHON,
son, b. 1/29/1887; fifth; Thomas Pachon (laborer, 28, Canada) and Emilie Custo (26, Canada)

PAQUIN,
John, b. 2/6/1952 in Rochester; fifth; stillborn; Henry Paquin (laborer, MI) and Henrietta Brewer (MA)
Linda M., b. 4/5/1954 in Rochester; Henry R. Paquin, Jr. and Heneretta Brewer
Robert L., b. 8/19/1956 in Rochester; Henry Paquin, Jr. and Henrietta Brewer
Rosemary E., b. 11/26/1949 in Rochester; fourth; Henry R. Paquin (carpenter, MI) and Henrietta Brewer (MA)

PEARSON,
Mark Allyn, b. 2/25/1969 in Portsmouth; James E. and Angela C. Pearson

PECKHAM,
Kelly Anne, b. 5/8/1979; Walter G. Peckham and Linda L. Tufts
Walter G., b. 2/28/1954 in Rochester; George B. Peckham and Eveline Stevens

PENNY,
daughter, b. 8/17/1888; second; Mark B. Penny (marble worker, 33, New Durham) and Lilla J. Burrows (23, Middleton); residence - Wakefield

PERKINS,
Emily Paige, b. 9/17/1994; Sheldon W. Perkins and Helen C. Newberry
Hazel A., b. 4/14/1898; first; Harry O. Perkins (laborer, 21, New Durham) and Lena Willey (17, Middleton)
Krisian A., b. 4/22/1987; Mikel Perkins and Cheryl White
Laurel Mitchel, b. 5/10/1908; first; Walter Percy Perkins (farmer, 28, So. Berwick, ME) and Sadie A. Mitchel (29, New Durham)

PETERSON,
Madisen Michael, b. 2/26/1991; Michael D. Peterson and Anne K. Lepene
Tess Elizabeth, b. 2/27/1998; Steven Peterson and Susan Armstrong

PLACE,
son, b. 11/1/1888; eighth; William Place (shoemaker, 40, Middleton) and Lydia Whitehouse (40, Middleton)
daughter, b. 11/24/1889; eighth; William B. Place (shoemaker, Middleton) and Lydia Whitehouse (Middleton)

PORTER,
Jamie Dea, b. 1/5/1989; Thomas Porter and Nancy Braasch
Shenna L., b. 2/25/1987; Thomas Porter and Nancy Braasch

POULIN,
Amy Louise, b. 4/17/1980; Alfred J. Poulin and Kathryn L. Walker
Derek Normand, b. 2/3/1998; Rocky A. Poulin and Kim Diane Theberge
Kevin Rocky, b. 9/9/1996; Rocky A. Poulin and Kim D. Theberge
Timothy David, b. 8/6/1962 in Rochester; Florian A. Poulin and Ramona A. Lafoe

POULIOT,
Sheena Marie, b. 6/29/1986; Ernest Pouliot and Linda Hoyt

PROSPER,
Daniel Ernest, b. 8/14/1998; Patrick Prosper and Sheri Prosper
Edwin M., b. 10/14/1977; Patrick R. Prosper, Sr. and Linda L. Harvey

PROULX,
David Mark, Jr., b. 9/15/1980; David M. Proulx and Sharon A. Baily

QUIMBY,
Christopher Michael, b. 11/25/1980; Michael F. Quimby and Deborah L. Bullis
Jennifer May, b. 4/13/1986; Michael Quimby and Deborah Bullis
Jessica Lynn, b. 4/13/1986; Michael Quimby and Deborah Bullis

RANCOURT,
Jacqueline Mae, b. 12/1/1970; John M. Rancourt and Frances E. Sanborn
Jean Noella, b. 9/19/1972; John M. Rancourt and Frances E. Sanborn
Mark J., b. 7/26/1973; John M. Rancourt and Frances M. Sanborn

RANDALL,
Sagan Leigh, b. 5/19/1988; Timothy Randall and Alisa Tetreault
Stephen M., b. 9/2/1977; Edgar E. Randall and Kathy J. Logan

REED,
Sandra Lee, b. 6/16/1946 in Rochester; first; Eugene Reed (US Marines, West Newfield, ME) and Janet Bullis (Haverhill, MA)

REYNOLDS,
Patricia Lynne, b. 7/10/1995; David A. Reynolds and Julie A. Goudreault

ROGERS,
Craig Everett, b. 10/24/1972; Kenneth G. Rogers and Joann C. Bean
Steven Lee, b. 10/18/1969; Kenneth G. and Joann C. Rogers

ROLLINS,
Micah Jesse, b. 6/7/1979; John S. Rollins and Sandra E. Shea

ST. PIERRE,
Jenna A., b. 6/28/1987; Bruce St. Pierre and Lesley Kreiensieck

SALISBURY,
Heather Lee, b. 8/18/1971; Wayne C. Salisbury and Sandra J.
    Goodwin
Heidi L., b. 2/15/1974; Wayne and Sandra J. Salisbury

SCALISE,
Nicholas Vincent, b. 7/29/1997; Richard A. Scalise, Jr. and Michelle
    L. Jolicoeur

SHACKFORD,
Jo-Ann Arlene, b. 12/16/1971; Joseph I. Shackford and Rosalyn A.
    Libby

SHAW,
Kathryn Rose, b. 10/21/1998; Christopher P. Shaw and Jo Anne
    Hamel

SHEA,
Donald E., b. 2/9/1952 in Rochester; third; Katherine Brewer (MA)
Patricia A., b. 4/11/1948 in Rochester; first; Millard J. Shea
    (woodsman, Bilmont, NY) and Katherine Brewer (Royalston,
    MA)

SHERWOOD,
Lance Bradbury, b. 11/18/1990; Bradbury Sherwood and Robin
    Collicutt
Nathan Wayne, b. 7/27/1996; Bradbury C. Sherwood and Robin Jo
    Collicott

SIMONDS,
Ruth M., b. 7/27/1890; first; George H. Simonds (laborer in shoe shop, Middleton) and ----- (Haverhill, MA); residence - Haverhill, MA

SINCLAIR,
Katie Lynne, b. 4/21/1980; David P. Sinclair and Evelyn A. Fowler
Tyler Timothy, b. 3/15/1991; Timothy C. Sinclair and Michelle L. Myers

SINDORF,
Amelia Rose, b. 1/25/1998; Jonathan E. Sindorf and Patricia D. Pringle
Dorothy C., b. 2/27/1960; Rev. John H. Sindorf and Dorothy Perry
Jonathan Edward, b. 5/30/1963; John Harman Sindorf and Dorothy Louise Perry
Joseph P., b. 12/16/1957; John H. Sindorf and Dorothy L. Perry
Peter John Richard, b. 12/12/1995; Jonathan E. Sindorf and Patricia D. Pringle

SMITH,
daughter, b. 4/25/1912; fourth; Guy A. Smith (clerk, 30, Franconia) and Clara M. Tufts (28, Middleton); residence - Franconia
Carl L., b. 9/17/1960; Robert L. Smith and Beulah M. Leighton
Gail M., b. 7/12/1956 in Rochester; Robert L. Smith and Beulah Leighton
Karl Welton, b. 12/29/1970; Loran E. Smith and Nancy J. Pearson
Loran Edward, Jr., b. 7/1/1961; Loran E. Smith and Nancy J. Pearson
Lorna Louise, b. 1/15/1965; Loran Smith and Nancy J. Pearson
Patricia L., b. 7/4/1955 in Rochester; Robert L. Smith and Beulah M. Leighton
Robert L., Jr., b. 8/26/1957; Robert L. Smith and Beulah Leighton
Stephen Paul, b. 10/29/1962 in Rochester; Loran E. Smith and Nancy J. Pearson
Thomas L., b. 12/3/1964; Robert L. Smith and Beulah M. Leighton

Warren S., b. 4/19/1910; third; Guy A. Smith (clerk, 28, Franconia) and Clara M. Tufts (26, Middleton)

Wilma L., b. 2/8/1959; Robert Smith and Beulah M. Leighton

STABILE,
David, b. 3/2/1986; David Stabile and Jeanmarie DiPrizio

Jason David, b. 3/11/1985 in Rochester; David Stabile and Jeanmarie DiPrizio

Jeremy David, b. 3/11/1985 in Rochester; David Stabile and Jeanmarie DiPrizio

Mark David, b. 4/30/1988; David Stabile and Jeanmarie DiPrizio

STEVENS,
daughter, b. 11/15/1892; second; Edgar N. Stevens (farmer, Middleton) and Annie Cleveland (housekeeper)

daughter, b. 12/13/1892; fourth; Warren Stevens (farmer, Middleton) and Etta Eaton (housekeeper, Brookfield)

daughter, b. 12/13/1892; fifth; Warren Stevens (farmer, Middleton) and Etta Eaton (housekeeper, Brookfield)

daughter, b. 11/14/1896; third; Thomas J. Stevens (farmer, 32, Middleton) and Lizzie A. Whitehouse (27, Middleton)

son, b. 3/9/1898; fourth; Edgar N. Stevens (lumber surveyor, 33, Middleton) and Annie Cleveland (26, Hillsboro)

daughter [Margaret E.], b. 7/20/1899; third; Albert Stevens (farmer, 31, Middleton) and Bernice Tufts (21, Middleton)

daughter [Alberta J.], b. 1/31/1901; fourth; Albert M. Stevens (farmer, 33, Middleton) and Bernice Tufts (24, Middleton)

son [Melvin E.], b. 6/22/1903; Albert M. Stevens (farmer, Middleton) and Bernice M. Tufts (Middleton)

son [Herbert J.], b. 12/17/1904; sixth; Albert M. Stevens (farmer, 36, Middleton) and Bernice M. Tufts (28, Middleton)

son [Sidney A.], b. 6/28/1906; seventh; Albert N. Stevens (farmer, 39, Middleton) and Bernice M. Tufts (29, Middleton)

daughter, b. 12/17/1911; tenth; Albert N. Stevens (farmer, 44, Middleton) and Bernice M. Tufts (36, Middleton)

daughter [Alice E.], b. 9/29/1914; eleventh; Albert M. Stevens
(farmer, 47, Middleton) and Bernice M. Tufts (38, Middleton)

son [Handy Andy], b. 12/30/1919; thirteenth; Albert M. Stevens
(farmer, Middleton) and Bernice M. Tufts (Middleton)

daughter, b. 4/3/1922 in Rochester; fourteenth; Albert M. Stevens
(farmer, Union) and Bernise Tufts (Middleton)

stillborn daughter [Ruth], b. 4/6/1930; second; Melvin E. Stevens
(lumberman, Middleton) and Maud P. Merrill (Wakefield, MA)

son, b. 3/2/1938 in Rochester; seventh; Melvin E. Stevens (laborer,
Middleton) and Maud P. Merrill (Wakefield, MA)

Albert M., b. 3/16/1938 in Rochester; fourth; Sidney A. Stevens
(cook, Middleton) and Marion E. Kinney (Springdale, NS)

Alvin Lee, b. 6/30/1934; fourth; Earl W. Stevens (laborer, Middleton)
and Elsie Ray (Hudson)

Arthur Leslie, b. 7/9/1907; eighth; Albert M. Stevens (farmer, 39,
Middleton) and Bernice M. Tufts (30, Middleton)

Betsy L., b. 9/4/1968; Leslie Stevens and Marcia Leary

Carleton Paul, b. 12/26/1936; sixth; Melvin Stevens (laborer,
Middleton) and Maud Merrill (Wakefield, MA)

Carrie Jean, b. 5/28/1979; Leslie A. Stevens and Marcia A. Leary

Cindy Lee, b. 2/1/1958; Earl F. Stevens and Janet A. Nason

Craig P., b. 7/15/1955 in Rochester; Carlton P. Stevens and Jane
Shaw

Earle Webber, b. 5/20/1908; third; Byron H. Stevens (farmer, 51,
Middleton) and Louise M. Webber (19, Milton)

Edwina, b. 5/18/1931; third; Melvin Stevens (mill hand, Middleton)
and Maud Merrill (Wakefield, MA)

Elwin R., b. 3/24/1896; first; Albert M. Stevens (farmer, 28,
Middleton) and Bernice M. Tufts (19, Middleton)

Eva, b. 6/18/1894; second; Hiram S. Stevens (labor, 30, Freeport,
ME) and Hattie Ross (25, Addison, ME)

Evelyn Louise, b. 8/2/1933; second; Sidney A. Stevens (farmer,
Middleton) and Marion E. Kinney (Springdale, NS)

George W., b. 3/27/1905; first; Byron H. Stevens (farmer, 47,
Middleton) and Louise M. Webber (16, Milton)

Hannah Grace, b. 12/25/1997; Leslie A. Stevens, Jr. and Holly E. Weed

James Walter, b. 7/4/1943 in Rochester; third; Arthur Leslie Stevens (lineman, Middleton) and Grace Gertrude Kinney (Westfield, ME)

Jane Betty, b. 5/20/1935; third; Sidney A. Stevens (factory worker, Middleton) and Marion E. Kinney (Springdale, NS)

Jeffrey K., b. 6/27/1977; Leslie A. Stevens and Marcia A. Leary

John, b. 3/15/1906; second; Byron H. Stevens (farmer, 49, Middleton) and Louise M. Webber (17, Milton)

Jones T., b. 5/14/1893; second; T. J. Stevens, Jr. (farmer, 28, Middleton) and L. A. Whitehouse (23, Middleton)

Julie Ann, b. 1/30/1962 in Rochester; Ronald E. Stevens and Irene L. Sprague

Julie Ann, b. 10/6/1970; Leslie A. Stevens and Marcia A. Leary

Kenneth D., b. 12/29/1960; Earl F. Stevens and Janet E. Nason

Lenora, b. 6/1/1916; twelfth; Albert M. Stevens (farmer, 48, Middleton) and Bernice Tufts (39, Middleton)

Leslie A., Jr., b. 5/14/1972; Leslie A. Stevens and Marcia A. Leary

Leslie Arthur, b. 1/21/1942 in Rochester; second; Arthur Leslie Stevens (lineman, Middleton) and Grace Gertrude Kinney (Westfield, ME)

Lydia Grace, b. 8/6/1909; ninth; Albert M. Stevens (farmer, 40, Middleton) and Bernice M. Tufts (29, Middleton)

Mark E., b. 12/1/1956; Earl F. Stevens and Janet Nason

Patricia Ann, b. 10/25/1938 in Rochester; first; Arthur L. Stevens (laborer, Middleton) and Grace G. Kinney (Westfield, ME)

Sally M., b. 3/14/1959; Earl F. Stevens and Janet E. Nason

Shirley Elizabeth, b. 1/12/1936 in Union; fifth; Melvin Stevens (laborer, Middleton) and Maud Merrill (Wakefield, MA)

Walter Ray, b. 4/13/1897; second; Albert Stevens (farmer, 29, Middleton) and Bernice Tufts (19, Middleton)

William H., b. 8/21/1932; third; Earl W. Stevens (laborer, Middleton) and Elsie A. Ray (Hudson)

STONE,
Eben Alexander, b. 10/1/1984

TALON,
Caitlin Leigh, b. 7/17/1990; Randy S. Talon and Toni L. Edgerly
Jared Travis, b. 9/24/1991; Randy S. Talon and Toni L. Edgerly

TANGNEY,
son, b. 12/23/1912; fourth; Ludger Tangney (laborer, 30, Canada) and
    Fernina Lerney (28, Canada)

TARDIFF,
Lillian Elizabeth, b. 2/27/1928; sixth; Donald Tardiff (laborer,
    Canada) and Carrie Grace (Tamworth)

TETREAULT,
Casey Lyn, b. 9/20/1978; Joel Armand Tetreault and Claire Beatrice
    Gelinas
Matthew Ryan, b. 7/24/1985 in Wolfeboro; Randolf Tetreault and
    Kathy Drew

THOMAS,
Leah Nicole, b. 2/6/1988; James Thomas and Pamela Dumont
Logan Paul, b. 11/10/1992; James E. Thomas and Pamela J. Dumont

THOMPSON,
Rachel Michelle, b. 7/17/1991; Wendell L. Thompson, Jr. and Cynthia
    A. Evans
Rebecca Marie, b. 7/17/1991; Wendell L. Thompson, Jr. and Cynthia
    A. Evans

THURBER,
Desra Raylene, b. 4/10/1972; Manfred W. Thurber and Frances E.
    Roy

TIBBETTS,
daughter [Hattie F.], b. 8/20/1906; second; Fred W. Tibbetts (mill
  hand, 26, Milton) and Myrtle E. Thurston (20, Madison)
Clifton Roswell, b. 3/23/1909; third; Fred W. Tibbetts (mill operative,
  28, Milton) and Myrtle E. Thurston (22, Madison)
Forest Walter, b. 3/24/1908; second; Albert M. Tibbetts (laborer, 33,
  Milton) and Lillian Tuttle (21, New Durham)
James Robert, b. 7/5/1969; Dorsity W. and Glenda J. Tibbetts
Melvin, b. 2/23/1911; third; Albert M. Tibbetts (farmer, 35, Milton)
  and Lillian D. Tuttle (22, New Durham)
Tracey Lyn, b. 7/27/1969; Robert O. and Judith L. Tibbetts
Verna Mildred, b. 11/27/1903; Fred W. Tibbetts (farmer, Farmington)
  and Myrtle E. Thurston (Madison)

TIVELL,
daughter, b. 3/29/1919; fifth; Charles Tivell (teamster, Salem, MA)
  and Goldie H. Stanley (Otis, ME)

TODD,
Angel, b. 3/19/1977; James R. Todd and Carole Ann Loughnane

TOMPSON,
Mica Ann, b. 5/6/1977; Wayne A. Tompson and Martha A. Kinney

TOWER,
Benjamin Talbot, b. 2/9/1989; Richard Tower, Jr. and Denise Talbot
Faith Elaine, b. 6/15/1986; Richard Tower and Denise Talbot

TOZIER,
Kelsey Autumn, b. 11/5/1985 in Rochester; Thomas Tozier and
  Sandra Ortman
Kurt Russell, b. 2/25/1984
Luke Thomas, b. 7/12/1990; Thomas Tozier and Sandra B. Ortman

TRIBOU,
Daniel Willard, b. 5/22/1918; second; George W. Tribou (carpenter, MA) and Ruth H. Jones (MA)

TUFTS,
son [Leon G.], b. 5/1/1888; seventh; George J. Tufts (farmer, 42, Middleton) and Emma F. Whitehouse (32, Middleton)
son [Franklin Isaac], b. 12/22/1889; first; Joseph W. Tufts (farmer, Middleton) and Cora P. Cook (Milton)
son [John D.], b. 7/7/1890; sixth; George J. Tufts (farmer, Middleton) and Emma Whitehouse (Middleton)
daughter [Mary R.], b. 7/26/1890; Charles D. Tufts (farmer, Middleton) and Nellie Corson
son [Clyde L.], b. 5/2/1902; first; Leon G. Tufts (laborer, 23, Middleton) and Addie M. Kimball (17, Middleton)
son, b. 9/28/1909; sixth; Leon G. Tufts (mill operative, 30, Middleton) and Addie M. Kimball (26, Middleton)
son [Myron K.], b. 11/25/1910; seventh; Leon G. Tufts (laborer, 31, Middleton) and Addie M. Kimball (27, Middleton)
son, b. 3/15/1913; ninth; Leon G. Tufts (farmer, 32, Middleton) and Addie Kimball (29, Middleton)
son [Roy J.], b. 7/25/1919; fifth; Joseph W. Tufts (farmer, Middleton) and Lillian D. Tuttle (New Durham)
daughter, b. 10/17/1923; fifth; Joseph W. Tufts (farmer, Middleton) and Lillian Tuttle (Farmington)
son [Frederick L.], b. 12/17/1923; sixteenth; Leon G. Tufts (farmer, Middleton) and Addie M. Kimball (Middleton)
Arthur William, b. 1/13/1941 in Rochester; fourth; Orrie Mott Tufts (laborer, Middleton) and Iris Isabelle Shepard (Acton, ME)
Barbara, b. 11/18/1921; second; John D. Tufts (farmer, Middleton) and Alice M. Hodges (Milton)
Beverly Alice, b. 8/25/1928; fourth; John D. Tufts (farmer, Middleton) and Alice Hodges (Milton)
Caleb Boston, b. 9/19/1989; Wilson Tufts and Debra Tufts
Cora Belle, b. 3/26/1917; fourth; J. Wright Tufts (farmer, 54, Middleton) and Lillian Tuttle (30, New Durham)

David A., b. 6/4/1952 in Rochester; second; Merton E. Tufts (truck driver, Farmington) and Geraldine R. Duprey (MA)

Doris Leona, b. 6/10/1921; seventh; Joseph W. Tufts (farmer, Middleton) and Lillian D. Tuttle (Middleton)

Elaine Allison, b. 1/25/1962 in Rochester; Woodrow W. Tufts and Marilyn J. Boston

Ellen Blanch, b. 5/3/1898; eleventh; George J. Tufts (farmer, 50, Middleton) and Emma Whitehouse (42, Middleton)

Ellen Maria, b. 12/22/1917; twelfth; Leon G. Tufts (farmer, 38, Middleton) and Addie M. Kimball (34, Middleton)

Elsie Ardena, b. 2/26/1912; eighth; Leon G. Tufts (mill operative, 31, Middleton) and Addie Kimball (28, Middleton)

Elsie Ardena, b. 2/3/1950 in Rochester; second; Stephen J. Tufts (lineman, Rochester) and Mary K. Marcoux (Milton)

Emma A., b. 5/29/1895; tenth; George J. Tufts (farmer, 47, Middleton) and Emma Whitehouse (30, Middleton)

Emma F., b. 11/23/1919; thirteenth; Leon G. Tufts (mill hand, Middleton) and Addie M. Kimball (Middleton)

Gail Andrea, b. 11/2/1938 in Rochester; second; George D. Tufts (cutter, Middleton) and Marion E. Shepard (Acton, ME)

George D., b. 8/14/1905; third; Leon G. Tufts (mill operative, 26, Middleton) and Addie M. Kimball (20, Middleton)

Georgianna G., b. 5/13/1948 in Rochester; first; Stephen J. Tufts (lineman, Rochester) and Mary K. Marcoux (Milton)

Geraldine, b. 6/8/1936; first; George Tufts (mill worker, Middleton) and Marion Shepard (Acton, ME)

Glenda Jacquet, b. 2/10/1940 in Rochester; first; Emma F. Tufts (Middleton)

Grace Thelma, b. 2/8/1907; fourth; Leon G. Tufts (mill operative, 27, Middleton) and Addie M. Kimball (22, Middleton)

Irene Elizabeth, b. 9/9/1916; eleventh; Leon G. Tufts (mill hand, 36, Middleton) and Addie M. Kimball (33, Middleton)

James G., b. 8/5/1960; Woodrow W. Tufts and Marilyn J. Boston

Joan Louise, b. 4/28/1937 in Rochester; first; Myron K. Tufts (leather stripper, Middleton) and Louise Kinney (Westfield, ME)

Joseph, b. 4/13/1888; first; Joseph W. Tufts (farmer, 28, Middleton) and Cora B. Cook (18, Milton)

Joseph Stephen, b. 9/27/1951 in Rochester; third; Stephen J. Tufts (lineman, Rochester) and Mary K. Marcoux (Milton)

June Kimball, b. 6/12/1921; fourteenth; Leon G. Tufts (mill hand, Middleton) and Addie M. Kimball (Middleton)

Keith Linwood, b. 10/17/1963; Woodrow W. Tufts and Marilyn Jean Boston

Lloyde S., b. 1/7/1904; second; Leon G. Tufts (mill operative, 23, Middleton) and Addie M. Kimball (19, Middleton)

Margaret Florence, b. 6/6/1940 in Rochester; third; Myron Kimball Tufts (stripper, Middleton) and Louise Evelyn Kinney (Westfield, ME)

Maurice W., b. 5/23/1929; second; Moses D. Tufts (farmer, Middleton) and Evelyn R. Nutter (Milton)

Michael A., b. 11/12/1956 in Rochester; Merton E. Tufts and Geraldine R. Duprey

Moses Davis, b. 4/25/1897; fifth; Joseph Tufts (farmer, 38, Middleton) and Cora B. Cook (27, Milton)

Nellie V., b. 3/6/1893; ninth; George J. Tufts (farmer, 47, Middleton) and E. F. Whitehouse (37, Middleton)

Orrie Mott, Jr., b. 5/13/1935; third; Orrie M. Tufts (laborer, Middleton) and Iris Shepard (Acton, ME)

Orrin Wesley, b. 4/18/1922; seventh; Joseph W. Tufts (farmer, Middleton) and Lillian D. Tuttle (New Durham)

Patricia Ann, b. 6/28/1951 in Rochester; first; Merton E. Tufts (truck driver, Farmington) and Geraldine R. Duprey (MA)

Patricia Ruth, b. 10/18/1927; first; Moses D. Tufts (farmer, Middleton) and Evelyn R. Nutter (Milton)

Pauline Dorothy, b. 6/11/1908; fifth; Leon G. Tufts (mill operative, 28, Middleton) and Addie M. Kimball (23, Middleton)

Phyllis E., b. 9/9/1919; first; John D. Tufts (farmer, Middleton) and Alice M. Hodges (Milton)

Priscilla Adams, b. 7/27/1922; fifteenth; Leon G. Tufts (farmer, Middleton) and Adeline M. Kimball (Middleton)

Ranson A., b. 6/12/1894; fourth; Joseph W. Tufts (farmer, 35, Middleton) and Cora B. Cook (22, Milton)

Richard Allen, b. 3/12/1939 in Rochester; second; Myron Tufts (leather stripper, Middleton) and Louise Kinney (Westfield, ME)

Robert L., b. 5/29/1959; Woodrow W. Tufts and Marilyn J. Boston

Roxanna A., b. 12/15/1965; Woodrow Tufts and Marilyn J. Boston

Ruby A., b. 9/26/1914; tenth; Leon G. Tufts (farmer, 35, Middleton) and Addie M. Kimball (30, Middleton)

Stephen J., b. 8/17/1929; seventeenth; Leon G. Tufts (farmer, Middleton) and Addie M. Kimball (Middleton)

Thelma, b. 7/9/1925; third; John D. Tufts (farmer, Middleton) and Alice M. Hodges (Milton)

Virginia F., b. 11/21/1923; first; Clyde L. Tufts (machinist, Middleton) and Evelyn Moulton (Farmington)

Wilson W., b. 5/29/1958; Woodrow Tufts and Marilyn J. Boston

TWOMBLY,

John, Jr., b. 3/21/1917; first; John Henry Twombly (mill hand, 30, W. Milton) and Ethel B. Whitehouse (21, Rochester); residence - Milton

VALLADARES,

Adam David, b. 9/30/1997; David A. Valladares and Carey Ann Vermette

VALRAND,

Julie Ann, b. 5/31/1979; Carl E. Valrand and Diane H. Venezia

Kerry L., b. 2/24/1975; Carl E. Valrand and Diane H. Venezia

VANDERHECKE,

Matthew Allan, b. 5/27/1984

VARNEY,

son, b. 5/8/1909; first; Nolan F. Varney (woodsman, 38, Farmington) and Lucy M. Hall (17, Rochester)

Kevin Phillip, b. 11/17/1998; Marc D. Varney and Nora Lee Paradis

Loyd Irving, b. 3/26/1911; sixth; Lewis N. Varney (sawyer, 34, Farmington) and Grace Pinkham (28, Middleton)

VEILLEUX,
Alyssa Rose, b. 5/18/1989; Steven Veilleux and Michelle Turmelle
Jacob Erik, b. 1/26/1995; Steven M. Veilleux and Michele M. Turmelle
Kelsey Michele, b. 6/10/1991; Steven M. Veilleux and Michele M. Turmelle

VOGE,
Justine Victoria, b. 10/6/1998; Jason Voge and Roxanne Voge

WALBRIDGE,
Alvin S., III, b. 11/9/1968; Alvin Walbridge, Jr. and Margaret Gagne

WEBSTER,
Albert Elmer, III, b. 10/2/1978; Albert Elmer Webster, Jr. and Patricia Leola Smith

WEEKS,
Alfred Robert, b. 3/17/1921; second; Guy B. Weeks (chauffeur, E. Wakefield) and Margaret E. Stevens (Middleton); residence - Wakefield
Malinda Lou, b. 4/2/1988; Duane Weeks and Diana Thomas

WEEMAN,
Fred H., b. 4/30/1954 in Rochester; Harris Weeman and Eunice F. Regan

WELCH,
Andrew David, b. 10/2/1992; Bruce D. Welch and Sheila J. Tuttle
Linda A., b. 7/20/1949 in Rochester; sixth; Sidney B. Welch (lumberman, NH) and Beth M. Sanborn (ME)

WELDY,
Carley Michelle, b. 9/15/1998; Norman Weldy and Allison Weldy

WENTWORTH,
Eugene William, b. 1/8/1937 in Rochester; second; William Wentworth (mold fitter, Union) and Blanche Reed (Canobie Lake)
Lawrence D., b. 4/17/1917; second; Joseph D. Wentworth (shoemaker, 27, Farmington) and Jennie May Savoie (19, Dover); residence - Farmington

WHITEHOUSE,
Gale D., b. 9/16/1965; Richard A. Whitehouse and Linda D. Drew
Norman J., b. 9/7/1916; first; Harvey J. Whitehouse (farmer, 21, Rochester) and Josephine A. Wallace (25, Middleton)
Richard, b. 3/22/1912; eighth; Harvey J. Whitehouse (farmer, 42, Middleton) and Isabelle Ellis (40, Alton)
Richard A., Jr., b. 12/20/1971; Richard A. Whitehouse and Lynda D. Drew

WHITTEN,
Shain Edward, b. 7/26/1986; Kenneth Whitten and Dianne LaRoche

WILKINSON,
Beatrice Mae, b. 6/17/1938; first; Melbourne Wilkinson (truck driver, Wakefield) and Edwina Young (Middleton)
Melbourne Albat, b. 5/30/1940; second; Melbourne Albat Wilkinson (truck driver, Wakefield) and Edwina Natalie Young (Middleton)

WILSON,
Christina Doris, b. 9/14/1994; Steven Wilson and Julie E. Wilkinson

WOODMAN,
son [Jesse], b. 5/14/1903; Frank Woodman (farmer, Plymouth) and Livonia Drew (Eaton)

WYLIE,
Lucas Ian, b. 10/6/1978; John Joseph Wylie and Patricia Katherine Doherty

YOUNG,
son [Perley L.], b. 6/5/1898; first; Lewis E. Young (farmer, 32, Middleton) and Effie A. Leighton (21, Middleton)
son [Eli S.], b. 8/2/1904; third; Lewis F. Young (farmer, 37, Middleton) and Effie A. Leighton (27, Middleton)
son [Herman], b. 10/15/1911; fourth; Lewis F. Young (farmer, 45, Middleton) and Effie A. Leighton (35, Middleton)
Chester, b. 1/4/1900; second; Lewis F. Young (farmer, 33, Middleton) and Effie A. Leighton (22, Middleton)
Cindy Lee, b. 2/28/1960; Roland W. Young and Stella Budroe
Mildred Doris, b. 9/27/1909; first; Fred R. Young (teamster, 18, Middleton) and Alice E. Heath (16, Union)
Roland Wilfred, b. 5/25/1917; fourth; Fred R. Young (farmer, 25, Middleton) and Alice Heath (24, Union)
Wilda, b. 8/9/1912; second; Fred R. Young (farmer, 21, Middleton) and Alice E. Heath (19, Union)

MIDDLETON MARRIAGES

ALLARD,
Charles Smith m. Tammy Lynn **Seale** 7/27/1996 in Rochester

ALLEN,
Michael R. m. Betsy J. **Tozier** 7/7/1979 in Rollinsford

AMES,
Fred m. Donna J. **Cameron** 8/26/1978 in Middleton
Fred L. m. Christine E. **LePage** 7/20/1991 in Middleton

ANDRUS,
Corey M. m. Susan M. **Peloquin** 7/2/1994 in Rochester

BALDWIN,
Richard G. m. Gail A. **Tufts** 3/19/1955 in Wakefield; H - 23; W - 16

BAUD,
James D. m. Virginia E. **Estes** 8/27/1977 in Farmington

BEAUDET,
Daniel N. m. Victoria J. **McLean** 8/24/1997 in New Durham

BELANGER,
Alphonse Charles m. Karen Ann **Gauthreau** 2/14/1970; H - b. 10/20/1951, s/o Louis J. Belanger and Ella M. Cox of West Lebanon, ME; W - b. 6/14/1953, d/o Edward D. Gauthreau and Catherine Deery of Middleton
Ronald Austin m. Kathleen Marie **Gauthreau** 7/4/1970; H - b. 6/25/1948, s/o Louis J. Belanger and Ella M. Cox of West Lebanon, ME; W - b. 6/14/1953, d/o Edward D. Gauthreau and Catherine M. Deery of Middleton

BELL,
James A., II m. Sharon B. **Suchocki** 10/21/1989 in Rochester

BIRNIE,
John D., II m. Christine M. **Sandin** 7/1/1996 in Middleton

BLAKE,
Richard A. m. Lorraine **Erickson** 6/21/1991 in New Durham

BLIDBERG,
Walter B. m. Debra T. **Nasuti** 8/25/1990 in Barrington

BLOUIN,
Michael m. Rosaria **Giusti** 8/16/1986 in Middleton

BODWELL,
Edward of Parsonsfield, ME m. Georgianna **Linscott** of Parsonsfield, ME 8/21/1897 in Milton; H - 39, printer, b. Acton, ME, s/o John E. Bodwell (Acton, ME, farmer) and Louisa J. Goodwin (Sanford, ME, housekeeper); W - 23, seamstress, b. Parsonsfield, ME, d/o David Linscott (Cornish, ME, farmer) and Mariam Linscott (Portland, ME, housekeeper)

BOLLES,
Clifford Roy of Middleton m. Helen Mabel **Eastman** of Middleton 2/4/1941 in Milton; H - 26, woodsman, 2d, b. Belmont, ME, s/o Sumner Bolles (laborer) and Lena M. Mayo (Dover-Foxcroft, ME, housewife); W - 17, housework, b. Middleton, d/o Charles F. Eastman (Milton, farmer) and Mary A. Tufts (Middleton, housewife)

BOUCHER,
Roger G. m. Marjorie H. **Howard** 9/9/1989 in Middleton

BOYD,
Joseph F. m. Cynthia N. **Varney** 9/23/1991 in Middleton

BRACKETT,
Herbert E. of Middleton m. Iva B. **Grace** of Farmington 12/16/1899 in Middleton; H - 30, stock-fitter, b. Middleton, s/o Moses D. Brackett (Acton, ME, watchman) and Sarah J. Perkins (Middleton, housework); W - 22, housework, 2d, b. Farmington, d/o Benjamin Grace (Middleton, shoemaker) and Lydia Frost (Middleton, housework)

BRADY,
Philip P. m. Karrie L. **Smith** 5/23/1998 in Union

BRANNAN,
Francis J. m. Florence C. **Chamberlain** 12/30/1961; H - s/o Norbert Brannan of Middleton; W - d/o Arthur Boucher of Durham
George P. m. Beverly A. **Rouleau** 2/21/1959 in Wakefield; H - 21, s/o Norbert Brannan; W - 17, d/o George Rouleau
George P. m. Judith E. **Young** 7/27/1963; H - s/o Norbert Brannan of Middleton; W - d/o Willard and Beatrice Young of Middleton
Gerard E. of Middleton m. Elizabeth A. **Cassell** of Gonic 7/19/1958 in Middleton; H - s/o Norbert Brannan; W - d/o Patrick Cassell
Jason J. m. Tammy L. **Wells** 7/26/1997 in Middleton
Norbert N. of Middleton m. Ruby A. **Tufts** of Middleton 4/10/1934 in Rochester; H - 33, chauffeur, b. E. Boston, MA, s/o James J. Brannan (NS, barber) and Catherine Lynch (NS, housewife); W - 19, at home, b. Middleton, d/o Leon G. Tufts (Middleton, mill worker) and Addie M. Kimball (Farmington, housewife)

BREWER,
Gene E. m. Rosalie S. **Beckman** 3/15/1968
Marcus H. of Middleton m. Bertha L. **Geary** of New Durham 12/22/1951; H - 20, lumber, b. MA, s/o Leslie S. Brewer and Harriett E. Whitman; W - 20, at home, b. NH, d/o Anthony W. Geary and Bessie K. Eastman

BRIERLY,
Martin L. m. Robin R. **Bruedle** 4/28/1984

BROOKS,
Carlyle G. of Rochester m. Martha K. **Hill** of Middleton 11/2/1946 in East Rochester; H - 27, laborer, b. Rochester, s/o Edward Brooks (Rochester, press worker) and Gladys York (Rochester, housewife); W - 20, b. Wakefield, d/o Waldo Hill (Wakefield, teamster) and Vila Kimball (Middleton, housewife)
George W. m. Lucille I. **Eastman** 5/24/1968
Louis W. m. Justine **Cameron** 1/11/1969
Louis Waldo m. Mary Louise **Fifield** 12/20/1964; H - 17, s/o Carlyle Brooks and Martha Hill of Middleton; W - 17, d/o Charles Fifield and Louise Drapeau of Union
Norman F. of Rochester m. Carlyne P. **Cook** of Middleton 12/10/1946 in Milton; H - 23, unemployed, b. Rochester, s/o Edward Brooks (Dover, mill worker) and Gladys York (Rochester, housewife); W - 18, at home, b. Union, d/o Clarence Cook (Middleton, truck driver) and Pauline Tufts (Middleton, shoe shop)
Samuel C. m. Kathleen J. **Hill** 10/16/1965; H - 17, s/o Carlyle Brooks; W - 16, d/o Norman Hill of Rochester
Samuel C. m. Sylvia A. **Amsler** 3/18/1972; H - 23, s/o Carlyle Brooks and Martha Hill; W - 25, d/o William H. Amsler, Jr. and Berdine A. Nyman

BROWN,
Harold of Middleton m. Henrietta **Fisher** of Haverhill, MA 7/17/1897 in Middleton; H - 19, shoecutter, b. Charlestown, MA, s/o John C. Brown (Boston, MA, drummer) and Annie C. Lougee (housework); W - 17, housework, b. Haverhill, MA, d/o Frederick S. Fisher (Hampstead, relaster) and Caroline J. Knight (Atkinson, housework)
Harold B. of Middleton m. Ambie G. **Hill** of Cornish, ME 7/21/1908 in Farmington; H - 30, farmer, 2d, b. Charlestown, MA, s/o John C. Brown (trav. salesman) and Hannah C. Lougee (Freedom, actress); W - 47, housework, 2d, d/o Asa Varney (farmer) and Sarah Clough (housework)

James G. m. Jean A. **Merrill** 12/7/1974; H - s/o William and June Brown; W - d/o Edward S. and Alice Merrill

John A. of Middleton m. Nellie **McDonald** of Middleton 8/26/1898 in Union; H - 22, farmer, b. Alton, s/o Charles H. Brown (farmer) and Angaline Rand (Alton, at home); W - 28, teacher, 2d, b. Farmington, d/o Warren Whitehouse (farmer) and Emma A. York (at home)

Wendell M. m. Priscilla J. **DiPrizio** 7/13/1980 in Farmington

William A., Jr. m. Janet M. **Potter** 9/5/1964; H - s/o William Brown and June St. Tufts; W - d/o Irving D. Potter and Elsie E. Norwood of Berwick, ME

William Alfred of Middleton m. June St. Clair **Tufts** 5/1/1941 in Berwick, ME; H - 25, laborer, b. New Durham, s/o William H. Brown (Madison, teamster) and Mabel R. Schully (Boston, MA, cleaner); W - 19, shoe worker, b. Middleton, d/o Leon G. Tufts (Middleton, laborer) and Addie M. Kimball (Middleton, housewife)

BRUNELLE,

Ralph G. of Laconia m. Geraldine G. **Tufts** of Middleton 1/18/1958 in Laconia; H - s/o Raymond Brunelle; W - d/o George D. Tufts

BRYANT,

Travis m. Kelly J. **Brown** 5/16/1998 in Farmington

BRYSON,

William E. m. Sharon L. **Christie** 11/14/1964; H - s/o James R. Bryson and Helen M. Ludwig; W - d/o Melvin Christie and Cora J. Kelley of North Rochester

BULLIS,

Eric Addison, Jr. of Middleton m. Elizabeth Edna **Eastman** of Middleton 11/4/1942 in West Milton; H - 19, laborer, b. Haverhill, MA, s/o Eric A. Bullis (Westminster, MA, shoe worker) and Viola F. Griffin (Haverhill, MA, housewife); W - 20, at home, b. Middleton, d/o Charles F. Eastman (Milton, farmer) and Mary A. Tufts (Middleton, housewife)

Merritt A. of Middleton m. Edith M. **Hughes** of Farmington 11/25/1939 in Berwick, ME; H - 70, shoe cutter, 2d, b. Rouses Point, NY, s/o Albert Bullis (Rouses Point, NY, deceased) and Amelia A. Amlaw (Rouses Point, NY, deceased); W - 68, housework, 3d, b. Ottawa, Canada, d/o Reuben Daily (Watertown, NY, deceased) and Harriett M. Topper (Ogdensburg, NY, deceased)

Richard A. m. Dorothy A. **Irish** 8/16/1963; H - s/o Eric A. Bullis, Jr. of Middleton; W - d/o Neal A. Irish of Farmington

Russell H. of Middleton m. Bertha M. **Eastman** of Middleton 5/8/1946 in Farmington; H - 21, lumberer, b. Haverhill, MA, s/o Eric Bullis (Westminster, MA, shoe shop) and Viola Griffin (Haverhill, MA, housewife); W - 28, at home, b. Middleton, d/o Charles Eastman (Milton, farmer) and Mary Tufts (Middleton, housewife)

Stewart W. m. Norma B. **Willey** 8/27/1955 in Rochester; H - 21; W - 19

BURBANK,
Paul H. m. Sally A. **Sullivan** 6/19/1957 in Farmington; H - s/o Edward J. Burbank of Farmington; W - d/o Mary T. Kimball of Farmington

BURKE,
Christopher F. m. Vicki-Lynn **Brewer** 9/9/1995 in Middleton
Michael J. m. Patricia K. **Stultz** 5/25/1998 in Middleton

BURNS,
Barry M. m. Rebecca J. **Furber** 7/13/1968

BURROWS,
David E. of Middleton m. Mina E. **Pinkham** of Middleton 2/27/1894 in Union; H - 32, farmer, b. Middleton, s/o David Burrows (Middleton, farmer) and Betsy Burrows (Ossipee, housekeeper);

W - 20, housekeeper, b. Middleton, d/o George E. Pinkham (Farmington, farmer) and Laura J. Pinkham (Milton, housekeeper)

George of Milton m. Janet Mae **Reed** of Middleton 7/3/1947 in Farmington; H - 26, store manager, b. Milton, s/o Carl Burrows (Milton, mill worker) and Marion Rand (housewife); W - 20, clerk, 2d, b. Haverhill, MA, d/o Eric A. Bullis (Westminster, MA, shoe shop) and Viola F. Griffin (Haverhill, MA, housewife)

Isaiah H. of Middleton m. Mamie A. **Battersby** of Middleton 5/30/1898 in Union; H - 26, farmer, b. Middleton, s/o David Burrows (Middleton, farmer) and Betsey Whitham (Ossipee, at home); W - 19, housework, b. New York, NY, d/o Allen B. Battersby (New York, NY, copper pounder) and Elizabeth Hance (Staten Island, NY, book-binder)

John A. of Middleton m. Millie Alice **Pervere** of Alton 6/26/1948 in New Durham; H - 37, woodman, b. Middleton, s/o David Burrows (Middleton, shoeshop) and Mina Pinkham (Milton, housewife); W - 23, shoe shop, b. No. Strafford, d/o Arthur Pervere (VT, shoeshop) and Emma Stone (No. Strafford, housewife)

Paul A. of Middleton m. Beverly R. **Wilmot** of Middleton 7/7/1973; H - 21; W - 18

Richard A. m. Kim W. **Dixon** 9/2/1978 in Middleton

BUTLER,
Kenneth Alan m. Lorette Rita **Morin** 6/5/1970; H - b. 1/5/1943, s/o Clifford Butler and Helen Eastman of Middleton; W - b. 7/27/1950, d/o Delmont Gagne and Irene Wyatt of Dover

CAMERON,
Donald A. m. Jean E. **Bullis** 11/6/1964; H - s/o Albert J. Cameron and Barbara L. Shaw of Farmington; W - d/o Eric A. Bullis, Jr. and Edna E. Eastman

Steven S. m. Darlene T. **Smith** 8/14/1988 in Rochester

CANDELARI,
John A. of Berwick, ME m. Pauline A. **Demers** of Middleton 10/3/1936 in Middleton; H - 22, shoe worker, s/o Robert Candelari (Italy, carpenter) and Katherine Bermei (Italy, housewife); W - 21, at home, d/o ----- W. Demers (Berwick, ME, deceased) and ----- E. Corson (Somersworth, deceased)

CARETTE,
Gary J. m. Dorothy R. **West** 7/2/1979 in Middleton

CARLETON,
Earle W. of Alton m. Evelene L. **Peckham** 11/30/1967; H - s/o Harold E. Carleton and Helen M. Bourne; W - d/o Sidney A. Stevens and Marione E. Kinney

CARON,
Jason P. m. Elizabeth A. **Randall** 2/14/1997 in Hampton

CARPENTER,
Stephen E., Jr. m. Sarah L.A. **Fox** 4/5/1997 in Middleton

CASAVANT,
Joseph of Middleton m. Florence **Moulton** of Middleton 7/1/1950; H - 33, woods, s/o Osman Casavant (MA) and Mary E. Brannan (MA); W - 26, shoe shop, d/o Frederick A. Moulton (NH) and Vivian E. Grace (NH)

Joseph W. of Middleton m. M. Dorothy **Fassett** of Farmington 10/23/1937 in Sanbornville; H - 19, shoeshop, b. Middleton, s/o Osman H. Casavant (Athol, MA, shoeshop) and Mary Brannan (E. Boston, MA, at home); W - 27, shoeshop, b. E. Boston, MA, d/o George M. Fassett (E. Boston, MA, salesman) and Mary J. Hubbard (Yarmouth, NS, at home)

Walter J. of Middleton m. Rita E. **Cope** of Middleton 9/6/1958 in Middleton; H - s/o Joseph Casavant; W - d/o Daniel Cope

CASSELL,
Jerome E. m. Wanda J. **Bartlett** 6/19/1998 in Concord

CHAMBERLAIN,
Elmore of Middleton m. Arlene E. **Young** of Middleton 1/17/1933 in West Milton; H - 26, farmer, b. Alton, s/o George Chamberlain (New Durham, farmer) and Maude Hurd (Alton, housewife); W - 18, at home, b. Farmington, d/o Fred R. Young (Middleton, mill worker) and Alice E. Heath (Union, housewife)

CHAMBERLIN,
Matthew J. m. Stacy L. **Paradis** 9/3/1994 in Middleton

CHAMPAGNE,
Richard m. Carol **McArthur** 9/27/1986 in Middleton

CHAPMAN,
Robert G. of Middleton m. Jane C. **Willard** of Crown Point 11/17/1951; H - 18, construction worker, b. NH, s/o Fred Chapman and Irene M. Acton; W - 17, at home, b. NY, d/o James H. Willard and Cancia M. Thebeague

CHASE,
Anthony J. m. Robin R. **Bierley** 9/8/1990 in Middleton
Carleton of Gonic m. Eunice **Regan** of Middleton 5/27/1950; H - 19, lumber worker, s/o Carl E. Chase (NH) and Lena R. Lesperance (NH); W - 17, shoe worker, d/o Francis M. Regan (MA) and Eunice M. Gilbert (NH)
David L. m. Hazel J. **Ellingwood** 4/14/1984

CHESLEY,
Gary J. m. Dorothy C. **Sindorf** 6/17/1978 in Farmington
James M. m. Debra Lynn **Frost** 4/27/1975 in Farmington; H - s/o Fred Chesley and Mary Stevens; W - d/o Jack Frost and Freda Jenness
Michael A. m. Tanya M. **Eaton** 4/25/1998 in Wakefield

CHICK,
Sumner L. m. Lillian E. **Mayo** 7/2/1994 in Middleton

CICCOTELLI,
Larry V. m. Paula L. **Brown** 2/17/1984

CICOLINI,
Peter Thomas m. Nancy Ann **Pennacchio** 1/23/1993 in Jackson

COLBATH,
Fred P. of Middleton m. Eliza S. **Thompson** of Springvale, ME 7/6/1906 in Union; H - 34, heel cutter, b. Middleton, s/o Leighton D. Colbath (Middleton, shoe maker); W - 25, shoe shop, 2d, b. Springvale, ME, d/o Charles S. Ricker (Shapleigh, ME, farmer)

Richard P. m. Virginia A. **Downs** 10/3/1954 in Farmington; H - 19; W - 23

COLEMAN,
Peter J. of New York m. Beatrice M. **Wilkinson** of Middleton 8/30/1958 in Milton Mills; H - s/o Peter Coleman; W - d/o Milborne Wilkinson

COOK,
Charles L. of Middleton m. Dorothy **Poore** of Landaff 12/25/1932 in Lisbon; H - 25, laborer, b. Middleton, s/o Edwin E. Cook (Middleton, farmer) and Ennie Jones (Middleton, housewife); W - 27, at home, b. Landaff, d/o Harry E. Poor (Landaff, dairy farmer) and Agnes Holmes (Whitefield, housewife)

Clarence E. of Middleton m. Pauline D. **Tufts** of Middleton 3/30/1926 in Union; H - 20, laborer, b. Middleton, s/o Edwin E. Cook (Middleton, farmer) and Ennie M. Jones (Middleton, housewife); W - 17, housework, b. Middleton, d/o Leon G. Tufts (Middleton, farmer) and Addie Kimball (Middleton, housewife)

Edward of Middleton m. Ena M. **Jones** of Middleton 5/9/1896 in New Durham; H - 29, farmer, b. Middleton, s/o Jacob H. Cook

(Middleton, farmer) and Pauline Ellis (Middleton, housekeeper); W - 16, housekeeper, b. Middleton, d/o Daniel B. Jones (Middleton, farmer) and Emma Perkins (Middleton, housekeeper)

George H. m. Judith K. **Holmes** 6/25/1966; H - 27, s/o Charles Cook of Middleton; W - 23, d/o Byron L. Holmes of Claremont

COOLIDGE,
Harland G. m. Cassandra M. **DiPrizio** 3/4/1989 in Union

COUTURE,
E.R. Paul m. Constance P. **Parent** 2/20/1960 in Sanbornville; H - 26; W - 19

CUNHA,
Paul m. Laura **Shambos** 6/14/1986 in Middleton

DAELLENBACH,
Michael J. m. Kim M. **Bailey** 11/22/1997 in Dover

DALRYMPLE,
Curtis J. m. Nancy L. **Reil** 8/22/1998 in Farmington

DAME,
Daniel Emerson of Middleton m. Minnie M. **Smith** of Middleton 11/25/1897 in Middleton; H - 24, weaver, b. Portsmouth, s/o John H.T. Dame (Portsmouth, shoemaker) and Fidelia A. Philbrick (Portsmouth, housekeeper); W - 18, housekeeper, b. Farmington, d/o Charles Smith (Dover, railroad hand) and Etta L. Brown (Farmington, housekeeper)

DANIELS,
William Henry m. Dorothy H. **Peters** 8/27/1976

DAUDELIN,
Lloyd M. m. Janet M. (Bullis) **Tatro** 6/7/1972; H - 49, s/o Victor Daudelin and Beatrice Brown; W - 46, d/o Eric A. Bullis and Viola Griffin

DAVIS,
Norman G. of Farmington m. Violet M. **Leighton** of Middleton 10/29/1928 in Union; H - 25, shoeworker, b. Farmington, s/o Charles F. Davis (Wolfeboro, laborer) and Ella Bunker; W - 23, shoeworker, b. Middleton, d/o Walter F. Leighton (Middleton, carpenter) and Elizabeth Drew (Middleton, housewife)

DECKER,
Patrick F. m. Betty Ann **Ringer** 5/28/1988 in Milton

DESIMONE,
Carlo M. m. Sandra L. **Bridges** 1/8/1978 in Farmington

DILLION,
James W. of Fairborn, OH m. Brenda M. **Harriman** of Middleton 4/20/1962 in Portsmouth; H - s/o James H. Dillion and Lillian J. Austin of Fairborn, OH; W - d/o Cyrus L. Harriman and Doris E. DePatra of Middleton

DIPRIZIO,
Charles, Jr. m. Sonia D. **Hector** 11/9/1957 in Rochester; H - s/o Charles DiPrizio of Middleton; W - d/o Edward Hector of Rutland, VT
Curt C. m. Jamie L. **Chesley** 9/26/1998 in Sanbornville
James J. m. Shirley J. **Murphy** 11/27/1977 in Farmington
John H. of Middleton m. Enid M. **Lowd** of Acton, ME 6/14/1947 in Acton, ME; H - 24, lumber yard, b. Middleton, s/o Charles DiPrizio (Italy, lumber dealer) and Louise Barlotta (Italy, housewife); W - 20, at home, b. Acton, ME, d/o Albert P. Lowd (Acton, ME, dairy farmer) and Doris Rowell (housewife)
Joseph C. m. Kimberly A. **Lefavour** 10/17/1976

Prisco C. of Middleton m. Phyllis E. **Davis** of Rochester 11/17/1962 in Rochester; H - s/o Constantino DiPrizio and Mary E. DiPrizio of Middleton; W - d/o Beverly H. Davis and Gertrude M. Tinker of Rochester

Prisco N. of Middleton m. Lois E. **Canney** of Farmington 8/4/1946 in Rochester; H - 22, farmer, b. Middleton, s/o Charles DiPrizio (Naples, Italy, contractor) and Louise Sarletta (Naples, Italy); W - 20, b. Farmington, d/o Ralph Canney (New Durham, poultry man) and Ethel Hayes (Milton, housewife)

DIXON,
Kelly D. m. Darlene M. **Twombly** 8/3/1991 in Middleton
Mark R. m. Tina L. **Dres** 10/27/1990 in Middleton

DOCKHAM,
Stephen W. m. Gayle L. **Bailey** 8/--/1974; H - s/o Raymond and Arlene Dockham; W - d/o Norman and Hazel Bailey

DOUGLAS,
Richard E. of Middleton m. Marianna R. **Scala** of Rochester 9/6/1958 in Rochester; H - s/o Gordon Douglas; W - d/o Michael Scala
Ronald G. m. Shirley L. **Williams** 8/4/1956 in Farmington; H - 18; W - 18

DOW,
Wayne E. m. Diane L. **Fioentino** 2/24/1994 in Middleton

DOWNS,
Fred W. of Wakefield m. Virginia A. **Stevens** of Middleton 11/3/1948 in Milton; H - 22, knife factory, b. Union, s/o Winifred E. Downs (Wolfeboro, mill employee) and Carrie Wentworth (Acton, ME, housewife); W - 18, waitress, b. Sandown, d/o Earl W. Stevens (Middleton, knife factory) and Elsie Ray (Hudson, housewife)

DREW,
Ellsworth of Middleton m. Flora M. **Bryant** of Freedom 7/9/1898 in Freedom; H - 28, farmer, 2d, wid., b. Eaton, s/o Thomas Drew (Eaton, farmer) and Sarah Bryant (Eaton, at home); W - 21, at home, b. Freedom, d/o Charles H. Bryant (Eaton, farmer) and Sarah Brooks (Freedom, at home)

Forest W. m. Linda O. **Stevens** 12/20/1957 in Union; H - s/o Christine Drew of Providence, RI; W - d/o John D. Stevens of Middleton

Robert B. of Middleton m. Grace M. **Lord** of Lebanon, ME 3/29/1924 in Somersworth; H - 19, farmer, b. Middleton, s/o Ellsworth Drew and Flora M. Bryant; W - 20, schoolteacher, b. Lebanon, ME, d/o J. Fred Lord and Sarah Warburton

William D. of Middleton m. Effie May **Thurston** of Middleton 1/14/1909 in Union; H - 23, farmer, b. Middleton, s/o Horace Drew (Eaton, farmer) and Maggie Walker (England, housework); W - 17, housework, b. Berwick, ME, d/o Josiah H. Thurston (Effingham, sawyer) and Silvia Ann Newhall (Wells, ME, housework)

DUBOIS,
Ronald R. m. Julie A. **Prosper** 12/7/1991 in Middleton

DUGGER,
R. Barclay, Jr. m. Signe L. **DiPrizio** 8/8/1998 in Farmington

DUPREY,
Louis W. m. Florence **Golledge** 6/19/1957 in Farmington; H - s/o Louis Duprey of Middleton; W - d/o Charles Golledge of Farmington

Louis W. of Middleton. m. Paula A. **Maddock** of Somersworth 8/11/1962 in Sanbornville; H - s/o Louis W. Duprey and Jeanette M. Ferraro of Farmington; W - d/o Paul J. Vachon and Pheobe LeFlannie of Somersworth

EASTMAN,

Charles F. of Middleton m. Mary A. **Tufts** of Middleton 6/2/1905 in Brookfield; H - 22, farmer, b. Milton, s/o Walter Tibbetts (farmer) and Harriett Downing (at home); W - 15, at home, b. Middleton, d/o Charles D. Tufts (Middleton, farmer) and Nellie Corson (New Durham, at home)

Harry H. m. Bernice A. (Ginn) **Boothby** 6/11/1971 in Middleton; H - s/o Charles A. Eastman and Mary Tufts; W - d/o Elwood Ginn and Alberta York

Harry Hanson of Middleton m. Evelyn May **Holman** of Wakefield 12/29/1945 in Farmington; H - 30, truck driver, b. Middleton, s/o Charles F. Eastman (Milton, retired) and Mary Adeline Tufts (Middleton, housewife); W - 18, store clerk, b. Lexington, MA, d/o George D. Holman (Lincoln, MA, knife factory) and Lillian M. Wood (Lexington, MA, housewife)

EDGERLY,

Lloyd A. m. Patricia G. **Delisle** 6/13/1987 in Middleton

Lloyd Q. m. Sandra **McFarland** 4/30/1977 in Middleton

Raymond C. of Middleton m. Deborah A. **Day** of Middleton 12/31/1985 in Middleton

EILA,

Sal R. m. Bette Gene **Stephens** 4/3/1976

ELLINGWOOD,

Danny L. m. Alana R. **Heald** 4/27/1991 in Middleton

Leland m. Joyce **Decker** 8/16/1986 in Middleton

ELLIOT,

Peter E. m. Michele R. **Armstrong** 11/17/1990 in Rochester

EMERY,

George E. of Middleton m. Addie **Simonds** of Middleton 7/26/1896 in Middleton; H - 40, farmer, b. Eaton, s/o Japhet Emery (Sanford, ME, farmer) and Mary E. Jenness (Eaton, housekeeper); W - 40, housekeeper, 3d, b. Middleton, d/o Stillman Simonds (Nashua, farmer) and Hannah Stevens (Middleton, housekeeper)

FARRINGTON,
Donald M. m. Doreen L. **Garland** 8/8/1992 in Middleton

FEERO,
Jesse L. m. Maureen **Taney** 4/5/1980 in Middleton

FERRARA,
Burton A. of Middleton m. Paula A. **Melanson** of Middleton 10/19/1985 in Hampton

FIFIELD,
George of Wakefield m. Livinia **Brewer** of Middleton 9/14/1950; H - 25, laborer, s/o George Fifield and Blanche E. Penny; W - 19, at home, d/o Leslie S. Brewer and Harriet E. Whitman

FORDER,
Robert of Middleton m. Shirley **Dixon** of Wakefield 9/16/1950; H - 23, US Army, s/o William John Forder (England) and Elizabeth Lloyd (England); W - 18, office worker, d/o George R. Dixon (NB) and Bessie F. Wiggin (NB)

FROST,
John H. m. Freda L. **Jenness** 5/27/1955 in Middleton; H - 28; W - 24
Newell E. m. Doris R. **Cram** 7/3/1960 in West Milton; H - 45; W - 46
Newell E. m. Charlotte E. **Heath** 11/18/1966; H - 51, s/o Elibous Frost; W - 27, d/o Llewellyn A. Buck of Rumford, ME

GARRETT,
Matthew D. m. Beth A. **Bourque** 8/13/1994 in Alton

GATES,
Charles Frederick m. Deborah Lee **Drapeau** 6/19/1976

GEARY,
Anthony W. of Middleton m. Bessie K. **Eastman** of Middleton 2/12/1931 in Union; H - 41, laborer, 2d, b. Waterboro, ME, s/o Sam R. Geary (Waterboro, ME, millwright) and Carrie B. Thomas (Limerick, ME, housework); W - 21, housework, b. Middleton, d/o Charles F. Eastman (Middleton, farmer) and Mary A. Tufts (Middleton, housework)

GERONAITIS,
William V. m. Teresa A. **Melanson** 4/18/1988 in Dover

GLIDDEN,
David O. m. Natalie L. **Brown** 7/11/1964; H - s/o Ounard L. Glidden and Elsie F. Fifield; W - d/o William A. Brown and June St. Tufts
David O. m. Mary J. **Tufts** 12/20/1975 in Wakefield; H - s/o Ormand L. Glidden and Elsie Fifield; W - d/o Harry Stanley and Ellen Otis
Dennis C. m. Deborah J. **Murphy** 6/20/1987 in Middleton

GOLDTHWAITE,
Karl Stanton m. Patricia Louise **Douglas** 6/22/1963; H - s/o Benjamin Goldthwaite of West Lebanon, ME; W - d/o Gordon Franklin Douglas of Middleton

GOODWIN,
John F., Jr. of Farmington m. Odabelle M. **Willey** of Middleton 11/27/1932 in Wakefield; H - 22, woodsman, b. Farmington, s/o John F. Goodwin (York, ME, shoeworker) and Inez J. Ham (Farmington, housewife); W - 24, at home, b. Middleton, d/o Henry D. Willey (New Durham, farmer) and Edith M. Ham
Keith A. m. Rhonda L. **Drew** 8/6/1977 in Farmington

GORDON,
Preston D. m. Melody L. **Peterson** 11/12/1989 in Albany

GRACE,
Chandler T. of Middleton m. Mary **Hess** of Portsmouth 11/8/1932 in Strafford; H - 30, chauffeur, b. Stratford, s/o Joseph S. Grace (Chatham, farmer) and Lodema Cates (E. Stratford, housewife); W - 18, at home, b. Brentwood, LI
Chandler T. m. Annie I. **Lamper** 4/13/1968
Joseph E. of Middleton m. Norma M. **Adams** of Rochester 3/4/1948 in Northumberland; H - 22, woodsman, b. Middleton, s/o Joseph S. Grace (Chatham, retired) and Lodena L. Cates (Strafford, housewife); W - 23, shoe shop, b. Guilford, ME, d/o Edgar N. Adams (Dover-Foxcroft, ME, carpenter) and Verne M. Willey (New Durham, housewife)

GRAY,
Bruce A. m. Tracy L. **Depalma** 5/19/1990 in Wakefield
Frank M. m. Anne-Marie **Gauthier** 9/2/1995 in Middleton

GREEN,
Steven B. m. Debra L. **Chesley** 3/3/1996 in Middleton

GREGOIRE,
Gerard R. m. Lenora W. **Lawrence** 9/1/1991 in Middleton

HALEY,
William R. m. Helen J. **Shave** 9/12/1987 in Middleton

HANCHETT,
Christopher A. m. Stephanie A. **Martin** 9/29/1995 in Somersworth
Larry A. of Farmington m. Linda D. **Tripp** of Middleton 3/17/1973; H - 19; W - 19
Larry A. m. Linda D. **Hanchett** 8/6/1976
Larry A. m. Linda **Hanchett** 1/1/1984

HANSON,
William F. of Middleton m. Mary E. **Penney** of Middleton 11/7/1887 in Wakefield; H - 37, laborer, b. Middleton; W - 28, b. New Durham

HARRIMAN,
Richard N. m. Carol E. **Kinney** 6/19/1966; H - 22, s/o Cyrus Harriman of Rochester; W - 17, d/o Walter V. Kinney of Middleton

HASKINS,
William C. m. Nancy Rae **Haskins** 4/15/1978 in Middleton

HATFIELD,
Timothy P. m. Karyn G. **Trudeau** 7/11/1987 in Middleton

HEALD,
Alfred P. m. Regina A. **Edgerly** 6/25/1966; H - 29, s/o James N. Heald, Jr. of Wolfeboro; W - 18, d/o Chester G. Edgerly of Middleton

Byron Jewett of New York, NY m. Marion **Gies** of Yonkers, NY 10/1/1942 in Middleton; H - 31, mason, b. Troy, ME, s/o James N. Heald (Troy, ME, blacksmith) and Edith Jewell (Westbrook, ME, housewife); W - 41, cook, 2d, b. Center Sandwich, d/o Warren Parker (ME, deceased) and Addie Brown (Conway, housewife)

HILL,
Craig m. Lorna **Smith** 2/15/1986 in Union

Waldo L. of Wakefield m. Vila S. **Tanner** 4/5/1924 in Rochester; H - 19, b. Wakefield, s/o Leon Hill and Ellen Willey; W - 24, 2d, b. Middleton, d/o George W. Kimball and Eliza S. Hanscom

Walter Freeman of Middleton m. Pauline Anita **Dodier** of Sanbornville 7/4/1945 in Wolfeboro; H - 20, laborer, b. Wakefield, s/o Waldo L. Hill (Wakefield, lumberman) and Vila L. Kimball (Middleton, housewife); W - 19, student, b.

Biddeford, ME, d/o Edward Dodier (Wakefield, chef) and Marie L. Brochu (St. Julian, Canada, housewife)

HOLDERNESS,
Richard O. m. Alice Jeanne **Nadeau** 1/7/1966; H - 34, s/o Charles Holderness of Rockland, ME; W - 25, d/o Elmer Drew of Milton

HOWARD,
Percy A. m. Shirley E. **Stevens** 11/28/1959 in West Milton; H - 39; W - 23

HUCKINS,
Shane E. m. Tina Mae **Chamberland** 7/15/1995 in Milton

HUNTER,
Bruce J. m. Rachel M. **Eldridge** 8/29/1998 in Milton
James B. m. Maureen R. **Leighton** 2/20/1959 in Farmington; H - 23, s/o Charles O. Hunter; W - 19, d/o William T. Leighton
Rockie J. of Middleton m. Darlene D. **Allen** of New Durham 2/16/1985 in Rochester

HURD,
Mervyn F. of Milton Mills m. Alice E. **Stevens** of Middleton 8/31/1931 in Rochester; H - 20, salesman, b. Milton Mills, s/o Ralph H. Hurd (Milton Mills, finisher in mill) and Florence E. Tuttle (Wakefield, housewife); W - 18, at home, b. Middleton, d/o Albert Stevens (Middleton, farmer) and Bernice Tufts (Middleton, housewife)

HUSSEY,
Edward S. of Middleton m. Rosalie A. **Wilmot** of Farmington 10/6/1973; H - 26; W - 18

JACKSON,
William V., Jr. of West Washington, ME m. Lillian M. **Chapman** of Middleton 8/21/1948 in Waldoboro, ME; H - 29, truck driver, b.

Boston, MA, s/o William V. Jackson (West Washington, ME, farmer) and Hazel Peasley (Waldoboro, ME, housewife); W - 32, shoe shop, 2d, b. Dresden, ME, d/o George Chapman (Dresden, ME, farmer) and Marjorie Cunningham (Wiscasset, ME, housewife).

JENNESS,
- Alden Gerard of Middleton m. Edith Natalie **Hunt** of Farmington 6/30/1945 in Farmington; H - 20, b. Middleton, s/o Elmer E. Jenness (Rochester, mill worker) and Lucinda M. Drew (Middleton, war worker); W - 20, shoe shop, b. Farmington, d/o Loran D. Hunt (Epping, retired) and Alice G. O'Connor (Haverhill, MA, housewife)
- Clarence E. of Middleton m. Barbara L. **Hunt** of Farmington 3/23/1946 in Farmington; H - 22, mill worker, b. Middleton, s/o Elmer Jenness (Rochester, millworker) and Lucinda Drew (Middleton, housewife); W - 23, clerk, b. Farmington, d/o Loren Hunt (Epping, no occ.) and Alice Connor (Haverhill, MA, housewife)
- Elmer of Rochester m. Lucinda **Drew** of Middleton 3/31/1923 in Somersworth; H - 28, mill operator, b. Rochester, s/o Isaac Jenness (Rochester, shoe repairer) and Sarah Howard (Rochester, housewife); W - 20, housework, b. Middleton, d/o Ellsworth Drew (Eaton, farmer) and Flora Bryant (Freedom, housewife)
- Leroy Stanley of Rochester m. Marion Elaine **Tufts** 11/12/1940 in Rochester; H - 18, logging, b. Rochester, s/o Wilbur H. Jenness (Rochester, woodsman) and Ethel R. Merrill (Nottingham, housewife); W - 17, housework, b. Middleton, d/o Joseph W. Tufts (Middleton, farmer) and Lillian D. Tuttle (New Durham, housewife)

JOHNSTON,
Dave Joseph m. April Elizabeth **Daudelin** 9/14/1993 in Dover

JONES,
Clyde F. m. Carlyne P. **Brooks** 7/8/1965; H - 44, s/o John Jones of East Lebanon, ME; W - 37, d/o Clarence Cook and Mrs. Leo LeClair of Middleton

JOY,
Frank T. of So. Berwick, ME m. Alice P. **Kimball** of Middleton 8/30/1905 in Wakefield; H - 23, fireman, b. So. Berwick, ME, s/o Owen Joy (So. Berwick, ME, farmer) and Sarah Abbott (So. Berwick, ME, at home); W - 18, weaver, b. Middleton, d/o George W. Kimball (Middleton, mill operator) and Eliza S. Hanscome (Dover, at home)

Kenneth D. m. Erica J. **Pratt** 7/26/1997 in Farmington

Mason S. of Union m. Mildred M. **Berry** of Middleton 3/12/1935 in Rochester; H - 18, laborer, b. Union, s/o Frank D. Joy (So. Berwick, ME, RR employee) and Alice Kimball (Middleton, housewife); W - 14, at home, b. New Durham, d/o Guy A. Berry (Wolfeboro, mechanic) and Eva A. Weymouth (Quincy, MA, housewife)

Phillip S. m. Lori L. **Harvey** 5/5/1989 in New Durham

KEATON,
James L. m. Holly B. **Kimball** 12/26/1991 in Danville

KEEGAN,
James R., Jr. m. Roxanne A. **Tufts** 9/10/1988 in Middleton

KELLEY,
Asa B. of Middleton m. Effie M. **Downing** of Middleton 6/26/1897 in Brookfield; H - 32, sawyer, 2d, b. Salem, s/o Asa Kelley (Salem, farmer) and Charlotte Smith (Hillsboro, housework); W - 21, housework, b. Middleton, d/o Luther Downing (Middleton, farmer) and Rosilla P. Hartford (East Rochester, housework)

KIMBALL,

Alphonse Lester of Middleton m. Priscilla Adeline **Tufts** of Middleton 8/16/1945 in Berwick, ME; H - 29, shoe shop, b. Alfred, ME, s/o Alphonse E. Kimball (Middleton, mill worker) and Ida Maxwell (Alfred, ME, deceased); W - 23, at home, b. Middleton, d/o Leon G. Tufts (Middleton, farmer) and Addeline M. Kimball (Middleton, housewife)

Alphonze of Middleton m. Ida **Littlefield** of Middleton 3/8/1915 in Milton Mills; H - 35, laborer, b. Middleton, s/o David Kimball (Farmington, shoemaker) and Nellie Hanscom (Farmington, housekeeper); W - 27, housekeeper, b. Alfred, ME, d/o Byron Maxwell (Alfred, ME) and Ellen Smith (Sanford, ME, housekeeper)

David L. m. Barbara Ann (Fifield) **Hodsdon** 6/11/1971 in Middleton; H - s/o Alphonso L. Kimball and Priscilla Tufts; W - d/o Charles Fifield, Sr. and Louise Drapeau

Elmer B. of Middleton m. Margaret **Wentworth** of Milton Mills 11/14/1923 in Milton Mills; H - 27, shoemaker, b. Middleton, s/o George W. Kimball (Middleton, farmer) and Eliza Hanscom (Dover, housewife); W - 22, school teacher, b. Milton Mills, d/o Hiram Wentworth (Milton Mills, carpenter) and Clara Pierce (Shapleigh, ME, housewife)

Ernest Alfred of Middleton m. Angie Emma **Colbath** of Middleton 5/2/1941 in Milton; H - 36, laborer, b. Union, s/o Alphonzo E. Kimball (Middleton, laborer) and Myrtle Glidden (New Durham, housewife); W - 21, at home, b. Lynn, MA, d/o Bert Dudley Colbath (Farmington, shoe worker) and Emma L. Kelley (Boston, MA, housewife)

George of Middleton m. Helen A. **LaBonte** of Middleton 7/26/1947 in Farmington; H - 33, laborer, b. Epping, s/o Walter Kimball (laborer) and Angeline M. Perkins (Northwood, housewife); W - 27, at home, 2d, b. New Durham, d/o Andrew Kleczek (Poland, farmer) and Mary Bresideski (Poland, housewife)

George B. of Middleton m. Gladys F. **Corson** of Milton 4/11/1921; H - 29, superintendent, b. Wakefield, s/o George W. Kimball (Middleton, farmer) and Eliza Hanscom (Dover, housewife); W -

23, governess, b. Milton, d/o John M. Corson (Milton, teamster) and Eva M. Postleton (Milton, housewife)

George B. m. Edith C. **Griffith** 11/24/1957 in Union; W - d/o Walter Harris of Wakefield

John m. Gertrude A. (Varney) **Hogan** 9/20/1971 in Ossipee; H - s/o Maurice Kimball and Louise Mullin; W - d/o Lewis Varney and Grace Pinkham

KING,
Oliver M., Jr. m. Bernice A. **Lessard** 7/3/1995 in Wolfeboro

KINNEY,
Arthur R. of Middleton m. Helen Mae **Burrows** of North Berwick, ME 6/22/1947 in Acton, ME; H - 21, auto mechanic, b. Newburyport, MA, s/o Allen Kinney (NS, carpenter) and Margaret Mullen (NS, housewife); W - 18, at home, b. Kittery, ME, d/o Arnold Burrows (Brattleboro, VT, auto mechanic) and Geneva Bowden (Eliot, ME, housewife)

Walter Vidito of Middleton m. Virginia Frances **Tufts** of Middleton 5/1/1943 in West Milton; H - 28, lineman, b. Westfield, ME, s/o Allen John Kinney (NB, carpenter) and Margaret Mullen (NS, housewife); W - 19, b. Middleton, d/o Clyde Linwood Tufts (Middleton, carpenter) and Evelyne Moulton (Farmington, dead)

KNOWLES,
Joseph H. of Middleton m. Hattie M. **Kimball** of Middleton 4/14/1890 in Milton; H - 48, farmer, b. Middleton; W - 34, b. Middleton

KOCHORIS,
Mark m. Linda M. **Dow** 3/31/1984

LABRECQUE,
Franklin D. of Rochester m. Gloria M. **Tufts** of Middleton 9/2/1949 in Middleton; H - 23, bus driver, b. NH, s/o Roland LaBrecque

(NH) and Alice Grenier (NH); W - 18, at home, b. NH, d/o Orrie M. Tufts (NH) and Iris E. Shepard (NH)

LACARRUBBA,
Emanuel m. Eleanor Louise **DiPrizio** 1/19/1963; H - s/o Salvatore LaCarrubba of Amagansette, NY; W - d/o Charles DiPrizio, Sr. of Middleton

LANDRY,
Gary J. m. Shelly Lee **Balwin** 1/20/1979 in Middleton

LAPIERRE,
Jeffrey A. m. Tina M. **Downs** 9/10/1994 in Farmington
Rene G. m. Shirley A. **Young** 11/24/1961; H - s/o Uldric LaPierre of Middleton; W - d/o Roland Young of Middleton
Richard R. m. Linda S. **Luongo** 11/18/1972; H - 21, s/o Ernest Lapierre and Lucille Bergevin; W - 18, d/o Victor Luongo and Gladys Ellis
Robert L. m. Carolyn **Wilkinson** 11/5/1960 in Sanbornville; H - 21; W - 18
Victor A. of Middleton m. Carol F. **Gaskell** of Farmington 9/1/1962 in Farmington; H - s/o Uldric A. LaPierre and Eva M. Broulott of Berwick, ME; W - d/o Joseph Gaskell and Irene G. Benoit of Farmington

LARSON,
Gene L. m. Mary B. **Williams** 10/12/1991 in Rochester

LAVOIE,
Edward Thomas of Rochester m. Marie Louise **Jolley** of Middleton 11/19/1943 in Sanford, ME; H - 55, painter, 2d, b. Canada, s/o Lazaar Lavoie (Canada, blacksmith) and Elabe Dubois (Canada, housewife); W - 38, shoe worker, 2d, b. Canada, d/o Alphonse Ouellette (Canadam farmer) and Fleurie Boucher (Canada, housewife)

LAWRENCE,
Matthew J. m. Suzanne **Ross** 6/1/1991 in Dover
Samuel A. of Middleton m. Flora M. **Drew** of Middleton 7/1/1924 in Exeter; H - 65, 2d, b. Meredith, s/o Samuel A. Lawrence and Ann V. Hunt; W - 48, 2d, b. Freedom, d/o Charles H. Bryant and Sarah J. Brooks
William P. m. Nancy A. **Lindsey** 4/25/1997 in Seabrook

LECLAIR,
Leo A. of Middleton m. Pauline Tufts **Cook** 10/2/1943 in Berwick, ME; H - 22, lineman, b. Nottingham, s/o Alphonse LeClair (Canada, laborer) and Florence Glover (Nottingham, housewife); W - 35, shoe worker, 2d, b. Middleton, d/o Leon Tufts (Middleton, millworker) and Addie Kimball (Middleton, housewife)

LEFEBRVE,
George H. m. Debra **Jones** 5/12/1979 in New Castle

LEIGHTON,
Charles A. of Middleton m. Georgia L. **Craft** of Haverhill, MA 6/26/1901 in Middleton; H - 28, sawyer, b. Rochester, s/o George Leighton (Farmington, farmer) and Lydia A. Pinkham (Dover Point, domestic); W - 26, domestic, b. Kentville, NS, d/o Simns Craft (Kentville, NS, farmer) and Bertha Ward (Kentville, NS, domestic)
Charles L. of Middleton m. Olivette T. **Pigott** of East Boston, MA 7/20/1896 in Sanbornville; H - 29, farmer, b. Middleton, s/o Charles H. Leighton (Middleton, farmer) and Annah E. Whitehouse (Brookfield, housekeeper); W - 29, b. Charlestown, MA, d/o Richard Piggott (Boston, MA, morocco finisher) and Hannah T. Locke (Rye, housekeeper)
Frank of Farmington m. Cora **Tufts** of Middleton 12/30/1932 in Milton; H - 21, laborer, b. Milton, s/o Fred Leighton (Farmington, laborer) and Grace Cotton (Milton, shoe operator);

W - 15, at home, b. Middleton, d/o J. W. Tufts (Middleton, farmer) and Lillian Tuttle (New Durham, housewife)

James P. of Middleton m. Etta M. **Young** of Middleton 6/15/1900 in Rochester; H - 25, laborer, b. Middleton, s/o Charles H. Leighton (Strafford, farmer) and Lucy A. Drew (Eaton, housework); W - 34, housework, 2d, widow, b. Middleton, d/o John H. Young (Wolfeboro, farmer) and Emily Cook (Middleton, housework)

Lewis F. of Middleton m. Helen M. **Cook** of Middleton 11/8/1904 in Brookfield; H - 25, mill operative, b. Middleton, s/o Charles H. Leighton (Middleton, farmer) and Lucy A. Drew (Eaton, at home); W - 17, at home, b. Middleton, d/o Dudley S. Cook (Middleton, watchman) and Lucy A. Hill (Wakefield, teacher)

Oscar W. of Middleton m. Carrie J. **Piggott** of Somerville, MA 1/18/1910 in Somerville, MA; H - 22, farmer, b. Middleton, s/o Charles F. Leighton (Middleton, farmer) and Lucy A. Drew (Eaton, housekeeper); W - 32, housekeeper, b. Charlestown, MA, d/o Richard Piggott (Charlestown, MA, merchant) and Elizabeth Lovell (Taunton, MA, housekeeper)

Presco F. of Middleton m. Gladys E. **Russell** of Milton 6/24/1923 in Milton; H - 24, laborer, b. Middleton, s/o Walter F. Leighton (Middleton, carpenter) and Elizabeth S. Drew (Middleton, housewife); W - 19, housework, b. Danvers, MA, d/o Arthur P. Russell (Danvers, MA, laborer) and Mary S. Kimball (Danvers, MA, housewife)

Rodney W. of Middleton m. Vickie A. **Lessard** of Middleton 6/23/1962 in Middleton; H - s/o William T. Leighton and Leona M. Grace of Middleton; W - d/o Forrest G. Lessard and Pauline Nutter

Walter F. of Middleton m. Lizzie S. **Drew** of Middleton 3/12/1892 in Farmington; H - carpenter, b. Middleton, s/o Charles H. Leighton (Middleton, farmer) and Hannah Whitehouse (Middleton, housekeeper); W - b. Middleton, d/o Horace Drew (Middleton) and Maggie Walker (Middleton, housekeeper)

William T. of Middleton m. Leona M. **Grace** of Middleton 4/25/1932 in Milton; H - 32, laborer, b. Middleton, s/o Walter F. Leighton (Middleton, carpenter) and Elizabeth Drew (Middleton, housewife); W - 30, b. Tamworth, d/o Joseph S. Grace (Chatham, farmer) and Lodema Cates (E. Stratford, housewife)

LEPENE,
Donald M. m. Patricia A. **Stevens** 9/28/1956 in Farmington; H - 18; W - 17

LESSARD,
Forrest G. of Middleton m. Marilyn J. **Noyes** of Farmington 12/14/1946 in Farmington; H - 24, lumberman, 2d, b. Middleton, s/o Dolphius Lessard (Somersworth, chef) and Edith Gage (Somersworth, housewife); W - 18, shoe shop, b. South Paris, ME, d/o Leland Noyes (So. Paris, ME, lumberman) and Gwendolyn Record (So. Paris, ME, housewife)
Kelly Francis m. Lori Lynn (Joy) Harvey **Craig** 4/19/1993 in Middleton
Kenneth m. Flora **Worth** 7/24/1986 in Farmington
Kenneth R. m. Bonnie Sue **Deuso** 6/17/1989 in Tuftonboro
Robert W. of Middleton m. Mary B. **Sullivan** of Farmington 6/7/1946 in Farmington; H - 22, shoe shop, b. Middleton, s/o Delphis Lessard (Somersworth, chef) and Edith Gage (Somersworth, housewife); W - 23, shoe shop, b. Berwick, NS, d/o Fred Sullivan (Berwick, NS, taxi driver) and Elizabeth Aldred (Berwick, NS, housewife)
Roger Leslie m. Charlotte Marie **Stevens** 11/28/1953 in Middleton; H - 27, lumber, Delphis Lessard and Edith M. Gage; W - 19, shoe shop, Melvin Stevens and Maude P. Merrill
William D. m. Betty J. **Weeks** 9/10/1966; H - 18, s/o Kenneth L. Lessard of Middleton; W - 18, d/o Kenneth W. Weeks of Wolfeboro

LIBBY,
Gregory G. m. Melissa A. **Peters** 10/8/1994 in Milton

LITTLEFIELD,
Robert M. of Union m. Sylvia L. **Hill** of Union 4/6/1946 in Milton Mills; H - 21, laborer, b. Enfield, ME, s/o Maynard Littlefield (Grand Falls, ME, mill worker) and Louise Preble (Lowell, ME); W - 19, at home, b. Rochester, d/o Waldo Hill (Wakefield, teamster) and Vila Kimball (Middleton, mill worker)

LUCIER,
Mark Charles m. Patricia Ann **Young** 5/29/1993 in Middleton

LUONGO,
James Ellis m. Lori Mae **Pike** 6/26/1976
James Ellis m. Lee Ann **Campbell** 4/6/1984
Nicola m. Marie **DiPrizio** 2/9/1957 in Sanbornville; H - s/o Joseph Luongo of Italy; W - d/o Charles DiPrizio

MARCOUX,
Joseph of Milton m. Janet **Chapman** of Middleton 5/13/1950; H - 23, machine tender, s/o Napoleon Marcoux (Wakefield) and Hazel M. Downs (Milton); W - 18, shoe shop, d/o Alfred Chapman (Haverhill) and Irene M. Action (Laconia)

MARQUIS,
Scott P. m. Darlene M. **Bruedle** 2/17/1995 in Farmington
Steven P. m. Barbara R. **Browne** 8/11/1990 in Middleton

MASSE,
Peter L., Jr. m. Janice A. **Scannell** 5/17/1984

MATHEWS,
Charles H. of Middleton m. Marion **Rice** of Middleton 4/21/1928 in Union; H - 31, factory hand, 2d, b. Keene, s/o John Mathews (Henniker, farmer) and Nellie Patterson (Sharon, housewife); W - 24, mill operative, b. No. Vassalboro, ME, d/o Leslie Rice (No. Vassalboro, ME, mill operative) and Eva Earl (E. Vassalboro, ME, housewife)

McDERMOTTROE,
Raymond D. m. Amy Lyn **Mailhoit** 11/3/1996 in Milton

McEACHERN,
Leon O. m. Anna E. **Kimball** 7/16/1960 in Wakefield; H - 31; W - 35

McENROE,
Donald F. of Middleton m. Edna M. **Anderson** of Hazardville, CT 8/23/1938 in Sanbornville; H - 24, medical student, b. Whitman, MA, s/o John F. McEnroe (Hanover, MA, shoe shop) and Eva M. Angie (Southbridge, MA, housewife); W - 32, nurse, b. Methuen, MA, d/o John Anderson (England, supt.) and Laura Sugden (England, housewife)

McMILLEN,
Edward J. m. Blanche A. **Grant** 6/14/1971 in Farmington; H - s/o Frank McMillen and Katherine O'Regan; W - d/o Henry Barraclough and Blanche Lewin

McPHERSON,
Kenneth m. Carol E. **Booth** 9/26/1965; H - 20, s/o Norman McPherson of Middleton; W - 17, d/o George W. Booth of Sanbornville

Russell E. m. Dianne H. **Lowell** of Rochester 11/4/1967; H - s/o Norman E. McPherson and Geneva Brewer; W - d/o Kenneth E. Lowell and Eleanor F. Moody

MERRILL,
Ralph H. of Middleton m. Mae E. **Major** of Middleton 6/1/1951; H - 49, laborer, b. MI, s/o Edward Merrill and Elizabeth Niciwonder; W - 35, shoe shop, 2d, b. NH, d/o Philip Stanton and Eva E. Howe

MESERVE,
Carl L. of St. Petersburg, FL m. Rose W. **Meserve** of Middleton 8/10/1985 in Farmington

MICHAUD,
Raymond L. m. Donna L. **Moulton** 12/3/1994 in Milton

MINCEY,
Joseph A., Jr. m. Kimberly D. **Main** 2/14/1997 in Middleton

MONNAT,
Brian K. m. Sheila D. **Riley** 11/7/1998 in Rochester

MONTOUR,
Martin L. m. Jennifer R. **Arlin** 3/21/1987 in Rochester

MOODY,
Alan m. Elena **Tavoulais** 6/6/1993 in Middleton

MOONEY,
Benjamin W. of E. Arlington, MA m. Helen **Knowles** of Middleton 1/27/1917 in Arlington, MA; H - 20, bank messenger, b. Somerville, MA, s/o William W. Mooney (Madison, mail service) and Emma McCrillis (Dexter, ME, housekeeper); W - 18, student, b. Milton, d/o Charles Knowles (Middleton, farmer) and Bessie Keyes (No. Conway, housekeeper)

MOORE,
Eli S. of Middleton m. Ethel I. **Wentworth** of Effingham 10/28/1897 in Ossipee; H - 29, farmer, b. Middleton, s/o Albert C. Moore (Middleton, farmer) and Sabina D. Seward (Wakefield, housework); W - 24, waitress, b. Lynn, MA, d/o George E. Wentworth (Lowell, MA, farmer) and Susan F. Merrill (Falmouth, ME, housework)

James D. of Middleton m. Lidelia A. **Dame** of Portsmouth 9/15/1887 in Wakefield; H - 62, farmer, 3d, wid., b. Middleton; W - 41, housekeeper, 2d, wid.

Roland R.E. of Middleton m. Dorothy M. **Whitehouse** of Middleton 2/10/1931 in Farmington; H - 19, farmer, b. Middleton, s/o Eli S. Moore (Middleton, farmer) and Ethel I. Wentworth (Lynn, MA, housework); W - 16, at home, b. Middleton, d/o Harvey Whitehouse (Middleton, farmer) and Isabell Ellis (Rochester, housework)

MORRILL,
Donald W. m. Candace M. **Long** 5/25/1996 in Milton Mills
Donald W., Jr. m. Sue A. **Yoder** 7/31/1997 in Farmington

MORRISON,
Charlie Harry of Middleton m. Rena May **Tuttle** of Middleton 11/8/1969 in Wakefield

MOULTON,
Fred A. of Middleton m. Vivian E. **Grace** of Middleton 6/2/1926 in Farmington; H - 20, laborer, b. Middleton, s/o Chester A. Moulton (Farmington, shoe operative) and Flora B. Howard (Farmington, housewife); W - 18, housework, b. Tamworth, d/o Joseph Grace (Chatham, farmer) and Lodema Cates (E. Strafford, housewife)

MURPHY,
William J., Jr. m. Doris E. **Nichols** 3/31/1979 in Farmington

NADEAU,
Robert A. m. Jeanne A. **Nadeau** 8/22/1964; H - s/o Benedict P. Nadeau and Rose A. Jacques of Somersworth; W - d/o Elmer E. Drew and Helen Pike

NASON,
Rodney E. m. Betty **Provencher** 3/17/1957 in Milton; H - s/o Edward Nason of Middleton; W - d/o Edward A. Provencher of Milton
Todd C. of Wakefield m. Christine M. **DiPrizio** of Middleton 8/4/1985 in Sanbornville

NELSON,
Eric S. m. Christine M. **Dodge** 9/18/1976

Eric S. m. Lauren A. **Corrozzo** 1/23/1984

NEPENI,
Albert G. m. Jane G. **Hulse** 6/17/1960 in Dover; H - 40; W - 33

NEWTON,
Dennis J. m. Cynthia D. **Walbridge** 7/13/1991 in Farmington

NUTTER,
John A. of Middleton m. Anna **Slingerland** of Middleton 4/1/1901 in Middleton; H - 46, farmer, 2d, div., b. Middleton, s/o Simson Nutter (Brookfield, farmer) and Paulina A. Ellis (Middleton, domestic); W - 35, domestic, 2d, wid., b. NY, d/o Allan Battersby (England, carpenter) and Mary Lawrence (St. Catherines, Canada, domestic)

O'KEEFE,
Owen M. m. Laurianne M. **Couture** 10/1/1988 in Middleton

OUELLETTE,
David R. of Sanbornville m. Donna L. **Petersen** of Middleton 3/16/1973; H - 32; W - 22

PAQUETTE,
Howard D. of Rochester m. Judith L. **Davis** of Middleton 9/22/1962 in Rochester; H - s/o Harry A. Paquette and Lena M. Filieu of Rochester; W - d/o Lester W. Davis and Marie E. Careno of Middleton

PATCH,
Glenn E. m. Annette J. **Poulin** 4/22/1989 in Middleton

PEAVEY,
Edward P. m. Cheryl A. **Corbett** 2/2/1991 in Barrington

PECKHAM,
Walter G. of Middleton m. Linda L. **Tufts** of Middleton 7/14/1973; H - 19; W - 20

PELLETIER,
Gideon J. of Middleton m. Theresa A. **Tache** of Salem, MA 9/25/1948 in Farmington; H - 46, truck driver, 2d, b. Salem, MA, s/o Gideon F. Pelletier (Canada, retired policeman) and P. LaPoint (Canada); W - 36, hairdresser, b. Salem, MA, d/o Albert Tache (Canada) and Corie Michaud (Canada, housewife)

PENNEY,
Joseph J. of Middleton m. Mary **Battersby** of New York, NY 12/11/1899 in Middleton; H - 72, farmer, 3d, b. Farmington, s/o Deborah Nutter (Rochester, housework); W - 68, housework, 2d, b. St. Catherines, Canada, d/o George Lawrence (St. Catherines, Canada, farmer) and Katie Birch (housework)

PERKINS,
Arthur R. of Middleton m. Myra E. **Getchell** of So. Wolfeboro 3/31/1906 in Wolfeboro; H - 24, laborer, b. So. Berwick, ME, s/o Samuel Perkins (Middleton, farmer); W - 19, housework, b. So. Wolfeboro, d/o Walter S. Getchell (So. Wolfeboro, painter)

Walter P. of Middleton m. Saddie A. **Mitchell** of New Durham 10/23/1905 in Alton; H - 26, laborer, b. So. Berwick, ME, s/o Samuel Perkins (Middleton, farmer) and Abbie Goodwin (Rollinsford, at home); W - 27, teacher, b. New Durham, d/o Thomas E. Mitchell (New Durham, farmer) and Lydia Perkins (Middleton, at home)

Walter P. of Middleton m. Margaret E. **Leighton** of Middleton 6/24/1922 in Milton; H - 42, farmer, 2d, b. So. Berwick, ME, s/o Samuel Perkins and Abbie J. Goodwin; W - 28, counter nestor, b. Rochester, d/o Walter Leighton and Elizabeth S. Drew

William W. of Middleton m. Eveline M. **Allen** of So. Berwick, ME 7/2/1892 in Middleton; H - 21, weaver, b. Dover, s/o Samuel Perkins (Middleton, farmer); W - 18, b. So. Berwick, ME

PERRY,
Paul P. of Middleton m. Susan A. **Mills** of Middleton 9/21/1985 in New Durham

PETERSEN,
Michael D. m. Anne K. **Lepene** 3/7/1987 in Middleton

PETERSON,
Steven J. m. Susan D. **Armstrong** 9/13/1997 in Deerfield

PIKE,
Alvah B. of Middleton m. Maud A. **Griffith** of Farmington 2/3/1901 in Middleton; H - 35, teamster, b. Milton, s/o James D. Pike (New Durham, farmer) and Susan L. Cloutman (Middleton, domestic); W - 37, domestic, 2d, wid., b. Syracuse, NY, d/o Elias Wilson (Cleveland, NY, glass blower) and Sarah A. Wilson (Coxsackie, NY, domestic)

Alvah B. of Middleton m. Nannie E. **Goodwin** of Kingston, MA 9/19/1914; H - 48, laborer, 2d, b. Wilton, s/o James D. Pike (New Durham, farmer) and Susan L. Cloutman (Middleton, housework); W - 38, housework, 2d, b. Kingston, d/o William P. Goodwin and Nannie E. Stevens (Kingston, housework)

John L. of Middleton m. Alice M. **Arnold** of Farmington 9/17/1887 in Acton; H - 21, shoemaker, b. Middleton; W - 17, b. Milton

PINKHAM,
George E. of Middleton m. Laura E. **Smith** of Farmington 12/27/1893 in Middleton; H - 42, farmer, 2d, b. Middleton, s/o Thomas Pinkham and Adeline Pinkham; W - 35, housekeeper, 2d, b. Farmington, d/o John Brown and Clarissa Brown

Herbert C. of Middleton m. Bessie **Vay** of Boston, MA 1/7/1912; H - 26, teamster, b. Middleton, s/o George E. Pinkham (Farmington, farmer) and Laura Maine (Milton, housekeeper); W - 25, housekeeper, 2d, b. Newfoundland, d/o John Vay (Newfoundland, sail maker) and Lottie Mercer (Newfoundland, housekeeper)

Herbert C. m. Abbie Ann **Colt** 9/11/1954 in Laconia; H - 68; W - 58

William E. of Middleton m. Luna B. **Drew** of Milton 9/26/1919 in Union; H - 42, farmer, 2d, b. Middleton, s/o George E. Pinkham (Farmington, farmer) and Laura E. Mane (Milton, housewife); W - 36, housekeeper, 2d, b. Middleton, d/o William Gray (chauffeur) and Emma Varney (Rochester, housewife)

PORTER,
Tom m. Nancy **Braasch** 12/20/1986 in Middleton

POTTLE,
Joseph E. m. Marsolie A. **Otis** 4/7/1966; H - 28, s/o Raymond Pottle of Dover; W - 37, d/o Raymond Otis of Portsmouth

PRATT,
David G. m. Michelle Lee **Nason** 1/29/1994 in Wakefield

PROSPER,
Patrick R., Jr. m. Sheri A. **Dexter** 7/25/1998 in Middleton

PUTNEY,
Dwayne E. m. Holly **Lineweber** 2/18/1984

QUIMBY,
Michael F. m. Deborah L. **Bullis** 3/19/1977 in Middleton

REAGAN,
James A. m. Shirley C. **Massingham** 6/27/1959 in Rochester; H - 19, s/o Francis Reagan and Mrs. Eunice M. Chapman; W - 20, d/o Arthur Massingham

Ronald M. m. Caroline J. **Wallace** 4/22/1955 in Farmington; H - 19; W - 18

ROBERTS,
Arthur B. m. Wanda **Hall** 5/27/1989 in Middleton

Douglas R. m. Catherine E. **Perrow** 3/16/1996 in Rochester

RUNNELS,
Robert D., Jr. of Milton m. Karen R. **Hill** of Middleton 11/10/1973; H - 18; W - 18

RZEPECKI,
Stanley J. m. Diane H. **Valrand** 4/9/1984

ST. LAWRENCE,
James A. m. Wendy Joyce **Woodman** 2/10/1996 in Rye

ST. PIERRE,
Donald N. m. Karen E. **Lamper** 12/20/1975 in East Rochester; H - s/o Joseph R. St. Pierre and Jeannine Marcoux; W - d/o Herbert Lamper and Waveltte Canwell

SEAVEY,
Arthur P. m. Linda O. **Drew** 7/1/1989 in Rochester

SHAW,
Christopher P. m. Jo Anne **Hamel** 8/24/1996 in Middleton

SHEPARD,
Clayton W. of Acton, ME m. Irene E. **Tufts** of Middleton 5/2/1936 in Acton, ME; H - 27, mule spinner, b. Acton, ME, s/o Olsen Shepard (Danville, VT, retired mule spinner) and Eva May Prince (Provincetown, MA, housewife); W - 19, at home, b. Middleton, d/o Leon G. Tufts (Middleton, mill hand) and Addie M. Kimball (Middleton, housewife)

SINDORF,
Jonathan E. m. Patricia D. **Pringle** 1/2/1988 in Farmington

SKALTSIS,
Peter J. m. Michelle A. **Bilodeau** 4/13/1987 in Wakefield

SMITH,
Robert L. m. Beulah M. **Leighton** 6/2/1955 in Tilton; H - 36; W - 18
Robert L., Jr. m. Robin M.H. **Allen** 1/14/1992 in Middleton

SNYDER,
Eric J. m. Joanne M. **DiPrizio** 10/17/1987 in Farmington

SPRAGUE,
Warren J. m. Shirley A. **Wiggins** 6/20/1998 in Farmington

STABILE,
David G. m. Jeanmarie **DiPrizio** 9/18/1977 in Farmington

STAPLES,
Howard V. m. Marilyn **Ouimette** 8/1/1970; H - b. 12/16/1929, s/o Clarence Staples and Elsie Robard; W - b. 7/26/1943, d/o Lewis Day and Florence Goodwin of Dover

STEVENS,
Albert M. of Middleton m. Bernice M. **Tufts** of Middleton 5/25/1895 in Union; H - 27, farmer, b. Middleton, s/o James F.D. Stevens (Middleton, farmer) and Lydia F. Brown (Bangor, ME, housework); W - 18, housework, b. Middleton, d/o George F. Tufts (Middleton, farmer) and Emma Whitehouse (Middleton, housework)
Albert M. m. Simone L. **Leveillee** 10/27/1956 in Farmington; H - 18; W - 18
Alvah J. of Middleton m. Lilla J. **Penney** of Middleton 9/1/1894 in Union; H - 26, mill hand, b. Middleton, s/o George W. Stevens (Middleton, farmer) and E. D. Whitehouse (Middleton, housekeeper); W - 36, housekeeper, 2d, b. Middleton, d/o David Burrows (Middleton, farmer) and Betsy Whitham (Ossipee, housekeeper)
Arthur L. of Middleton m. Grace G. **Kinney** of Middleton 9/24/1935 in Milton; H - 27, laborer, b. Middleton, s/o Albert M. Stevens (Middleton, farmer) and Bernice M. Tufts (Middleton, deceased);

W - 17, at home, b. Westfield, ME, d/o Allen J. Kinney (Moncton, NB, carpenter) and Margaret Mullen (New Tusket, NS, housewife)

Byron H. of Middleton m. Jennie A. **Hatch** of Tuftonboro 5/3/1903 in Brookfield; H - 46, farmer, b. Middleton, s/o Thomas J. Stevens (Middleton, farmer) and Mary E. Whitehouse (Middleton, housework); W - 44, housework, 2d, b. Alton, d/o Hiram C. Kenney (shoemaker) and Clara E. Dorr (housework)

Byron H. of Middleton m. Louise M. **Webber** of Middleton 11/1/1904 in Brookfield; H - 47, farmer, 2d, b. Middleton, s/o Thomas J. Stevens (Middleton, farmer) and Mary Whitehouse (Middleton, at home); W - 16, housework, b. Milton, d/o George F. Webber (Philadelphia, PA, cigar maker) and Lydia E. Jones (Milton, at home)

Earl F. m. Janet E. **Nason** 12/23/1954 in Sanbornville; H - 25; W - 19

Earl W. of Middleton m. Elsie A. **Ray** of Middleton 3/10/1929 in Union; H - 20, farmer, b. Middleton, s/o Byron Stevens (Middleton, farmer) and Louise Webber (Milton, housewife); W - 16, in shoe shop, b. Hudson, d/o Frank H. Ray (Hudson, MA, teamster) and Sarah L. McLaren (Sandown, housewife)

Edgar N. of Middleton m. Annie M. **Cleveland** of Concord 12/24/1888 in Boscawen; H - 23, lumber surveyor, b. Middleton; W - 16, mill girl, b. NB

George W. of Middleton m. Grace M. **Mooney** of Middleton 10/10/1924 in Union; H - 19, b. Middleton, s/o Byron H. Stevens and Louisa Webber; W - 29, b. Somerville, MA, d/o William W. Mooney and Emma McCrillis

Howard of Middleton m. Elizabeth L. **Bishop** of Middleton 11/26/1947 in Union; H - 41, mechanic, 2d, b. Boston, MA, s/o Hermon Stevens (Belfast, ME, salesman) and Arsula K. Souther (Hingham, MA, housewife); W - 49, housework, 2d, b. West Somerville, MA, d/o Alexander H. Dadmun (MD, photographer) and Edith L. Guilford (W. Thornton, NH, housewife)

Handy Andy of Middleton m. Sarah Margaret **Lyons** of Rochester 7/3/1940 in Rochester; H - 20, tractor driver, b. Middleton, s/o A. M. Stevens (Middleton, retired) and B. M. Tufts (Middleton, deceased); W - 20, shoe shop, b. Rochester, d/o Fred Lyons (Danville, ME, box shop) and Florence Stanhope (Dennysville, ME, housewife)

Henry D. of Middleton m. Bertha F. **Runnels** of Wakefield 4/25/1900 in Union; H - 26, livery man, b. Middleton, s/o Thomas J. Stevens (Middleton, farmer) and Mary E. Whitehouse (Middleton, housework); W - 19, housework, b. Cherry Valley, MA, d/o Samuel Runnels (Wakefield, blacksmith) and Edna A. Platt (Andover, MA, housework)

Herbert J. of Middleton m. Lillian **Campbell** of Rowley, MA 6/11/1927 in Union; H - 22, farmer, b. Middleton, s/o Albert M. Stevens (Middleton, farmer) and Bernice M. Tufts (Middleton, housewife); W - 18, no occ., b. Rowley, MA, d/o Daniel Campbell (Glasgow, Scotland, fireman) and Grace Farley (Rowley, MA, cook)

Hiram S. of Middleton m. Hattie B. **Ross** of Middleton 3/21/1890 in Rochester; H - 26, mill hand, b. Middleton; W - 21, housekeeper, b. Middleton

John I. m. Kathleen M. **Berry** of Rochester 12/14/1967; H - s/o Byron H. Stevens and Louise M. (Webber) Willey; W - d/o John J. Donaldson and Margaret Marshall

Leslie A., Jr. m. Holly E. **Weed** 9/28/1996 in Middleton

Leslie Arthur m. Marcia Agnes **Leary** of Farmington 10/21/1967; H - s/o Arthur Stevens and Grace Kinney; W - d/o Kenneth R. Leary and Nelzina Miller

Melvin E. of Middleton m. Maud P. **Merrill** of Farmington 9/1/1928 in Union; H - 25, laborer, b. Middleton, s/o Albert M. Stevens (Middleton, farmer) and Bernice Tufts (Middleton, housewife); W - 16, b. Wakefield, MA, d/o Paul Merrill (Winchester, MA, St. RR conductor) and Rachel (Wakefield, MA, housewife)

Melvin E. m. Eleanor M. **Reid** 4/12/1959 in Farmington; H - 55, s/o Albert M. Stevens; W - 21, d/o MacMillen Reid

Sidney A. of Middleton m. Marion E. **Kinney** of Sanbornville 7/3/1930 in Lebanon, ME; H - 24, cook, b. Middleton, s/o Albert M. Stevens (Middleton, farmer) and Bernice Tufts (Middleton, housewife); W - 18, at home, b. Springdale, NS, d/o Allen Kinney

(Moncton, NB, carpenter) and Margaret Mullen (Newtusket, NS, housewife)

Walter R. of Middleton m. Mabel A. **Swift** of Union 12/20/1919; H - 22, butcher, b. Middleton, s/o Albert M. Stevens (Middleton, farmer) and Bernice M. Tufts (Middleton, housewife); W - 19, housework, b. Waterboro, ME, d/o Arthur Swift (Windham, ME, laborer) and Maude Morse (Skowhegan, ME, housewife)

William Huntley m. Kathleen Ellen **Sprague** 12/6/1952; H - 20, lumberjack, s/o Earl W. Stevens and Elsie A. Ray; W - 16, at home, d/o Louis E. Sprague and Madelaine F. Adjutant

STONE,
John J. m. Brenda I. **Cochran** 8/5/1988 in Middleton

STOWE,
David W. m. Roxana R. **Roy** 11/15/1975 in Middleton; H - s/o John Stowe and Barbara Bean; W - d/o Leo Roy and Eleanor Grant

SULLIVAN,
Donald R. m. Pati R. **Young** 10/11/1968

SWINERTON,
Lawrence of Middleton m. Anna M. **Adjutant** of E. Wolfeboro 2/4/1934 in Milton; H - 20, farmer, b. Milton, s/o Jacob M. Swinerton (Worcester, MA, shoemaker) and Emma McKinstrey (Worcester, MA, housewife); W - 22, at home, b. E. Wolfeboro, d/o Martin B. Adjutant (E. Wolfeboro, farmer) and Hattie M. Hooper (Wakefield, housewife)

TANNER,
Charles E. of Milton m. Viola **Kimball** of Middleton 3/27/1919 in Rochester; H - 24, mill work, b. Rochester, s/o Hervey E. Tanner; W - 18, b. Middleton, d/o George Kimball (Middleton, millhand) and Eliza S. Hanscomb (Dover, housewife)

Lloyd Cecil of Middleton m. Sarah Jane **Fifield** of Union 5/19/1945 in Wakefield; H - 26, machine operator, b. Wakefield, s/o Charles

E. Tanner (Wakefield, Navy Yard) and Vila L. Kimball
(Middleton, housewife); W - 22, assembler, b. Wakefield, d/o
George R. Fifield (Conway, stone mason) and Blanche E. Penney
(E. Lebanon, ME, housewife)

TARDIFF,
Donald of Middleton m. Carrie E. **Remick** of Milton 5/11/1925 in
Union; H - 27, woodsman, b. Canada, s/o Joseph Tardiff
(Canada, farmer) and Azidda Martineau (Canada, housewife); W
- 25, housekeeper, 2d, b. Albany, d/o Frank L. Grace (Chatham,
farmer) and Lizzie B. Willey (Albany, housewife)

TAYLOR,
Matthew L. m. Debrah S. **Sterns** 9/16/1989 in Rochester

TELLES,
Matthew S. m. Christine P. **Bonia** 9/11/1995 in Durham

TEMPLETON,
Harold of Wakefield m. Thedora C. **Libby** 4/5/1949 in Milton; H - 42,
mechanic, 2d, b. NH, s/o Bert Templeton (NH) and Annie Knox
(NH); W - 34, at home, b. MA, d/o Thomas P. Libby (MA) and
Daisy M. Hansen (NH)

TETREAULT,
Randolph R. m. Kathy L. **Drew** 10/21/1979 in Middleton

THIBEDAU,
Chester m. Sandra **McFarland** 2/14/1986 in Milton

THOMAS,
David E. m. Dionne D. **Williams** 10/26/1991 in Franconia
James E. m. Pamela J. **Dumont** 1/23/1987 in Rochester

TIBBETTS,
Albert M. of Middleton m. Lillian D. **Tuttle** of Middleton 11/14/1908 in Farmington; H - 34, mill operative, b. Milton, s/o Walter S. Tibbetts (New Durham, farmer) and Hattie L. Downing (Milton, housework); W - 22, housework, b. New Durham, d/o William B. Tuttle (Middleton, farmer) and Mazina D. Colomy (housework)

Clifton R. of Middleton m. Irene **Day** of Kezar Falls, ME 3/22/1927 in Conway; H - 17, laborer, b. Middleton, s/o Fred Tibbetts (Milton, mill hand) and Myrtle Thurston (Madison, housewife); W - 22, millworker, b. Kezar Falls, ME, d/o George Day (woolen mill) and Hattie (Kezar Falls, ME)

Clifton R. of Middleton m. Thelma F. **Moran** of Danbury 6/27/1937 in Wilmot; H - 28, laborer, 2d, b. Middleton, s/o Fred Tibbetts (Middleton, laborer) and Myrtle Thurston (Madison, at home); W - 26, at home, 2d, b. Danbury, d/o Frank Dici (deceased) and Myrtle Dici (Danbury, at home)

Dorsity W. m. Glenda J. **Burns** 6/11/1965; H - 33, s/o Charles Tibbetts of Somersworth; W - 25, d/o George Burns of Middleton

Leander E. of Middleton m. Gertrude May **Drew** of Farmington 6/11/1899 in Middleton; H - 48, farmer, 4th, b. Brookfield, Asa Tibbetts (Brookfield, farmer) and Esther Abbott (Ossipee, housework); W - 20, housework, b. Rochester, d/o Frank J. Drew (Gilmanton, shoemaker) and Lizzie H. Young (Rochester, housework)

Leander E. of Middleton m. Frances J. **Sprague** of Springvale, ME 5/8/1910; H - 59, teamster, 4th, b. Brookfield, s/o Asa Tibbetts and Esther Abbott; W - 43, housework, 2d, b. So. Wayne, WI, d/o Alphonzo James and Lucy Fogg

Melvin L. of Middleton m. Mabel B. **Brown** of Wolfeboro 7/31/1936 in Milton; H - 25, shoe shop, s/o ----- Tibbetts (Milton, laborer) and ----- Tuttle (New Durham, housewife); W - 24, housewife, 2d, d/o ----- Brown (NB, laborer) and ----- Folsom (New Boston, housewife)

TITCOMB,
George Benjamin of Middleton m. Dorothy Ruth **Stanhope** of Middleton 6/28/1939 in Farmington; H - 21, sheet metal worker, b. W. Newbury, MA, s/o Charles L. Titcomb (W. Newbury, MA, carpenter) and Charlotte M. Gile (Conway, housewife); W - 20, at home, b. Lynn, MA, d/o Everett Stanhope (Lynn, MA, electrician) and Ruth A. Peoples (Claremont, housewife)

TOMPSON,
Wayne A. m. Martha A. **Kinney** 10/21/1966; H - 19, s/o Carl A. Tompson of Rochester; W - 18, d/o Arthur R. Kinney of Middleton

TRIPP,
Leroy F., Jr. m. Stacie K. **Sandstrom** 6/11/1989 in Middleton

TRUDEAU,
Gary J. m. Karyn G. **Osborne** 7/5/1980 in Rochester

TSALTAS,
Michael G. m. Elisabeth M. **Carter** 9/23/1989 in Rochester

TUFTS,
Clyde L. of Middleton m. Eva E. **Moulton** of Middleton 6/9/1928 in Union; H - 26, mill operative, b. Middleton, s/o Leon G. Tufts (Middleton, farmer) and Addie Kimball (Middleton, housewife); W - 20, mill operative, b. Middleton, d/o Augustin Moulton (Farmington, shoeworker) and Flora Howard (Farmington, housewife)

Franklin D. m. Octavia A. **Richardson** 11/8/1975 in Middleton; H - s/o Myron Tufts and Louise Kinney; W - d/o Oliver Richardson and Edith Wallingford

Franklin D. m. Julie Ann **Cyr** 10/16/1993 in Farmington

George D. of Middleton m. Marion E. **Shepard** of Manchester 11/4/1935 in Milton; H - 30, mill worker, b. Middleton, s/o Leon G. Tufts (Middleton, farmer) and Addie M. Kimball (Middleton, housewife); W - 20, at home, b. Acton, ME, d/o Olen Shepard (Danville, VT, at home) and Ina M. Prince (Horne's Mills, deceased)

Herbert G. of Middleton m. Linnie M. **Smith** of Middleton 8/30/1911 in Brookfield; H - 20, farmer, b. Middleton, s/o Joseph W. Tufts (Middleton, farmer) and Cora Belle Cook (Milton, housework); W - 20, housework, b. Acton, ME, d/o Charles Irving Smith (Shapleigh, ME, farmer) and Mandy M. Hussey (Acton, ME, housework)

John D. of Middleton m. Alice M. **Hodges** of Milton 11/28/1918 in Milton; H - 28, farmer, b. Middleton, s/o George J. Tufts (Middleton, farmer) and Emma Tufts (Middleton, housewife); W - 20, schoolteacher, b. Milton, d/o Edgar C. Hodges (Ossipee, mill operative) and Carrie L. Corson (Lebanon, ME, housewife)

John R. of Alton m. Edna **Tufts** of Middleton 12/20/1919 in Farmington; H - 52, farmer, 2d, b. Alton, s/o Samuel Tufts (Middleton, shoemaker) and Susan Chamberlin (Alton, housewife); W - 24, housekeeper, b. Middleton, d/o Charles Tufts (Middleton, farmer) and Nellie Corson (Milton, housewife)

Joseph W. of Middleton m. Hattie S. **Foss** of Barnstead 10/7/1901 in Rochester; H - 40, farmer, 4th, wid., b. Middleton, s/o Davis Tufts (farmer) and Adaline D. Horne (domestic); W - 27, domestic, 2d, wid., d/o John Varney (farmer) and Emma Corson (domestic)

Joseph W. of Middleton m. Lillian D. **Gilbert** of Middleton 9/8/1918 in Middleton; H - 60, farmer, 5th, b. Middleton, s/o Davis D. Tufts (Middleton, farmer) and Adeline D. Horne (Middleton, housekeeper); W - 30, housekeeper, 2d, b. New Durham, d/o William B. Tuttle (New Durham, farmer) and Mazina M. Colomy (New Durham, housekeeper)

Merton of Farmington m. Geraldine **Duprey** of Middleton 11/3/1950; H - 22, laborer, s/o Isaac Frank Tufts (Middleton) and Lucy E. Goodwin (Alton); W - 19, office worker, d/o Louis W. Duprey (Adams, MA) and Jeanette M. Lasano (Saugus, MA)

Moses D. of Middleton m. Evelyn A. **Jones** of Alton 3/13/1918 in Farmington; H - 20, farmer, b. Middleton, s/o Joseph W. Tufts

(Middleton, farmer) and Cora Belle Cook (Milton, housewife); W - 17, housekeeper, b. Alton, d/o King Jones (Alton, lumberer) and Carrie Lowell (New Durham, housekeeper)

Moses G. of Middleton m. Evelyn R. **Nutter** of Milton 1/12/1927 in Union; H - 29, farmer, 2d, b. Middleton, s/o Wright Tufts (Middleton, farmer) and Cora B. Cook (Milton, housewife); W - 20, teacher, b. Milton, d/o Frank J. Nutter (Berwick, ME, mill operative) and Gertrude Wentworth (Milton, housewife)

Myron K. of Middleton. m. Louise E. **Kinney** of Middleton 12/24/1936 in Union; H - 26, farmer, b. Middleton, s/o Leon G. Tufts (Middleton, mill hand) and Addie M. Kimball (Middleton, housewife); W - 20, maid, b. Wakefield, d/o Allen J. Kinney (Moncton, NB, carpenter) and Margaret F. Mullen (New Tusket, NS, housewife)

Orrie M. m. Beverly A. **Brannan** 2/8/1964; H - s/o Orrie M. Tufts and Iris Shepard; W - d/o George Rouleau and Inez Eldridge

Orrie M., Jr. of Middleton m. Linda J. **Valleton** of Rochester 8/30/1958 in Chichester; H - s/o Orrie Tufts; W - d/o John Valleton

Ransom of Middleton m. Muriel Lee **Hodgdon** of Middleton 7/14/1947 in Farmington; H - 53, woodsman, b. Middleton, s/o Joseph W. Tufts (Middleton, farmer) and Belle Cook (Barnstead, housewife); W - 49, housework, 3d, b. Rothesay, NB, d/o George A. Kirkpatrick (Gondola Pt., Canada, farmer) and Annie P. Kidey (Philadelphia, PA, housewife)

Roy Joseph of Middleton m. Estelle C. **Danahy** of Farmington 1/22/1949 in Farmington; H - 29, woodsman, b. Middleton, s/o Joseph W. Tufts (NH) and Lillian D. Tuttle (NH); W - 35, burling, 2d, b. MA, d/o Willard E. Newcomb (MA) and Clare W. Wilson (England)

Stephen J. of Middleton m. Mary K. **Marcoux** of Milton 11/11/1947 in Farmington; H - 21, lineman, b. Rochester, s/o Leon G. Tufts (Middleton, farmer) and Addie Kimball (Middleton, housewife); W - 17, at home, b. Milton, d/o Napoleon Marcoux (Wakefield, employed in mill) and Hazel Downs (Milton, employed in mill)

Stephen J. m. Rita S. **Marcoux** 8/31/1957; H - s/o Leon Tufts of Middleton; W - d.o Hazel Marcoux of Milton

William D. of Middleton m. Dollie May **Wallace** of Farmington 4/2/1911 in Farmington; H - 22, farmer, b. Middleton, s/o Charles D. Tufts (Middleton, farmer) and Nellie M. Corson (Middleton, housework); W - 21, shoe shop op., b. Milton, d/o John C.F. Wallace (Middleton, teamster) and Dora Perkins (Middleton, housework)

Wilson W. m. Debra E. **Ebert** 3/1/1980 in Middleton

Woodrow W. m. Marilyn J. **Boston** 4/5/1957; H - s/o Leon G. Tufts of Middleton; W - d/o Robert O. Boston of Alburn, AL

TUTTLE,

Levi W. of Middleton m. Fannie **Walker** of Middleton 3/1/1890 in W. Lebanon, ME; H - 26, farmer, b. Middleton; W - 17, b. Middleton

Levi W. of Middleton m. Joan L. **Rollins** of Middleton 9/19/1905 in Farmington; H - 41, farmer, 2d, b. New Durham, s/o Stephen M. Tuttle (Middleton, farmer) and Mary A. Berry (New Durham, at home); W - 27, at home, 2d, b. New Durham, d/o Alonzo Lowell (farmer)

TWOMBLEY,

Steven m. Tina L. **Pridham** 7/3/1987 in Middleton

VACHON,

Joseph M., Jr. of Farmington m. Beverly A. **Tufts** of Middleton 12/20/1946 in Farmington; H - 21, shoe shop, b. Wolfeboro, s/o Joseph Vachon (Lancaster, woodsman) and Inez Elliott (Lancaster, shoe shop); W - 18, at home, b. Rochester, d/o John Tufts (Middleton, mill worker) and Alice Hodges (Milton, housewife)

VANDER BLOEMEN,

James S. m. Onna Lee **Dalrymple** 4/15/1978 in Middleton

VARNEY,
Marc D. m. Nora L. **Paradis** 11/1/1997 in Rochester
William R. of Middleton m. Sylvia A. **Adkins** of Northfield 3/3/1962 in Tilton; H - s/o William G. Varney and Eleanor M. Newcome of Berwick, ME; W - d/o Roland A. Routhier and Evelyn S. Bagley of Torrence, CA

WADE,
Alston of Dover m. Ruth E. **Eastman** of Middleton 1/23/1949 in Dover; H - 42, janitor, 2d, b. Sandwich, s/o Frank Wade (NH) and Mary Clough (NH); W - 30, housework, b. Middleton, d/o Charles Eastman (NH) and May Tufts (NH)

WALKER,
Adam of Middleton m. Annie A. **Labonte** of Middleton 7/4/1890 in Middleton; H - 44, printer, b. Scotland; W - 31, housekeeper, b. Middleton

WASHBURNE,
Ivan m. Patricia **Kelsey** 12/5/1987 in Middleton

WATTS,
Donald W. m. Brenda L. **Lavoie** 7/27/1991 in Middleton

WEBSTER,
Albert E., Jr. m. Patricia L. **Smith** 6/24/1978 in Rochester

WEEMAN,
Harris Eugene m. Eunice Francis **Chase** 4/25/1953; H - 24, steel work, Howard A. Weeman and Ella M. Smith; W - 20, shoe shop, Francis Martin Reagan and Eunice May Gilbert

WELCH,
Bruce D. m. Sheila J. **Tuttle** 8/18/1990 in Hanover
Mark E. m. Jane B. **Stevens** 9/9/1956 in Rochester; H - 23; W - 21
Stanley E. m. Annie R. **Wiggin** 6/2/1956 in Middleton; H - 25; W - 27

WELSH,
Keith R. m. Helen M. **Goodfield** 12/6/1990 in Middleton

WENTWORTH,
Joseph of Farmington m. Jennie May **Savoir** of Middleton 10/17/1914 in Farmington; H - 24, shoemaker, b. Middleton, s/o Joseph Wentworth (Middleton, shoemaker) and Martha Wentworth (Middleton, housekeeper); W - 16, at home, b. Dover, d/o Joseph Savoir (Dover, conductor) and Delia Savoir (Middleton, housekeeper)

WHEELER,
Charles W. m. Freda L. **Frost** 12/11/1998 in Farmington

WHITEHOUSE,
Charles W. of Middleton m. Melissa A. **Perkins** of Middleton 3/12/1905 in Middleton; H - 40, mill operator, 2d, b. Middleton, s/o Warren H. Whitehouse (Middleton, farmer) and Emma A. York (Newmarket, at home); W - 32, at home, b. Middleton, d/o Samuel Perkins (Middleton, farmer) and Abbie J. Goodwin (Rollinsford, at home)

Charles W. of Middleton m. Lilla J. **Stevens** of Dover 12/22/1912 in Barnstead; H - 48, mill operative, 3d, b. Middleton, s/o W. H. Whitehouse (Middleton, farmer) and Emma A. York (Newmarket, housework); W - 45, housework, 3d, b. Middleton, d/o David Burrows (Middleton, farmer) and Betsy Witham (Ossipee, housework)

Fred L., Jr. of Farmington m. Ellen M. **Tufts** of Middleton 5/28/1938 in Milton; H - 19, box maker, b. Rochester, s/o Fred L. Whitehouse (Strafford, box maker) and Georgie I. Berry (Farmington, deceased); W - 20, shoe shop, b. Middleton, d/o Leon G. Tufts (Middleton, mill hand) and Addie M. Kimball (Middleton, housewife)

Richard of Middleton m. Gladys S. **Moore** of Middleton 7/12/1931 in Farmington; H - 19, farmer, b. Middleton, s/o H. J. Whitehouse (Middleton, farmer) and Isabelle Ellis (Rochester, housewife); W

- 28, teacher, b. Middleton, d/o Eli S. Moore (Middleton, farmer) and Ethel I. Wentworth (Lynn, MA, housewife)

Richard A. m. Linda D. **Drew** 6/5/1964; H - s/o Richard Whitehouse and Gladys Moore; W - d/o Donald K. Drew and Viola B. Sprague of Sanbornville

WHITNEY,

James E. of Salem m. Edith E. **Randlett** of Middleton 1/1/1938 in Salem; H - 62, mastr. mechanic, 2d, b. Quincy, MA, s/o Charles C. Whitney (Baldwinville, MA, carpenter) and Rhoda A. Perry (Roseway, NS, housewife); W - 48, heel coverer, 2d, b. Haverhill, MA, d/o Arthur E. Lord (Exeter, printer) and Alma F. Kimball (Salem, housewife)

WICKS,

Walter W. m. Rosemarie D. **Hunter** 4/2/1984

WIGGIN,

Raymond W., Jr. of Middleton m. Annie R. **Jenness** of Middleton 12/6/1946 in Milton Mills; H - 20, mill worker, b. Lebanon, ME, s/o Raymond Wiggin (Rochester, laborer) and Anita Gerry (Kingston, MA, housewife); W - 18, at home, b. Middleton, d/o Elmer Jenness (Rochester, mill worker) and Lucinda Drew (Middleton, housewife)

WILKINSON,

Melbourne A. of Wakefield m. Edwina N. **Young** of Middleton 11/18/1937 in West Milton; H - 21, truck driver, b. Wakefield, s/o Frank Wilkinson (Freedom, RR employee) and Lucy M. Roles (Ossipee, at home); W - 18, at home, b. Middleton, d/o Fred Young (Middleton, mill operator) and Alice Heath (Wakefield, at home)

Wilfred Arthur of Wakefield m. Yvonne Frances **Bullis** of Middleton 11/18/1939 in Milton; H - 26, laborer, b. Wakefield, s/o Frank S. Wilkinson (Freedom, RR employee) and Lucy M. Roles (Ossipee, housewife); W - 18, at home, b. Haverhill, MA, d/o

Eric A. Bullis (Westminster, MA, shoe shop) and Viola F. Griffin (Haverhill, MA, housewife)

WILLEY,

Charles R. of Middleton m. Ennie M. **Cook** 1/18/1926 in Union; H - 48, woodchopper, b. Middleton, s/o Edward LaBonte (shoemaker) and Annie A. Willey (Middleton, housekeeper); W - 44, housework, 2d, div., b. Middleton, d/o Daniel B. Jones (Middleton, shoemaker) and Emma Perkins (Middleton, housekeeper)

Earl B. of Middleton m. Mary **LaMay** of Newport 7/11/1917 in Farmington; H - 20, farmer, b. New Durham, s/o Henry D. Willey (New Durham, farmer) and Gertrude Randall (Canada, housekeeper); W - 19, shoe operative, b. Manchester, d/o Frank LaMay (Canada, farmer) and Ida Bishop (Canada, housekeeper)

George H. of Middleton m. Eva E. **Roberts** of Farmington 11/24/1894 in Milton; H - 31, RR hand, 2d, b. Middleton, s/o Jonas D. Willey (New Durham, farmer) and Abbie Horne (Middleton, housekeeper); W - 27, housekeeper, 2d, b. Farmington, d/o J. O. Nute (Milton, leather cutter) and Martha Welch

Henry D. of Middleton m. Flora **Howard** of Farmington 3/9/1911 in Farmington; H - 42, blacksmith, 2d, b. New Durham, s/o John W. Willey (New Durham, blacksmith) and Mary E. Tufts (Middleton, housework); W - 26, housework, b. Farmington, d/o Charles Howard (Farmington, wood chopper) and Belle (Farmington)

WILMOT,

Rosco E. of Farmington m. Alice M. **Staples** of Farmington 9/12/1973; H - 21; W - 18

WOODMAN,

Frank W. of Middleton m. Livonia **Drew** of Middleton 3/25/1903 in Farmington; H - 49, farmer, 2d, b. Tilton, s/o Frank S. Davis (Alton, mechanic) and Mirah B. Plummer (Lakeport, housework);

W - 37, housework, b. Eaton, d/o Thomas Drew (Eaton, farmer) and Sarah L. Bryant (Windham, ME, housework)

WORSTER,
Robert Orman m. Ina May **Brannan** 2/14/1970; H - b. 10/21/1951, s/o George Worster and Doris Burries; W - b. 12/18/1949, d/o Norbert Brannan and Ruby Tufts of Middleton

YERAKES,
James m. Lisa M. **Corvino** 4/30/1988 in Farmington

YOUNG,
Fred G. of Cambridge, MA m. Margaret E. **Leary** of Cambridge, MA 8/24/1910 in Middleton; H - 21, barber, b. Alton, s/o Herbert S. Young and Susie Petigrew; W - 21, stenographer, b. Amesbury, MA, d/o John Leary and Mary F. Haden
John H. of Middleton m. Mary M.C. **Pike** of Middleton 6/23/1898 in Rochester; H - 58, farmer, 2d, wid., b. Wolfeboro, s/o Jeremiah Young (Wolfeboro, farmer) and Mary A. Jackson (Holderness, at home); W - 52, at home, 2d, wid., b. Middleton, d/o William H. Cloutman (Rochester, carpenter) and Lucinda Stevens (Middleton, at home)
Lewis F. of Middleton m. Effie A. **Leighton** of Middleton 3/27/1896 in Farmington; H - 29, farmer, b. Middleton, s/o John H. Young (Wolfeboro, farmer) and Mary E. Cook (Middleton, housekeeper); W - 18, housework, b. Middleton, d/o Charles H. Leighton (Middleton, farmer) and Lucy A. Drew (Eaton, housekeeper)
Roland Wilfred of Middleton m. Stella Marjorie **Budroe** 8/31/1940 in West Milton; H - 23, lumberman, b. Middleton, s/o Fred R. Young (Middleton, mill employee) and Alice E. Heath (Union, housewife); W - 18, waitress, b. Wolfeboro, d/o Edward J. Budroe (Conway, woodsman) and Sadie G. Elliott (Alton, housewife)
Samuel of Middleton m. Mary A. **Lougee** of Middleton 9/29/1892 in Middleton; H - 50, farmer, 3d, b. New Durham, s/o Joel Young

(Farmington, blacksmith) and Mary Durgin (Middleton); W - 48, housekeeper, 2d, b. Acton, ME

Willard A. m. Paulette E. **Tremblay** 7/1/1961; H - s/o Willard and Beatrice Young of Middleton; W - d/o Dennis Tremblay and Ann LaFurienia of Rochester

Willard J. of Middleton m. Dorothy M. **Cooper** of Middleton 8/31/1962 in So. Berwick, ME; H - s/o Fred R. Young and Alice Heath of Middleton; W - d/o Ernest M. Ward and Sadie Keene

Willard J. m. Abbie **Kidder** 11/13/1965; H - 46, s/o Fred Young of Middleton; W - 42, d/o Mrs. David Carson of FL

MIDDLETON
DEATHS

ANDREWS,
Clarence L., Jr., d. 9/19/1996 in Rochester; b. 6/6/1931*

ARSENAULT,
Joseph A., d. 9/10/1993 in Dover; b. 3/22/1925*

AUCLAIR,
Ethel B., d. 10/29/1984; b. 11/6/1904*

BABCOCK,
John H., d. 12/25/1995 in Wolfeboro; b. 6/14/1906*

BAKER,
Albert S., d. 9/15/1895 at 60/11/15; spinal meningitis; farmer; widower; b. Westmoreland; Larkin Baker (Westmoreland) and Celina Cobb (Westmoreland)

BARTLETT,
Everett E., d. 8/29/1988 in Middleton; b. 3/7/1935*

BARTSCH,
Pauline M., d. 1/29/1969 at 39; w/o Albert I. Bartsch

BEAUDRY,
Alice F., d. 3/22/1979; w/o James Beaudry; b. 5/15/1897*
James E., d. 9/6/1980; wid/o Alice Beaudry; b. 6/11/1899*

BELL,
Byron Franklin, d. 11/18/1950 at 30/8/28; shoe worker; married; b. Rochester; Frank Bell and Margaret Stanhope
Doris B., d. 2/1/1958 at 49; housewife
Edwin, d. 1/28/1916 at 0/3; Robert Bell and Elizabeth Worden

BODGE,
Daniel J., d. 8/6/1901 at 58; alcoholism; shoemaker; widower; b. Tuftonboro; Jesse Bodge (Lee) and Hattie Jones (Tuftonboro)

BOODY,
Rebecca W., d. 3/13/1910 at 87/0/1; housework; widow; b. Randolph, VT; Joseph Chamberlain (VT) and Nancy Hale

BRADBURY,
A. Caroline, d. 7/23/1973 at 64; ----- Tucker; w/o Milton Bradbury

BRADFORD,
Annie, d. 4/19/1919 at 34/7/24; cancer; housekeeper; married; b. Exeter; Samuel Lawrence (Meredith) and Augusta A. Horne (Middleton)

BRANNAN,
Catherine, d. 2/26/1958 at 85; housewife; widow
James, d. 4/22/1936 at 72; b. NS; Nickelson Brannan (NS)
Norbert N., d. 5/16/1973 at 72; h/o Ruby Tufts Brannan
Thomas Vincent, d. 4/24/1957 in Farmington; Norbert Brannan

BRUEDLE,
Ruth P., d. 4/16/1994 in Wolfeboro; b. 10/30/1906*

BRYANT,
Charles H., d. 5/16/1926 at 84/10/24; farmer; widower; b. Eaton; Ephraim Bryant and Mary A. Drew

BRYSON,
Helen M., d. 12/29/1996 in Ossipee; b. 9/26/1907*

BUDROE,
Sadie G., d. 4/22/1955 at 54; Henry Elliott

BULLIS,
E. Edna, d. 5/4/1973 at 51; ----- Eastman; w/o Eric A. Bullis, Jr.
Edith M., d. 10/2/1954 at 83; Reuben Dailey and ----- Topper
Eric A., d. 11/14/1971 at 75; Merritt Bullis and Addie Barnes
Merritt A., d. 5/6/1958 at 89; Albert Bullis and Amelia Amlau

Viola F., d. 1/23/1967 at 67; w/o Eric A. Bullis, Sr.

BURNS,
Emma F., d. 9/15/1998 in Wolfeboro at 78**
James W., d. 12/3/1945 at 0/3/20; b. Rochester; George W. Burns (Providence, RI) and Emma F. Tufts (Middleton)

BURROWS,
Betsey, d. 5/5/1924 at 88/4/1; b. Ossipee; Alexander Witham (Ossipee) and Mehitable Moody (Moultonboro)
Daniel, d. 11/24/1913 at 81/0/17; lesion of heart; farmer; b. Middleton; William Burrows (Middleton) and ----- Downs (Middleton)
David, d. 11/2/1907 at 77/4/12; old age; farmer; married; b. Middleton; David Burrows (Lebanon, ME) and Hannah Nutter (Newington)
Isaiah H., d. 5/25/1907 at 35/8/0; typhoid fever; woodsman; divorced; b. Middleton; David Burrows (Middleton) and Betsy Witham (Ossipee)
John, d. 8/15/1889 at 34/9/20; liver trouble; RR hand; married; b. Providence, RI
John Andrew, d. 5/9/1996 in Wolfeboro; b. 10/25/1910*
Lorraine Mary, d. 4/1/1951 at 0/0/3 in Rochester; b. Middleton; John Burrows (Middleton) and Millie Pervere (No. Stratford)
Millie A., d. 1/16/1976; w/o John Burrows; b. 8/19/1924*

BUSWELL,
Abbie, d. 3/4/1996 in Wolfeboro; b. 10/27/1911*

BUTLER,
Clifford R., d. 4/13/1986 in Rochester; b. 3/9/1914*

CAMPBELL,
Ralph, d. 6/26/1952 at 59 in Hanover; John Campbell and Sadie Potter

CANNEY,
Henrietta, d. 6/2/1936 at 63/4/0 in Dover; housewife; widow; b. NB; William H. Gillespie (Bangor, ME) and Emily Carolyn Keeyer (NB)

CARDEN,
Arthur H., Jr., d. 12/26/1998 in Salem

CARDINAL,
Erric M., d. 4/1/1926 at 0/0/11; b. Middleton; John Cardinal, Jr. (Epping) and Helen Burrows (Middleton)

CARLIN,
Frank, d. 1/23/1926 at 59/11/28; sawyer; single; b. Barnard, VT; Thomas Carlin (Ireland) and Annie Churchey (Ireland)

CASAVANT,
Florence E., d. 4/6/1985 in Rochester; Fred Moulton and Vivian Grace; b. 9/1/1924*
Joseph W., d. 2/7/1973 at 55; h/o Florence E. Casavant

CHAMBERLAIN,
Elmore H., d. 1/5/1958 at 51; George Chamberlain and Maud Hurd

CHANEY,
Francis A., d. 8/19/1906 at 73/10/19; Bright's disease; housework; widow; b. Portsmouth; Oliver Ayers (Greenland) and Martha Cotton (Portsmouth)

CHESLEY,
James M., d. 8/1/1996 in Brownsville, TX

CHOUINARD,
Alfred J., d. 9/4/1965 at 60; Peter Chouinard and Marie Gagon; h/o Annette Chouinard

CLOUTMAN,
Polly, d. 2/1/1890 at 75/11; apoplexy; housekeeper; widow; b. Middleton
William H., d. 10/15/1890 at 75/11; old age; carpenter; widower; b. Middleton

COLBATH,
Elizabeth H., d. 11/18/1890 at 87/0/12; old age; housekeeper; widow; b. Rochester
Emma L., d. 10/28/1949 at 71; housework; widow; b. Boston, MA; David Kelley
Leonard, d. 4/3/1889 at 72/5; shock; farmer; married; b. Middleton
Lydia M., d. 8/15/1889 at 82/8; erysipelas; housekeeper; widow; b. New Durham

COLE,
Lula M., d. 10/29/1971 at 79; m/o John Cole

COOK,
Charles L., d. 1/16/1907 at 69/1/6; heart disease; farmer; married; b. Middleton; Lewis Cook (Milton) and Nancy Jones (Durham)
Charles L., d. 1/1/1961 at 53; Edwin Cook and Ennie Jones; h/o Dorothy Poor Cook
Dudley S., d. 10/11/1898 at 43/2; septic peritonitis; watchman; married; b. Milton; Jacob H. Cook (Milton) and Hannah L. Furber (Middleton)
Edwin, d. 5/26/1929 at 63/0/21; farmer; divorced; b. Middleton
Eva May, d. 10/4/1901 at 0/3/15; bronchitis; b. Middleton; Edward Cook (Middleton) and Eunie M. Jones (Middleton)
Flora, d. 4/20/1903 at 0/1/13; indigestion; b. Middleton; Edwin Cook (Middleton) and Ennie M. Jones (Middleton)
George, d. 8/30/1928 at 59/0/29; farmer; single; b. Wakefield; Samuel J. Cook (Middleton) and Rebecca Downs (E. Rochester)
Jacob H., d. 11/26/1904 at 72/0/24; cancer of mouth; farmer; married; b. Middleton; Isaiah H. Cook (Middleton) and Johanna Pike (Middleton)

Lucy A., d. 7/10/1913 at 64/0/12; chronic nephritis; housewife; b. Wakefield; James W. Hill (Wakefield) and Eliza Weymouth (Saco, ME)

Mary E., d. 10/11/1913 at 79/1/25; Bright's disease; housewife; b. Tuftonboro; Jeremiah Horne (Tuftonboro) and Annie Canney (Tuftonboro)

Mary E., d. 12/14/1928 at 86/8/25; housekeeper; widow; b. Middleton; Mark L. Furber (Farmington) and Eliza A. Ricker

Norman E., d. 3/20/1927 at 0/7/25; broncho pneumonia; b. Middleton; Clarence E. Cook (Middleton) and Pauline D. Tufts (Middleton)

COON,
William M., d. 12/5/1964 at 73; George Coon and Deborah Martin; h/o Anne Coon

CORSON,
Charles A., d. 5/17/1888 at 36; consumption; shoemaker; married; b. Middleton; Albert Corson (Milton) and Betsey Ham (New Durham)

Woodbury, d. 11/7/1925 at 63/5/4; laborer; married

CRITO,
Victor, d. 1/31/1907 at 6/10/1; displacement; b. Canada; Philip Crito (Canada) and Josephine Abrold (Canada)

CURRIER,
Sherburne M., d. 8/12/1988 in Middleton

DANIELS,
William H., d. 6/9/1990 in Boston, MA; b. 12/11/1919*

DAUDELIN,
Victor E., d. 4/13/1974 at 71

DAVIS,
Elizabeth L., d. 5/14/1935 at 90/0/26; at home; divorced; b.
 Middleton; Jeremiah Colbath (Middleton) and Lydia Webster
 (Durham)
Lester W., d. 2/8/1975 at 66; Charles Davis and Josephine Jameson;
 h/o Marie Davis
Lloyd K., d. 9/11/1986 in Middleton
Marie Emma, d. 10/5/1996 in Portsmouth; b. 10/29/1913*
Meander H., d. 5/16/1931 at 68/7/16 in Farmington; lumberman;
 married; b. Middleton; Charles W. Davis (Tuftonboro) and Emily
 E. French (Middleton)

DEARBORN,
Hannah, d. 5/10/1898 at 80/0/10; dropsy and old age; at home;
 widow; b.Milton; John Whitehouse (Milton) and Betsey
 Wentworth (Wakefield)

DECOSTER,
Peter Joseph, d. 7/20/1970 at 66; Rene DeCoster and Lucia DeVits;
 h/o Mary J. DeCoster

DEXTER,
Tina Marie, d. 7/5/1975 at 0/0/0; Ernest Dexter and Patricia Taylor

DIPRIZIO,
Albert Charles, d. --/--/1970 at 21; John H. DiPrizio and Enid Lowd
Amelia, d. 3/11/1957; w/o Prisco DiPrizio
Anthony V., d. 12/21/1995 in Wolfeboro; b. 1/15/1937*
Charles, d. 6/3/1984; b. 10/4/1895*
Louise, d. 7/26/1984; b. 8/29/1897*
Prisco, d. 3/24/1971 at 78; fa/o Evelyn DiPrizio
Rosemary T., d. 1/23/1985 in Dover; John Long and Mary Russo; b.
 7/9/1933*
Sonia H., d. 5/26/1984; b. 7/15/1935*

DORE,
James, b. 6/29/1893 at 84; dropsy; widower; b. Middleton
Sally, d. 4/29/1893 at 86; old age; married; b. Middleton

DOW,
James Israil, d. 5/12/1911 at 51; burning building; laborer

DOWLING,
Myrtle E., d. 10/22/1985 in NJ; b. 11/16/1914*
Thomas, d. 4/1986 in AL; b. 3/20/1912*

DOWNING,
George W., d. 2/8/1898 at 76/4/16; paralytic shock; farmer; widower; b. Middleton; Samuel Downing (Middleton) and Mary Davis (New Durham)
L. E., d. 5/23/1894 at 20/3/18; consumption; single; b. Middleton; L. H. Downing (farmer, Middleton) and Rosilla P. Hartford (Conway)
Luther Hale, d. 6/16/1910 at 61/0/19; farmer; married; b. Middleton; George W. Downing (Middleton) and Caroline Colbath (Middleton)

DOWNS,
Fred C., d. 4/1/1962 at 87; fa/o Hazel Marcoux of Milton

DRAWBRIDGE,
Edward F., d. 4/17/1947 at 74/6/23; retired; married; b. Worcester, MA; George D. Drawbridge (Lewes, England) and Abagail Littlefield (Kennebunk, ME)
George D., d. 11/23/1910 at 75/10/3; decorator; married; b. Lewes, England; David Drawbridge (England) and Elizabeth (England)

DREW,
Annie E., d. 2/7/1913 at 64/8/24; lesion of heart; housework; b. St. Andrews, NB; Hugh Maloney (St. Andrews, NB) and Mary Clark (St. Andrews, NB)

Benjamin M., d. 12/9/1937 at 82/8/21; farmer; widower; b. Eaton; Thomas Drew (Eaton) and Sarah Bryant (Freedom)
Ellsworth, d. 7/12/1922 at 52/7/19; farmer; married; b. Eaton; Thomas Drew (Eaton) and Sarah Eaton (Eaton)
Forrest W., d. 9/13/1985; Christina Drew; b. 3/3/1936*
Horace, d. 9/23/1911 at 62/2/5; chronic nephritis; farmer; widower; b. Eaton; Thomas Drew (Eaton) and Sara Bryant (Eaton)
Maggie, d. 9/20/1911 at 58/3/28; heart disease; housework; married; b. Ireland; John Walker (England) and Elizabeth Black (England)
Sarah, d. 2/4/1905 at 75/5/20; la grippe; at home; widow; b. Eaton; John Bryant and Sarah Cilley
Thomas, d. 6/11/1897 at 71/3/6; apoplexy; farmer; married; b. Eaton; Thomas Drew

DROUIN,
Joseph Arthur, d. 5/19/1970 at 17; Raymond O. Drouin and J. Claire Allard

DUDLEY,
Earle V., III, d. 9/22/1992 in Portsmouth

DUNN,
Donald L., d. 4/28/1986 in Wolfeboro; b. 12/4/1920*

EASTMAN,
Charles Franklin, d. 10/15/1950 at 67/6/14 in Rochester; farmer; widower; b. Milton; Walter Tibbetts
Haskett, d. 4/17/1910 at 66/11/16; farmer; married; b. No. Conway; Stephen Eastman and Dorothy Cook
Leo P., d. 11/3/1910 at 0/0/6; b. Middleton; Charles F. Eastman (Milton) and Mary A. Tufts (Middleton)
Loyde R., d. 4/21/1967 at 50; h/o Lucille Beamis Eastman
Mary R., d. 8/13/1948 at 58/0/18; housewife; married; b. Middleton; Charles D. Tufts (Middleton) and Nellie Corson

Ruth A., d. 11/30/1918 at 66/10/12; chronic interstitial; housewife; widow; b. Middleton; Davis Tufts (Middleton) and Adeline D. Horn (Middleton)

ELLINGWOOD,
May E., d. 1/5/1986 in Rochester; b. 12/31/1921*

ELLIOTT,
George Everett, d. 5/8/1908 at 0/0/19; bronchitis; b. Middleton; Frank H. Elliott (Stoneham, MA) and Minnie Graton (Manchester)

EMERY,
Mary E., d. 1/12/1899 at 70/5/6; general debility; housewife; widow; b. Eaton; Henry Jenness and ----- Eastman

FENERTY,
Stanley W., d. 4/23/1989 in Portsmouth

FORTIER,
Richard M., d. 5/30/1991 in Manchester; b. 7/4/1935*

FOSTER,
Augustus, d. 8/18/1951 at 83/7/12; shoe shop; married; b. FL; Peter Foster and Maria Williams

FRANCOEUR,
Donald E., d. 1/6/1961 at 51; Eldridge Francoeur and Mabel Magnan; h/o Berniece Colclough
John D., d. 7/27/1960 at 40; Eldridge Francoeur and Mabel Magnan
Lawrence A., d. 9/12/1964 at 53; Eldridge Francoeur and Mable Magnon

FRANKLIN,
David J., d. 5/6/1984; b. 9/23/1958*

FRASER,
Daniel D., d. 6/19/1928 at 78; carpenter; widower; b. NS

FRAWLEY,
George Thomas, d. 7/13/1953 at 75 in Strafford; poultry man; married; b. Bridgewater, MA; Thomas Frawley and Ellen A. Donnell

FROST,
Hiram B., d. 2/7/1892 at 78; la grippe; farmer; widower; b. Middleton
John H., d. 2/7/1988 in Manchester; b. 6/23/1926*
Phebe A., d. 4/1/1896 at 70/2/12; paralysis; housekeeper; married; b. Middleton; Robert Ellis (Middleton) and Hannah Wentworth (Middleton)

FULLER,
Christine Mary, d. 8/22/1996 in Middleton at 45**
Donald P., d. 2/12/1985 in Rochester; Phillip Fuller and Rubye Fuller; b. 10/1/1940*
Peter, d. 12/18/1996 in Middleton at 50**

FURMAN,
Charles J., d. 6/24/1994 in Rochester at 66**

GARDNER,
Gerard, d. 1/19/1994 in Farmington at 83**
Irene Mae, d. 8/7/1992 in Rochester; b. 8/21/1907*

GATES,
Ellsworth C., d. 1/12/1978; h/o Pearl E. Gates; b. 10/25/1896*

GAUTHIER,
Eugene Noel, d. 4/23/1997 in Laconia; b. 12/27/1929*
Robert, d. 10/16/1984

GIBBS,
John W., d. 4/9/1907 at 78/1/8; neuralgia of heart; laborer; married; b. Waterboro, ME; Israel Welch

GILBY,
Edward F., d. 9/13/1941 at 76/2/1; farmer; widower; b. Waterville, ME; Freeman Gilby (Waterville, ME) and Marguerette Derrah (Waterville, ME)

GRACE,
Chandler Timothy, d. 4/14/1970 at 67; Joseph Grace and Lucy Lodena Cates
David Lee, d. 6/18/1949 at 0/0/0; b. Middleton; Joseph Grace (Middleton) and Norma Adams (ME)
Joseph S., d. 2/27/1953 at 81 in Strafford; farmer; widower; b. Chatham; Chandler P. Grace and Abbie Bean
Lodena Lucy, d. 9/21/1950 at 64/5/24 in Rochester; housewife; married; b. Stratford; Benjamin Cates and Matilda Dickie

GRANT,
Frances M., d. 3/17/1975 at 85; Stephen Roma and Ann Manette

GREATRIX,
Paul B., d. 12/3/1986 in Wolfeboro; b. 11/15/1906*

HANRAHAN,
Dr. William, d. 10/24/1937 at 58; dentist; married; b. Woonsocket, RI; William J. Hanrahan (Ireland) and Mary Reynolds (Lawrence, MA)

HANSCOM,
John, d. 4/4/1889 at 60; dropsy; farmer; widower; b. Dover

HANSON,

Bulah M., d. 10/1/1894 at 0/7/8; cholera infantum; b. Wakefield; William F. Hanson (mill hand, Middleton) and Mary E. Penney (New Durham)

W. Furber, d. 4/8/1938 at 87/4/11 in Dover; laborer; b. Middleton; William S. Hanson (Middleton) and Hannah L. Hanson (Middleton)

HARRIMAN,
Cyrus L., d. 1/8/1963 at 53; h/o Doris Depatra Harriman
Richard N., d. 1/12/1998 at 55** in Rochester

HART,
Emily Ellsworth, d. 9/26/1997 in Rochester; b. 4/23/1924*
William H., d. 2/10/1992 in White River Junction, VT; b. 8/2/1925*

HASKINS,
Christopher W., d. 12/16/1974 at 0/3/16; William Haskins

HEAD,
Fannie M., d. 7/10/1913 at 41/4/6; paresis; b. Farmington; Andrew Walker and Hannah Berry

HILDRETH,
Della Jane, d. 12/27/1989 in Rochester

HILL,
Penny Lee, d. 1/13/1961 at 0/0/28; Alfred Hill and Dorothy Smith

HILTON,
Adelaide, d. 5/22/1907 at 84/7/21; jaundice; housewife; widow; b. Tuftonboro; David E. Davis and Sally W. Pike (Middleton)

HOLMES,
Frank H., d. 12/4/1945 at 65/4 in Lynn, MA; cattle dealer; widower; b. Strafford; Herbert Holmes (Strafford) and Sarah F. Hayes (Farmington)

Nellie M., d. 4/12/1944 at 59/0/15 in Manchester; housewife; married; b. Lynn, MA; Alton Chase (Augusta, ME) and Sybil C. Pease (Bealding, ME)

HOOPER,
Lyle F., d. 4/18/1962 at 62; Richard Hooper and Alice Johnson

HORNE,
David F., d. 5/16/1888 at 86; dropsy; farmer; married; b. New Durham; Jacob Horne (New Durham) and Polly French (Farmington)
Jethro E., d. 3/17/1911 at 66/11; pneumonia; farmwork; widower; b. Middleton; John D. Horne (Middleton) and Mary Chase (Wolfeboro)

HORTON,
Agnes M., d. 10/10/1910 at 0/7/6; b. Manchester; Herbert Horton (Franklin) and Olive M. Melanson (Dorchester)

HOULE,
Barbara Jean, d. 9/1/1996 in Middleton at 53**

HOWARD,
Charles, d. 11/9/1928 at 71/4/27; laborer; widower; b. Newmarket; Frank Howard (Newmarket) and Hannah Brown (Barrington)

HOWE,
Marie Clara, d. 6/11/1960 at 65; w/o Raymond Howe
Pauline M., d. 3/9/1955 at 68; Elber Hurd and Frances Cain
Raymond G., d. 7/31/1980; f/o Robert Howe; b. 7/11/1904*
Richard, d. 5/3/1957 in Manchester

HOYT,
Robert R., Jr., d. 6/22/1975 at 30; drowned; Charles W. Hoyt and Margaret Twombly; residence - Dover

HUCKINS,
Anita M., d. 3/7/1997 in Milton; b. 6/1/1942*

HURD,
son, d. 11/19/1937 at 0/0/1 in Sanford, ME; b. Sanford, ME; Mewyn Hurd (Milton Mills) and Alice Stevens (Middleton)

HYNES,
Edmund Carl, d. 3/5/1976; h/o Ann Hynes; b. 2/28/1898*

JEAN,
Patricia M., d. 1/12/1990 in Middleton

JENNESS,
Lucinda, d. 1/19/1979; w/o Elmer Jenness; b. 10/10/1902*

JOHNSON,
Edna, d. 2/6/1998 at 54** in Orlando, FL
Myrtie, d. 3/25/1955 at 75; Moores Brown
Thomas F., d. 4/13/1993 in Dover; b. 6/15/1912*

JOLLEY,
Leander N., d. 2/24/1943 at 51/2/22; box shop; married; b. Keene; John F. Jolley (Keene) and Mary Veganer (Keene)

JONES,
Addie L., d. 5/2/1933 at 73/9/1; at home; widow; b. Middleton; America Lane (Norway, ME) and Eliza Furber (Middleton)
Charles H., d. 7/3/1892 at 35; consumption; farmer; b. Middleton
Emma H., d. 6/18/1907 at 56/10/14; gangreen rectum; housekeeper; widow; b. Middleton; Steven Perkins (Middleton)
John, d. 6/9/1890 at 83; old age; farmer; married
Sidney, d. 3/21/1887 at 2/10; b. Middleton; Charles Jones (Middleton) and Lizzie Kimball

JOY,
Jessie-Ann, d. 8/22/1998 at 66** in Sanbornville

KELLEY,
Cecelia, d. 3/26/1997 in CA; b. 2/22/1943*
Effie M., d. 11/13/1906 at 30/2/22; phthisis; housework; married; b. Middleton; Luther H. Downing (Middleton) and Rosa Hartford (Middleton)
Ruth G., d. 7/25/1955 at 73; Alvah Garland

KILTON,
Viola E., d. 6/23/1989 in Wolfeboro; b. 3/14/1921*

KIMBALL,
daughter, d. 2/24/1898 at 0/0/0; stillborn; George Kimball (Middleton) and Eliza Hanscom (Dover)
Annie C., d. 11/10/1917 at 53/5/27; lobar pneumonia; dressmaker; single; b. Middleton; Nehemiah Kimball (Middleton) and Martha B. Ham (Middleton)
Charlotte T., d. 9/30/1940 at 70/6/13 in Dover; housewife; married; b. Halifax, NS; Nicholas Breen (Halifax, NS) and Ellen McLaughlin (Halifax, NS)
Eliza S., d. 3/31/1930 at 75/8/0; housewife; married; b. Dover; John Hanscom (Dover) and Maria Stevens (Middleton)
Elmer B., d. 12/7/1971 at 75; h/o Margaret W. Kimball
George W., d. 1/6/1937 at 80/9/23; widower; b. Middleton; Washington Kimball (Middleton) and Martha Ham (New Durham)
Herbert, d. 2/4/1965 at 75; David Kimball and Nellie Hanscom
Ida, d. 12/1/1889 at 12; heart disease; scholar; single; b. Middleton
Lester E., d. 10/20/1915 at 22/3/10; injury to side; mill hand; single; b. Wakefield; George Kimball (Middleton) and Eliza Hanscom (Middleton)
Lizzie, d. 4/--/1887 at 30; b. Middleton; Washington Kimball and Martha Kimball

Ralph M., d. 7/14/1951 at 69/5/11 in Dover; laborer; single; b. Middleton; David S. Kimball and Nellie S. Hanscom

Woodbury, d. 9/20/1963 at 51; br/o George M. Kimball

KINNEY,
Allen J., d. 7/12/1967 at 83; wid/o Margaret Mullen Kinney
Arthur R., d. 1/14/1984; b. 11/20/1925*
Margaret F., d. 9/8/1956 at 72; Vidite Mullen and Mary Pime; w/o Allen Kinney
Virginia F., d. 10/10/1995 in Rochester; b. 11/21/1923*
Walter V., d. 3/12/1975 at 60; Allen Kinney and Margaret Mullen; h/o Virginia Kinney

KIRTHLEY,
Mary E., d. 5/11/1913 at 69/7; ver. hemorrhage; housework; b. Middleton; David Tufts and Adeline Horne

KNOWLES,
Joseph H., d. 3/2/1902 at 59/3/3; diabetes mellitus; farmer; married; b. Milton; Parker Knowles and Susan Corson (Milton)

LAMPER,
Annie I., d. 4/30/1968 at 70; w/o Chandler T. Grace

LANE,
America, d. 9/21/1910 at 78/9/29; carpenter; widower; b. Oxford, ME; Ami Lane (Oxford, ME) and Eliza Whitehouse (Oxford, ME)
Eliza Ann, d. 6/6/1910 at 73/5/19; at home; married; b. Middleton; Mark L. Furber (Farmington) and Eliza Ricker (Farmington)

LANGEVIN,
John, d. 2/25/1942 at 77/0/11; weaver; widower; b. Stanstead, Canada

LANGLEY,
Adam W., d. 8/23/1991 in Rochester

LAPIERRE,
Jeffrey A., d. 7/22/1995 in Middleton

LAVERTUE,
John R., d. 11/15/1967 at 64; Joseph Lavertue and Florence Downs

LAWRENCE,
Annie, d. 8/2/1921 at 74/11/17; housekeeper; married; b. Middleton; John D. Horne (Middleton) and Mary Chase (Wolfeboro)
John E., d. 10/11/1989 in Rochester

LEGERE,
Gerard A., d. 1/21/1995 in Fort Kent, ME at 47**

LEIGHTON,
son, d. 11/20/1929 at 0/0/1; b. Middleton; Presco Leighton (Middleton) and Gladys Russell (Danvers, MA)
Bennie W., d. 12/31/1937 at 6 hrs. in Wolfeboro; b. Wolfeboro; William Leighton (Middleton) and Leona Grace (Tamworth)
C. Chaney, d. 1/11/1889 at 14/11/5; farmer; single; b. Middleton
Carry V., d. 5/23/1897 at 26/2/22; childbirth; housekeeper; married; b. Portland, ME; Charles Guilford (Hollis, ME) and Rebecca Tucker (Saco, ME)
Charles H., d. 12/8/1925 at 83/7/17; farmer; married; b. Middleton; V. H. Leighton (Strafford) and Dorothy Jones
Charles Lorenzo, d. 1/5/1951 at 83 in Wolfeboro; farmer; married; b. Middleton; Charles Leighton and Anna Whitehouse
Delwin H., d. 3/28/1969 at 73; b. 12/24/1895*
Elizabeth S., d. 9/4/1945 at 71/5/29; housewife; married; b. Middleton; Horace Drew (Eaton) and Margaret Walker (England)
Etta M., d. 2/24/1932 at 68/0/15; housekeeper; widow; b. Middleton; John H. Young (Middleton) and Mary E. Cook (Middleton)
James P., d. 4/14/1908 at 32/8/27; pneumonia; farmer; married; b. Middleton; Charles H. Leighton (Middleton) and Lucy N. Drew (Eaton)

Olivette, d. 9/20/1947 at 80/4/23; married; b. Charlestown, MA;
    Richard Piggott (Limerick, Ireland) and Hannah S. Locke (Rye)
Walter Frank, d. 7/7/1953 at 88 in Strafford; farmer; widower; b.
    Middleton; Charles H. Leighton and Anna Whitehouse
William T., d. 5/4/1984; b. 2/9/1901*

LESSARD,
Edith M., d. 1/29/1978; mo/o Robert and Roger Lessard; b. 5/2/1903*
Forrest L., d. 10/21/1947 at 0/0/22; b. Norway, ME; Forrest L.
    Lessard (Middleton) and Marilyn Noyes (So. Paris, ME)

LLOYD,
Robert A., d. 12/22/1969 at 55; h/o Lydia Lloyd

LOTHROP,
Ethelda T., d. 10/22/1930 at 66/6/28; housewife; married; b. NB;
    John C. Wells (Eastport, ME) and Rebecca Calhoun
John M., d. 6/6/1936 at 82/6/0; carpenter; b. Cambridge, MA; George
    B. Lothrop (Chocetuate, MA) and Eunice Wheeler (Concord,
    ME)

LUONGO,
Angelina, d. 8/7/1971 at 79; m/o Nicholas Luongo
Gladys V., d. 5/18/1991 in Dover

LYTLE,
John W., d. 1/8/1971 at 79; h/o Gladys Lytle
William, d. 11/21/1924 at 87/1/25; b. Hants County, NS; William
    Lytle (NS) and Margaret Dodge (NS)

MACDONALD,
Hugh J., d. 11/22/1945 at 64/1/28; lumberman; single; b. NS; Allen
    MacDonald (NS) and Mary MacDonald (NS)

MAHONEY,
Robert H., d. 9/22/1988 in Middleton; b. 11/19/1915*

MALKIN,
Bertha, d. 11/25/1994 in Middleton; b. 2/18/1909*

MANCUSO,
William A., d. 5/8/1989 in Dover; b. 2/24/1920*

MARQUES,
Eunice M., d. 5/30/1975 at 58; John Mitchell and Lena Livingston; w/o William J. Marques

MARTINEAU,
Forest, d. 11/17/1912 at 15/1/5; typhoid fever; single; b. Middleton; Napoleon Martineau (Quebec, Canada) and Josephine Brown (Ossipee)

MASKELL,
Alan A., d. 5/30/1975 at 32; fire; Alton R. Maskell and Lucy Downs

MASON,
Frank, d. 7/11/1896 at 46; struck by lightning; woodchopper; married; b. Canada

MAXFIELD,
Frances Mary, d. 3/7/1997 in Rochester; b. 6/8/1913*

McCONNELL,
Donna M., d. 2/16/1995 in Rochester; b. 9/23/1953*

McCULLOUGH,
John R., d. 7/1/1946 at 67/10/8; supt. of county farm; married; b. Philadelphia, PA; Alexander McCullough (Ireland) and Maria Query (Philadelphia, PA)

MELLOWS,
Katie E., d. 11/9/1889 at 34/4/; Bright's disease; housekeeper; married; b. Rochester

MESERVE,
Robert L., d. 2/21/1978; h/o Rose Meserve; b. 3/9/1910*

MESSIER,
Carrie M., d. 4/13/1939 at 67/3/25; housewife; married; b. Charlestown, MA; John Boyce (Worcester, MA) and Martha Baker (Charlestown, MA)

MITCHELL,
Hazel E., d. 8/19/1974 at 58

MONAHAN,
Mary, d. 9/3/1906 at 32; phthisis pulmonia; single; b. Lynn, MA; Michael Monahan (Ireland) and Mary Gallagher (Ireland)

MOONEY,
Dorothy, d. 9/7/1919 at 0/0/8; congenital debility; b. Middleton; Benjamin W. Mooney (Somerville, MA) and Marion Knowles (Milton)
Elinor I., d. 1/13/1921 at 0/6/12; b. Middleton; Benjamin F. Mooney (Somerville, MA) and Marion Knowles (Milton)
Richard, d. 12/5/1997 in Dover; b. 4/18/1930*

MOORE,
Albert C., d. 9/30/1910 at 80/9/25; farmer; widower; b. Middleton; Randall Moore (Canterbury) and Mary C. Hill (Northwood)
Charles W., d. 1/22/1971 at 80; fa/o Mrs. Frederic Auclair
Eli S., d. 8/3/1925 at 56/10/27; farmer; married; b. Middleton; Albert C. Moore (Middleton) and Sabrina Seward (Wakefield)
Emma C., d. 12/13/1933 at 69/5/5; housekeeper; single; b. Middleton; Albert C. Moore (Middleton) and Sabrina Seward (Wakefield)
Ethel I., d. 4/9/1967 at 93; ----- Wentworth; wid/o Eli Moore
James D., d. 7/15/1914 at 89/6/11; cardiac insufficiency; farmer; b. Middleton; Randall Moore (Canterbury) and Mary C. Hill (Northwood)

Lydia A., d. 2/7/1940 at 69/11/16; housekeeper; single; b. Middleton; Albert Moore (Middleton) and Sabrina Seward (Wakefield)

Mary E., d. 11/9/1962 at 64 in Rochester; w/o Thomas Moore

Roland E., d. 11/16/1998 in Manchester

Sabrina D., d. 4/19/1904 at 71/8/23; exhaustion; at home; married; b. Wakefield; Samuel Seward and Betsey Wentworth

MORIARTY,
Edith M., d. 7/19/1984
William Edward, d. 7/19/1984; b. 9/21/1919*

MOULTON,
Evelyn, d. 11/30/1923 at 19/8; shoeworker; single; b. Middleton; ----- Moulton and Flora Howard

Maud E., d. 2/24/1911 at 31/11; tobes dorsalis; housework; married; b. Farmington; Clarence Ham (Farmington) and ----- (Tuftonboro)

NICOLA,
Harold G., d. 2/27/1992 in Middleton; b. 6/21/1900*

NUTTER,
Charles E., d. 2/5/1899 at 38/4/3; diabetes mellitus; farmer; single; b. Middleton; Simpson Nutter (Wakefield) and Paulina Ellis (Middleton)

John N., d. 11/27/1940 at 83/11/2; farmer; widower; b. Middleton; Simpson Nutter and Polina Ellis

ORNE,
Adeline L., d. 11/6/1907 at 83/3/3; old age; housework; widow; b. Middleton; Joseph Tufts (Lee) and Rebecca Stevens (Middleton)

Augustus G., d. 4/8/1894 at 77/4/3; pneumonia; farmer; married; b. Tuftonboro; Isaiah G. Orne (farmer, Wolfeboro) and Sarah R. Rainard (England)

Frederick A., d. 6/5/1914 at 76/8/11; heart disease; farmer; b.
Tuftonboro; Augustus G. Orne (Moultonboro) and Sallie Caverly (Tuftonboro)

PALISI,
Delores M., d. 5/17/1989 in Wolfeboro

PARENT,
Conrad O., d. 7/25/1964 at 48; Edward Parent and Celinare Caron; h/o Jeannette Parent

PEASE,
Lydia E., d. 4/5/1889 at 49; apoplexy; b. So. Newmarket

PENNEY,
Almira B., d. 4/20/1894 at 66/3/1; shock; housewife; married; b. Middleton; Isaiah H. Cook (farmer, Middleton) and Joanna M. Pike (Middleton)
Joseph J., d. 11/30/1903 at 76/9/21; angina pectoris; married; b. Farmington; ----- and Deborah Nutter (Rochester)
Lewis, d. 9/5/1887 at --; b. Middleton

PERKINS,
Abbey Jane, d. 5/17/1910 at 67/10/11; housework; widow; b. Rollinsford; William Goodwin (So. Berwick, ME) and Mary Dore (Rollinsford)
Arthur M., d. 4/2/1967 at 78; h/o Villa Quimby Perkins
Charles M., d. 6/10/1931 at 79/10/27 in Farmington; shoe maker; widower; b. Middleton; John D. Perkins (Middleton) and Harriett A. Garland (Middleton)
John J., d. 3/15/1934 at 75/11/12; laborer; married; b. Middleton; Stephen Perkins (Middleton) and Martha Straw (Tuftonboro)
Joseph F., d. 11/5/1987 in Rochester; b. 8/17/1919*
Joseph L., d. 12/30/1889 at 57/6; insanity; farmer; widower; b. Middleton

Laurel M., d. 9/22/1908 at 0/4/12; cholera infantum; b. Middleton; Walter Perkins (So. Berwick, ME) and Sadie Mitchell (New Durham)

Samuel, d. 9/8/1908 at 77/6; chronic diarrhea; farmer; married; b. Middleton; Solomon Perkins (Middleton) and Mary Perkins (Middleton)

Samuel, Jr., d. 8/4/1936 at 67/0/23; b. Middleton; Samuel Perkins (Salmon Falls) and Abbie J. Goodwin (Eliot, ME)

Violet L., d. 8/31/1925 at 0/2/8; Lester A. Perkins (Wolfeboro) and Elizabeth Lord (Acton, ME)

Walter P., d. 5/28/1954 at 74; Samuel Perkins and Abigail Goodwin

PIKE,

Altie S., d. 4/27/1911 at 39/4/4; septic fever; housekeeper; divorced; b. Middleton; James D. Pike (New Durham) and Susan L. Cloutman (Middleton)

Ebenezer S., d. 3/23/1890 at 78/5/23; apoplexy; farmer; married; b. Middleton

James D., d. 11/10/1914 at 80/10/7; cardiac dilation; farmer; b. New Durham; Jacob J. Pike and Deborah Davis (New Durham)

John S., d. 2/24/1896 at 58/8/7; apoplexy; farmer; married; b. Middleton; John L. Pike (Middleton) and Abigail (Middleton)

Mattie, d. 12/3/1887 at 21; single; b. Middleton; E. S. Pike (Middleton) and Drazilla Pike (Middleton)

PINKHAM,

Charles E., d. 2/19/1892 at 51; la grippe; farmer; b. Farmington

George E., d. 1/31/1924 at 74/0/6; farmer; widower; b. Farmington; Thomas Pinkham (New Durham) and Adeline Hodgdon

Herbert C., d. 5/20/1956 at 70 in Rochester; George Pinkham and Laura J. Main; h/o Abbie Pinkham

Orrin, d. 2/28/1925 at 69/7/25; laborer; divorced; b. Farmington; Thomas Pinkham (New Durham) and A. Hodgedon

PLUMMER,
M. M., d. 4/26/1894 at 0/9/14; "fitts"; b. Milton; Hazen Plummer (shoe maker, Milton) and Nettie Pike (Middleton)

QUIMBY,
Jessica L., d. 7/11/1986 in Boston, MA
Louise J., d. 12/15/1977; mo/o Michael Quimby; b. 3/26/1925*

RICH,
Christine Jane, d. 2/13/1996 in Ossipee; b. 12/18/1907*

ROACH,
Dorothy, d. 2/4/1990 in Rochester; b. 2/5/1921*

ROBERTS,
Elizabeth V., d. 10/20/1958 at 91; bookkeeper; single

ROWE,
Karen Gamage, d. 5/2/1993 in Dover; b. 7/5/1932*

SABANS,
Ormond Atwood, d. 3/20/1996 in Wolfeboro

SCHOFIELD,
Hildred C., d. 9/9/1958 at 69; Enor Peterson and Sarah McDonald

SHAW,
Thelma M., d. 3/21/1998 at 87** in Wolfeboro

SHEPARD,
Clayton W., d. 10/25/1980; h/o Irene Shepard; b. 3/16/1909*
Olin, d. 5/19/1939 at 77/2/7; spinner; b. Danville, VT; William Shepard

SICORD,
David R., d. 3/19/1962 at 77; fa/o Mildred Secord

SIMONDS,
Stillman, d. 12/30/1907 at 79/7/13; old age; farmer; married; b. Dunstable; Moses Simonds (Nashua) and Susan Blood (Nashua)

SINCLAIR,
Chester J., d. 8/27/1973 at 60; h/o Josephine Francoeur Sinclair
Jeannette F., d. 5/26/1980; mo/o David Sinclair; b. 8/1/1915*

SINDORF,
Rev. John Harmon, d. 9/17/1998 at 77** in Manchester

SLATTERY,
George, d. 10/17/1930 at 65/10/10; farmer; single; b. MA

SMITH,
James F.D., d. 8/6/1905 at 77/11/13; apoplexy; farmer; widower; b. Middleton; Isaac Stevens and Margaret Butler
Warren S., d. 4/20/1910 at 0/0/0; b. Middleton; Guy A. Smith (Franconia) and Clara M. Tufts (Middleton)

SPAHN,
Marie J., d. 1/30/1987 in Middleton; b. 6/6/1920*

STEVENS,
son, d. 3/9/1898 at 0/0/0; stillborn; Edgar N. Stevens (Middleton) and Annie Cleveland (Hillsboro)
daughter, d. 4/3/1922 at 0/0/0 in Rochester; Albert M. Stevens (Union) and Bernise M. Tufts (Middleton)
daughter [Ruth], d. 4/6/1930 at 0/0/0 in Farmington; b. Farmington; Melvin Stevens (Middleton) and Maud Merrill (Wakefield, MA)
son, d. 3/2/1938 at 4 3/4 hrs. in Rochester; b. Rochester; Melvin E. Stevens (Middleton) and Maud P. Merrill (Wakefield, MA)
Albert M., d. 2/7/1941 at 73/1; farmer; widower; b. Middleton; James F.D. Stevens (Middleton) and Lydia F. Brown (Benton, ME)
Arthur L., d. 8/7/1973 at 66; h/o Grace Kinney Stevens
Aurore P., d. 3/23/1957; w/o John I. Stevens

Bernise M., d. 4/3/1922 at 44/4/16 in Rochester; housewife; married; b. Middleton; George J. Tufts (Middleton) and Emma Whitehouse (Middleton)

Byron H., d. 5/3/1940 at 82/5/2; farmer; married; b. Middleton; Thomas J. Stevens (Middleton) and Mary Whitehouse (Middleton)

Edgar Nash, d. 10/7/1943 at 77/9/21; farmer; married; b. Middleton; James F.D. Stevens (Middleton) and Lydia Brown (Benton, ME)

Edwina, d. 5/19/1931 at 0/0/1 in Rochester; b. Rochester; Melvin Stevens (Middleton) and Maud Merrill (Wakefield, MA)

Elwin R., d. 3/31/1896 at 0/0/7; spasms; b. Middleton; Albert M. Stevens (Middleton) and Bernice M. Tufts (Middleton)

Eva, d. 3/4/1919 at 24/8/14; influenza; schoolteacher; single; b. Middleton; Hiram S. Stevens (Freeport, ME) and Hattie B. Ross (Farmington, ME)

George W., d. 2/9/1902 at 54/10/27; chronic nephritis; farmer; married; b. Middleton; George W. Stevens (Boston, MA) and Hannah Whitehouse

Grace G., d. 9/9/1987 in Dover; b. 8/30/1918*

Handy Andy, d. 12/2/1940 at 20/11/2; laborer; married; b. Middleton; Albert M. Stevens (Middleton) and Bernice Tufts (Middleton)

Herbert, d. 1/26/1932 at 27/1/9 in Wolfeboro; farmer; married; b. Middleton; Albert M. Stevens (Middleton) and Bernice Tufts (Middleton)

Hiram S., d. 10/6/1942 at 78/9/24; retired RR man; married; b. Freeport, ME; Benjamin F. Stevens (Middleton) and Statira Wilson (ME)

James W., d. 9/19/1943 at 0/2/15; b. Rochester; Arthur Stevens (Middleton) and Grace Kinney (Westfield, ME)

Jennie A., d. 1/24/1904 at 45/6; pulmonary consumption; at home; married; b. Alton; Hiram Kenney and Clara E. Dore

Jonathan B., d. 3/7/1897 at 70/9/19; cancer of stomach; farmer; married; b. Middleton; John D. Stevens (Middleton) and Martha Buzzell (Middleton)

Lydia F., d. 6/8/1904 at 78/3/23; neuralgia of heart; at home; married; b. Benton, ME; Nathaniel Brown (Benton, ME)

Mary E., d. 9/26/1901 at 65/2/3; meningitis and Bright's disease; domestic; married; b. Middleton; R. W. Whitehouse (Middleton) and Elizabeth Kimball (Middleton)

May Sevilla, d. 10/21/1950 at 60; housewife; widow; b. Sunny Corner, NB; James Johnston and Josephine White

Melvin E., d. 8/7/1958 at 56; Albert M. Stevens; h/o Eleanor Reid Stevens

Melvin E., Jr., d. 3/25/1929 at 0/1/27 in Wakefield; b. Rochester; Melvin E. Stevens (Middleton) and Maud Merrill (Wakefield, MA)

Pearl May, d. 7/16/1943 at 15/7/9; student; single; b. Union; Herbert Stevens (Middleton) and Lillian Campbell (Rowley, MA)

Sidney A., d. 12/16/1978; h/o Marion Stevens; b. 6/28/1906*

Viola J., d. 7/29/1946 at 79/3/2; housewife; widow; b. Farmington; Charles Dudley (Somersworth) and Lydia Tibbetts (Tamworth)

STILES,
Louise E., d. 1/5/1985 in Dover; Percy Cunningham and Minnie Williams; b. 6/12/1908*

SWEENEY,
Michael, d. 2/19/1985; Sidney Sweeney and Lillian Weiss; b. 6/11/1939*

SYMONDS,
Hannah, d. 5/25/1924 at 88/4/1; b. Middleton; Isaac Stevens and Margaret Butler (Hampstead, E.)

TALBOT,
Pauline M., d. 11/25/1995 in Middleton; b. 1/31/1926*

TAYLOR,
Charles B., d. 11/1/1951 at 68/0/4; woolen mill; married; b. England; Ramsden Taylor and Mary Dyson

THIVIERGE,
Theodore, d. 10/10/1985 in Rochester; Adelard Thivierge and Marie Routhier; b. 4/5/1917*

TIBBETTS,
Harold, d. 6/24/1931 at 26/9/15 in Danbury; woodsman; single; b. New Durham; Lillian D. Tuttle (New Durham)
Leander, d. 7/4/1921 at 70/4/27; farmer; married; b. Brookfield; Asa Tibbetts (Wolfeboro) and Esther Abbott (Ossipee)
Sarah G., d. 3/26/1897 at 56/5; cardiac dropsy; housekeeper; married; b. Middleton; Thurston Garland (Middleton) and Mary Cook (Middleton)
Vira E., d. 12/29/1984; b. 9/9/1902*

TREMBLAY,
Lauretta, d. 2/7/1991 in Boston, MA

TUFTS,
son, d. 4/9/1887 at 5; b. Middleton; Charles D. Tufts (Middleton)
Addie M., d. 6/20/1963 at 78; wid/o Leon G. Tufts
Charles D., d. 1/17/1943 at 88/1/13; farmer; widower; b. Middleton; Davis Tufts and Adeline D. Horne
Clyde L., d. 12/22/1987 in Rochester; b. 5/2/1902*
Cora Belle, d. 6/22/1900 at 28/10/17; blood poison; housewife; married; b. Milton; Moses Cooke (Milton) and F. S. Downing (Holderness)
David [Davis], d. 10/31/1896 at 76/11/8; ulceration of stomach; farmer; widower; b. Middleton; Joseph Tufts (Hampton) and Rebecca Stevens (Middleton)
Ellen M., d. 6/10/1919 at 59/7/6; ptomaine poison; housewife; married; b. Milton; Eli Corson
Elsie A., d. 11/7/1913 at 1/8/10; pneumonia; b. Middleton; Leon G. Tufts (Middleton) and Addie M. Kimball (Middleton)
Eva E., d. 7/3/1978; w/o Clyde Tufts; b. 7/25/1907*
Frederick L., d. 8/24/1989 in Farmington; b. 12/17/1923*

George David, d. 6/16/1970 at 64; Leon Tufts and Addie Kimball; h/o Marion Shepard Tufts

George J., d. 3/29/1931 at 83/0/17; farmer; married; b. Middleton; David Tufts (Middleton) and Adeline Horne

Grace Thelma, d. 9/25/1910 at 3/7/16; b. Middleton; Leon G. Tufts (Middleton) and Addie M. Kimball (Middleton)

John D., d. 11/11/1975 at 85; George J. Tufts and Emma Whitehouse; h/o Alice Tufts

Joseph W., d. 12/26/1888 at 0/8/13; fits; b. Middleton; Joseph W. Tufts (Middleton) and Belle Cook (Milton)

Leon G., d. 8/11/1952 at 73; farmer; married; b. Middleton; George L. Tufts and Emma F. Whitehouse

Lloyde S., d. 2/16/1904 at 0/1/10; septicemia; b. Middleton; Leon G. Tufts (Middleton) and Addie Kimball (Middleton)

Marion E., d. 5/3/1988 in Portsmouth; b. 1/25/1915*

Maud, d. 6/24/1895 at 10/6; scholar; single; b. Middleton; Charles D. Tufts (Middleton) and Nellie Corson (Middleton)

Moses D., d. 2/12/1972 at 74; Joseph Tufts and Corabell Cook

Myron K., d. 11/20/1968 at 57; h/o Louise Kinney Tufts

Ransom L., d. 8/10/1973 at 79; h/o Muriel Kirkpatrick Tufts

Robert L., d. 7/12/1992 in Rochester at 33**

TUTTLE,
Langdon I., d. 5/20/1904 at 51/1/1; acute tuberculosis; laborer; single; b. Middleton; Ivory Tuttle (Middleton) and Belinda J. Cook (Milton)

Mary A., d. 12/27/1905 at 83/8/24; senectus; widow; b. New Durham; William Berry (Strafford)

Phillip, d. 11/4/1968 at 43; h/o Rena Kimball Tuttle

WALKER,
Elizabeth, d. 5/13/1887 at 58; widow; b. Middleton

WEISS,
Josef, d. 11/25/1971 at 93; f/o Robert Weiss
Robert, d. 12/3/1996 in Middleton; b. 11/12/1914*

WELCH,
Eleanor E., d. 8/19/1976; w/o Otis Welch; residence - Rochester
Otis R., d. 8/19/1976; h/o Eleanor Welch; residence - Rochester

WENTWORTH,
Eliza A., d. 2/4/1896 at 56/3; cardiac dropsy; housekeeper; widow; b. Middleton; Samuel Twombly (Milton) and Eliza York (Middleton)

WHALEN,
Barry James, d. 7/16/1996 in Rochester; b. 10/17/1948*

WHITEHOUSE,
Bertram O., Sr., d. 11/22/1994 in Farmington; b. 1/14/1929*
Charles, d. 8/14/1893 at 33/8/3; peritonitis; single; b. Middleton; R. Whitehouse (Middleton) and Clarissa Frost (Middleton)
Clarissa D., d. 2/8/1892 at 73; la grippe; housekeeper; widow; b. Middleton
Eliza H., d. 2/2/1910 at 93/10; old age; housework; widow; b. Middleton; Samuel Colbath and Mary Garland
Harvey J., d. 11/10/1946 at 78/7/8; farmer; widower; b. Middleton; Jones Whitehouse (Middleton) and Abbie Harvey
Ida M., d. 5/11/1934 at 74/4/10; housewife; married; b. Wolfeboro; Frank Johnson (Wolfeboro) and Elizabeth Sanborn (Gloucester, MA)
Melissa, d. 3/29/1907 at 34/4/27; cardiac syncope; housekeeper; married; b. Middleton; Samuel Perkins (Middleton) and Abbie Goodwin (Middleton)
Ralph, d. 12/28/1900 at 0/10/0; pulmonary tuberculosis; b. Rochester; H. J. Whitehouse (Middleton) and Lizzie B. Ellis (Alton)
Richard, d. 1/20/1970 at 57; h/o Gladys Moore Whitehouse
Richard A., Sr., d. 10/18/1994 in Wolfeboro; b. 5/6/1944*
Robert P., d. 12/13/1889 at 75/11; old age; farmer; married; b. Middleton

W. H., d. 1/22/1907 at 64/9/24; prostatis abscess; farmer; married; b. Middleton; A. W. Whitehouse (Middleton) and Eliza Colbath (Middleton)

Wesley J., d. 6/5/1951 at 67/4/21 in Wolfeboro; farmer; single; b. Wolfeboro; Edwin Whitehouse and Ida Johnson

WIGGETT,
Ernest A., d. 12/26/1964 at 65; h/o Leona Wiggett

WILLEY,
Abigail, d. 5/19/1900 at 87/1/15; general debility; housewife; widow; b. New Durham; ----- Grace and ----- Willey

Bartholomew, d. 6/13/1914 at 79/2/14; arterios chrosis; farmer; b. New Durham; Bartholomew Willey (New Durham) and Polly Willey (New Durham)

Charles R., d. 7/7/1929 at 53/2/29; farmer; widower; b. Middleton; Edward LaBonte and Annie A. Willey (Middleton)

Fitz E., d. 3/15/1894 at 34/10/2; spinal; trader; single; b. Middleton; Jonas D. Willey (farmer, New Durham) and Abbie Horne (Middleton)

Flora, d. 10/8/1974 at 89

Henry D., d. 11/7/1934 at 66/2/23; blacksmith; married; b. New Durham; John D. Willey (New Durham) and Mary A. Tufts (Middleton)

Jonas D., d. 7/12/1910 at 74/2/8; farmer; married; b. New Durham; Charles Willey (New Durham) and Abby Grace (New Durham)

Sarah A., d. 5/10/1923 at 64/1; housewife; married; b. Farmington; Leonard Babb and Martha Emerson

WORTH,
George M., d. 7/10/1980; h/o Flora Worth; b. 11/30/1921*

WRIGHT,
Chester A., d. 3/16/1962 at 78 in Rochester; h/o Alice Wright

WYATT,
Charles H., Jr., d. 3/2/1993 in Middleton; b. 12/12/1927*

YORK,
Susan M., d. 10/28/1955 at 52; Edgar Scranton and Doris Knight

YOUNG,
Alice, d. 5/5/1979; m/o Willard Young; b. 3/6/1893*
Beatrice, d. 9/6/1961; w/o Willard Young
Chester, d. 5/11/1900 at 0/4/7; abscess middle ear; b. Middleton;
    Lewis F. Young (Middleton) and Effie Leighton (Middleton)
Dorothy Mae, d. 8/22/1963 at 58; w/o Willard Young
Fred R., d. 12/20/1974 at 83; h/o Alice Young
John H., d. 11/14/1915 at 75/11/13; carcinoma of stomach; farmer;
    widower; b. Tuftonboro
Mary E., d. 3/30/1894 at 54/6/23; consumption; housekeeper;
    married; b. Middleton; Lewis Cook (farmer) and Nancy Jones
Sarah M., d. 2/6/1892 at 60; cancer; housekeeper; married; b. Dover
Wilda, d. 1/20/1913 at 0/5/11; pneumonia; b. Middleton; Fred R.
    Young (Middleton) and Alice E. Heath (Union)

Other Heritage Books by Richard P. Roberts:

Alton, New Hampshire Vital Records, 1890-1997

Barnstead, New Hampshire Vital Records, 1887-2000

Barrington, New Hampshire Vital Records

Dover, New Hampshire Death Records, 1887-1937

Gilmanton, New Hampshire Vital Records, 1887-2001

Marriage Records of Dover, New Hampshire, 1835-1909

Marriage Records of Dover, New Hampshire, 1910-1937

Milton, New Hampshire Vital Records, 1888-1999

Moultonborough, New Hampshire Vital Records

New Castle, New Hampshire Vital Records, 1891-1997

New Hampshire Name Changes, 1768-1923

New Hampshire Name Changes, 1923-1947

Ossipee, New Hampshire Vital Records, 1887-2001

Rochester, New Hampshire Death Records, 1887-1951

Vital Records of Durham, New Hampshire, 1887-2002

Vital Records of Effingham and Freedom, New Hampshire, 1888-2001

Vital Records of Farmington, New Hampshire, 1887-1938

Vital Records of Lyme and Dorchester, New Hampshire, 1887-2004

Vital Records of New Durham and Middleton, New Hampshire, 1887-1998

Vital Records of North Berwick, Maine, 1892-2002

Vital Records of Orford and Piermont, New Hampshire, 1887-2004

Vital Records of Tamworth and Albany, New Hampshire, 1887-2003

Vital Records of Tuftonboro and Brookfield, New Hampshire, 1888-2005

Vital Records of Wakefield, New Hampshire, 1887-1998

Vital Records of Warren, New Hampshire, 1887-2005

Wolfeboro, New Hampshire Vital Records, 1887-1999

www.ingramcontent.com/pod-product-compliance
Lightning Source LLC
Chambersburg PA
CBHW051624230426
43669CB00013B/2167